Sexuality and Victorian Literature

Sexuality and Victorian Literature

Edited by Don Richard Cox

The University of Tennessee Press / Knoxville

85--51688

"On the Enrichment of Poor Monkeys by Myth and Dream; or, How Dickens Rousseauisticized and Pre-Freudianized Victorian Views of Childhood," copyright © 1984 by Mark Spilka.

Publication of this book has been aided by a grant from The Better English Fund, established by John C. Hodges at The University of Tennessee, Knoxville.

Since its inception in 1956, the distinguished series, "Tennessee Studies in Literature," sponsored by the Department of English at the University of Tennessee, Knoxville, has published 26 volumes. Beginning with Volume 27, the series is presented in a new format. Each book deals with a specific theme, period, or genre, for which the editor of that volume has invited contributions from leading scholars in the field. No longer an annual series, the volumes will be published as they are ready. As with all University of Tennessee Press books, the "Tennessee Studies in Literature" volumes are printed on paper that meets the guidelines for permanence and durability of the Committee on Production Guidelines for Book Longevity of the Council on Library Resources, and binding materials are chosen for strength and durability.

Library of Congress Cataloging in Publication Data
Main entry under title:
Sexuality and Victorian literature.
    (Tennessee studies in literature ; v. 27)
    Includes index.
    1. English literature—19th century—History and criticism—Addresses, essays, lectures. 2. Sex in literature—Addresses, essays, lectures. I. Cox, Don Richard. II. Series.
PR469.S4S49 1984   820'.9'353   83-21655
ISBN 0-87049-424-4
ISBN 0-87049-438-4 (pbk.)

Tennessee Studies in Literature

Preface

The age that a historian once called the "world of our fathers" has now become the world of our grandparents, perhaps the world of our great-grandparents. But the Victorian period still holds an attraction for us, because it is in the nineteenth century that we find the true origins of our twentieth-century world and sensibilities.

The essays in this volume examine the sexuality of the Victorians from a literary perspective, interpreting their experience from the distance of a hundred years. During that hundred years we have moved from a time when the term *Victorian* symbolized "prudery," to a time when the period is often equated with prostitution, pornography, and "secret lives." Although both stereotypes are no doubt exaggerated (or perhaps it would be more correct to say that both stereotypes are only partially true), it would be incorrect to say that we do not understand Victorian sexuality. It would also be incorrect, however, to say we now understand all we ever will about it. The late twentieth century finds us, some believe, preoccupied with our own sexuality. In such a time, as these essays demonstrate, the "world of our grandparents" still has much to offer in assisting us to understand ourselves.

Don Richard Cox

Contents

x   Contents

Sexuality and Victorian Literature

Morton N. Cohen

Lewis Carroll and Victorian Morality

A few years ago a well-known writer came to talk with me about Lewis Carroll. He was writing a biography of Carroll, and, as I was then editing Carroll's letters, he thought that I might be able to help him. Most of all, he wanted to know about Carroll's sex life. He asked me a long string of pointed questions, and he wanted specific, factual answers. I could not, in all honesty, supply them, and I fear he was disappointed. I did not know whether Carroll had sexual dreams; I could not speculate about Carroll's sexual fantasies or even say if he had any.

And yet, in spite of those negative and uninformative replies, I believe that I know Carroll as well as anyone else does and that, on the basis of twenty years' work with the man's published writings, his diaries, and his letters, I can be fairly sure about his likes and dislikes, his political and religious views, his social outlook, and the general pattern of his relationships. It follows, too, that I can venture some reasoned views about his attitude to sex as it emerges from a careful examination of his personal writings.

One uncontrovertible fact is that Lewis Carroll was a model Victorian. He was born in 1832, five years before Victoria ascended the throne; he died in 1898, three years before the Queen herself. But Carroll was a model Victorian in more than chronology; he was particularly Victorian in his voluminous record keeping. The Victorian age was an age of record, perhaps the last in the conventional sense, the last age of paper record. With the telephone not yet in common use, people still wrote letters to one another. But besides that, the Victorians were obsessed with the need to write things down, as if to keep score, to justify themselves to themselves.

Lewis Carroll himself was a record keeper of mind-boggling proportions. One wonders, indeed, how he managed to perform his duties as Mathematical Lecturer at Christ Church, Oxford, to carry out his clerical tasks, to write twenty or so books, to take hundreds of photographs, and to do all the other things he did, indeed, to live so full a life and still maintain his voluminous records. The detailed diaries that he kept for half of the nineteenth century must have taken an inordinate amount of his time. And then there is the myriad of letters he wrote. But even they offer no reasonable explanation of how he managed to do all that he did.

We all write letters, and certainly the Victorians wrote more of them than we do, but Carroll was one of the most formidable letter writers who ever lived. When he was nearing his twenty-ninth birthday, in 1861, he began keeping a letter register, where he assigned a number to every letter he wrote and received and entered beside the number a précis of the letter's contents. He kept the register until he died, thirty-seven years later. The last entry in that register, which accounts for his letters for just over half his life, numbered 98,721.

By examining Carroll's diaries and letters, we get a fairly comprehensive view of this Victorian, and we learn a good deal about his milieu, the age in which he lived, and, in particular, Victorian Oxford. But most of all, we get to know the man who created the *Alice* books. We learn how he thinks, what he believes in, and we become acquainted with his opinions, his manner of living, and, perhaps most important for our purpose here, with his emotional responses.

One obstacle that stands in the way of seeing Lewis Carroll plain is, ironically, the critical attention he has received. Sad to say, most literary critics who write on Carroll, like my visitor, bring to their work a good many preconceptions, if not misconceptions. And many of them appear less interested in knowing Carroll than they are in grinding away at some theory they have, whether based on fact or not. Everyone who has read *Alice's Adventures in Wonderland* knows that it contains levels of feeling and meaning that are not readily accessible. Critics have been working overtime trying to get at that inaccessible substructure of the books, most particularly critics with a psychoanalytical bent. But the fact is that the more one reads of these critics' work, the more confused one grows. If we take them seriously, we enter a world of chaos.

One critic has conclusively proved that *Alice* was not written by Lewis Carroll at all and that the real author was Queen Victoria. An earlier writer toys with the notion that *Alice's Adventures in Wonderland* is an allegory of the Oxford Movement, another an allegory of Darwinian evolution. Still another tells us that the story of Alice represents Charles Dodgson's own birth trauma in the isolated Cheshire rectory where he was born. Other psychoanalysts tell us that the book is about a woman in labor, that falling down the rabbit hole is a hidden expression of Dodgson's secret wish for coitus, that Alice is a phallus (that one, at least, rhymes), or that she's a fetus. Or, if we prefer, we can take the view that she is a transvestite Christ. A more recent essay claims that Dodgson was the first "acidhead," while Kenneth Burke tells us that the story is about toilet training and bowel movements.[1] It's almost as though these analysts are competing to advance the most unusual, some would say the most outrageous or fantastic, interpretation of Dodgson the man and his brainchild *Alice in Wonderland.* I listened not long ago to a paper on Alice as a symbol of the fallen woman. Well, after all, she does fall down the rabbit hole.

There is no consensus; nowhere do we find even the hope of agreement on what the story really means. Certainly the day will come when we shall have better techniques for understanding the real meaning of the book and what Dodgson's subconscious was getting at here. But our tools and techniques are not yet sufficiently refined for that exercise; we do not yet know how to interpret Dodgson's psychological pyrotechnics in the story.

We are all products of our own time, and I confess that when I first began to work on Carroll, I thought that some of these critics might be right. After all, Dodgson did prefer the company of little girls to adults, and perhaps we could learn about that preference through psychoanalytical speculation. I half expected to find suspicious, or at least ambiguous, evidence about his relationships with his child friends in the letters that he wrote to them. Actually, at first my expectations seemed to be working out when photocopies of the letters started pouring in. A huge proportion of the letters were addressed to little girls, and some of the girls were saluted as "Darling," "My own Agnes," and the like. But with closer acquaintance, I had to abandon my earlier suspicions.

In fact the psychologists and the psychoanalysts have not helped me to understand Carroll. My understanding has come from my work with original material, Carroll's diaries, his letters, and the reminiscences that the little girls themselves have left behind. For one thing, I have grown convinced in the process that we have more to learn about Carroll and his fellow-Victorians by seeing them in their day-to-day dealings with one another, that is by examining their conscious lives, than we can from symbol hunting and psychological theorizing. Most of these intelligent Victorians were exceptionally self-conscious, and they constantly sought to assess their own worth, to justify their behavior. Lewis Carroll is a good case in point: he is most revealing when he appraises himself to himself, to the society in which he lived, and to God.

I don't mean to suggest that we should look at these people in a vacuum; indeed the surroundings they grew up in are extremely important. Oddly

enough, some of Dodgson's biographers have failed to examine his environment carefully and have not dealt sufficiently with two powerful influences
that helped to shape him.

The first important influence was the Yorkshire rectory where Charles
Dodgson spent his childhood. Dodgson's father was the curate of a Yorkshire congregation (later he became Archdeacon of Richmond and Canon
of Ripon). Dodgson *père* had come from a long line of clergymen, among
them a sprinkling of bishops, and it seemed quite natural that three of his
four sons should go into the church. The family in the rectory was a large
one of eleven children; Lewis Carroll was the third child, the eldest son.
It was a "good" family on both sides, with family trees going back for centuries. It was conservative, steeped in tradition, pious, devoted to social
service—and morning, noon, and night the family prayed together. Although
we know that Carroll's father could be witty on occasion and display a good
sense of fun, the essential picture we get of him is of a strong, solid, authori-
tarian, rather gloomy high and dry churchman.

We know less about Carroll's mother. She died before he was nineteen.
She must have been a gentle creature, and, what with eleven children, a
very busy one. In the few allusions that Carroll makes to her, he shows genuine affection. But it is clear from the evidence that Carroll's relationship
with his father was one of the powerful facts of his life. The two developed
close mutual sympathies and understanding early, and the father soon became
a model for the son to emulate. The father died in 1868, when Carroll was
thirty-six, but even years later, when Carroll himself was an older man, he
characterized the loss of his father as "the greatest sorrow of my life."

Dodgson certainly had pleasant memories of childhood. After all he had
a good number of sisters and brothers to play with, and we know that he
enjoyed walks and rambles in the Yorkshire countryside. He was adept at
mechanical things, and he built a miniature railway in the back garden and
a puppet theater for which he wrote original plays. We know, too, that he
was a constant reader, had a good memory, liked to sketch and to write poetry and short stories. But perhaps most of all, he had learned, early, under
his father's guidance, to live a purposeful life. It was a life of prayer and
charity and duty and love. Selflessness and hard work were part of the code
by which he lived. Today we would say that Charles Dodgson and a large
number of his contemporaries never really had any childhood—they had to
study too long, they had to pray too much and too often, they had to perform too many rituals, and they had to work too hard. But they did not
object: this was the only way to live. They enjoyed reading the Bible (it
was, after all, the best of all storybooks), and they even looked forward to
the Sunday sermon almost as much as children in our time look forward to
Sesame Street on television. They believed in Christ as a real phenomenon;

He was, in a sense, a member of the family. And they genuinely strove to do good deeds and to think noble thoughts.

When we teach about the Victorian age, some of us tend to characterize it as a time when all the traditional values, and especially traditional religious faith, came under severe attack. The new science, the developmental theory, Benthamism, Darwinism, Agnosticism, the new geology, Higher Criticism – these new movements called everything into doubt. And indeed they did, but the truth is that they called everything into doubt for only a handful of top-drawer intellectuals like Alfred Tennyson, Matthew Arnold, George Eliot, and a few others. For most people, the traditional faith endured, and when the onslaught from all the 'isms began, they turned, in panic, back to the old verities. They had earlier been shocked by the outrages of the Regency, and they had already barricaded themselves against the sins of the world. Now it only remained for them to reinforce the barricades against the new threats.

The Victorians' faith reached back to the Puritans, beyond the moral looseness of the eighteenth century, and the Puritan scenario was what it had always been. The protagonists were a jealous God and an omnipresent Devil who fought for the human soul. One's conduct here on earth ultimately earned a reward in Heaven or punishment in Hell. The old faith was based on authority: God, parents, elders, betters, upper classes. It had nothing to do with any modern notions of democracy or equality. Most Victorians were not taught to cultivate open minds, to consider all sides of a question. The flexible, searching mind was truly exceptional; most minds were rigid, dogmatic. They feared new ideas; they sensed danger and evil in change and innovation.

Earnestness was an essential Victorian characteristic, transcending the limits of specific religions, and it underscored everyone's behavior, regardless of his or her religious convictions. Kingsley, Newman, Matthew Arnold, George Eliot, Tennyson, Browning – even they, while they cultivated different spiritual vineyards, all emerged with a central concern for the way one must behave. They all endorsed the same quality of living, the same moral code. And the ordinary Victorians as well as the great thinkers all agreed on an uncompromisingly Christian ethic that required self-discipline and good habits, that demanded that all action conform to a Christian conscience and all behavior be characterized by honesty, good manners, and generosity. You might not believe in God, but you behaved according to His Commandments anyway.

Lewis Carroll embraced this ethic at an early age, in the family circle in Yorkshire, with his father setting the tone and spirit of his faith. He was, to begin with, a bright lad, but he must have worked unremittingly, for when he left home to go to Richmond School at the age of twelve, he was already proficient in higher mathematics and could read and write Latin easily. He entered his school with more in his head than most young people today have in theirs when they enter—some would say leave—college.

But what about the whimsey that was to make him famous? Where does that come in? Well, that is there as well, or the roots of it are. The youthful jottings that survive are delightful, the compositions, the stories, the verse, the drawings are all inventive, clever, spellbinding. Yes, the moral tone is always present too.

The Dodgsons, like other good Victorian families, produced family magazines. The earliest one is appropriately entitled *Useful and Instructive Poetry,* and it was composed entirely by the young Lewis Carroll, aged thirteen, especially for a younger brother and sister. It contains a string of humorous verses and some pencil sketches. Three of the verses are entitled "Punctuality," "Charity," and "Rules and Regulations." While the verses are often clever and witty, some of the titles and the accompanying moral tags couch the fun in an earnest context. The first verse in the magazine is entitled "My Fairy":

> I have a fairy by my side
>   Which says I must not sleep,
> When once in pain I loudly cried
>   It said, "You must not weep."
>
> If, full of mirth, I smile and grin,
>   It says, "You must not laugh,"
> When once I wished to drink some gin,
>   It said "You must not quaff."
>
> When once a meal I wished to taste
>   It said "You must not bite,"
> When to the wars I went in haste,
>   It said "You must not fight."
>
> "What *may* I do?" At length I cried,
>   Tired of the painful task,
> The fairy quietly replied,
>   And said "You must not ask."
>
>   *Moral*: "You mustn't."

This playful rhyme is an apt comment on Victorian childhood and, by implication, on Victorian parenthood and adulthood. After all, these children who were taught that they *mustn't* did in time go on to become adults, and they carried the lesson of *mustn't* to the four corners of the earth. Certainly *mustn't* becomes one of the strongest themes of Charles Dodgson's mature life.

Carroll remained at the Richmond Grammar School for only a year and a half, boarding with the headmaster and his huge family in what was surely a close replica of his own home. When he left Richmond, the headmaster wrote to Carroll's father: "I shall always feel a peculiar interest in the gentle, intelligent, and well-conducted boy who is now leaving us." [2] The emphasis on good behavior was not perfunctory.

Carroll spent the next three years at Rugby. Those years did much to convince him that all he had learned in his family circle was absolutely and irrevocably true. Biographers have missed much in not examining more carefully the influences that must have impinged upon Carroll at Rugby: they offer us some of the more important insights into Carroll's personality and indeed into the shaping of Victorian character generally.

In the second quarter of the nineteenth century, Rugby was enjoying the result of the reforms initiated by Dr. Thomas Arnold. Arnold came to Rugby in 1828 determined to turn the school, which had been labeled a "nursery for vice," into a training ground for Christian gentlemen. In Arnold's view the school's chapel was as important as its classrooms: Christian faith and Christian learning would, if blended well, produce a superior breed of man, a new brand of Englishman. To achieve his goal, Arnold made changes: he instituted the preceptor system, he selected his staff carefully, and he instilled in them and in the boys they taught a missionary zeal. His Sunday sermons in chapel—he was Rugby's chaplain as well as its headmaster— bore a distinct, martial tone, and the boys later recorded that they often felt that the headmaster was speaking to each one of them personally. Arnold told the boys that this life on earth was no fool's paradise: it was a battle-field where everyone must fight and where the stakes were enormous.

The boys listened, they were mesmerized, they quaked. They well knew Arnold's list of six supreme evils, which included sensual wickedness and evil companionship. They learned, too, that Arnold placed religious and moral behavior ahead of gentlemanly conduct, and gentlemanly conduct ahead of intellectual achievement. Arnold also taught a kind of spiritual introspection: he believed that all sinners must look for help within themselves even as they must constantly vindicate themselves to themselves. He sought to build strong individual temples in his boys. He believed that if they cultivated strong wills, strong minds and strong bodies would follow automatically. Truthfulness was one of Arnold's special values, and no one came in for so much reproof and punishment as a boy caught lying. It is no secret that Arnold's army of private soldiers went forth to become the eminent Victorians and that Rugby became the model for all good schools, not only in England but in the entire English-speaking world.

Lewis Carroll never actually heard Dr. Arnold preach. He arrived at Rugby in 1846, three years after Arnold's death, and his headmaster was

A.C. Tait, who, if he did not possess Arnold's fiery personality, certainly matched Arnold's dedication to high ideals. Tait, too, made the chapel the heart of the school and in his eight years there did much to reinforce Arnold's missionary spirit. No mean preacher himself, Tait soon went on to become the Archbishop of Canterbury. It was he whom Lewis Carroll heard preach at Sunday chapel. But we can be sure that Carroll also read Arnold's sermons, published in 1848, while Carroll was a Rugby boy.

Certainly not all Rugby boys emerged in their headmaster's image, but Lewis Carroll needed no prodding in his conduct or his studies. He had formed his habits earlier, in Yorkshire. What is especially interesting, in reading the Dodgson diaries and the letters, is that one finds echoing in these pages the very principles that Dr. Arnold had laid down before Dodgson ever arrived at Rugby. By some quirk of descent, Dodgson becomes, in some respects, a reflection, at least spiritually, of the headmaster he never knew. Life for Dodgson is indeed an armed battle against the Devil, and one wins that battle by being ever vigilant, by exercising a strong will, by practicing merciless self-denial, by engaging in constant and unremitting labor, and by living in perpetual communion with God in thought and in prayer.

We have no diary for the years Dodgson was at Rugby, but we do have one for his early years as a mathematical lecturer at Christ Church, beginning in 1855. On one occasion he writes: "With God's help I desire to begin (1) daily reading and meditation of the Bible (best before chapel), (2) cleaning off arrears of lecture-work before doing anything else, (3) denying myself indulgence in sleep in the evenings, (4) methodically preparing outlines of sermons. Oh God," he concludes, "I repent of my past life: I long to do better . . . for Jesus Christ's sake. Amen."[3] Similar resolutions appear regularly in the diaries, and they are accompanied by hasty, modest entries about his accomplishments: his working at mathematical problems, the proofs he has readied for the printer, and, here and there, an account of the number of hours he has worked that day, on some days as many as fourteen.

Here is another entry from the diary: "I here record my intention of beginning, next term, a habit of evening work, and also of trying the experiment of taking regular Sunday duty" (January 24, 1865). Another entry: "Term begins tomorrow. I must try to get into regular habits, and a life of more direct preparation for the Ministry. Oh God, purify me, and help me to live ever as in thy sight, for thy dear Son's sake" (October 17, 1862). On the last day of 1863: "Here, at the close of another year, how much of neglect, carelessness, and sin have I to remember! I had hoped, during the year, to have made a beginning in parochial work, to have thrown off habits of evil, to have advanced in my work at Christ Church—how little, next to nothing, has been done of all this! Now I have a fresh year before me: once more let me set myself to do some thing worthy of life 'before I go hence, and be no more seen.' Oh God, grant me grace to consecrate to Thee, during this new year, my life and powers, my days and nights, myself. Take me, vile and worthless as I am: use me as Thou seest fit, help me to be Thy servant, for Christ's sake. Amen" (*D,* I, 208). The humility, the deep and genuine religious feeling and devotion was his to the end. Less than six years before he died, he writes, after preaching in church on Sunday: "Once more I have to thank my heavenly Father for the great blessing and privilege of being allowed to speak for Him! May He bless my words and help some soul on its heavenward way" (April 3, 1892).

By most standards, Dodgson's life was one of considerable accomplishment. Most people know his two children's classics and some know that he wrote some works on mathematics and logic. But few realize that his bibliography contains some three hundred separately published items. Apart from his writing, he taught mathematics diligently and, although he never had his own curacy, he took his clerical duties seriously and often preached in church. On a number of occasions, in fact, he filled St. Mary's, Oxford, to capacity with a university congregation. He served for almost ten years as Curator of Christ Church Common Room, and he made a name for himself as one of the earliest art photographers and certainly the finest photographer of children in the nineteenth century.

Dodgson constantly befriended the poor and visited the sick, and, we are told, when he realized that his children's books would bring in a modest income for the rest of his life, he actually asked Oxford University to reduce his salary. All his life he lived simply in college rooms, allowed himself pleasures but no extravagant indulgences, ate little when he ate at all, and usually dressed in black. Only once in his life did he travel abroad. For most of his life he helped support his six unmarried sisters and a good many other people — relatives, friends, even strangers. He always took on new students to teach and was ready, however modestly, to offer young and old alike religious or spiritual instruction. In Dodgson, Dr. Arnold's lofty Victorian standards were incarnate: we never find an allusion to anything sensual, and he holds truthfulness to be as noble a virtue as Arnold did.

Dodgson's faith, like Arnold's, had been worked out logically: if his faith could not stand the test of logic, it was not worth having, and there was no place for compromise or exceptions. He knew precisely what he believed in and why. "I believe, *first and before all,*" he wrote a friend, "that there is an absolute, self-existent, external, distinction between Right and Wrong. . . . By 'Right' and 'Wrong,' I mean what *we ought to do,* and *ought not to do,* without any reference to rewards or punishments. . . . Secondly, I believe I am responsible to a *Personal Being* for what I do. . . . Thirdly, I believe that Being to be *perfectly good.* And I call that perfectly good Being 'God.'"[4]

And so what have we here in this selfless, hard-working, devout Victorian —a saint? Hardly. Although he is charitable and understanding, he is not flawless. As good a man as he is, he is equally beset by foibles and short-comings. His own exceptional abilities make him impatient with those of lesser gifts. His uncompromising standards frequently turn him into a prig. His determined honesty leads him sometimes to deal with others brusquely. He is a snob. Occasionally he writes testy, disagreeable letters to tradespeople, to the Steward of Christ Church, to Oxford colleagues, to hosts and hostesses, to fellow-clerics (once to a`bishop) complaining about their behavior.

Even for Victorian England, when formality reigned, Carroll's social stance is stiff and unbending. Imagine, never, not once in his life, did he address an adult outside his family by a first name. No friend, no colleague ever got called John or Fred or Harry. In spite of his multifarious interests—in the theater, in photography, in medicine, in art—he lived a carefully ordered life. He not only regulated his outer behavior but imposed strict rules upon his inner life as well. He kept his emotions in check, harnessed, and while this uncompromising rigor turned him into a thoroughly repressed human being, that was the only possible way for Carroll to live. "God has implanted sexual desires [in us all]," he wrote in an essay, "[and] . . . God forbids us to arouse or encourage these desires except for the object for which He gave them, marriage."[5] Carroll's repression was probably good for his art, but it could not have added to his happiness as a human being. We have no evidence anywhere that he ever lost control or that his defenses ever crumbled.

When we discuss Carroll's emotional life, we at once encounter the little girls. If Dodgson's posture was so stern, his principles so uncompromising, how do these little girls fit into the life? Some part of the answer is to be found in the Victorian man's attitude toward women and children generally.

Never since the Middle Ages had woman been worshipped for her innocence and for her goodness as she was in Victorian times. After all, she and her sisters composed a breed of humanity closer to angels than men; they were models of virtue. They had no sexual appetites to plague them, and their instincts were unsullied. They could even draw men heavenwards and help them achieve salvation. And so men nurtured and admired these blessed beings; they shielded their sisters, their wives, and their daughters from the gross and brutish world; they protected and cherished their natural piety.

Along with this cult of feminine purity came the cult of childhood innocence which the Victorians inherited from the Romantics. They read their Blake, Wordsworth, and Coleridge, and they knew that the child, and especially the female child, was a sprite living an idyllic existence. She had recently come from God and she still possessed a modicum of divine knowledge. And so the Victorian male devoted himself to the child's needs, thought himself privileged to witness the visionary gleam inherent in these creatures, and encouraged the expanding heart and mind. Men valued the prerogatives of helping to mold the child's mind, of loving those beautifully natural beings, of being loved by them, of devoting one's energies to educating them, to amusing them, and to making them laugh.

When Dodgson first discovered his deep affinity for the child, we do not know, but it was probably in the Yorkshire rectory where he grew up with his younger brothers and sister. It must have been a remarkable event, for he went on to devote much of his life to children. Over and over again, one is astonished at his patience and his willingness to endure the rebuffs, the impetuous outbursts, and the thoughtlessness both of the children he knew and of their mothers. But all the while, he reveals an almost magical insight into the hearts and minds of the children. He built his friendships with them carefully, always aware that they could come tumbling to the ground like a house of cards. "It takes some time to *understand* a child's nature," he wrote to the mother of a young girl, "—particularly when one only sees them all together, and in the presence of their elders. I don't think anybody, who has only seen children so, has any idea of the loveliness of a child's *mind.* I have been largely privileged in tête-à-tête intercourse with children. It is very healthy and helpful to one's own spiritual life: and humbling too, to come into contact with souls so much purer, and nearer to God, than one feels oneself to be" (*L*, II, 980).

But there is another side to Dodgson's friendships with these little girls, a less earnest side, that appears when he meets with them or when he writes them letters or stories from afar. Say that Dodgson was an arrested child himself, if you wish, or, like Kipling and Barrie, a permanent adolescent. But what is more important is that these children sparked his creative fire. The little girls were natural, honest creatures: they laughed easily, and he enjoyed making them laugh. What is more, he felt thoroughly relaxed and at ease with them: in their presence his stammer often disappeared. I shudder to think how many original Lewis Carroll stories have been lost—the dozens, perhaps hundreds, that he invented for these little girls on the spur of the moment, as he did *Alice in Wonderland,* but which he never wrote down. But I suppose we must not be greedy; at least we have a great many of his letters to the little girls, overflowing as they do with fantasy upon fantasy that he created for them.

How serious was he really about these child friends? Enormously serious. He pursued these youngsters, he negotiated with their parents for visits with them, and he took them on railway journeys, on outings to the theater, to art galleries, for long walks. He fed them, he gave them inscribed copies of his books, he sent them presents, he paid for some of their French lessons, art lessons, singing lessons, and he even paid some dentist bills. He made sketches of them; he photographed them. He entertained them in his rooms at Christ Church; he wrote them amusing and loving letters; he cuddled them; he kissed them.

Certainly eyebrows were raised, there was gossip, and some mothers complained. But Dodgson was no fool. In face of the criticism, he defended himself. He had committed no sin; his friendships with little girls gave them and him only pleasure; why should he deny his friends or himself that pleasure?

Dodgson's married sister, Mary Collingwood, learned that he was having child friends to stay with him at the seaside (he rented rooms in the home of a proper Victorian landlady in Eastbourne, and this landlady's maid looked after all the needs of his young guests), and when his sister wrote to inquire about these guests of his, Dodgson replied directly:

> I *do* like getting such letters as yours. I think all you say about
> my girl-guests is most kind and sisterly, and most entirely proper
> for you to write to your brother. But I don't think it at all advis-
> able to enter into any controversy about it. There is no reasonable
> probability that it would modify the views either of you or of me.
> I will say a few words to explain my views: but I have no wish
> whatever to have "the last word": so please say anything you like
> afterwards.
>
> You and your husband have, I think, been very fortunate to
> know so little, by experience, in your own case or in that of your
> friends, of the wicked recklessness with which people repeat
> things to the disadvantage of others, without a thought as to
> whether they have grounds for asserting what they say. I have met
> with a good deal of utter misrepresentation of that kind. And
> another result of my experience is the conviction that the opinion
> of "people" in general is absolutely worthless as a test of right and
> wrong. The only two tests I now apply to such a question as the
> having some particular girl-friend as a guest are, first, my own
> *conscience,* to settle whether I feel it to be entirely innocent and
> right, in the sight of God; secondly, the *parents* of my friend, to
> settle whether I have their *full* approval for what I do. You need
> not be shocked at my being spoken against. *Any*body, who is
> spoken about at all, is *sure* to be spoken against by *somebody:* and
> any action, however innocent in itself, is liable, and not at all
> unlikely, to be blamed by *somebody.* If you limit your actions in
> life to things that *nobody* can possibly find fault with, you will
> not do much! (*L,* II, 977–78)

In spite of the gossip and in spite of his sister's concern, Dodgson simply went on entertaining child guests and making new child friends. After all, he had no misgivings about the friendships: he never forced them upon anyone; he kept them alive only when both parties enjoyed them and only when he had approval from the parents in every detail. If he happened to talk to a pretty child in the charge of her governess, on the beach, in a railway carriage, or wherever, he immediately wrote a note to the child's mother reporting the incident and requesting permission to see the child again. Then, depending on how the friendship ripened, he asked permission to write to the child, or he sent a letter to the child by way of the mother, requesting that the mother hand the letter to the child if she wanted the friendship to continue. If all went well, he invited the child to his rooms for tea or dinner, to look at photograph albums. Later, he asked to "borrow" the child for a day's outing in London. If he thought the child beautiful, he asked permission to photograph her, and on some occasions to photograph her "without drapery," that is, nude. But in this delicate circumstance, he preferred always to have the mother or someone else present "to arrange the dress," by which he means to undress the child.

He knew, of course, that photographing children in the nude, and in his college rooms to boot, would cause tongues to wag. But here, too, he defended himself eloquently. Here is an explanation he wrote to the mother of a group of sisters he hoped to photograph:

> Here am I, an amateur-photographer, with a deep sense of admiration for *form*, especially the human form, and one who believes it to be the most beautiful thing God has made on this earth—and who hardly ever gets a chance of photographing it! . . . and now at last I seem to have a *chance* of it. I could no doubt hire *professional* models in town: but, first, they would be ugly, and, secondly, they would *not* be pleasant to deal with: so my only hope is with *friends*. Now your Ethel is beautiful, both in face and form; and is also a perfectly simple-minded child of Nature, who would have no sort of objection to serving as model for a friend she knows as well as she does me. So my humble petition is, that you will bring the 3 girls, and that you will allow me to try some groupings of Ethel and Janet . . . without any drapery or suggestion of it. . . . I need hardly say that the pictures should be such as you might if you liked frame and hang up in your drawing-room. On no account would I do a picture which I should be unwilling to show to all the world—or at least all the artistic world. . . . If I did not believe I could take such pictures without any lower motive than a pure love of Art, I would not ask it: and if I thought there was any fear of its lessening *their* beautiful simplicity of character, I would not ask it.

> ... I fear you will reply that the one *insuperable* objection is
> "Mrs. Grundy" – that people will be sure to hear that such pic-
> tures have been done, and that they will *talk*. As to their *hearing*
> of it, I say "of course. All the world are welcome to hear of it,
> and I would not on any account suggest to the children not to
> mention it – which would at once introduce an objectionable ele-
> ment" – but as to people *talking* about it, I will only quote the
> grand old monkish . . . legend: They say: Quhat do they say? *Lat
> them say!*
>
> It only remains for me to add that, though my *theories* are so
> out-of-the-way (as you may perhaps think them), my *practice* shall
> be strictly in accordance with whatever rules you like to lay
> down – so you may at any time send the children by themselves,
> in perfect confidence that I will try *no* experiments you have not
> previously sanctioned. (*L*, I, 338–39)

Seen in the historical context, Dodgson's sketching and photographing
undressed children is not all that exceptional. Anyone who works with Victorian illustrated books is accustomed to encountering frequently drawings
and paintings of unclothed, sexless children. It is simply another offshoot
of the cult of worshipping childhood innocence. After one of his photographic
sessions, Dodgson wrote to the mother of the girls who sat for him: "Their
innocent unconsciousness is very beautiful, and gives one a feeling of reverence, as at the presence of something sacred" (*L*, I, 381).

In the pre-Freudian air of Victorian England, cuddling and kissing children was accepted behavior, and it is not surprising that Dodgson sat children on his knees and kissed some of his young friends. "Being entrusted
with the care of Ethel for a day is such a great advance on mere acquain-
tanceship," Dodgson wrote to the child's mother, "that I venture to ask if
I may regard myself as on 'kissing' terms with her, as I am with many a girl-
friend a great deal older than *she* is. . . . Nevertheless, if I find you think
it wiser that we should only shake hands, I shall not be *in the least* hurt.
Of course I shall, unless I hear to the contrary, continue to shake hands only"
(*L*, II, 1062–63). Here is a much earlier entry in the diary: "I promised a
[copy of *The Hunting of the*] *Snark* to a quite new little friend, Lily Alice
Godfrey, from New York, aged 8, but talked like a girl of 15 or 16, and de-
clined to be kissed on saying goodbye, on the ground that she 'never kissed
gentlemen.' It is rather painful to see the lovely simplicity of childhood so
soon rubbed off: but I fear it is true that there are no children in America"
(*D*, II, 390).

Whatever one chooses to think about Lewis Carroll's subconscious, one
must conclude from the evidence that he followed some perfectly clear pre-

cepts in ordering his life and that these precepts governed both his inner responses as well as his outer behavior. Love was a strong force in his life, love of innocence and purity. But this innocence and purity were strongly tied to his personal God. Beauty to him is the beauty of nature, and nature is a creation of God. When innocence and beauty exist together, then for him a supreme, even divine, joy results.

What about marriage? And what about sex? Indeed Carroll thought much about marriage. He recorded some of those thoughts in his diaries. For instance, on July 31, 1857, when he was twenty-five, he consulted his father on the subject of taking out life insurance: should he and, if so, when? Both being accomplished mathematicians, they had no difficulty in deciding that it would be best for Carroll to "save at present, and only insure when the prospect [of marriage] becomes a certainty" (D, I, 117).

Carroll wrote an essay entitled "Marriage Service,"[6] in which he considered carefully the problem of who might and who might not marry for a second time and which conditions, in the eyes of God, permitted remarriage and which did not. He set down some remarkably sensible guidelines.

In Carroll's works and, perhaps more significantly, in his diaries and in his letters, he uses the language and the imagery of marriage both seriously and whimsically. Two examples from the letters will suffice here. In a letter to a friend aged twenty-three, Carroll wrote: "Dear Miss Dora Abdy, May I have the pleasure of fetching you, for a tête-à-tête dinner some day soon? And if so, will you name the day?" In a postscript, he adds: "Now please don't go and tell all your friends, in the strictest confidence, 'I've just had a letter from a gentleman, and he asks me to name the day!'" (L, II, 1058). In another letter, one that Carroll wrote in 1889 to an earlier child friend who was by this time a grown woman, he reports to her on a visit paid him at Eastbourne, in his summer lodgings by the sea, by Isa Bowman, a child actress he had befriended: "Isa is one of my *chiefest* of child-friends," he wrote. "I had her with me at Eastbourne last summer . . . for a week's visit, nominally: but we got on so well together, that I kept writing to Mrs. Bowman for leave to keep her longer, till the week had extended to *five*! When we got near the end of *four*, I thought 'At any rate I'll keep her over the normal *honey-moon* period!'" (L, II, 730). Carroll was, by his own confession, at the time he wrote these two letters, "a *very* old fogey," and all hopes of real marriage and honeymoons had fled. But marriage and honeymoons were nonetheless the language of thought, perhaps of dreams, for him still.

I would contend that, although Dodgson never married, he was a family man, a marrying man, and he remained a bachelor only because his efforts to marry were thwarted, because he never won the hand of someone he wished to marry. I recently tried to show that he may very well have expressed an interest in a possible alliance with Alice Liddell, but that Dean and Mrs.

Liddell, related to the aristocracy and being extremely ambitious for their daughters, would have rejected a mere Oxford mathematics don with no important family connections and, what is more, hampered by a stammer and a deaf right ear.[7] I believe he may also have proposed marriage to one or possibly two other friends.

Carroll was denied marriage and, given his standards, denied sexual experience as well. That meant that he had to retain a strict hold upon his outer behavior and his inner instincts. A letter he wrote to a young friend in 1893 is illuminating. He first assures her that he has remembered his promise to pray for her. "I have done so ever since, morning and evening," he writes, and then goes on to another subject:

> Absence of temptation is no doubt sometimes a blessing: and it is
> one I often thank God for. But one has to remember that it is
> only a short breathing-space. The temptation is sure to come
> again: and the very freedom from it brings its own special
> danger—of laying down the weapons of defence, and ceasing to
> "watch and pray": and then comes the sudden surprise, finding us
> all unprepared, and ready to yield again. (L, II, 952)

Lewis Carroll fought his battles with the Devil—and, as we know, for the Victorians, sex was often the Devil. I am convinced that Carroll won his battles. Search as one may through the nine volumes of the diaries, through the thousands of letters, and through the mound of reminiscences that his young friends later added to the record, absolutely nothing indicates that he ever lost a single skirmish. He had exiled the Devil early, when a boy, and there was no place for him in Carroll's life thereafter. It had to be that way. Somewhere deep down inside, Carroll knew that, given his preference for the friendship of children, if he once succumbed to any temptation, he would never be able to befriend them again. His own uncompromising standards, his forthright, pious nature would not permit it. Besides he loved innocence so, how could he ever violate it? He was not, as James Joyce would have him be, Lewd Carroll. He was a sort of Victorian Catcher in the Rye, but he was not a Humbert Humbert. In him came together the stern Puritan godliness of home and the lofty spirit of militant Christianity of Rugby. These Victorian forces produced a man so thoroughly controlled that we find it difficult to believe in him as he really was. But the fault, as someone once said, lies not in the stars, but in ourselves. The evidence is there, in the written record, and in Carroll's case, the written record brings us closer to the object than do the surviving papers of most luminaries. Dodgson kept his diaries as a way of accounting to God for what he did in His service and as a way of prodding himself on to greater work in the service of his Savior. They tell the truth, for Dodgson knew as well as anyone that you could not lie to God.

The truth is that he loved much and many, and his love helped a succession of young people find their footing in life and grow up happier and more self-confident than they might have done had he not trod this earth. He also left two great children's classics, which, in their way, try to do for all children of all places and all times what Charles Dodgson was able to do for the relatively few that he knew personally. Perhaps he would have been happier had he married and given expression to his sexual promptings. But that was not to be. As a celibate, he left behind a greater and kinder legacy than most men are able to do who lead what we think of as more conventional lives.

Notes

I owe a special debt to two books that do not appear in the notes below: Walter E. Houghton, *The Victorian Frame of Mind* (New Haven: Yale Univ. Press, 1957), and David Newsome, *Godliness & Good Learning* (London: John Murray, 1961). Lewis Carroll's diaries and letters are the private property of the C.L. Dodgson Estate; the excerpts here may not be reproduced without permission.

1. Most of the writings by critics alluded to are anthologized in *Aspects of Alice,* ed. Robert Phillips (London: Penguin, 1974), including Burke's essay, "From 'The Thinking of the Body.'"

2. Stuart Dodgson Collingwood, *The Life and Letters of Lewis Carroll* (London: T. Fisher Unwin, 1898), p. 26.

3. Nine of Dodgson's thirteen diary volumes survive and are now in the British Library. Almost three-fourths of the text appears in *The Diaries of Lewis Carroll,* ed. Roger Lancelyn Green, 2 vols. (London: Cassell, 1953). Dodgson wrote this entry on February 6, 1863, and it appears almost entirely in the published edition (I, 191). The quotations from the *Diaries* (*D*) that appear below carry citations in the text. When the text in fact includes material from the manuscript diaries only, merely the date of the entry appears after the entry. When the quotation in the text includes material not in the published version, that material comes directly from the manuscript diaries.

4. This letter, dated June 28, 1889, appears in full in *The Letters of Lewis Carroll,* ed. Morton N. Cohen (New York: Oxford Univ. Press, 1979), II, 746–47. In subsequent quotations from the *Letters* (*L*), the volume and page numbers appear at the end of the quotation.

5. "Theatre Dress," *Lewis Carroll Circular,* no. 2 (1974), 10–11.

6. Ibid., 12–13.

7. "Who Censored Lewis Carroll?" *The Times,* Jan. 23, 1982, p. 9.

Alan P. Johnson

"Dual Life":
The Status of Women
in Stoker's *Dracula*

Leonard Wolf has described exactly the theme in Bram Stoker's *Dracula* (1897) which seems to account for the novel's widespread and persistent appeal: "energy without grace, power without responsibility."[1] "Dracula is considerably more," Wolf points out, "than a sexual danger. Stoker insists on his brooding, primordial animality—he is antirational, childlike, instinctual," and, "in Christian terms he is a creature cut off from God because, for the sake of breath and motion, he has abjured salvation." A rebel against the limits of mortal life, Dracula is "a hero of despair" (pp. 220, 233). As Mina Harker says in the novel itself, "[H]is action is based on selfishness."[2] *Dracula* may be read as an epic struggle between the Count and the forces of western civilization led by Dr. Van Helsing or as a *Bildungsroman* in which Jonathan Harker and the novel's other young men learn to know and control the energy personified in Dracula.[3] The division of materials in the novel, however, implies that the significance of Dracula as an embodiment of "energy without grace, power without responsibility," is rooted importantly in the experience of his two victims, Lucy Westenra and Mina.

Despite the novel's focus on Jonathan in Transylvania in its first four chapters, the narrative in the remainder of the book forms a diptych—a portrait first of Lucy and then of Mina—which invites the reader to dwell upon and compare the two women, especially with regard to their respective involvements with Dracula. Chapters 5–16 focus upon Lucy in London and in Whitby, where Dracula lands by ship and attacks her, and then in London again, where her several male admirers, led by Dr. Van Helsing, gather to try to release her from Dracula's demonic influence and to find and destroy him. When, in Chapter 17, Mina and her husband Jonathan join the search after Lucy's death and exorcism, the focus shifts to Mina as Dracula's second victim and as an indispensable aid to the men in the pursuit and destruction of Dracula. In this diptych each woman develops what Van Helsing at one point calls a "dual life" (p. 206)—a life of conscious and willing conformity to her society and yet also a life of largely subconscious rebellion against it. In the case of each woman, Dracula symbolizes her inner rebelliousness, and its crisis coincides with her commerce with Dracula. The diptych also shows, however, that each woman's rebellion is justified and has been provoked by the undue constraints and condescension which have been inflicted upon her by her society, chiefly by the men around her and chiefly because the thinking of the society is dominated by anachronistic notions of social class and chivalry. By the end of the novel Dracula's significance as a symbol of selfishness includes the male characters as well as Lucy and Mina, but, with regard to the two women, the facts that he is a male and an aristocrat mirror of the kind of power that frustrates Lucy and Mina, and thus the kind of power they would like to wield. Both are frustrated by male prerogative: Lucy is expected to make an aristocratic marriage, and Mina is simultaneously apotheosized and nullified by the men's chivalry. *Dracula* is a complex book, but in the main it is not the sadistic exercise in misogyny for which it has sometimes been mistaken.[4] On the contrary, with the aid of some remarkable psychological symbolism, it presents an incisive and sympathetic analysis of the frustration felt by women in late-nineteenth-century Britain.

In general the historical counterpart of Lucy's and Mina's rebelliousness is the complex of frustrated hopes and resentment which must have motivated and accompanied British women's slow, uphill struggle toward equal status with men in the last half of the nineteenth century. Stoker was definitely interested in this long, wide-ranging effort, but his novel seems particularly to be a response to the concept of the "New Woman" which became hotly controversial in the early 1890s. The frustrating slowness of the general progress toward equality for women is evident in the lapse of forty-eight years between the first Parliamentary defeat of women's suffrage in 1870 and its passage in 1918, and in the long lapse between the first listing of a woman (Elizabeth Blackwell, who held a U.S. medical degree) in the Medical Register of the United Kingdom in 1859 and the decision of the Royal College of Physicians and Surgeons to grant their diplomas to women in 1908. Women were far less free to enter professions such as medicine and law than to become nurses and teachers, who were honored but underpaid, and clerical workers, who could find "a new type of employment created by such technical inventions as the . . . typewriter" (first marketed by E. Remington and Sons, for example, in 1874) without competing with an established male work force.[5]

Even as a youth Stoker must have been aware of the practical abilities of Victorian women and aware that they merited self-sufficiency if they wished it. His biographer, Harry Ludlam, notes that Stoker's mother, Charlotte, was active in Dublin in "social welfare work and determined championing of the weaker sex."[6] In her published lecture, *On Female Emigration from Workhouses* (Dublin, 1864), she advocated government-supported emigration for Irish pauper girls in order to "equalize the sexes" numerically. While she recognized marriage as "the true and legitimate end of a woman's existence," she did not rank marriage as "by any means the first (much less) the only object of emigration." For her, emigration and numerical equalization were "the best and surest means" by which pauper girls and other "young women of good character" might become "self-supporting young wom[e]n" and attain "that independence in other countries from which they are debarred in this" (pp. 8–9). Ludlam states that Bram himself spoke on the issue of votes for women at the Trinity College (Dublin) Philosophical Society in the late 1860s, but he does not tell us which side Bram took (p. 27).

While Stoker was certainly aware of the late-Victorian women's movement in general and had Charlotte's precedent for sympathy toward it, *Dracula* seems clearly a response particularly to the "New Woman" controversy of the 1890s because he mentions the "New Woman" in the novel (p. 99) and focuses upon precisely the sort of frustration depicted repeatedly in the so-called "New Woman" fiction published in the first half of the decade. According to Linda Dowling, the "New Woman" concept was a demand for "sexual equality and self-development" for women and a challenge to the traditional Victorian marriage arranged for money and position, to the subservience of wives to their husbands, and even in some cases to the ideas of motherhood and distinctively womanly human "nature." The "New Woman" concept, Dowling says, was expressed in fiction such as George Egerton's *Discords* (1893), Mona Caird's *The Daughters of Danaus* (1894), Grant Allen's *The Woman Who Did* (1895), and, from a critical viewpoint, Hardy's *Jude the Obscure* (1895). Dowling points out that the outspoken defiance of "established culture" by this fiction created "deep cultural anxiety" in contemporary reviewers and commentators and moved them to respond with an "apocalyptic vocabulary" in which they compared the novelists' attacks to the French Revolution and the decline of Rome. In *The New Woman and the Victorian Novel*, Gail Cunningham emphasizes that in the "New Woman" novels the usual consequence of the heroine's struggle for sexual and social independence is that she suffers "nervous disorder, disease, and death" as a result of her opposition to the society she lives in.[7]

Nervous disorder is precisely what Stoker's two heroines are driven to suffer by the clash between their aspirations and social rejection, and in Lucy's case he adds not only disease and death but also a period of postmortem vampirism. His handling of feminine rebellion differs from the "New

Woman" fiction in three notable ways, however. First, despite his sympathetic understanding of the causes of the rebellion, he resembles the "New Woman's" anxious critics by characterizing the rebellion with the "apocalyptic" figure of an alien vampire. Like the journal, *Lady's Realm,* which characterized the modern woman of 1887 as "this feminine Frankenstein" (Calder, p. 164), Stoker is ultimately conservative, as the novel's ending will show, although he implies that the traditional family and social structure should be conserved by means of reform. Second, neither Lucy nor Mina is literally a full-fledged "New Woman." Lucy is a traditional, upper-class, Victorian young woman and is consciously unconcerned with feminist reform, whereas Mina is aware of, and has strong affinities with, the "New Woman," but desires only recognition within a freely chosen marriage rather than radical sexual and social independence. And, third, since Stoker has chosen to show that women like Lucy and Mina who are consciously and outwardly conformists feel the same rebellious impulse displayed by the overt, radical rebels of the "New Woman" fiction, he has introduced the element of dual personality within each of his heroines. In responding to the "New Woman" controversy, then, he sees the broad scope of feminine rebellion and focuses upon its subconscious and barely conscious, rather than polemical and overt, mode, and he attempts to suggest changes which will obviate feminine rebellion and preserve the ideal of family-centered society.

Stoker depicted the public, fully conscious personalities of Lucy and Mina with a wealth of detail. As Stephanie Demetrakopoulos has pointed out, Lucy is what Peter Cominos has called the Victorian "Womanly Woman" in *Suffer and Be Still.* Lucy is the fragile, feminine "angel in the house" whose activities are never more than trivial. In the eyes of those around her, Lucy in her normal, public character is repeatedly "sweet," for example.[8] Her family has some continuity socially as her father, who is dead at the time of the story, has inherited an entailed estate (*Dracula,* p. 174). The family is at least modestly wealthy, for they have servants, a home called Hillingham in the London area, and perhaps a second residence at 17 Chatham Street, London, and they take rooms for the summer in a house at the Crescent in Whitby. In Whitby Lucy goes out "visiting with her mother" on "duty calls" (p. 74) and in London Lucy goes "a good deal to picture-galleries and for walks and rides in the park" and to the "pops" or popular concerts (p. 64; cf. 103, 116). Her vocation is apparently to be courted, and, although she receives proposals from Dr. Seward and Quincey Morris before Arthur Holmwood proposes, it seems understood by her mother and Lucy that she will marry Arthur, the only son of Lord Godalming, an aging peer. Early in the novel, Lucy writes to Mina that Arthur "and mama get on very well together; they have so many things to talk about in common," and Lucy goes on, "Mina, I love him," although she doesn't say why (pp. 64, 65).

In contrast to Lucy, Mina, even in her public, conscious role, resembles the "New Woman," but not in the sexually advanced mold of Grant Allen's Herminia in *The Woman Who Did* or Hardy's Sue Bridehead. Rather, Stoker's characterization of Mina recalls George Eliot's heroines or, more precisely, Wilkie Collins' Marian Halcombe, the independent, practical young woman who helps the young art teacher, Walter Hartwright, in solving the mystery of her helplessly "feminine" half-sister Laura's supposed death and in rescuing her from incarceration in an asylum by her fortune-hunting husband in *The Woman in White* (1860).[9] Probably the type of woman Stoker intends to represent in Mina is described in his remark in his printed lecture, *A Glimpse of America* (London, 1886), that American women are not bound by "those petty restraints which, with us, are rather recollections or traditions than social needs, or the logical outcome of the spirit of the age. In the United States, a young woman is, almost if not quite, as free to think and act for herself as a young man is. This personal freedom is of course based on a large measure of education, practical as well as of book-learning, and has its correlative in a very stringent law of personal discretion" (pp. 24–25).

In her journal Mina jokes about the "New Woman's" disapproval of the conventional feminine appetite for "severe tea" and about the "New Woman's" probably wanting to do the proposing of marriage; but Mina also adds, "And a nice job she will make of it, too! There's some consolation in that" (pp. 99–100).[10] Mina's status as "New" is suggested in the fact that she is an orphan and "never knew either father or mother" (p. 164). All that is known of her background is that she and Lucy have been childhood friends. Mina's "New Woman" status is established mainly by her practical competence. She supports herself at the novel's beginning as an "assistant schoolmistress" (p. 63), and, when she marries, she chooses a rising solicitor rather than an artistocrat who might give her vacuous leisure. As Harker's fiancée she has learned typing and stenography so as to "be able to be useful to Jonathan" (p. 63), and after their marriage she memorizes train schedules "so that [she] may help Jonathan in case he is in a hurry" (p. 192; cf. 343). After joining the alliance of Lucy's friends in pursuit of Dracula, she puts all their information in chronological order, types all of it in triplicate, and, except for a brief and disastrous interval, acts as "secretary" to the group.

As Professor Van Helsing soon sees, Mina "has a man's brain," but she also has "a woman's heart" (p. 241; cf. 344). Her engagement to Harker is a *donnée* at the outset of the story, and her devotion to him in her public, conscious role is a pattern of romantic fidelity. She marries him when he is a mental wreck in Budapest after his escape from Castle Dracula and sustains him through his subsequent self-doubt by "keeping up a brave and cheerful appearance" (p. 165). When she learns that she has been infected with vampirism, she is stricken with "horror and distress," and when she sees "some sure danger to him: instantly forgetting her own grief, she seize[s] hold of him and crie[s] out:— . . . 'Stay with these friends who will watch over you!'" (p. 289). To the young men who have courted Lucy, Mina acts as an affectionate, maternal, and sisterly comforter. Along with her romantic fidelity and perhaps her feminine sympathy, her religious faith and a ludicrous sense of propriety also set her off from the "New Woman." She shows the religious fiber of her character, for example, as she writes about her marriage: "Please God, I shall never, never forget . . . the grave and sweet responsibilities I have taken on me" (p. 115). After becoming consciously aware that Dracula has attacked her, she cries out, "What have I done to deserve such a fate, I who have tried to walk in meekness and righteousness all my days" (p. 294), and she persistently reassures her allies "that it is in trouble and trial that [their] faith is tested . . . and that God will aid [them] up to the end" (p. 295; cf. 301, 313, 321). Mina's propriety is a curious oddity. When she leads Lucy back from a sleepwalking in Whitby's parish churchyard, for example, and has put her own shoes on Lucy's bare feet, Mina daubs her own feet with mud "using each foot in turn on the other, so that . . . no one, in case we should meet any one, should notice my bare feet" (p. 102). Nevertheless, Mina's practical competence makes her a self-sufficient woman in the style, for example, of Collins' Marian Halcombe and Stoker's own *Glimpse of America* and an obvious contrast to Lucy.

Although *Dracula* presents the traditional, Victorian, womanly ideal in Lucy and an approximation of the "New Woman" in Mina, both Lucy and Mina are led by the conflict between their personal wishes and their social surroundings to develop a mainly unconscious, egocentric rebelliousness whose crisis coincides with, and is symbolized by, Dracula's attacks upon each character. In giving Lucy and Mina each a powerful, subconscious mental life distinct from her conscious self, Stoker drew upon the general notion of double personality, or dissociation, which had been developed in recent psychology—for example, by Jean Charcot, who is mentioned in *Dracula* (p. 197)[11]—and had been popularly immortalized in Stevenson's *The Strange Case of Dr. Jekyll and Mr. Hyde* (1886). Stoker's awareness of double personality within one person in the years preceding *Dracula* is suggested in his *Personal Reminiscences of Henry Irving* (1906) in references to Irving's opinion that while performing a role an actor should have "'a double consciousness, in which all the emotions proper to the occasion may have full sway, while the actor is all the time on the alert for every detail of his method.'" Stoker discussed his employer Irving's views with him at least by 1889 and probably read them in Irving's preface to Diderot's *Paradox of Acting* edited by W.H. Pollock in 1883.[12] Stoker made explicit use of the literary "double," a character who is an external embodiment of a "self" which exists naturally within the mind of another character, in the playful story "Crooken Sands," published in 1894. In it, the central character not only sees his own "double," but also reads what seems to be a book invented by Stoker, "Die Döppleganger [sic,] by Dr. Heinrich von Aschenberg."[13] In *Dracula* Stoker uses not only the notions of "dual life" and the external double, Dracula, but also the notion of "unconscious cerebration." According to Leonard Wolf, the term was used by nineteenth-century physicians to label thought processes which were examined in contemporary research such as Dr. Thomas Laycock's *Treatise on the Nervous Diseases of Women* (1840) (*The Annotated Dracula*, p. 71, n.27). In *Personal Reminiscences of Irving*, Stoker once uses the term synonymously with "dual consciousness" (I, 265). In *Dracula* Dr. Seward uses the term twice to refer to the thought processes of his patient, Renfield (pp. 79, 276). The rebellious selves of Lucy and Mina seem to be largely the product of their unconscious cerebration as they respond to their social surroundings. After their discontentment develops to the stage of strong rebellion, Dracula appears and attacks each character. He is thus in this context a symbolic double of each woman's rebellious egoism, and the literal vampirism which results from his bite represents the change in personality produced by the egoism.

Lucy's duality first shows itself in the novel in her sleepwalking at Whitby and culminates in her funeral vault, where Arthur, under Van Helsing's direction, hammers a three-foot stake through her heart and sees "Lucy as she [lies] there; the pointed teeth, the bloodstained, voluptuous mouth . . . the whole carnal and unspiritual appearance," change to "Lucy as we had seen her in her life, with her face of unequalled sweetness and purity" (pp. 220, 222). Between her death and the exorcism, Van Helsing sums up her condition as a polarity of sleeping and waking: "[H]ere is some dual life. . . . She was bitten by a vampire when she was in a trance, sleep-walking . . . in a trance could he best come to take more blood. In trance she died, and in trance she is Un-Dead, too" (p. 206). To the reader who focuses upon Dracula as a literal creature with extraordinary powers, Lucy's sleepwalking and trances may seem to result simply from his influence. The novel suggests, though, that the sleepwalking precedes his influence. Lucy's sleepwalking first occurred in her childhood, and, during the seven-month period of the novel's present-time action, the sleepwalking recurs shortly before July 26, twelve days before Dracula's move upon England. He probably does not and cannot know of her existence until he disembarks from the *Demeter* on the night of August 7 and becomes aware of her at the funeral of the *Demeter* captain in the Whitby parish churchyard on August 10. She is apparently first attacked by Dracula on the night of August 10.

The emergence of Lucy's "vampire" self is a product of her feelings of vigorous sexual desire and a disinclination for the constraint of marriage which confronts her as a girl who is attractive, about to turn twenty, and comfortably placed in polite society, but it is also a product of the ineffectuality of her fiancé, Arthur, and the impercipient selfishness of her mother, who promotes Lucy's and Arthur's marriage. Writing to Mina in a mood of playful vanity in May, Lucy boasts of "*Three* proposals in one day!" and later comments, "Why can't they let a girl marry three men, or as many as want her . . . ?" (pp. 65, 68). Although her tone is still playful, the comment reflects her genuine sexual attraction to Seward and Morris, whom she has refused. She has found Seward "handsome . . . one of the most resolute men I ever saw, and yet the most calm" (p. 64), and she reflects, "[I]t isn't at all a happy thing when you have to see a poor fellow, whom you know loves you honestly, going away . . . and to know that . . . you are passing quite out of his life" (p. 66). With regard to Morris, whom she regards as "manly," she "would worship the very ground he trod on . . . if [she] were free" (pp. 68, 69).

When Mina first refers to Lucy's sleepwalking in July, she mentions at the same time that "Lucy is to be married in the autumn" to Arthur "and . . . is already planning out her dresses and how her house is to be arranged," noting that Arthur is expected to join them soon at Whitby (p. 81). Apparently to Lucy the house she is in at Whitby represents the coming marriage since her sleepwalking takes her outside, and when her somnambulism is frustrated by Mina, Lucy "tries the door, and . . . goes about the room searching for the key" (p. 82; cf. 103). Her antipathy to the social role she is expected to assume is underscored in the sleepwalking section of the novel by her similarity to the "white lady" who, according to local legend, haunts Whitby Abbey. The white lady is supposedly the nun described in Walter Scott's poem "Marmion" who was unfaithful to her vows by plotting with Marmion in an attempt to win his love and was punished by being immured in the abbey. Like the lady, Lucy characteristically wears white. The parallel is recalled later when Lucy, after her death, becomes the "Bloofer Lady" or beautiful lady attacking children in London, again wearing white. The fact that her victims are all children suggests that her animosity, like the rebelliousness of the most radical heroines in "New Woman" fiction, is directed not only at the vows and legal constraints of the role she has been expected to assume but at motherhood itself.

The importance of Arthur as an effective cause of Lucy's rebellion is implied by the extreme destructiveness of her intention when, on her deathbed, she invites him in a "voluptuous" voice to kiss her (pp. 167–68) so that she may draw out his blood and infect him, too, with vampirism. In fact, he has given her reason to regard him not only as a prime agent of social constraint because he is her fiancé, but as a mere nullity as well. When Arthur visits Lucy at the end of August, he takes her on a merely conventional round of diversions—"walks and drives, and rides, and rowing, and tennis, and fishing" (p. 116)—and before and after that visit he is detained at the bedside of his dying father. When the illness that accompanies Lucy's vampirism appears during Arthur's visit at the end of August, he calls in Seward and returns to his father for a week. He returns briefly on September 7 and gives blood at Van Helsing's request but immediately goes away again to his father until Lucy calls him to her deathbed on September 19. Although Van Helsing sees Arthur as "stalwart . . . and . . . strong" and eager to help at the time of the transfusion (p. 130), Stoker's management of the story hints that Arthur's attachment to the class system of the past keeps him from thoroughly effective action in the present.[14] Lucy frequently proclaims her love for Arthur, but she reserves her specific adjectives of praise for Seward and Morris. Her antipathy becomes murderously evident when Arthur approaches her deathbed, and after her death she repeats her offer of a fatal kiss, now with a mocking tone, when Arthur sees her as a vampire returning to her tomb on what would have been their wedding night.

By means of the conclusion of Lucy's story, in which Arthur hammers a stake through her heart, Stoker suggests that her rebellion could have been prevented by the presence of a strong self-dependent fiancé. Van Helsing apparently insists that Arthur perform the exorcism and that the phallic stake be used in order to teach him the masculine strength he has lacked. However, because Arthur's ineffectuality was largely a result of his subordination of personal interest in Lucy to aristocratic family duty, Stoker seems to imply that the aristocratic duties prevent vigorous, independent, procreative, life-sustaining action and should be thrown off or transcended. In the words of *A Glimpse of America*, Arthur has been governed by outmoded "tradition" rather than "social needs, or . . . the spirit of the age." Although he retains the title he inherits from his father, Arthur subsequently takes an active part in the hunt for Dracula and devotes distinctly aristocratic contributions to its success: terriers to destroy Dracula's rats, the weight of the Godalming title to persuade a locksmith to open Dracula's Piccadilly house, and a steam launch which Arthur stokes, repairs, and pilots himself. While he learns through the exorcism to use the resources of his class in a self-dependent, socially beneficial way, his "mercy-bearing stake" seems to release Lucy's waking self, now her soul, from the domination of her rebellious, vampire self by assuring her that the aristocracy could have provided her with a strong partner worthy of her submission to the constraints of marriage and motherhood.

Arthur is an important cause of Lucy's rebellion and almost becomes the first victim of her vampirism, but her rebelliousness seems to be brought to the intensity of vampirism by her antipathy toward Mrs. Westenra. Although Lucy never speaks against her, Lucy must see Mrs. Westenra as repressive, outdated, and selfish. In mid-August Mina writes that Mrs. Westenra expects to die of heart disease "within a few months" and "is rejoiced that [Lucy] is soon to have some one [Arthur, that is] to protect her" (p. 105). Lucy will have little choice but to accept this protection because Mrs. Westenra has altered her will so as to leave her entire estate, against her lawyer's advice, to Arthur rather than Lucy. Mrs. Westenra's domination by the past is suggested generally, as is old Lord Godalming's, by failing health but especially by her tampering with the garlic with which Van Helsing tries to protect Lucy from Dracula. Because of Mrs. Westenra's heart trouble, the physicians Seward and Van Helsing conceal from her any information about Lucy's sickness which might upset Mrs. Westenra and cause her "sudden death" (p. 127). Since she has not been told that the garlic wreath which Van Helsing puts around Lucy's neck and the garlic seal on her closed window are protection against a vampire, Mrs. Westenra removes the wreath and opens the window "to let in a little fresh air" (p. 142), as she says, exposing Lucy to an attack by Dracula. Mrs. Westenra's reasoning is traditional, and her error suggests that the traditional social ideal which she embodies cannot comprehend or cope with a threat to its existence such as Lucy's rebelliousness. Moreover, the fact that the error allows Dracula to enter through the window suggests that Lucy's rebelliousness is directly fostered by her mother's traditionalism.

Mrs. Westenra's selfishness appears clearly when Dr. Seward introduces Van Helsing to her as his consultant about Lucy's illness. Seward notes that Mrs. Westenra is "alarmed, but not nearly as much as I expected. . . . Here, in a case where any shock may prove fatal, matters are so ordered that . . . things not personal . . . do not seem to reach her." Seward calls her attitude "an ordered selfishness" (p. 129). Later on, when a wolf which Dracula has freed from the London Zoo thrusts his head through Lucy's window while her mother is with her, Mrs. Westenra, according to Lucy's report of the incident, "crie[s] out in fright . . . and clutche[s] wildly at anything that would help her," including the protective garlic wreath which she tears from Lucy's neck (p. 151).

Lucy's antipathy toward her mother is strongly suggested in Lucy's affection for a particular seat in the Whitby parish cemetery and is suggested also in the episode of the wolf. The cemetery seat is introduced in a scene in which Mina and Lucy, sitting in the seat, talk with Mr. Swales, an old native, who argues that epitaphs are usually untrue. To prove his claim he points to the epitaph of George Canon on a slab under their feet. The epitaph says that the slab and seat were "erected by his sorrowing mother to her dearly beloved son" and that he "died, in the hope of a glorious resurrection." Swales states that "the sorrowin' mother was a hell-cat that hated him . . . an' he hated her so that he committed suicide in order that she mightn't get an insurance she put on his life." Although George Canon was outspoken in his filial rebellion, the antagonism between him and his hypocritical mother parallels closely the implicit antagonism between Lucy and Mrs. Westenra. Lucy's response to Swales is revealing: "Oh, why did you tell us of this? It is my favourite seat, and I cannot leave it; and now I find I must go on sitting over the grave of a suicide" (pp. 76–77).

While Lucy occupies the cemetery seat nine days later on August 10, Dracula apparently becomes aware of her for the first time and draws her blood. He has come from Transylvania on the *Demeter*, has taken refuge in George Canon's grave, and thus is there when Lucy and Mina use the seat during the funeral of the *Demeter* captain on the morning of the tenth. On the evening of the tenth, Mina discovers that Lucy has sleepwalked and finds her "half reclining with her head lying over the back of the seat" with Dracula bending over her (p. 101). Four days later the two girls see his "dark figure" on the seat, and in the evening Lucy is attacked a second time (pp. 104–05). Stoker's use of the seat and his timing of events suggest that the suicide's grave symbolizes Lucy's antipathy toward her mother and that psychologically Lucy progresses from resisting marriage with Arthur, to the antipathy against her mother for promoting the marriage, to a climactic indulgence in selfish hatred toward her mother which is symbolized by the advent of Dracula from the grave.

The later episode in London in which the wolf thrusts himself into Lucy's window reiterates the suggestion that her submission to Dracula – that is, her rebellious egoism – is partly and importantly a response to her mother's actions. As literal narrative the episode is a peculiar combination of events. Prior to the episode, Van Helsing has successfully protected Lucy in her room at night by means of garlic, and Dracula has released a wolf, "Bersicker," from the London Zoo. In the episode Mrs. Westenra looks in on Lucy at night, and as they lie together in Lucy's bed for warmth, they hear "the flapping and buffeting" of Dracula in the form of a bat at the window. Bersicker breaks in, and Mrs. Westenra clutches at Lucy's garlic wreath, then dies. As she falls, her head strikes Lucy's, making the young woman "dizzy for a moment or two." Lucy sees the wolf withdraw, and "a myriad of little specks [seem] to come blowing in through the window." The specks are a characteristic vampire form, as Van Helsing later explains (p. 245). Lucy at first feels as if she is under "some spell" and is unable to move, but she "recover[s] consciousness" and places all her garlic flowers on her mother's body (pp. 151–52).

In the literal narrative the wolf is Dracula's means of creating a passage through the window, which apparently has been sealed with garlic, but because Dracula has become symbolic of Lucy's rebellious egoism, the wolf is perhaps symbolic of her potentiality for physical violence. This meaning is supported emphatically by the zoo-keeper's description of Bersicker, which precedes the episode. Bersicker is docile to his trainer and so accustomed to captivity that he "ain't . . . used to fighten' or even providin' for hisself," but "you can't trust wolves no more nor women," the zoo-keeper says, and he fears that if Bersicker cannot find food during his escape, he might devour an untended baby in the park (pp. 145, 148). With reference to Mrs. Westenra, the wolf's intrusion through the window seems to suggest that she now perceives the potential violence in Lucy's character as they lie in Lucy's bed. With reference to Lucy, Stoker's use of the wolf suggests that she feels a desire to destroy her mother completely, whereas the vampirism which expresses Lucy's essential egoism drains the victim of his power but permits him to exist. The events following Bersicker's intrusion suggest that Lucy advances to a new affirmation of her vampirish rebelliousness. As she is literally stunned by her mother's fall, so apparently is Lucy stunned by the revelation of selfishness in her mother's clutching at the garlic wreath. At this point Dracula enters in the form of specks — that is, Lucy's egoism rises climactically within her — and this development seems to determine her next action. She puts the protective flowers on her dead mother and away from herself even though they can do her mother no good and even though Lucy recalls Van Helsing's instructions to wear them. As she is recalling her experience immediately afterward, "the air seems full of specks." Although she has "recovered consciousness" and goes on to pray for divine help, she has apparently given her allegiance decisively to her rebellious impulse in response to her mother's self-revealing clutch at personal survival.

The characterizations of Arthur and Mrs. Westenra which emerge from their relationships with Lucy suggest that Stoker does not intend his presentation of her to be a simple excoriation of a lustful woman whose mask of superficial propriety falls away. Of course, Lucy begins with a vigorous sexual vitality and, after her infection with vampirism, becomes seethingly "voluptuous," and Stoker's lurid rendering of Arthur's driving a stake through her heart suggests that a lustful woman must be shown her place with a vengeance. The intensity of the imagery strongly supports speculation that Stoker wrote under the grip of an Oedipal fantasy or saw female sexuality as what Phyllis Roth calls the "pre-Oedipal threat" of the *vagina dentata* of folk lore.[15] The totality of Lucy's story, however, represents her as a victim before she becomes a villainess, a victim not only of her own vitality and vanity but especially of the class system which is perpetuated by Arthur's subordination of himself to aristocratic duty and by Mrs. Westenra's egocentric, socially ambitious management of Lucy's life. Lucy's story suggests that the ideal courtship would be one between an independent man and woman, both oblivious of aristocratic concerns — that is, between a man and woman like Jonathan and Mina.

Having shown that aristocratic concerns block the way to satisfactory marriage and evoke rebellion even in a thoroughly conventional, relatively unthinking young woman like Lucy, Stoker shifts his focus to Mina and shows that even in the seemingly ideal marriage of an independent, freely choosing man and woman, the woman encounters reluctance on the part of the men around her, including her husband, to accept her as an able, self-determining person. The dual life which such reluctance evokes in Mina passes through two phases: its emergence, culminating in her commerce with Dracula, and the extension of her dual life from the time the men discover her vampirism until they destroy Dracula at the end of the novel. The emergence of Mina's dual life is a clear, direct result of her exclusion from the pursuit of Dracula by Jonathan, Van Helsing, Seward, Arthur, and Quincey Morris because of their chivalric preconceptions about her proper role.

The men's exclusion of Mina is foreshadowed by their persistent protectiveness toward and apotheosis of her. Jonathan, for example, writing journal entries during his adventures in Transylvania at the beginning of the novel, wishes to spare Mina "the pain" of learning about his "wicked, burning desire" to be kissed by the vampire women there (p. 46) and supposes that although "Mina is a woman," she has "nought in common" with "those awful women" (p. 61). Similarly when Seward meets Mina and she asks him to inform her about Lucy's death, he thinks of Mina as "a sweet-faced, dainty-looking girl" whom he "must be careful not to frighten" (p. 226), although he is soon struck by her "courage and resolution" and gives her his full journal to read (p. 229). Quincey Morris, at his first meeting with Mina, expresses his admiration for her but diminishes her with the title, "'Little girl' — the very words," Mina reflects, "he had used to Lucy" (p. 237). Van Helsing is the most florid of the men in the exercise of paradoxically condescending courtliness. To him, at his first meeting with Mina when he visits her in Exeter to acquire information about Lucy, Mina is "one of God's women, fashioned by His own hand to show us men and other women that there is a heaven where we can enter, and that its light can be here on earth. So true, so sweet, so noble, so little an egoist . . . in this age, so sceptical and selfish" (p. 194, cf. 191 and 225). He has greeted her with a "courtly bow" and has been surprised that she seems to have a "good memory for facts, for details[, since i]t is not always so with young ladies" (p. 189). When the men and Mina gather at Seward's London asylum to raid Dracula's house, Carfax, next door and to discover his other lairs, Van Helsing proposes that Mina be excluded and is supported by the other men. On September 30, the eve of the Carfax raid, he says to Seward, "[A]fter to-night she must not have to do with this so terrible affair . . . it is no part for a woman. Even if she be not harmed, her heart may fail her. . . . And, besides, she is . . .

not so long married; there may be other things to think of some time, if not now" (p. 241). "[Y]ou must be our star and our hope," Van Helsing tells her, "and we shall act all the more free that you are not in danger" (p. 248). Jonathan is "relieved" by the exclusion since the men's work "is too great a strain for a woman to bear" (pp. 248, 260; cf. 254, 268), and Seward reflects after the Carfax raid that "if she had remained in touch with the affair, it would in time infallibly have wrecked her" (p. 262; cf. 241).

Ironically, it is by being put out of touch with the pursuit of Dracula that Mina indeed is "infallibly . . . wrecked." Her response to the exclusion is foreshadowed in her reaction to Van Helsing's underestimation of her ability to remember facts at their first meeting at Exeter. In an uncharacteristically discourteous act, Mina shows him the area of her competence and his ignorance by handing him her diary to read in shorthand. As she describes the action in her journal, she notes her similarity to Eve: "I could not resist the temptation of mystifying him a bit—I suppose it is some of the taste of the original apple that remains still in our mouths" (p. 189). Later, the exclusion of Mina is followed immediately by her overt cooperation but also by her conscious displeasure and covert commerce with Dracula. When Van Helsing announces the exclusion on September 30, she sees it as "not . . . good . . . a bitter pill for me to swallow," but she agrees because the men's "minds were made up," and, she writes, "I could say nothing, save to accept their chivalrous care of me." Their instruction for her "to go to bed and sleep" as they set off for Carfax she describes immediately afterward as "manlike" (p. 248). While the men count coffins and kill the rats with which Dracula decoys them in the Carfax chapel, Mina experiences Dracula's first attack upon her, which she recalls confusedly as a dream of a "pillar of cloud" from which emerge two fiery red eyes and then a "livid white face" (pp. 264–65). The image of the phallic pillar suggests her desire to exercise the power which the men reserve for themselves. Consciously, the following morning, Mina continues to assent to the exclusion although she finds herself, she says, "crying like a silly fool" (p. 262).[16]

As the exclusion continues through the two days, October 2 and 3, Dracula's visits continue during the nights, culminating in what Van Helsing calls Mina's "baptism of blood" (pp. 327, 347). Although the episode is not without puzzling details, it clearly implies a magnification of Mina's rebellious desire for power. She is awake rather than sleeping when Dracula enters her room, and, although she is "bewildered" when he prepares to take a "little refreshment," she recalls later that "strangely enough, I did not want to hinder him." When he finishes he tells her, "You shall be avenged in turn; for not one of them but shall minister to your needs." Somewhat puzzling are the facts that when Mina tries to awaken Jonathan, who sleeps next to her, she cannot, and that Dracula forces Mina to drink from a wound he makes in his own chest. By the depth of Jonathan's sleep, Stoker perhaps intends to represent the stolidity of Jonathan's misconception of Mina's needs and abilities. Mina's forced drinking of Dracula's blood seems to suggest that when Mina has yielded up her energies to her wish for egocentric power, then, next, the newly energized wish for power forces itself upon her conscious, everyday mind and begins to energize it.[17]

As soon as Van Helsing and the other men discover Mina's vampirism, they see that their exclusion of her has been a mistake and include her once again in their councils "in full confidence" (p. 296). This rectification of the condition which was the immediate cause of her discontent and consequent vampirism does not, however, halt or reverse the effects of her vampirism. Her teeth elongate, for example, and she discovers that she has a telepathic connection with Dracula. When, before departing to ambush Dracula at his Piccadilly house, Van Helsing touches Mina with a sacramental wafer to protect her and it burns her forehead, the Cainlike "mark of shame" it leaves convinces Mina and the others that she is still "unclean" even in the eyes of God (p. 302, cf. 290). While the vampire, or rebellious, self persists in Mina, her pious and loving self rises in reaction to it to the level of saintly martyrdom, but without freeing her from the vampirism. She repeatedly expresses religious hope, for example, and she offers her telepathic link with Dracula as a means of locating him. Realizing that it may be a danger to the men and that she must obey if Dracula summons her, she vows, with eyes that "sh[i]ne with the devotion of a martyr," to die at the first "sign of harm to any that [she] love[s]" (p. 296). She also excludes herself from the men's councils, asks for posthumous exorcism, and memorializes her self-sacrifice by having Jonathan read a burial service for her in the presence of the other men. Even her saintly, martyrlike intentions, however, do not break the telepathic link or erase her Cainlike mark until Jonathan's and Quincey's knives destroy Dracula in the final scene in Transylvania.

The persistence of Mina's dual life implies that even after the men redress their error of excluding her they remain guilty of their chivalric prejudice or of the egoism from which it sprang. The second, saintly phase of Mina's rebellion, then, calls attention to the fact that Dracula has been available throughout the novel as a symbol of egoism in the men as well as in the women. The nature of the men's error is suggested by their lack of control over Dracula. He himself points out their freedom from his domination when they confront him at his Piccadilly house and he taunts them: "Your girls . . . are mine already; and through them you and others shall yet be mine—my creatures" (p. 312). While his threat prophesies that the men will become his subjects, it also admits that they are not yet under his power. He, however, is not under their power either. All they have succeeded in doing is to identify him as their enemy. Van Helsing has learned of

Dracula's identity by reading Jonathan's Transylvanian diary and documents pertaining to Dracula's acquisition of Carfax and has taught Seward, Arthur, and Quincey "to believe" in Dracula's reality when they discover Lucy returning to her tomb in vampire form. In the novel's opening chapters, Jonathan has found Dracula in his box of earth in Transylvania and attempted to destroy him with a shovel but has been "paralyse[d]" by his look so that "the shovel turn[s] in [Jonathan's] hand" and merely wounds Dracula's forehead (p. 60). Later Jonathan comes to wonder whether he has imagined Dracula's existence until Van Helsing assures Jonathan, "[I]t is *true*." With the reassurance, Jonathan feels himself to be "a new man . . . I was in doubt," he says, "and . . . did not know what to trust, even the evidence of my own senses" (pp. 192–94). Neither Jonathan nor the other men, however, succeed in seizing Dracula when they confront him at his Piccadilly house, and, after that confrontation, they cannot pursue him without Mina's help. Jonathan and the other men have learned to believe in the reality of egoistic energy but apparently have not learned how to grasp and eradicate it as it lingers elusively within themselves.

The fact that, as Dracula flees to Transylvania, Jonathan and the other men can track him only by means of the telepathic link between Dracula and Mina suggests that the men can know and master the egoistic energy in themselves only by studying it in Mina and letting what they see in her guide them on a psychic journey into themselves or perhaps into a species of collective unconscious.[18] Perhaps at the novel's end, Stoker assigned the exorcism of the sensual, Transylvanian vampiresses to Van Helsing because of his earlier mental philandering when he jokes, for example, about his blood transfusion to Lucy as a sort of marriage. And perhaps Quincey, who is repeatedly characterized by rough-and-ready resolution, assists at the destruction of Dracula to stress that Jonathan has acquired that quality as his knife shears the Count's throat. In any case, the pursuit of Dracula into Transylvania suggests the sort of psychic journey which Rider Haggard implied in *She* (1886) and Conrad would depict in "The Heart of Darkness" in 1899. A journey into the underworld of the mind is suggested, for example, by Mina's, Jonathan's, and Seward's comments that, since Dracula's escape, "it is almost impossible to realise that the cause of all [their] trouble is still existent" (p. 327). Later, as Jonathan journeys upriver during the pursuit he comments, "We seem to be drifting into unknown places and unknown ways; into a whole world of dark and dreadful things" (p. 361). Moreover, a psychic journey is implied not only by Mina's telepathy but also by the fact that Van Helsing taps the telepathic link by hypnotising Mina. The telepathy, he tells her, is a "power . . . you have won from your suffering," and the hypnosis is his "volition" – that is, his desire to learn what she has suffered (p. 347). Mina's telepathy provides the clues to Dracula's escape from

London into Transylvania and makes the men's journey possible. Without her telepathy, Van Helsing's epic struggle would fail, and his and the younger men's education would fall short of self-knowledge and self-mastery.

The persistence of Mina's dual life until the men destroy Dracula implies, then, that the rebellion of an intelligent, good woman may be the only means by which she and the men who slight her can destroy the egoism which the men inadvertently admit from their own psychic depths and evoke from hers. In the context of *Dracula* as a whole, the men's chivalric preconceptions, which frustrate Mina's desire for acceptance as an able, independent person, recall the outworn concerns with social class which were a major cause of Lucy's rebellion against her conventionally Victorian, arranged, socially advantageous marriage to an ineffectual husband. Whereas Stoker symbolized the constructive male response in Lucy's case with the phallic stake, representing a strong, self-dependent transcendence of the obligations of class, at the novel's end the emasculating knife symbolizes a rejection of the male egoism implicit in the chivalric ideal. The ideal which the novel affirms is summed up in its final vignette of solidarity among its "little band of men" and Mina, and in the procreative, married love between Mina, the novel's "New Woman," and its "new man," Jonathan, who are equal in their marriage and equally capable in the larger society.

Notes

1. *A Dream of Dracula: In Search of the Living Dead* (Boston: Little, Brown, 1972), p. 302.

2. *Dracula* (1897; rpt. New York: New American Library, 1965), p. 347. Unless otherwise noted, all page numbers cited in text are from this edition. For a photo-offset edition of the first edition (second printing) and textual notes, see *The Annotated Dracula*, ed. Leonard Wolf (New York: N. Potter, 1975). The NAL edition omits the first edition's untitled, unsigned 77-word prefatory note which states that the book is a sequence of records written by persons who were contemporary with, and close to, the events they describe. The only serious typographical error in the NAL edition is *madams* on p. 123 for *The Annotated Dracula's madmans*.

3. See, e.g., Richard Wasson, "The Politics of Dracula," *English Literature in Transition*, 9 (1966), 24–27, and Mark M. Hennelly, Jr., "*Dracula*: The Gnostic Quest and Victorian Wasteland," *English Literature in Transition*, 20 (1977), 13–26, which provocatively argues that Van Helsing leads the novel's young men through an initiation into the mystery of procreative force and that Dracula embodies that force.

4. See especially Daniel Farson, *The Man Who Wrote Dracula: A Biography of Bram Stoker* (New York: St. Martin's Press, 1976), pp. 212–16, 233–35; Stephanie Demetrakopoulos, "Feminism, Sex Role Exchanges, and Other Subliminal Fantasies in Bram Stoker's *Dracula*," *Frontiers: Journal of Women's Studies*, 2 (1977), 104–13; Phyllis A. Roth, *Bram Stoker* (Boston: Twayne, 1982), pp. 111–26; Judith Weissman,

"Women and Vampires: *Dracula* as a Victorian Novel," *Midwest Quarterly*, 18 (1977), 392–405; and Gail B. Griffin, "'Your Girls That You All Love Are Mine': *Dracula* and the Victorian Male Imagination," *International Journal of Women's Studies*, 3 (1980), 545–65. My essay is not a blanket contradiction of these works but differs from them by focusing upon evidence of Stoker's understanding and disapproval of victimization of women by men.

5. *Encyclopaedia Britannica*, 1911 ed., s.v. "nursing," s.v. "women"; ibid., 15th ed., *Macropaedia*, s.v. "typewriter," s.v. "women, status of."

6. *A Biography of Bram Stoker, Creator of Dracula* (London: New English Library, 1977), p. 14, retitled from *A Biography of Dracula: The Life Story of Bram Stoker* (1962). I am indebted to Miss Ann Stoker for permission to use the pamphlet by Charlotte Stoker, cited below in my text.

7. Linda Dowling, "The Decadent and the New Woman in the 1890s," *Nineteenth-Century Fiction*, 33 (1979), 434–53, esp. pp. 438, 446, 450, 453, and 446–48. Gail Cunningham, *The New Woman and the Victorian Novel* (New York: Barnes and Noble, 1978), p. 49. See also ch. 12 of Jenni Calder, *Women and Marriage in Victorian Fiction* (New York: Oxford Univ. Press, 1976), and Lloyd Fernando, *"New Women" in the Late Victorian Novel* (University Park: Pennsylvania State Univ. Press, 1977), esp. pp. 1–25, 129–33. Although Calder and Fernando use "New Woman" to refer broadly to the "modern" woman of the last quarter or so of the nineteenth century, their quoted uses of "New Woman" come from the 1890s.

8. Demetrakopoulos, "Feminism . . . in *Dracula*," p. 109.

9. I am indebted to Professor Elaine Showalter for the comparison between Mina and Marian and the suggestion that Stoker's two young women may derive from Collins'. It is generally recognized that he borrowed Collins' concept of the novel as a collection of documents written by various characters and edited by one of them. Stoker's MS notes for *Dracula* do not mention Collins or his work but do show that from the start Stoker planned to include a "girl," who becomes Lucy in a plan dated March 8, 1890, and a shrewd, skeptical woman, who seems to become Mina, Lucy's "Schoolfellow" and a "teacher" in the March 8 plan. His inclusion of a "detective inspector," Cotford, in the notes may suggest *The Moonstone* (1868) as his model, however. The fact that Stoker associates Lucy with "the white lady" who allegedly haunts Whitby Abbey (p. 72) is probably a misleading clue. The MS notes show that he learned the legend of the white lady from three fishermen in Whitby on July 30, 1890, at least four months after planning the novel. Thus the question of his specific debt to *The Woman in White* remains open. For permission to use and quote from Stoker's MS notes for *Dracula*, I am indebted to Ann Stoker and to the Phillip H. and A.S.W. Rosenbach Foundation of Philadelphia and its assistant director, Walter C. Johnson. For the materials cited, see Notes, bk. 1, p. 35; bk. 2, n.p., slip dated 30/7/90; and book lists and reading notes in bks. 2 and 3.

10. As Phyllis Roth notes (*Bram Stoker*, p. 48), Stoker based his novel *The Man* (1905) on a foolish and egocentric proposal of marriage by a "modern" girl who ultimately learns that true feminine love is submissive and sexual. The novel, however, does not reject her desire for a useful education and social function and portrays her as an intelligent, capable person. Stoker is also highly sympathetic toward the

"modern" woman while advocating the submissiveness and sexuality of true feminine love in *The Mystery of the Sea* (1902) and *Lady Athlyne* (1908).

11. See ch. 10, "Psychiatry from Pinel and Mesmer to Charcot," in Gardner Murphy and J.E. Kovach, *Historical Introduction to Modern Psychology*, 3rd ed. (New York: Harcourt Brace Jovanovich, 1972); Edwin O. Starbuck, "Double-Mindedness," in *Encyclopaedia of Religion and Ethics*, ed. James Hastings (Edinburgh: T. T. Clark, 1911); Bernard Hart et al., "The Concept of Dissociation," *British Journal of Medical Psychology*, 6 (1926), 241–63; and Ralph Tymms, *Doubles in Literary Psychology* (London: Bowes and Bowes, 1949), ch. 3, esp. p. 95.

12. *Personal Reminiscences of Henry Irving*, 2 vols. (New York: Macmillan, 1906), II, 1, 19–21; see also I, 149, 170, 265. The only distinctly psychological work mentioned in Stoker's MS notes for *Dracula* is *Theory of Dreams* (attr. to Robert Gray, Bishop of Bristol), 2 vols. (London: F.C. and J. Rivington, 1808), from which he abstracts such anecdotes as reports of a woman who became cataleptic twice daily and of a man able to die and revive at will (Notes, bk. 3).

13. Bram Stoker, *Dracula's Guest* (1914; rpt. London: Jarrolds, 1966), p. 185, originally titled *Dracula's Guest and Other Weird Stories* (see *The English Catalogue of Books*: vol. 9, London: Publishers' Circular, Ltd., 1916, p. 1306). *Crooken Sands* (New York: T.L. De Vinne, 1894) is listed in *The National Union Catalogue, Pre-1956 Imprints*, vol. 570 (London: Mansell, 1978), p. 623. For the concept of the literary double see especially Angus Fletcher, *Allegory: The Theory of a Symbolic Mode* (Ithaca: Cornell Univ. Press, 1964), pp. 151, 192–95; Edwin Honig, *Dark Conceit: The Making of Allegory* (1959; rpt. New York: Oxford Univ. Press, 1966); and C.F. Keppler, *The Literature of the Second Self* (Tucson: Univ. of Arizona Press, 1972), esp. pp. 1–13, 182–210. For its use in Victorian literature generally, see Masao Miyoshi, *The Divided Self* (New York: New York Univ. Press, 1969).

14. Arthur's ineffectuality and subordination to his father are noted as an example of the Oedipal pattern by Richard Astle, "Dracula as Totemic Monster: Lacan, Freud, Oedipus and History," *Sub-stance*, 25 (1980), 99. Astle also notes, as I do in the text below, Arthur's demonstration of strength later in the novel.

15. Roth, *Bram Stoker*, p. 123; cf. Demetrakopoulos, "Feminism . . . in *Dracula*," p. 108. For Oedipal fantasy, see Astle, "Dracula as Totemic Monster"; Maurice Richardson's seminal "Psychoanalysis of Ghost Stories," *Twentieth Century*, 166 (1959), 419–31; C.F. Bentley, "The Monster in the Bedroom: Sexual Symbolism in Bram Stoker's *Dracula*," *Literature and Psychology*, 22 (1972), 27–34; Royce MacGillivray, "*Dracula*: Bram Stoker's Spoiled Masterpiece," *Queen's Quarterly*, 79 (1972), 518–27; and Joseph Bierman's untenable "Dracula: Prolonged Childhood, and the Oral Triad," *American Imago*, 29 (1972), 180–98.

16. Gail Griffin ("'Your Girls That You All Love Are Mine,'" 461–62) notes the "bitter pill" exchange and other provocation of Mina cited in my text in order to argue that the men's "chivalric glorification of womanhood" causes Mina and Lucy to assert their sexuality. My point is that, as their vampire mate, Dracula serves as a symbol of their self-concern (their indignation), which may include an assertion of sexuality but is not limited to it.

17. The parallel between Mina's "baptism of blood" and fellatio is often noted,

and, like the staking of Lucy, it supports speculation that Stoker was gripped by Oedipal fantasy (see, e.g., Bentley, "Monster in the Bedroom," p. 30) or fear and hatred of women (Roth, *Bram Stoker*, p. 122). As a symbol for Mina's psychological experience, however, the "baptism" is consistent with the preceding narrative's presentation of her increasing resentment toward the men's chivalry and represents an act of mind.

18. For anticipations of the collective unconscious in the 1890s, see Yeats's postulation of an Anima Mundi as reported in his *Autobiography* (New York: Macmillan, 1953), p. 158; also see Oscar Wilde's "collective life of the race . . . race-experience . . . the dreams, and ideas, and feelings of myriad generations," in "The Critic as Artist" (1890) in his *Poems and Essays* (London: Collins, 1956), pp. 319–21, which is noted by Wendell Harris in "Arnold, Pater, Wilde, and the Object as in Themselves They See It," *Studies in English Literature*, 11 (1977), 745.

Jenni Calder

Cash and the Sex Nexus

In George Meredith's *Diana of the Crossways* (1885) the occasion of the hero-ine's most intensely expressed sexuality is also a moment of political crisis and excitement. She is a thinking and high-principled woman, proud of her association with politically influential men. She considers herself above the sexual and financial maneuvers of the marriage market. Percy Dacier, her lover, brings her exciting and confidential political news, and watches its effect on her.

> She was radiant with her dark lightnings, yet visibly subject to him under the spell of the news he had artfully lengthened out to excite and overbalance her: – and her enthusiasm was all pointed to his share in the altered situation, as he well knew and was flat-tered in knowing.

Her admiration, she thinks, is all for the political hero, the success of the man with whom she is anticipating a comradely union.

Of all late Victorian novelists Meredith perhaps most minutely explored relations between male and female. He took a more generous, forgiving and ironic view than Henry James, who was equally relentless in his pursuit of evidence on the associations of men and women. His florid style can be offputting for the late-twentieth-century reader, whose eager quest for mod-ernity leads more readily to James, but Meredith has a wisdom and a frank-ness which are rewarding. He also has a delectable sense of comedy, which, as he himself was acutely aware, is one of the writer's most powerful weap-ons. Unlike James his observations of social and sexual mores were a chal-lenge as well as a comment.

Transported by the exciting prospect of political triumph, Diana is vulnerable and irresistible. The two often go together. "Her glowing look doated on the faithful lieutenant." And the faithful lieutenant responds. Meredith does not *tell* us that Percy lays hands on his heroine, but we do not need to be told.

Meredith's talent is nothing if not dramatic, indeed his language often has the combination of staginess and nuance that we find in the Greeks.

> "Ah! no," she joined her hands, wondering whither her armed majesty had fled; "no softness! no payments! Flatter me by letting me think you came to a head—not a silly woman's heart, with one name on it, as it has not to betray. I have been frank; you need no proofs . . . ." The supplicating hands left her figure an easy prey to the storm, and were crushed to a knot on her bosom. She could only shrink. "Ah! Percy . . . you undo my praise of you—my pride in receiving you."

Diana has no need of proof that she is physically attractive, and she demands to be admired for her mind. The demand is part of her armory, for she *is* susceptible. In spite of the suggestion of the male predator Diana is no victim. She is vulnerable precisely because the attraction is a two-way current. Her view of man as hero, and she could love no less than hero, idealizes his sexuality. It is not that she denies its existence, but that she demands its control. "I am flesh and blood after all," protests Percy, to which she replies, "You drive me to be ice and door-bolts." But within the scene, in the very language of rejection, she radiates physical magnetism. Throughout the novel her beauty and power to attract men has been emphasized. The confrontation here simply underlines this.

What Meredith projects here is not Victorian prudery. It is not a refusal to acknowledge sex, or a revulsion against it, but a determination to master it. Diana, though long separated from her husband, is married. Gossip has described her as the mistress of a powerful politician, now dead. She has ridden out that storm, yet she is independent; she associates freely with the men who interest her. There are no witnesses to this midnight scene, yet she must be true to her view of herself, and of her situation.

> "I wish to respect my hero. Have a little mercy. Our day will come; perhaps as wonderfully as this wonderful news. My friend, drop your hands. Have you forgotten who I am? I want to think, Percy!"
>
> "But you are mine."
>
> "You are abasing your own."

"No, by heaven!"

"Worse, dear friend; you are lowering yourself to the woman who loves you."

"You must think me superhuman."

"I worship you — or did."

"Be reasonable, Tony [Diana's nickname]. What harm! Surely a trifle of recompense? Just to let me feel I live! You own you love me. Then I am your lover."

"My dear friend Percy, when I have consented to be your paramour, this kind of treatment of me will not want apologies."

Percy employs a traditional male argument. Diana's response betrays her susceptibility. Her use of "my friend" attempts to emphasize what she considers paramount in their relationship. What is remarkable about this scene, and about so much of Meredith's writing, is the language of his heroine. It may not be naturalistic, although one could argue for that, but like few other writers of the period, including women, he caught precisely a woman's strength and her defenselessness, her potential, and the challenges before her.

When Percy has gone Diana dwells on her humiliation, and it disturbs her the more when she reflects honestly on the extent to which she has set out to attract him. The territory which Meredith explores is not new to the novelist, nor is it essentially different from the territory that remains a major concern one hundred years later. Diana's strength and her vulnerability are tied up with sex and status. As a beautiful woman she has an influence on men, and thus on the affairs of men, which can easily be used unscrupulously. (Although it is interesting that the confrontation scene with Percy is followed immediately by Diana's entry into an area of the world of men — journalism — where she finds herself totally ignored and is valued only if she can supply something newsworthy. She is irritated when she finds her femininity ignored; she is not used to it.) It is a traditional role for women.

As a clever woman she is distrusted by men, though some respect her intelligence and others discount it in favor of her beauty. As an independent woman who has been unhappily married, in a union that clearly provided neither sexual nor intellectual satisfaction, she sees marriage as a threat to individuality. Yet she idealizes love and enjoys having a powerful influence on men. She uses her femaleness. She needs money to maintain her independence, and for her independence to make some impact she needs a considerable amount of money. She writes for a living, an occupation she is well aware is open to compromise. While she uses sex, she feels the need to guard herself from her own sexuality — hence the repelling of Percy. While she values the status that money can buy, and needs it, she wants to consider herself above the fraught male world of competitive money-making. By all the rules of the game she shouldn't win. She is, as she so painfully recognizes, a hypocrite. But then, so are men, and they win. And Meredith's heroine *does* win, in a sense. She chooses marriage, both in the sense that she commits herself both to an institution and to a man. Significantly, however modest a gesture, she kisses her husband-to-be (not Percy) on the arm. Meredith leaves his heroine at the traditional happy-ever-after moment. What is important is not that we believe in her future wedded bliss – and her marriage inevitably suggests compromise – but that she believes in what she is doing, and her husband believes in her and in her belief. We can hardly ask for more.

Meredith was a revolutionist. In his own way he wanted to overthrow society, challenge conventions, uproot traditions. His view was that this could be done through comedy, and women. He was not directly concerned with sexuality as such, but he was certainly concerned with sex as a powerful current in society. The making and marring of marriages and extramarital unions was the making and marring of society. Very rarely does he bring a man and a woman together out of sheer sexual attraction. A stronger attraction is that of companionship, the ability of a man and a woman to share on a equal basis the same interests and activities. He challenged Victorian convention because it made that kind of free association so difficult, and made it so difficult because of the forces of sexuality, which it could never allow out into the open for long enough to examine and assess. Meredith wanted to close the gulf between men and women, not by allowing women a specifically sexual freedom but by allowing them independence (for which money was essential), freedom of movement, a positive and vigorous existence, side by side with the men of their choice if they should so choose.

Yet in all his heroines and in the heroes who win them he strongly communicates sexuality, through their expressiveness, their energy, and their sensitivity. He emphasizes the physical, activity, fresh air. This emphasis may have its hints of the right-minded person's alternative to masturbation, but it nevertheless projects the inhabitants of his novels as, to use Percy Dacier's phrase, "flesh and blood." *Diana of the Crossways* was Meredith's first real success after thirty odd years of writing, and the fact that it was successful reflects the climate of opinion at the time. By the 1880s the debate about love, marriage, and equality was current, and acknowledgment of a woman's right to sexual pleasure was not unknown. But it would be a mistake to make the assumption that until the last quarter of the century novelists, except when writing about prostitutes and fallen women (which they did remarkably often), skirted the "problem" of sexuality. That the major voices were troubled by it – we need only look at Dickens who got himself so thoroughly and productively hung up on female sexuality – is clear. But that women themselves could communicate it is also clear. Maggie Tulliver must be one of the most sexual beings in the whole of Victorian fiction. Jane Eyre and Shirley, and a host of forgettable heroines in novels by forgettable female novelists who quarried the romantic vein Charlotte Bronte so powerfully exposed, convey themselves by thought, look, and gesture, by a physical expressiveness, that attracts attention to themselves as sexual beings, if not always conventionally attractive. Men too could be conveyed, within Victorian conventions, as sexual beings without the suggestion that they were at the mercy of barely controllable appetites. Unlike the excitable Percy, Redworth, Diana's eventual mate, expresses his maleness through a combination of rather somber control and certain kinds of physical prowess — as a horseman, for example. There is a clear knightly suggestion of both the courtly and the courageous. In the case of both men and women the conventions for the expression of sexuality were readily available, and were often put to suggestive use.

We do not need explicitness to tell us about sex. There are of course moments in Victorian novels when the evasion of explicitness is gross — *Tess* is the obvious example, but one certainly cannot argue that Hardy is repressing sexuality. It is an elemental current in most of his novels, especially in those agonizing sterile confrontations between men and women who are doomed to discord. We are ourselves, in the 1980s, hung up on the sexual act, to the extent that we see sexuality only in terms of the act itself or imitations thereof. We regard with distrust or mockery the Victorian inclination to subsume sex into either the conventional structure of society or into romanticism (which they were much more likely to do than veil it with prudery). We assume that novelists who wanted to be frank were leant on by their publishers and their public, and this was true in Hardy's case. We look at what we now know about the nature of Victorian society — the number of prostitutes, the number of women led to the marriage bed like lambs to the slaughter, and the number of marriages that were sustained by the samplings of errant husbands — and we ask, why did Victorian novelists not write about these things? The answer of course is that they did. Fallen women, marital infidelity, the sterility of sexual relations are all insistent themes in the Victorian novel. But perhaps the most insistent theme of all, and the theme that in a sense explodes in the last quarter of the century, just at the time when, if attitudes were not radically changing at least a debate was surfacing, was the theme of sex and cash. It might be argued that sexual explicitness was not the victim, by the 1880s, of prudery and repression, but of class and economics.

One could put it another way, and say it was the victim of social values. Marriage was valued more as a social and economic institution than as a personal or sexual union. Meredith challenged this by attempting to disrupt conventional views of society and to offer as an alternative an ideal of companionship, indeed of comradeship, in an idealogical union. George Eliot accepted the inevitability of the repressiveness of marriage: Maggie Tulliver dies; Dorothea is ironically consigned to a "romantic" union; Gwendolen Harleth is almost destroyed by marriage. Later novelists, Marie Corelli, for instance, challenged the economic marriage with portrayals of romantic love. A fierce debate raged between the pragmatists and the romanticists.

The dominant view of conventionally accepted unions between men and women presented an arrangement of mutual comfort, a prop of society and the state, and supported by society and the state. Many Victorian novelists recognized that within this convenient arrangement lay a vast potential for lack of fulfillment, frustration, neglect, cruelty. Marriage, it might have been said, was a collusion between the state and the individual to make the territory of human relations habitable. Take from sexual union its institutional character and its economic convenience and an uncharted continent would be laid bare, featuring perhaps ravishing mountains and gloriously rushing rivers, but full also of swamps and chasms that would claim the unwary. It was the novelists above all who explored this territory.

This was the terrain that George Gissing painfully hacked his way into, against the background of his own unhappy attempts to break free from the social strictures of the marital institution, only to find himself in a far more tortured personal situation. In his novels he gives the impression of a dogged determination to represent certain kinds of neglected realities. His characters certainly *articulate* their sexual needs but perhaps do not communicate them as strongly as the creations of some earlier novelists. His novels quiver with the grating against each other of society and the individual, of convention and emotion, of stasis and rebellion, of idealism and the reality that drags human beings into self-destruction. In many ways he goes hand in hand with his contemporary Hardy, although the physical landscape of Hardy's novels is so different. Gissing tends to be harshly urban. But the emotional landscape is very similar. It is the individual's battle with society, and the union between men and women is the battleground. Again, the emotional cannot be separated from the economic. The bitterness of so many of Gissing's characters, the rebellion and usually defeat of so many of his men and women, arises from just this. If money makes women sexually vulnerable, it can make men sexually aggressive and lead them to blame their lack of success with women on their lack of cash. Gissing's projections of sexuality are full of anger and resentment; Hardy's are often similar, although he is better at communicating straightforward lust. (It is interesting that both the rebellious and the romantic reactions to sexual repression leave out tenderness.) Lying behind the anger and resentment was an acute sensitivity toward the economics of class. To approach sexual relations closely is not just a question of throwing off inhibitions. Society is less likely to avert its eyes in horror at the exposure of carnality as it is to look at it with cool assessment in terms of cash and property.

The proprietorship of sex was another of Meredith's themes, most scintillatingly in *The Egoist* (1879). Sir Willoughby Patterne only wants a wife to complete his sense of himself. His impending marriage is seen entirely in terms of possession: a wife will add the finishing touch to his estate, his mansion, his interior design. The prospective wife refuses to be owned, and turns society's assumptions about appropriate union upside down. This was one of the aspects of social and sexual relations that deeply disturbed Robert Louis Stevenson, at the same time one of the most honest and the most reticent (in his published writings) of late Victorian writers. He could not reconcile sexual needs, the sexual generosity of the prostitutes he associated with in his youth, and marriage as an economic institution sanctioned by middle-class mores. He hated what he saw as middle-class hypocrisy. He hated the idea of the cozy middle-class household turning its back on the raw realities of the backstreet jungle. So did Gissing. Stevenson detected within the coziness not only the potential for sexual excess, but for violence. He experienced intimately the Calvinist insistence on the suppression and diversion of the less controllable areas of human emotion and behavior. He also detected the collusion in the exploitation of women, both in the home and in the backstreet.

He wrote about this in a number of ways, and it would be unfair to suggest that he dodged the issue of sex, although it is violence and family hostilities that he explores most deeply. When he writes about rebellion against middle-class values, as in "The Misadventures of John Nicolson" (1888) or, notoriously, in *The Strange Case of Dr Jekyll and Mr. Hyde* (1886), the eruption against repression results in murder, not in orgiastic sex—although sexual gratification is implied in *Jekyll and Hyde*. But in *The Master of Ballantrae* (1889) the sexual magnetism of the Master is clear. So, in *Kidnapped* (1886), is that of the insouciant Alan Breck Stewart. Women are drawn to these vigorous males, but only toward the end of his life—and then when there was not enough of his life left to explore it fully—did Stevenson start to feel able to communicate female sexuality. He had always felt that his readers could not take an honest approach to sex, and so had tended to avoid it altogether—although he got himself into difficulties over *Catriona* (1893), where his young hero and heroine live together in a state of innocent but powerful affection. In his desire not to offend, Stevenson verges on coyness. Even when he is able to communicate frankly female sexuality, he is uneasy with young girls—as he had possibly been in his own life. It is the sexuality of mature women that he expresses strongly, the elder Kirstie in *Weir of Hermiston* (1896), the tavern landlady in the fragment *The Young Chevalier*, unfinished at his death. The exception is Uma in *The Beach of Falesa* (1893), whose sexual awareness is simple and straightforward, but there Stevenson was operating within an entirely different social ambience, and there is no doubt that he found it liberating.

Toward the end of his life Stevenson wrote in a letter to his cousin Bob, who had shared many of his youthful experiences, about sexual attitudes.

> If I had to begin again—I know not—si jeunesse savait, vieillesse pouvait—I know not at all—I believe I should DO AS I HAVE DONE—EXCEPT THAT I believe I should try TO BE MORE CHASTE IN EARLY YOUTH, and honour Sex more religiously. THE DAMNED THING of our education is that Christianity does not recognise and hallow Sex. It looks askance at it, over its shoulder, oppressed as it is by reminiscences of hermits and Asiatic self-torturers.

Christian, or Calvinist, repression led to the exploitation and repression of women. By denying the importance of sex in human impulse and behavior, men were driven underground in their search for experience and well brought up women were denied the opportunity to discover and enjoy their own sexuality. Stevenson's awareness of this was a major influence in his life and had begun to be an influence in his writing when he died. In fact, it might be said to have been a negative influence in his writing from the beginning, governing what he felt he could write about. He was deeply grateful for the generosity of women who sold their bodies, and enjoyed the company of women who could be relaxed and realistic about sex, yet found the idea of the sexual marketplace, both in the brothel and in the drawing room, deeply offensive. It was never likely that he would marry a girl of his own class and background: that would have seemed to him too close to exploitation. One senses that he could never have brought himself to be the man responsible for destroying the armor of inexperience. It is not irrelevant that the women he fell in love with were older than himself, and married.

What did Stevenson mean by "honouring" sex "religiously"? I think he meant that he would have tried to be more honest about sex—something he always wanted to be—and that he intended "religiously" in a larger sense than Christian. I think he meant also that he would have tried to do justice to sex, to its importance and value in human relations. In another letter to Bob he talked of "the prim obliterated polite face of life, and the broad, bawdy, and orgiastic—or maenadic—foundation." Strong feelings reined in by social, political and economic harness, emotion eroded by money, the elemental fact of procreation covered over by nursery wallpaper: his awareness of all this was underlined by his awareness of his own inability to make sense of it. Stevenson was not alone in detecting a vast social conspiracy to defuse the profoundest human impulses. Anthropologically and historically we can see that every social unit has evolved its own devices for controlling what Stevenson called the "maenadic" foundations of human behavior. Yet twentieth-century readers join with these late Victorians in seeing the nineteenth century as peculiarly dishonest about sex.

Stevenson was not an avowed feminist, yet one aspect of all this that disturbed him deeply was female vulnerability, and the way that the exploitation of women was built into the social structure. We know that Meredith and Stevenson spent some time together, and perhaps this was something that they talked about. Stevenson developed a profound admiration for Meredith (whose work had a not altogether happy influence on Stevenson's), and Meredith saw Stevenson as a rising talent, indeed gave him a part as such in one of his own novels. Another personal association takes us to perhaps the strongest voice in late nineteenth-century literature, to Henry James, a close and encouraging friend of Stevenson.

James discourses not of sexuality but of social sexual relations. His characters would crumple into little heaps if it were not for the social environment that holds them up. Indeed, that is his view of individuals and society. As a novelist he approaches his task as an observer, and that is precisely his strength. But he is an observer within the ranks, unlike any of the novelists mentioned so far, who in their very different ways were all outsiders or intruders. James interprets for us the tiny flickers of attraction and repulsion that send their dangerous ripples through the drawing room, and he can do it with such precision and certainty because he is on home ground. Because he is an observer he is cool, not a rebel, like Meredith, Gissing, Hardy, and Stevenson, who all approach, from different directions, the possibility of overthrow. But his long and illuminating look at the sex nexus is perhaps the more valuable for its lack of personal commitment.

James's advantage is that he never questions that the sex nexus is the cash nexus. Marriages are made in the market place, not in heaven or in bed, and not only marriage, but most relations between men and women on the upper levels of society. Given that, it is absurd to look for something other than marketplace morality. Emotions cannot be separated from economics. Beautiful men and beautiful women are like beautiful art objects: they can be bought, most likely by rich Americans, or they can be collected, by those with the environment, if not the means, to sustain them. The more sensitive his men and women are the more likely they are to insist on something "better" than natural attraction, and look for refinement, an aesthetic sense, a noble tradition, to substantiate, or even to substitute for, physical attraction. In a form of subtle paradox that James delights in, precisely this sensitivity has the effect of condoning the ethics of the marketplace.

In most of James's novels aesthetic values operate and absorb social values. One novel in which this does not occur is *What Maisie Knew* (1897).

Here there is a minimum of sustaining environment, a minimum of controlling values, whether artificial or natural. We watch a kaleidoscopic sexual ballet, as couples shift and money and property change hands, through the eyes of a child, ironically the nearest James could get to a totally disinterested observer. It is like a play being performed before an audience of one, who boos or applauds, and takes a fancy to one of the leading actors, the matinée idol who must be nice because he is so attentive to his audience, willingly suspends disbelief, and loves the excitement of it all. All the time she senses that she belongs on the stage with the others, is herself a part of the drama.

James refers to Maisie as the witness of "gross immoralities." What she sees are not naked bodies or rumpled beds, with which James has little concern, for he sees sexual intimacy in terms of social alliance, how society sees, and society does not see the rumpled beds. Maisie witnesses the bargaining in human flesh, in which she herself is involved. She both solicits and is solicited. She is not so much a pawn in an adult game as both stockbroker and stock, and to know how she stands she has to do her sums right. "Her choice . . . was there before her like an impossible sum on a slate. . . ." To do the sum she requires aid—she is a child. She has to fall back on the "dingy decencies" of Mrs. Wix, her governess; but Mrs. Wix has a stake in the bargaining also. Everyone does. To avoid doing the sum she needs to be shielded by the charm of Sir Claude (the matinée idol) as a continuing presence, Sir Claude in his fresh light clothes and his straw hat, who remains, remarkably, as the battle rages for possession of Maisie, as the stakes are raised and the bidding soars, if not uncontaminated at least morally responsive. He loses Maisie and gains the abominable Mrs. Beale.

And this is the cash/sex nexus, red in tooth and claw, without a hint of warmth or attractiveness, except in Sir Claude himself, and even his charm is of a kind to appeal to a child, a fairy story hero, "the perfect gentleman and strikingly handsome." And "charm" itself becomes a cold, devalued word, as a succession of ladies attempt to be charming to Maisie, and they charm and are charmed by various men. The ladies are painted social objects (social, not sex objects) the most blatant being Maisie's own mother. Sir Claude, insisting on Maisie's freedom to choose her future, is implicated in the bargaining, not only by his association with Mrs. Beale. He is implicated further because Maisie tries to bargain for *him*. She is not just the victim of the nexus, but plays an active role.

Over and over again it is the abrasiveness of human relations that James exposes, suggesting continually that, in spite of whatever good intentions, social and economic realities force these sparks and currents of hostility to play in the atmosphere like an electric storm. The currents are in their way sexual, but James seems often to dwell on the repellent rather than the attracting. And always he is presenting a situation that is in a state of constant movement. There is no suggestion of marriage as a stable refuge, which had in a previous generation appeared to be an ideal. It is at best a momentary pause in the restless shifting of relationships, yet as an *institution*, as a structure, it remains solid enough to provide society's foundations. And in that there is a horrible irony.

So James, like others, saw the collusion between society and the individual to maintain an acceptable formalization of sexual relations, but also he saw this formalization as a positive encouragement to immoral transactions (and the immorality came from the bargaining, not from the sex) on an horrendous scale. *The Wings of the Dove* (1902) is an example of this. The scale of the bargain here, where the impecunious Kate Croy, who marries her lover to a wealthy girl whom they both know is going to die, on the understanding that ultimately she will gain both love and money, is of melodramatic proportions – the dramatic boldness of many of James's plots is often overlooked as one attends to the intricacies of his detail. But can you have love and money, other than by lucky accident? Does the behavior that society condones, if not actively approves, allow room for both? In this case the transaction appears to erode the emotion: the money market seems to be more stable than the emotional one. Character can subvert emotions – and morality – and in *The Wings of the Dove* it is Milly Theale, the third party concerned, who quite unconsciously interferes with the course of true negotiation.

Perhaps the novel in which the morality is most elusive is *The Golden Bowl* (1904). The Prince from Italy is valued and bought by Adam Verver for his daughter Maggie. He accepts the terms of the bargain, that he will lend distinction, like other collected pieces, to a museum in the raw new American City. The rough edges of the marketplace are smoothed away, for these are refined and civilized people, who have absorbed fashions of discreetly clothing vulgarities. Father and daughter love each other, and value the Prince, symbol of an historical and artistic richness. The union of American cash and Italian culture produces a child, doated on by the collector grandfather, the perfect justification of such intercourse.

Sexuality can often be communicated *in reverso*. We are told that the Prince is handsome; we see that he is appealing. But it is through another woman, Charlotte Stant, that we become fully aware of him as a sexual being.

> She could have looked at her hostess with such straightness and brightness only from knowing that the Prince was also there – the discrimination of but a moment, yet, which let him take her in still better than if she had instantly faced him. He availed himself

of the chance thus given him, for he was conscious of all these things. What he accordingly saw for some seconds, with intensity, was a tall, strong, charming girl who wore for him, at first, exactly the look of her adventurous situation, a suggestion, in all her person, in motion and gesture, in free, vivid, yet altogether happy indications of dress from the becoming compactness of her hat to the shade of tan in her shoes, of winds and waves and custom-houses, of far countries and long journeys, the knowledge of how and where and the habit, founded on experience, of not being afraid. He was aware, at the same time, that of this combination the "strong-minded" note was not, as might have been apprehended, the basis: he was now sufficiently familiar with English-speaking types, he had sounded attentively enough such possibilities, for a quick vision of differences. He had, besides, his own view of this young lady's strength of mind. It was great, he had ground to believe, but it would never interfere with the play of her extremely personal, her always amusing taste. This last was the thing in her—for she threw it out positively, on the spot, like a light—that she might have reappeared, during these moments, just to cool his worried eyes with. He saw her in her light: that immediate, exclusive address to their friend was like a lamp she was holding aloft for his benefit and his pleasure. It showed him everything—above all her presence in the world, so closely, so irretrievably contemporaneous with his own: a sharp, sharp fact, sharper during these instants than any other at all, even than that of his marriage, but accompanied, in a subordinate and controlled way, with those others, facial, physiognomic. . . .

This is the woman who commands the prince, not the pleasing daughter of an American millionaire. She is physically and intellectually impressive and challenging. His response to this adventuring woman, who might also be described by some as an "adventuress," tells us more about the Prince than anything else. Nowhere else, in fact, do we see him so responsive. She is a strong presence, physically, emotionally, psychologically. But Charlotte Stant, like the Prince, is penniless, and being people so substantive they require also to be substantial. They require it, materially and psychologically, his background and her sureness require it, and society expects it. Without the prop of society's expectations they become nothing of significance.

Just before Charlotte Stant's arrival (and they have of course been lovers; this is no first meeting) the Prince has been described: he is "noble," a "beautiful personal presence, that of a prince in very truth, a ruler, warrior,

patron, lighting up brave architecture and diffusing the sense of a function."
Both the Prince and Charlotte are firmly associated with an image of light:
mutual illumination is the way their attraction is presented. But the Prince's
function depends not on tradition and nobility, however appealing they may
be, but on money. His status as warrior and ruler needs her confident and
modern approach. The problem is solved. The Prince marries Maggie,
Charlotte marries Maggie's widowed father, the Prince and Charlotte remain lovers. There is cash and property enough for all; there is a child to
satisfy the needs of the two who value a child—Maggie and her father, who
innocently (or perhaps it is not innocence) collude in the relationship of
their respective spouses by being so absorbed in each other. It might seem
to be a logical and mutually satisfactory arrangement, neatly sidestepping
the interference of moral judgment.

Yet of course it can't work. It doesn't work because to manipulate sex
and finance with real success requires an emotional armor-plating that only
social sophistication can provide, and father and daughter are without it.
In that sense they are innocents. It is this innocence, culpable as it may
be, that first allows room for the arrangement, and then closes in on it. It
is Maggie who detaches herself from the quartet and watches them, "her
father's wife's lover facing his mistress . . . her father sitting, all unsounded
and unblinking." They are playing cards. Social custom provides them with
a game that is compatible with their disloyalties. Significantly Maggie has
never been good at cards.

> She was asking herself at last how they could bear it—for, though
> cards were as nought to her and she could follow no move, so
> that she was always, on such occasions, out of the party, they
> struck her as conforming alike, in the matter of gravity and
> propriety, to the stiff standard of the house.

If cards provide the Prince and Charlotte with a kind of immunity, it is in
a sense her inability to play that gives Maggie an immunity to the "stiff standard" of the house. It is because she does *not* conform that she sees the truth
that conformity is hiding, and suffers, and is enlarged in the reader's eyes.
And it is because she does not conform that she has strength to look straight
at the truth and not be shifted by it. Maggie's suppression of the"vulgar
heat of her wrong," the "wild eastern caravan, looming into view with crude
colours in the sun, fierce pipes in the air, high spears against the sky" means
that she denies herself a cloak for the full horror of the situation.

The horror is complex. Sexual jealousy is there, we understand, as she
denies herself "the rages of jealousy, the protests of passion" (and in her denial we appreciate her passion) "terror and disgust" at the deceit. The reader
sees, as perhaps Maggie doesn't, the profounder horror that society is so

well equipped to provide the means not just for the practicalities of sexual infidelity but, looking at James's work as a whole, for a vast range of humanly damaging relations, ruthlessly driven by the need for sexual, social, and financial gratification.

There is of course a quantity of evidence on Victorian reticence, fear and hypocrisy on sexual matters. James analyses sexual relations without really talking about sex at all. Stevenson was always troubled by the fact that he was, he felt, prevented by his public from writing frankly about sex, one of the reasons why he could only write about the contemporary scene in the distant and anarchic world of the Pacific. We know that Gissing was angered and agonized by society's inadequacy in sexual matters. Hardy tried to write about "free love" but found it hard to describe mutually satisfying sexual relations. By the end of the century men and women were looking for more openness, challenging the hypocritical multiple standards of society, writing about extramarital sex and contraception and female sexuality. But without underestimating the damage of Victorian sexual repression, or the value of the reaction against it, it is perhaps as well not to overestimate sexual motivation, even toward the end of the century. James was a chronicler as well as an analyst, but his is not the only voice that tells us, with irony or anger, with amusement or with bitterness, both that social and financial needs were often stronger than sexual, and that the relationship between sex and money was often more intimate than that between men and women. Finance could provide a highly satisfactory displacement activity.

Loralee MacPike

The Fallen Woman's Sexuality: Childbirth and Censure

> Although the eighteenth- and nineteenth-century novel may be said to move toward marriage and the securing of genealogical continuity, it often gains its particular narrative urgency from an energy that threatens to contravene that stability of the family on which society depends [by] . . . an act of transgression that threatens the family—namely, adultery.
>
> Tony Tanner, *Adultery in the Novel*

> Wherever [the fallen woman] appears, and for whatever overt moral purpose, her story reveals underlying sexual attitudes.
>
> Sally Mitchell, *The Fallen Angel*

> "Novels are very often stories about the loves of men for other men's wives."
>
> George Moore, *Esther Waters*

Consider Anna Karenina. Her vibrant sexuality draws her from a loveless marriage into an intense but destructive sexual relationship. The pivot of her existence is her sexuality; but the point upon which Tolstoy's evaluation of her sexuality rests is its legality. *Anna Karenina* is one of the few nineteenth-century novels in which childbirth is actually shown. Both Anna and Kitty give birth, in ways and under circumstances and to children that are part of a metaphor used by Tolstoy to help create the emotional climate within which his readers can judge Anna.

While married to Alexei Karenin, Anna bears one child, a son, Sergei, whom she loves deeply and devotedly. From her liaison with Alexei Vronsky she bears a second child. Tolstoy merely outlines this second confinement but describes its aftermath graphically: puerperal fever, the scourge of childbearing women. Anna's hair is cut; her beautiful face and hands grow thin; her vitality is stilled. The child is a girl, named after her mother in obvious reference to the sins of the parents. From its birth Anna is unable to love it. She is too ill to nurse it and too tied up in her sexual relationship with Vronsky to care for it as she did for Sergei. Her legally fecund sister-in-law Dolly notes when she visits Anna that Anna does not even know how many teeth her daughter has—a sure sign of neglect. In the end Anna destroys both her sexual self and her parent self beneath the wheels of a train. Tolstoy thought the ending both unavoidable and appropriate.

But Anna is not the only woman who bears a child in the pages of *Anna Karenina*. Kitty Levin's confinement is presented in detail; Tolstoy abates not one cry or pang, as Levin paces nervously outside the door and curses himself for the sexuality that brought his Kitty such suffering. Kitty calmly assures him that the event, suffering and all, is the normal and natural result of legitimate sexuality, and that she welcomes it as she had welcomed the loving that caused it. The child is a boy, and Kitty takes him to breast with a flood of maternal instinct that does not wane as time passes; months later her body automatically responds to his hunger cries even when she is too distant to hear them. For Levin, nothing is more inspirational than the sight of mother and son and the knowledge that they are his.

The contrast between these two portraits of mothering is obvious and intentional. Tolstoy wishes to make a statement about the exercise of female sexuality and finds that the statement can most clearly be made by contrasting legitimate and illegitimate sexuality through the event of childbirth.

For Tolstoy, children are not merely symbolic—standing as "a visible sign of something invisible"[1]—but metaphoric of values, values that cannot be contained within the confines of a symbol or group of symbols but expand into a web of relational meanings of which symbols form a part but never the whole. In fact, "the symbol is a type of metaphor" and "metaphor is a source of knowledge of reality."[2] In some cases, particularly poetry, a full understanding of the tensions that make up reality can only be expressed through metaphor. James Dickey has said,

> Poets believe that the things of this world are capable of making connections between each other that not God but men see, and they say so. . . . And it is in the language of metaphor charged with specific emotions that the poet makes his statement and creates, out of the world as it is, the world that he must, because he is what he is, bring to birth.[3]

The metaphor, then, is something distinctly human-created in order to speak its creator's sense of meaning in the world without reducing to literality the intuitive terms in which that world exists. In this way, Stephen Brown says, metaphor

> may express a portion, or at least an aspect, of the truth which would not otherwise find expression. By means of it . . . an imaginative and emotional element which is really in the mood is put into the expression of the mood. Without this element the expression would be inadequate, that is, less completely expressive of the object of thought as affected by the mood or frame of mind, and so less completely true.[4]

Metaphor thus allows the reader to capture the feeling of tension arising from a simultaneous understanding of several unresolved conflicts or beliefs. Robert Rogers, in a psychoanalytic study of metaphor, has found that most metaphors have to do with body imagery and sexuality, for the sense of body and self is the most primary human emotion and the one most re-

ive to the "expanded boundary" or "potential space" that the metaphor
s,[5] within which the mood or emotion associated with an unspoken
_esolved issue can be made accessible to the intellect and the feelings
of the reader simultaneously. I find the idea of "potential space" most useful
here because it suggests that rather amorphous, difficult-to-define area that
metaphor inhabits. It encompasses Dickey's "specific emotions" and Brown's
"mood" by suggesting that the likeness or relationship the metaphor implies is not a congruity of tenor and vehicle but instead an approach of the
one to the other. The reader's own intuition fills in the potential space, makes
the connection. When a suggested likeness calls forth a connection or causes
the reader to fill in a potential space and create a link, a metaphor is born.
Childbirth can become one such metaphor, with both the woman's and the
child's bodies creating a potential space in which to think about the nature
of human beings within a biological system which must use sexuality as
a means of continuation but at the same time assigns it a social, familial
value. There is a great potential space between what can be said about childbirth technically and medically, and what it represents within a society—in
other words, between the physical body of the childbearer and the accepted
social values of childbearing. It may be that the nineteenth century's reticence about physical functions and physical bodies actually enlarged the
space around childbirth and made possible the metaphor by which Tolstoy
judged Anna and Kitty. For Tolstoy's deliberately parallel childbirth experiences are consciously used metaphors for evaluating the complex mood
created by legitimate and illegitimate exercises of sexuality within the context of the family, society, and interpersonal relationships.

The advent of childbirth as a source of moral evaluation is linked less
to what we commonly think of as Victorian prudery than to what Michel
Foucault, in *The History of Sexuality*, has called the "rhetoric of allusion
and metaphor" which clothed nineteenth-century discussion of sex in order
to mask the "transforming of sex into discourse."[6] Foucault argues persua-
sively that, just as the seventeenth century confessional had created a new
discourse of detail which required more, rather than less, thought about sex,
so the nineteenth century, through medicine and psychiatry and economics, created a multitude of ways to speak (or at least to think) about sex that
had not previously existed. Because sexuality determined inheritance and
thus governed such a great portion of the economic life of nations just becoming conscious of the economic base of nationhood, both its exercise and
its control became quasi-public matters. I say quasi-public because, although
what could politely be said or done was definitely and often drastically pro-
scribed, the very existence of these proscriptions required constant discourse,
constant awareness of what not to do or say or think or feel. And so childbirth, a mere fact of life in the eighteenth century and shown as merely that

in novels like *Tristram Shandy*, became a means of talking about sexuality and thus lent itself to the formation of metaphor.

A study of childbearing in the nineteenth-century novel reveals a wide use of this basic metaphor within a surprisingly, and perhaps artifically, narrowed potential space.[7] Good women bear sons, bad women daughters who cannot carry on the family line, thus ensuring that negative qualities in the parents (particularly the mother) will not be part of the moral "genealogical continuity" of which Tanner speaks in the first epigraph to this essay. Good women have pleasant (or at least easy) childbirths and suffer no ill effects from parturition, as if to suggest that the childbirth process itself is related to the mother's moral fitness to reproduce her personal qualities. Good women feel a primary and primal connection to their children and through childraising contribute to the continuity of the social fabric.[8] All three facets of the metaphor of childbirth are connected to control of female sexuality, the first genealogically, the second physically, and the third socially.

The metaphor itself, as applied to both married and unmarried mothers in the novel, has wide currency during the nineteenth century and indeed becomes an unspoken statement of judgment which can be superimposed upon the "realistic" framework of the story to direct or control reader response. The reader, filling in the potential space between the realistic depiction of childbearing and the outcome of the childbearer, accedes almost unwittingly in the metaphor-making author's moral design. It is with the fallen woman that we see most clearly how judgment of female sexuality operates through the metaphor of childbirth. Anna Karenina's adultery is punished by the difficult birth of a girl child whom Anna does not love, while Kitty's legitimate sexuality is rewarded by the joyful birth of a son whom she cherishes. Adultery exists. It cannot be kept out of the realistic novel, and so it must be contained and controlled. The metaphor of childbirth is one such container.

The most obvious and frequent attitude toward adultery is condemnation. For this purpose, an intuitively understood metaphor of childbirth could be adopted wholesale. I want to look briefly at such adoptions, to outline what the metaphor encourages its users to say and believe about the free exercise of female sexuality, and then to turn to ways the metaphor has been used to condone or redeem the fallen woman and to speculate on why it isn't more used and how this failure delineates, in part, the outermost limits of the novel's power.

The metaphor of childbirth within a realistic framework begins even before the start of the nineteenth century. In America in 1791, Susanna Haswell Rowson wrote *Charlotte Temple*. Today we like to dismiss this book as the maundering of a sentimental pen dipped into the ink of a stereotypical

mind, but in fact it is both typical and innovative: typical of the popular novel, which largely defined the reading horizons of a rapidly changing society,[9] and innovative in its attempt to create a realistic form through which the author might speak truth to her readers.[10] The subtitle of *Charlotte Temple* is "A Tale of Truth," and Rowson both saw and intended it to convey the same sort of truth that Tolstoy would later convey through Anna Karenina's fate.

Though a virtuous child of strict moral upbringing, Charlotte is misled by the bad advice of a self-serving friend and elopes with Montraville to America. Of course, he has no intention of marrying her, for her fortune is too small and she is not mistress of the fashionable social airs which soon distract Montraville. Pregnant and cast out of her lodgings by poverty, she is helped by a poor family and in their hovel gives birth to a daughter and then dies. Rowson maintains Charlotte's spiritual purity throughout the novel, and she redeems her daughter Lucy through Lucy's subsequent resistance to corruption in *Charlotte's Daughter* (1828); but Charlotte herself must die for her sins.

Charlotte Temple sets the tone of virtually all subsequent novels dealing with fallen women. The woman must be punished for her fall, even though it was engineered by others and despite her own deep repentance. Rowson wanted to "give her audience an honest look at what they might experience in reality."[11] As founder of a girls' school, lifelong teacher of young girls, and one of the first American writers to create works specifically for girls, Rowson wrote to alert women to the dangers of sexuality and candidly to influence their actions. She saw ungoverned premarital sexuality as such a dangerous problem that she developed a fictional, realistic mode of presenting its punishment—the birth of a child. Charlotte bears a daughter and dies from the effort. After her confinement she "lay for some hours in a kind of stupor" and soon "evinced the total deprivation of her reason"—what one critic has called a "postpartum psychosis."[12] She "took [not] the least notice of her child" until the very end, when she consigned it to her father's care, adjuring him not to love it but to "protect" it—the most one can hope for an "offspring of disobedience."

Charlotte Temple creates a recognizable potential space between the fallen woman and her childbearing that is the beginning of metaphor. Charlotte's immorality becomes the vehicle, and the outcome of her childbearing the tenor, of a metaphor of childbirth that is to prevail throughout the century.

Nor is it only in popular fiction that the metaphor appears. In 1844 Balzac, in "A Woman of Thirty," uses it as baldly as Arnold Bennett does in *The Old Wives' Tale* in 1907, more than a decade after the "Victorian novel" has begun its transition to what is called The Modern Novel. Balzac's novella well illustrates the most conventional attitude toward a woman's sexual behavior. Julie d'Aiglemont marries a man she does not love and bears a daughter; marriage without love is a misuse of legitimate sexuality. The offspring of her first passionate affair is not only a girl but one so depraved by her mother's illicit sexuality that she jealously drowns her younger half-brother (Julie's illegitimate son by a second lover), thus negating any possibility of paternal succession through illegitimacy. By her husband Julie bears three more children: both sons die in battle, and the daughter precipitates her mother's death by forming an illicit alliance with the wastrel son of Julie's second lover (the father of the drowned son). Beneath Balzac's sentimentality lies a reaffirmation of the eternal verities about a woman's sexual sphere: she who is wanton pays. And his reaffirmation comes through the metaphor of childbirth. George Lukács has said of Balzac's characters that they are purposely overstated and "can never pertain to single human beings, only to social forces."[13] In "A Woman of Thirty," Balzac presents Julie as such a social force through the misuse of her sexuality.

And of course there is *The Scarlet Letter* (1850). Hester Prynne's punishment for her unrepented sexuality includes Pearl, "emblem and product of sin." Hester believes it might have been better to kill Pearl, and she is never able to understand or control the child. Hawthorne shows through Hester the tensile relationship between sexuality and intellect, then undercuts it by Pearl's own ungovernable female mind. The potential space created by the scarlet letter as symbol is intensified and enlarged when Hester bears a girl and remains sexually unregenerate. Puritan society knew how to deal with Hester because it could fill the potential space with righteous condemnation; Hawthorne steps back to allow the reader to make a judgment and then directs that judgment by use of the childbirth metaphor.

Then there is Hardy. Both *Tess* (1891) and *Jude the Obscure* (1895) reflect Hardy's stoical representation of "natural consequences." Critic Douglas Brown has noted that Hardy's novels seem to concern themselves "with *responsible* married life, and the breeding of children."[14] The contrast in these two novels is between an honest but illicit sexuality and a hard sexlessness that withdraws from the implications of its oppression. It seems likely that Hardy preferred the mindless fecundity of Tess's mother Joan; Tess's own baby is a boy (Tess *is*, after all, honest and loving), but he dies because Tess cannot give him the proper care. She must be punished, for in Hardy's world the sin of uncontrolled sexuality cannot be expiated. Bridehead's is a more extreme case of unleashed sexuality. Hardy presents Sue as classically torn between Jude and Phillotson, unable to consent to respectable boredom but unwilling to brand herself by illicit passion. Jude's first-born, licit and male although unknown to Jude because he too flees from the respectability of a marriage without passional substance, becomes the means of vengeance upon Sue and Jude's illegitimate children. It is as if through killing them and hanging himself he expresses the world's ultimate and utter refusal to acknowledge their validity as members of a society whose rules their parents have flouted. Sue is a good mother, but such goodness avails not, and even that which she has not is taken from her, for "a child had been prematurely born, and . . . it, like the others, was a corpse." It is of course perfectly appropriate in Hardy's universe that the lawful son and heir should be the one to exact the price of his father's unhallowed passion and restore society and succession to their wonted paths. Both Sue and Tess are doomed to suffer the classic consequences of their sexual freedom; the use of the metaphor of childbirth prevents the reader from imagining a reality for either heroine in which she might build a life for herself within the world of the Hardy novel. Hardy's use of the metaphor of childbirth reflects his deepest intentions.

Of course, condemnation of sexuality doesn't require a heroine as hardened as Sue or Anna. Among the "tribe of scribbling women" who provided Mudie's with a constant stream of semi-romantic novels, Adeline Sergeant was both prolific and popular as she described the tribulations of women who loved. In *Esther Denison* (1889) she presents a totally sympathetic heroine who, when her true love Sebastian marries sweet but shallow Nina La Touche, becomes a successful writer and a compassionate friend of the downcast. Sergeant's intent is not to mystify but to illuminate, for early on she tells the reader that Esther and Sebastian will eventually marry, but with no hope of the happiness that could have been theirs had the way been smooth for each to love only the other. At this point the book ceases to be merely a romance and becomes an exploration of the ways love and legality affect happiness. When Sebastian's wife and infant child are lost in a shipwreck, Esther allows herself to love him and marry him in the knowledge that although he loves her best, he did not love her first. Nina's surprise return makes of Esther a fallen woman. That the stain of this position can never quite be removed is part of the point of Sergeant's book. Although Esther legally marries Sebastian after Nina's death, the metaphor of childbirth confirms her position as a fallen woman. It is no surprise that the fruit of such a union is a daughter who cannot carry on the family name. Esther is condemned — lightly, to be sure, but still condemned — for taking advantage of a situation whose consequences she could not know. Her years of waiting and faithfulness do not count in the face of a desperately desired marriage that was no marriage. And while Sergeant does not damn Esther outright, she does see that even an unintentional lapse cannot be quite forgiven and chooses the metaphor of childbirth to embody the sin.

This same sort of situation is shown in a much harsher way by moralist George Meredith in *One of Our Conquerors* (1891). Nataly Radnor is not a bad woman. She adores Victor and tries to shield their daughter Nesta from the awful truth that must come out when she decides to marry—that her mother and her father are not lawfully wed. In fact, if anyone deserves disapproval, it is Victor Radnor, for his relentless push to join the ranks of the moneyed and the social despite the existence of a lawful wife, Nataly's obvious disinclination, and the need to protect Nesta from the world's discovery of her illegitimacy. When the expectable happens and Nesta is wooed by a young man about to come into an earldom, Nataly is forced to reveal the falseness of her position. Of course the young man, finding his beloved covered with the "cleaving green slime" of her mother's infamy, abandons the courtship. Meredith is broad-minded enough to not to visit the sins of the parents upon the child, so he allows Nesta eventually to find a husband. But he does not spare Nataly. Even with Victor's wife on her deathbed, Meredith can foresee no marriage for the faithful, meek, loving Nataly; she dies before Nesta achieves her happiness and Victor his freedom. It should no longer be surprising to the reader that Nataly and Victor's illegitimate child is a girl or that the author can at best offer her the most minor of happinesses. The unlawful child retires and is lost in small domesticity; the erring mother dies. And what of the erring husband? Victor is coldly capable of believing that not to sin by joining himself to Nataly sexually would have been the ultimate sin. In fact, he sees their act as a means of "glorifying" Nataly for her helpless acquiescence to a force, a current, stronger than either of them. His is clearly an individualist, worldly morality whose shallowness Meredith exposes through Nataly's death. Only Nataly herself comprehends the magnitude of their sin: "Nothing that she could do; no devotedness, not any sacrifice, and no treaty of peace, no possible joy to come, nothing could remove the shadow from her child." And this, of course, is why it is fitting, to her as well as to Meredith, that she die. She and her creator subscribe to the same set of values.

Many critics, writing about adultery in the novel, imply that there is a difference between the wife who is sexually incontinent and the single woman who falls through sexual indulgence. This brief sample of novels in which illegitimate children are born suggests that there is little difference. The punishment for both is the same. Certainly adultery threatens the specific existing social structure of currently intact families. But any female sexual license threatens a society in which marriage and childbearing must be controlled to insure the continuation of that society in its present form. Therefore, the sexual conduct of unmarried women is of as great concern to the novel as is the adulterous behavior of married women. Both are equally bad, and both, as we have seen, are commensurately punished.

Once the metaphor of childbirth has allowed for a dialogue between writer and reader and has filled the metaphor's potential space with a traditional interpretation, it can become a polemic as well as an artistic tool. I will mention but two such polemic uses as brief examples of the remarkable versatility of the metaphor: August Strindberg's *Confessions of a Fool* (1893) and Gabriele d'Annunzio's *The Triumph of Death* (1896).

In the former, mysogynist Strindberg fictionalizes his complaints against his wife. He sees a sexual mother as an insult and believes that female lust, which he calls "nymphomania," causes a woman to conceive illegitimately. The Baroness is very ill after the birth of her first child, a daughter, and the child dies of brain fever after her mother deserts her. A second illegitimate daughter dies two days after birth, apparently the victim of "indifference and neglect." Two more daughters are referred to only in passing; the last-born, a son, comes too late to redeem the mother. "She detested children; in her eyes motherhood was degrading. . . . Her race was doomed to extinction because she was a degenerate, in the process of dissolution." As a confirmed mysogynist, Strindberg can be expected to marshall every force, realistic and psychological, to sway readers to his view of female sexuality. The existent metaphor of childbirth offers an ideal potential space for creating a reader response that will validate the author's own prejudices.

D'Annunzio's use of the metaphor is even more interesting. For him childbirth becomes a justification of his peculiar *fin-de-siècle* decadence. George Aurispa creates a morality in which Hippolyte Sanza is glorified for leaving her family and living in sin with him. The very hugeness of their lawlessness delineates the extent of their love. Hippolyte's pregnancy is the ultimate demonstration of their lawlessness and the ultimate justification of their sexuality, but George cannot bear its social implications: a family structure, legal inheritance, a formal tie that places the lovers squarely within the society they are rebelling against. And so, as their housemaid cries out in the pangs of childbirth, George throws himself and the pregnant Hippolyte off a cliff into the sea, clasped in one another's arms and bound together in a love doomed to death by pregnancy. No child is born, but the mere fact of pregnancy dooms Hippolyte. D'Annunzio's novels seem almost a justification of his own life, an attempt to create a philosophy to glorify self-indulgence. By using the metaphor of childbirth as a means of negatively judging the fallen woman, d'Annunzio couples readers' belief in Hippolyte's badness with an implicit belief in the relative innocence of George, who, although himself the father of the unborn child (a fact he seems conveniently to forget), strikes a blow for some sort of "morality" by destroying the sinning woman and her illegitimate child. Like Strindberg, d'Annunzio exploits the metaphor to shape reader response. And only a fully established metaphor with an implicit moral to fill its potential space can lend itself to such polemics.

In the novels I have examined so far, the metaphor of childbirth carries a thoroughly understandable meaning which can underline an author's condemnation and even offset explicit (but often spurious) shows of sympathy. Once such a traditional usage has been established for the metaphor, however, it can also become a powerful tool in the novelist's attempt to refashion social values. For if good women bear and love their sons, might not a bad woman's love of her son redeem her?

The nineteenth century was not so universally prudish as we often seem to find it convenient to believe. With a crusading sense of the injustice of blanket condemnation of female sexuality, some authors chose to use the metaphor of childbirth as a potential vehicle for change outside its established context. Two very popular novels—Elizabeth Gaskell's *Ruth* (1853) and George Moore's *Esther Waters* (1894)—use the birth of an illegitimate but beloved son as a means of redemption of the erring mother and reform of a society equally erring through self-righteous condemnation of women whose only fault was to have been denied the social and moral education that would have prevented seduction by unscrupulous men. In both books, the child becomes not a punishment but a blessing. This inversion of the traditional childbirth metaphor creates a subconscious reader identification with the fallen woman; under the spell of the novelists' use of the metaphor, it becomes difficult for the reader to condemn blindly, and the author has a potentially powerful tool for the reshaping of social values.

In *Ruth,* Ruth is virtually driven to the life of a fallen woman. She is a penniless orphan, without education or skills. Gaskell shows the inhumanity of her dressmaking apprenticeship; in fact, it is her mistress's stern disapproval of so innocent an activity as a walk to her childhood home that strips Ruth even of the stultifying apprenticeship and leaves her nowhere to turn but the arms of Mr. Bellingham. Bellingham is of a class that averts its eyes from minor dalliances with dressmakers, so only Ruth is surprised when his mother swoops down to rescue her son, saying, "If she has no friends, and is the creature you describe, . . . the best place for her is, as I said before, the Penitentiary." Such is the opinion of the world of Gaskell's readers, and she does not hesitate to evoke it in contrast to her own portrait of Ruth's worth. Fortunately, Ruth's sunny disposition leads to her rescue by a crippled Dissenting minister, Thurstan Benson. When she discovers she is going to bear a child, her first act is a cry of joy to God for His blessing. Thurstan immediately sees the child as a "purification" of Ruth's sins. And while he will not attempt to deny one jot of her sinfulness, he is hopeful of her redemption because he does not "confuse the consequences with the sin." He can look upon the child as innocent and holy, apart from its unhallowed conception.

After a completely healthy and normal pregnancy, Ruth bears a son, "a new, pure, beautiful, innocent life, which she fondly imagined, in that early passion of maternal love, she could guard from every touch of corrupting sin by ever watchful and most tender care." Ruth's fitness as a mother never varies from the moment the child is placed in her arms. Rearing Leonard gives her a dignity and a glory: "she might have been placed among the highest in the land, and would have been taken by the most critical judge for their equal"—and all this because "her whole heart was in her boy." The child brings her closer to God and enables her to efface herself to do God's work, first as a teacher and then, when her horrible secret is discovered by the town's Philistines, as a nurse during a plague epidemic. She sacrifices herself, first for her boy and then for the townspeople, and eventually for Bellingham himself when he falls ill of typhoid. Her love for her son and her sacrifices for the society that spurns her bring Ruth her redemption. She earns his entry into society as a surgeon; he in turn is the source of her redemption. This grand redemption is only slightly undercut by Ruth's death. Having shown that Ruth was the equal of any lady, Gaskell spares the world the difficulty of taking Ruth herself to its bosom by leaving it with only the memory of her goodness. The book closes with a text from Revelation to prove that God welcomes sinners and seats them, spotless, at his right hand. Truly, as Thurstan Benson said in his most impassioned moment, "not every woman who has fallen is depraved."

Gaskell uses the metaphor of childbirth to underline that a fallen woman can be redeemed by her child. The famous Dissenting minister Frederick Denison Maurice found the book true "to the divinest morality." [15] And it may well have inspired George Moore in his depiction of the young serving-girl Esther Waters, who is carried away by passion and ale and William's broad shoulders. Moore is careful to express Esther's sense of the shame of her position: "hers was the unpardonable sin." In the course of only nine pages Moore speaks of "shame," homelessness, "trouble," desperation, "sin," and "adversity" and prophesies loss of character and the need to "bear your cross." Esther herself knows "it is always a woman's fault" and acknowledges that the suffering of childbirth is the curse laid upon female sexuality. Esther's mother, slowly dying from constant childbearing, speaks for all women: "Ah, we poor women have more than our right to bear with! . . . It is the children that breaks us poor women down altogether." Of course the pregnant Esther is dismissed from her situation and cast upon the world's conscience.

But the world's conscience is twisted and flawed, for Esther "never imagined other than that her child would be a boy" and that she would love it very much. And indeed, after a short labor which the coarse interns and midwives dismiss as too easy to be interesting and which is aided by the judicious use of chloroform to prevent the pain a poorer, more fallen woman in the next bed suffers, Esther gives birth to a son. From the first she "thought she must die of happiness" when looking at the child, and when she nursed it her face "took on an expression of holy solicitude." "Her personal self seemed entirely withdrawn; . . . her senses swooned with love." From the moment of Jackie's birth, his mother faultlessly devotes herself to his welfare. Although she loses situation after situation because she insists on keeping and raising her son, Esther continues to revile only the sin, never herself. The child redeems her through his purity and innocence. "It is none of the child's fault if he hasn't got a father, nor is it right that he should be deserted for that" for "he at least was innocent." As she sinks into poverty, Moore calls hers "a heroic adventure." She is repaid for her faithful suffering by William's return, their eventual marriage, and seven good years in which Jackie grows to manhood. The turning point comes with William's remark that, after all, "it may not be a woman's fault if she falls." Esther rises to something near happiness, and even William's death and her subsequent poverty cannot change the fact that she has cared for and thus been redeemed by her son, who becomes a soldier. Looking at him in his uniform, she was "conscious that she had accomplished her woman's work — she had brought him up to man's estate; and that was her sufficient reward." Moore argues, as Gaskell did, that condemnation and ostracism do not eradicate the problem of the fallen woman. We must hate the unlawful exercise of sexuality, but not the sexuality itself.

Interestingly enough, the attitude of Gaskell and Moore is not confined to the "serious" novel; it is adopted in a significant number of the popular novels of the day and in fact becomes a romantic as well as a realistic metaphor. Amelia Opie's stilted, melodramatic novelette *Father and Daughter* (1801) is a good example. Opie acknowledges that

> some brilliant and persuasive . . . writers, of both sexes, have
> endeavoured to prove that many an amiable woman has been for
> ever lost to virtue and the world . . . merely because her first fault
> was treated with ill-judging and criminal severity. This assertion
> appears to me to be fraught with mischief. . . . And it is surely as
> false as it is dangerous. I know many instances, and it is fair to
> conclude that the experience of others is similar to mine, of
> women restored by perseverance in a life of expiatory amendment,
> to that rank in society which they had forfeited by one false step,
> while their fault has been forgotten in their exemplary conduct as
> wives and *mothers* [emphasis mine].

The story on which this moral is based shows Agnes Fitzhenry succumbing to her seducer, bearing a son, and returning home to nurse her insane father and regain the esteem (if not the visiting cards) of her neighbors. Unlike

Ruth or Esther, she loses both her figure and her looks and is doomed to poverty forever, but her son is clearly the badge of her redeemability.

I would not wish to discount the value of such redemptions of fallen women, nor to deny their effects on their readers. But I do not think it is coincidental that all these heroines were single, were victims of seduction, bitterly repented their wrongdoing, and denied themselves any further exercise of sexuality outside marriage. It is such women we must be sorry for, not the Anna Kareninas of the world who continue to live in sin, to flaunt their sexual selves and deny their maternal and social identities. Ruth, Esther, and Agnes are single and innocent when they fall, so they harm no existing family structures. I would suggest that only non-adulterous female sexuality could be treated as leniently as Gaskell, Moore, and Opie treat it. The adulterous wife is always condemnable.[16]

Gaskell, Moore, and Opie were able to take the metaphor of childbirth one step further than more conventional novelists, but in the end they failed to move more than that single step toward expansion of the metaphor to encompass its full potential space by dissociating female sexuality from its biological consequences. It is easy to imagine such a dissociation: Tolstoy might have given Anna and Vronsky a son and allowed Anna to create a marriage with Vronsky. But we have no such heroines. It appears possible to rehabilitate a fallen woman who conceived unaware, who repented her fall, and who devoted herself to the welfare of child and society; it is doubtful whether the nineteenth century could forgive a woman who wantonly continued to consume forbidden fruit following the cautionary conception of a child. Anna Karenina is certainly a case in point: Tolstoy could find no other end for her than the iron wheels of a train, for she would not accept Karenin's forgiveness and moral shelter but preferred her own sexual gratification. And her daughter, neglected and nameless, is the symbol of her wantonness.

What might happen to an ideal Anna in an ideal world where her sexual expression belonged to her alone? Grant Allen, in *The Woman Who Did* (1895), creates such a heroine. When she first attracts Alan Merrick's attention, Herminia Barton is in body, mind, and soul a truly free woman, self-supporting and capable of subtle moral and intellectual discernments. Grant Allen emphasizes Herminia's intrinsic human superiority to Alan. Her presentation of the logic of her situation—that to marry would be to deny the rights and freedoms of all women—overwhelms his own feeble attempt to defend the common morality of the times, and the two carry on a liaison in which Herminia retains her own home and her teaching job. But when she becomes pregnant, Allen's rhetoric and his treatment of Herminia both change. He begins to speak of her inabilities—inability to understand Italian art, inability to appreciate the dusty beauties of Alan's beloved Perugia—and places Alan in the ascendance morally and logically, as he persuades her to give up her job and go to Italy for her confinement. It seems natural to Grant Allen that "she yielded the point . . . to his masculine judgment" for "it must always be so. The man must needs retain for many years to come the personal hegemony he has usurped over the woman. . . . Deep down in the very roots of the idea of sex we come on that prime antithesis, — the male, active and aggressive; the female, sedentary, passive, and receptive." It is almost shocking to come upon such a sudden denial of the very qualities Allen has professed to admire in Herminia. But as the book progresses, it becomes clear that he painted her as wonderful only to show the root falseness of such a wonder. It is one thing for a woman to engage in a sexual liaison; that might be very advantageous to a man. But a woman who refuses to marry the man whose child she bears is clearly stepping beyond the allowable — or enjoyable — bounds of acceptability. Alan dies; Herminia refuses his father's help and, penniless, awaits the child's birth. The Herminia of the first third of the novel would have borne a son; but Grant Allen, having already shown that he feels Herminia has exceeded even the vast license he would allow her, gives her a girl. It is true that "she longed to fondle it" even before its birth and believed it would "regenerate humanity" because of the freedom from convention into which it was to be born. And she works hard to support Dolores. However, even her poor provisions are not enough, for the very circumstances of the child's birth cut it off from society. It is Herminia's misfortune — and her creator's secret delight — that Dolores grows up to covet all the world has to offer and scorn the principles for which Grant Allen praised a childless Herminia. But of course there is a world of difference between Herminia and Dolores. Herminia was the daughter of the Dean of Dunwich. Blessed by legitimacy, she could for herself espouse causes and seek freedom, secure in the world's approval. Dolores has not that approval and so cannot flout a legitimacy she does not possess. Allen may call Dolores' behavior "atavism" and paint her as a shallow creature, but he bestows upon her the book's ultimate success — the Merrick family name and fortune, and an advantageous marriage. Given the metaphorical significance of the sex of Herminia's illegitimate child, it is not at all ironic that Allen should end his novel with Herminia's quite gruesome death, from a self-administered dose of prussic acid, as she removes the last obstacle to Dolores's accession to social acceptability. Like Tolstoy, Allen wants to admire a woman who is able to overleap the barriers of social custom; but like Tolstoy, he is compelled to punish her, in exactly the same way society does. Unlike Ruth and Esther, Herminia chose her sexual licentiousness, chose at every point not to accept the redemptions society offered in the form of marriage (to Alan or, later, to Harvey Kynaston) and legitimacy of offspring (Alan's father had offered to adopt the child and legitimatize it). In spite of the obvious rightness of Herminia's reasons for her actions, such wanton disregard of all the social sanctions of sexuality could only bring to the author's lips Dolores' despairing cry: "Illegitimate! Illegitimate! Dishonored from her birth! A mark for every cruel tongue to aim at! Born in shame and disgrace! And then, to think what she might have been, but for her mother's madness!" It is clear that Allen subscribes, after all, to the creed that "it is a woman's ancestral part to look up to the man; she is happiest in doing it." Herminia's refusal to look up, her insistence on maintaining control of her own body and of her sexuality, brings curses from the lips of her own daughter and the bitter, bitter sting of prussic acid in the throat. It is difficult to imagine a more severe or shocking denouncement of woman's sexuality. The ultimate freedom, it seems, must bring the ultimate punishment.

For most writers in the nineteenth century, childbirth thus served a metaphoric function, creating a potential space in the mind of the reader which came to be filled with a single moral judgment. That judgment could be differed from, could be turned—as by Gaskell and Moore—to show its obverse, but it could not be dissociated from the metaphor of childbirth until childbirth ceased to be a metaphor. William Starbuck, a moderately successful mid-century writer of semi-romances, nicely sums up the metaphor's content in *A Woman Against the World* (1864). Of his heroine, a fallen woman doomed to unhappiness, he says: "When a woman falls from her purity there is no return for her—as well may one attempt to wash the stain from sullied snow. Men sin and are forgiven; but the memory of a woman's guilt cannot be removed on earth."

Because childbirth was so bound up with social and economic definitions of women, the childbirth metaphor had to await the loosing of those bonds before it could change. Two novels which both showed and helped to shape such a loosing are Kate Chopin's *The Awakening* (1899) and Olive Schreiner's *The Story of an African Farm* (1883). In *The Awakening*, Edna Pontellier's children are sons, but they are not symbols of approval or disapproval of Edna's choices. She leaves her husband, has an affair with another man, and falls in love with a third; but these sexual activities are only part of Edna's search for a foundation of selfhood. Failing to find it in love, in motherhood, or in art, she chooses suicide—a statement about the lack of meaning in women's lives in general, not about Edna's sexuality. Likewise, Lyndall in *The Story of an African Farm* becomes pregnant while away at school. Two men woo her, but Lyndall feels no need for social protection against the results of her sexuality. She chooses to bear her child unwed. Schreiner specifically gives Lyndall a son. He lives but three hours, and she contracts a fatal fever while visiting his grave, suggesting that there is yet no place in the world Schreiner paints for a freedom like Lyndall's. Yet Lyndall can imagine such a freedom and can move toward it, and Schreiner allows her to do so by presenting and judging Lyndall on grounds other than her sexuality, grounds of ability and grace and sensitivity, which can expand women's horizons beyond the doom of a Lyndall, who cannot yet singlehandedly oppose the world. But, with imaginings like Chopin's and Schreiner's, the world begins to change.

Although childbirth as a metaphor outlives the nineteenth century in the works of such authors as Arnold Bennett, who remained a mid-Victorian for his whole career, it survives in the twentieth century largely in pulp romances, which, as Northrop Frye has pointed out, are the final pulse of a dying genre. Its disappearance as a serious artistic metaphor is not a result of twentieth-century scorn of marriage or approval of the free exercise of female sexuality, for these we have achieved neither in our novels nor in our lives. Rather, the novel has followed Chopin's and Schreiner's lead in adopting different metaphors for the assessment of moral value. The metaphor of childbirth closed upon itself in such works as *Ruth* and *Esther Waters* and especially *The Woman Who Did*, crystallizing the potential space which gave it its initial power, and it died in Chopin's and Schreiner's re-evaluations of female morality. Today—in Margaret Drabble's *Thank You All Very Much* (1973), for example—an illegitimate daughter's birth can be the fullest possible measure of the unmarried heroine's human value and the path to her greatest achievements.

No metaphor can survive outside the society whose unstated judgments allow the existence of its potential space, and it can be used creatively only by those authors who wish to change the potential space by altering the society that created it. A fascination with female sexuality can exist only in a world that believes in its licentiousness. This is why the metaphor of childbirth is at once so powerful and so suggestive for the nineteenth-century author. It allows the saying of the unsayable and may perhaps also lead toward the thinking of the unthinkable. But by its elusive nature a metaphor can never quite close that potential space and show the unthinkable. Its power is its limitation, just as the power of female sexuality in the nineteenth century shaped its restriction.

Notes

1. *Webster's New Collegiate Dictionary*, 1962.

2. Warren A. Shibles, *An Analysis of Metaphor in the Light of W.M. Urban's Theories* (The Hague: Mouton, 1971), pp. 39, 62.

3. James Dickey, *Metaphor as Pure Adventure* (Washington, D.C.: Library of Congress, 1968), pp. 13–14.

4. Stephen J. Brown, *The World of Imagery: Metaphor and Kindred Imagery* (London: Kegan Paul, 1927), p. 73.

5. Robert Rogers, *Metaphor: A Psychoanalytic View* (Berkeley: Univ. of California Press, 1978), p. III.

6. Michel Foucault, *The History of Sexuality* (New York: Random House, 1978), p. 17.

7. See Loralee MacPike, "Childbirth as a Metaphor in the Nineteenth-Century Novel," *International Journal of Women's Studies,* 3, no. 2 (March/April 1980), 113–30.

8. The same metaphor applies to fathers, albeit to a much lesser extent, probably because they have alternate ways of proving their value as social beings.

9. Helen W. Papashvily, *All The Happy Endings* (New York: Harper, 1956), p. 24.

10. Dorothy Weil, *In Defense of Women: Susanna Rowson* (Univ. Park: Pennsylvania State Univ. Press, 1976), p. 10. Weil's is a major revision of Rowson's reputation as a novelist.

11. Ibid., p. 15.

12. Ibid., p. 135.

13. George Lukács, *Studies in European Realism* (London: Hillway, 1950), p. 83.

14. Douglas Brown, *Thomas Hardy* (London: Longmans, 1961), p. 98.

15. Elizabeth Gaskell, *Ruth* (New York: Putnam's, 1906; rpt. 1972), introduction, xii.

16. Adulterous husbands fare far better. Victor Radnor, for instance, had cause to be glad over Nataly's death, for he had had his eye on another attractive woman for some time.

Ellen Miller Casey

"Other People's Prudery":
Mary Elizabeth Braddon

In a seminal article on minor Victorian fiction, Louis James suggested that "the most penetrating and imaginative writers transform social reality in their art. . . . The 'bad' writer on the other hand cannot either apprehend or express the social reality."[1] In James's sense, Mary Elizabeth Braddon is neither good nor bad. She apprehends social reality clearly, but does not transform it. As a result she reveals much about the fears of the Victorians and the devices of their novelists. Braddon is one of those novelists who fit well into Richard Altick's category of minor novelists who can be examined "with profit to our understanding both of the nature of popular literature itself and of the frustrations and conflicts that were at work in the ordinary Victorian's subconscious."[2]

A.O.J. Cockshut suggests that if we wish to investigate Victorian standards of moral sensibility and decency we must examine their "half-hearted and unwilling adherent . . . since the willing adherents of the prevailing ethos will be slow to give us any idea of what they are concealing."[3] In her life Braddon absolutely refused to accept Victorian sexual conventions. She lived with publisher John Maxwell for fourteen years, bearing him five illegitimate children. In her novels, however, Braddon was more half-hearted. Although both Victorian and contemporary critics have recognized that Braddon perceived the secrets which underlay respectable Victorian society, she never fully succeeded in transforming that recognition into great art. In her early sensation novels such as *Lady Audley's Secret* (1862) and *Aurora Floyd* (1863) and in her later domestic ones such as *Vixen* (1879), Braddon stopped short of accepting the implications of what she saw, pulling back to a more conventional posture. Nonetheless, her work is worth investigating, for her struggles with the restraints of conventional morality reveal much about both the Victorians and their novels.

Recently, feminist critics have been adding much to our understanding of Braddon's method of operating within the constraints of popular morality. Elaine Showalter, for example, argues that *Lady Audley's Secret* is "a carefully controlled female fantasy of rebellion and power."[4] In her recent book on the sensation novel, Winifred Hughes argues similarly that Braddon deliberately undermines the traditional moral assumptions: "Instead of abandoning the popular conventions, she circumvents them, using them against themselves, investing them with a new ironic significance."[5] Certainly it is true that Braddon is one of those novelists who express what U.G. Knoepflmacher calls the asocial and amoral "counterworld" of Victorian society, who "repudiate yet indulge rebellious attitudes at odds with the dictates of accepted behavior."[6]

Despite her struggle with the restraints which society placed on the expression of such subversive sub-texts, Braddon never totally succeeded in transforming social reality. Her chafing under the constraints of popular morality was evident to critics of her early, sensation novels. The *Reader*, for example, recognized the difficulties of writing a novel such as *Aurora Floyd* in England rather than in France, for an English author was forced to preserve her heroine's "nominal purity," no matter how unrealistic that purity might be.[7] The reviewer of *The Lady's Mile* (1866) in the *Christian Remembrancer* made a similar point: "In comparing themselves with French novelists, our writers must feel at a cruel disadvantage, and must often be ashamed of the clumsy expedients they are driven to by punctilio, the necessities of the publisher, or whoever else feels the pulse of popular morality."[8]

Braddon first excited that pulse with her sensation novels. In these she defied convention by writing of murders and bigamies committed by beautiful women who were regarded semi-sympathetically. Despite the outrage of some readers, Victorian critics recognized that Braddon's sensation novels were responding to their readers' desires rather than defying them. In a review of *Aurora Floyd*, for instance, Henry James suggested that Braddon's popularity was a result of "observing a strictly respectful attention to her readers" and keeping up with the "delicate fluctuations of the public taste."[9]

Braddon kept up with these "delicate fluctuations" by carefully limiting what she wrote. Her subjects were shocking, but she maintained the proprieties by limiting the amount of detail which she provided, by legitimatizing passion with marriage, even if a bigamous one, and by taking care that at the end of the novel the good were rewarded and the evil punished. In other words, she provided a stimulus to Victorian imaginations with a wink for the knowing and a carefully proper surface for the censors.

Limiting detail is an obvious way to maintain the proprieties. It is one thing to assert that Aurora Floyd has eloped with her father's groom; it is quite another to detail the subsequent events. It is one thing to present Lady Audley pushing her husband into a well to prevent the detection of her bigamy; it is quite another to depict in graphic detail the process of drowning. The difference between Victorian and modern novels often lies less in the situations depicted than in the amount of detail provided to flesh out those situations. As A.H. Japp noted in 1867, one could write of immorality so long as one did it objectively, without passion.[10]

To legitimatize passion with marriage is perhaps a less obvious way to placate the moralists. Henry James pointed to this technique in his 1865 essay on Braddon when he attributed her success to her strict morality: "If one of her heroines elopes with a handsome stable-boy, she saves the proprieties by marrying him. This may be indecent if you like, but it is not immoral."[11] As Margaret Oliphant recognized, the English Victorians had a preference for crime over vice and preferred bigamy—an indictable crime —to something plainer.[12] Braddon clearly perceived this national preference. Indeed, Oliphant declared that Braddon began "the reign of bigamy as an interesting and fashionable crime."[13] There is no simple, enjoyable fornication in Braddon's novels. Always the appearances are preserved.

Rewarding the good and punishing the evil is, of course, the most common way to satisfy Victorian sensibilities. In this context it is important to note that poetic justice served social more than religious ends. True, such justice affirmed the providence of God, but more importantly it justified society's values and compensated for earlier impropriety in a novel. Elizabeth Gaskell's *Ruth* and Charles Reade's *Griffith Gaunt* were regarded as much more shocking than anything by Braddon because in both novels those who violated the sexual mores were accorded understanding and sympathy and ended less than tragically. Braddon was occasionally accused of making her readers sympathize with criminals,[14] but she made no mistakes at the ends of her novels. Her villainesses were always punished, thus satisfying the code that is well represented by Robert Buchanan's comment in the *Fortnightly Review:* "Where there is sin in literature and no suffering, the description is false, because in life the moral implication of sin is suffering. . . . "[15]

After 1870, Braddon moved in accordance with popular taste from the sensation novel to the domestic one. One of the best of these later novels is *Vixen,* which appeared in weekly installments in *All the Year Round* from 5 October 1878 to 14 June 1879, and in standard three-volume form in February 1879.[16] With its wealth of detail about the manners and mores of the time, *Vixen* is probably more representative of Braddon's natural taste than the earlier sensation works. (James perceptively compared her to Jane Austen, for example.)[17] In any case *Vixen* was one of Braddon's favorite novels.[18]

In *Vixen,* Braddon abandoned the sensation mode and her attempts to use what Showalter describes as her subversive sub-texts of feminine rebellion. She did not, however, abandon subversion, though as in her earlier novels she did not pass the barrier from expression to transformation of social reality. For understanding the sexual ethos of the Victorian Age, however, and the constraints which it placed on its novelists, *Vixen* is at least as valuable as the earlier novels. Braddon is here writing of ordinary life, not of crime, but her awareness of passion and its possible effects is still present, all the more intriguing because it is repressed, not breaking out in criminal actions. *Vixen* is a nice, quiet, domestic romance whose very real power comes from sexual energy and whose very real failure comes from an inability or unwillingness to acknowledge that energy forthrightly.

Vixen unfortunately confirms Michael Sadleir's judgment that Braddon would have written better novels in an atmosphere of greater freedom in which she would not have had to submit to "other people's prudery." [19] Sadleir and Lionel Stevenson both recognize that although Braddon did not share her readers' "moral prejudices," she nonetheless avoided impropriety by "an unconvincing twist . . . to the story" and "implausible manipulation of the plot." [20]

Certainly the plot of *Vixen* is a contrived one. Two lovers are separated by a variety of incidents including their own misapprehensions. Needless to say, all is resolved happily at the end. At the opening of the novel Violet Tempest, called Vixen by her beloved, fox-hunting father because of her red hair, is just shy of fifteen. She is infatuated with her neighbor Roderick (Rorie) Vawdrey, nineteen, who is resisting his mother's pressure to marry his sophisticated cousin Lady Mabel Ashbourne. Two years later, Vixen's father dies of a sudden heart attack on Rorie's twenty-first birthday, and Vixen is comforted by Rorie's assurance that, contrary to rumor, he is not engaged to Mabel.

Another two years pass. Vixen is "out" and courted by Captain Conrad Carmichael. She spurns him, and he vows that "it shall be measure for measure." Vixen returns home to learn that Rorie's mother has died and that Rorie and Mabel have become engaged to satisfy her dying wish. Carmichael visits and successfully woos Vixen's mother. Despite his threats, Carmichael's only action against Vixen after the marriage is to institute a strict system of economy so that he need not suffer when she inherits the estate on her twenty-fifth birthday.

When Vixen refuses the proposal of Carmichael's friend Lord Mallow, Carmichael is infuriated. During the course of berating Vixen for her improper conduct in spending her time riding with Rorie, Carmichael reveals that she is the only woman he has ever loved. In the course of the subsequent argument, Vixen drops a lamp which sets the house on fire but does not destroy it. Carmichael then banishes Vixen to the desolate house of his eccentric aunt, Miss Skipwith. On the day when Rorie and Mabel are to marry, Rorie suddenly appears there, freed by Mabel's elopement with Lord Mallow. Rorie proposes to Vixen, who immediately accepts him. Vixen's mother dies; Carmichael leaves; Rorie rents his house to Lord and Lady Mallow; and Rorie and Vixen live happily ever after in her old and much beloved home.

Victorian reviewers found *Vixen* slight, readable, and respectable. The *Athenaeum* included *Vixen* among its "Novels of the Week," commenting that the novel had ingenuity of description but a slight plot. "The interest consists in marking how a writer who thoroughly understands her business can make a respectable three-volume novel out of so little material."[21] The *Academy* also had a short notice of *Vixen* in its "New Novels." It described the novel as "in Miss Braddon's later and better manner, put together with but a small stock of incidents, and yet vivid and readable."[22] The *Saturday Review*, Braddon's long-standing opponent, was rather snide, expressing amazement that there was no crime from Miss Braddon this time and asking rhetorically how she managed to fill her pages. It added ironically, "Let Miss Braddon only go on in this most respectable course, and we shall yet have the pleasure of seeing her books given away as prizes in a school for young ladies."[23] Clearly *Vixen* aroused no storms of opposition or approbation.

One must agree with these reviews; *Vixen*, while readable, is no great work of art. Yet this judgment of the novel isn't totally satisfactory, for *Vixen* has a power that is not encompassed by the tepid approbation of the reviewers. This power does not come from clever characterization or vivid description, though both are present. Rather *Vixen's* power comes from the underlying sexual passions which the novel acknowledges but doesn't develop.

In *Vixen*, the refusal to accept Victorian propriety takes several forms. As in most of her novels, Braddon uses irony extensively.[24] She maintains an ironic stance toward the whole notion of romantic passion without sexual involvement, largely by repeated allusions to great lovers of literature. An ironic contrast to the novel's respectability is provided by frequent references to Shakespeare's *Hamlet* and *Antony and Cleopatra*, Tennyson's *Idylls of the King*, and Dante's story of Paolo and Francesca. We laugh, as Braddon surely intends that we should, at Vixen's overblown language when she thinks of *Antony and Cleopatra:* "that story of a wild undisciplined love grand in its lawless passion—its awful doom. To have loved thus, and died thus, seemed a higher destiny than to do right, and patiently conquer sorrow, and live on somehow to the dismal end of the dull blameless chapter" (p. 308). We also laugh when Mrs. Carmichael, in rebuking Vixen for riding with Rorie, utters one of the greatest lines of Victorian respectability: "it is worse than a crime, Violet; it is an impropriety" (p. 216). No further evidence should be needed to prove Braddon an unwilling adherent to the prevailing sexual ethos.

Despite her irony, however, Braddon does adhere to that ethos. This is most evident in her use of the common Victorian ploy of setting up suggestive situations that prove to be innocent.[25] This ploy is akin to Anne Radcliffe's treatment of the supernatural—after scaring, prove things rational. For the Victorians the motto might well have been—after shocking, prove things innocent.

Braddon begins this pattern of suggesting shocking things with the character of Vixen herself. By a number of hints Vixen is presented as a woman capable of any daring; as a result we expect her to break out in violence. Decorum prevails, but we are always aware of the suppressed violence in Vixen's character. Braddon repeatedly stressed Vixen's tempestuousness. Her name—Violet (Vixen) Tempest—is part of this pattern, as are her red hair and the description of her as a "pretty horsebreaker," a common euphemism for a prostitute. Captain Carmichael describes Vixen as "this fair devil of a daughter, who looks capable, if offended, of anything in the way of revenge, from a horse whip to slow poison" (p. 89). Despite the hints, however, Vixen is not a sensation heroine, though Braddon is clearly exploiting the convention which she helped to establish.

Another situation which is presented and then evaded is the relationship between Vixen and Rorie. He is engaged to Lady Mabel and yet spends his time riding in the forest with Vixen. Mrs. Carmichael reprimands Vixen for her companionship with Rorie: "Violet, you must know that all talk about brother and sister is sheer nonsense" (p. 216). Captain Carmichael is even more direct: "I will come between you and your lover, Roderick Vawdrey. Your secret meetings, your clandestine love-making, shall be stopped" (p. 229). In point of fact there has been no love-making, and when Rorie breaks through their reserve to propose to Vixen she rejects him because he is engaged, reminding him of his duty and honor. The words with which she does so are stilted and unbelievable, especially when set in the context of the heightened descriptions of their idyllic ride: "You and I must part, Rorie. This night ride in the forest must be our last. Never any more, by sun or moon, must you and I ride together. It is all over, Rorie, the old childish friendship. I mean to do my duty, and you must do yours" (p. 225). It may be that Braddon intends by this stilted language to indicate that she too finds Vixen's renunciation of Rorie improbable; unfortunately the inappropriate clichés falsify the entire situation and create a sense that art has been sacrificed to propriety.

The most interesting relationship in *Vixen* is that between Vixen and her stepfather. Again, however, Braddon evades the logical consequences of the situation she creates. Captain Carmichael proposes to Vixen and, after she rejects him, marries Vixen's mother. He becomes a tyrannical husband and father, insisting that he will "tame" Vixen. The situation verges on the incestuous. As Carmichael explains to Vixen: "You are the girl I would have periled my soul to win – the girl who rejected me with careless scorn. . . . If you had been my wife, Violet, I would have been your slave. You forced me to make myself your stepfather, and I will be master instead of slave" (p. 229). Despite this melodramatic language, nothing happens. Carmichael does not rape Vixen, does not beat her mother. He only keeps a tight watch on the budget, tries to marry Vixen to his friend Lord Mallow, and sends Vixen off to stay with his aunt. The discrepancy between the potential and the actual is so immense that it is unbelievable. Braddon succumbs to decorum and plays herself false.

Besides creating irregular situations which are never carried to their logical ends, Braddon uses another common Victorian technique for suggesting passion without offending the proprieties. She employs alternative expressions, metaphors, for the passion which she cannot express directly. Although the conventionality of its plot and the weakness and implausibility of Rorie and Captain Carmichael move *Vixen* firmly in the direction of tepid propriety, the sexual metaphors, like the hints about Vixen's character and situation, create a sense of genuine passion. An examination of the central metaphors of Vixen – horseback riding and fire – is valuable for what these metaphors suggest about Victorian fiction in general.

Braddon's metaphors of riding and fire are not, of course, original, having been used by other authors as metaphors for sexual passion in a number of earlier works. For example, riding is used in Browning's "The Last Ride Together" (1855), Reade's *Griffith Gaunt* (1866), and Eliot's *Daniel Deronda* (1876),[26] while fire appears in Collins's *The Woman in White* (1860), Dickens's *Great Expectations* (1862), and Reade's *Hard Cash* (1863). Though Braddon may be drawing on these precedents, she makes the metaphors her own by adding significant symbolic details.

Horseback riding becomes in *Vixen* virtually the synonym for passion. Lord Mallow, for example, falls in love with Vixen while she leads him on a day-long ride. More important, riding substitutes for the words that Vixen and Rorie cannot say. This is perhaps clearest in their ride home after Rorie has proposed and Vixen has refused him:

> It was a long grassy ride, safe only for those who knew the country well, for it was bordered on each side by treacherous bogs. Violet knew every inch of the way. Arion scented his stable afar off, and went like the wind; Blue Peter stretched his muscular limbs in pursuit. It was a wild ride along the grassy track, beside watery marshes and reedy pools that gleamed in

the dim light of a new moon. The distant woods showed black against the sky. There was no light to mark a human habitation within ken. There was nothing but night and loneliness, and the solemn beauty of an unpeopled waste. A forest pony stood here and there—pastern-deep in the sedges—and gazed at these two wild riders, grave and gay, like a ghost. A silvery snake glided across the track, a water-rat plunged, with a heavy splash, into a black pool as the horses galloped by. It was a glorious ride. Miserable as both riders were, they could not but enjoy that wild rush through the sweet soft air, under the silent stars.
(p. 226)

One doesn't need to be a Freudian to recognize the symbolic nature of this landscape. The watery marshes and reedy pools through which the horses with muscular limbs rush on a grassy track describe an archetypal sexual landscape. If that is not enough, one also has the silvery snake and the water-rat plunging into a black pool. The ride is the substitute for a direct expression of the passion the propriety prohibits. One might even suggest that it is more effective in its suggestiveness than a more explicit love scene. In any case, the passage makes clear why Braddon was so frequently praised for her power of description and suggests what she might have been able to accomplish in a more permissive situation which would have allowed her to bring events to a climax.

Horses play their part in another metaphor for passion. Captain Carmichael repeatedly compares Vixen to a horse which he will tame and ride. Before he has given up the ideal of marrying Vixen, Carmichael thinks: "She is like that chestnut mare that threw me six times before I got the better of her. . . . There are two conquests a man can make over a woman—one to make her love him, the other—" (p. 86). The thought is never completed, unless implicitly a page later: "But I conquered the chestnut, and I'll conquer Miss Tempest—or make her smart for it" (p. 87). After he decides to marry Vixen's mother, Carmichael still uses the metaphor. Mrs. Tempest complains to him how much Vixen opposes the wedding. Carmichael anwers, "Your daughter has a noble nature, but she has been spoiled by too much indulgence: Even a racehorse—the noblest thing in creation—has to be broken in, not always without severe punishment. Miss Tempest and I will come to understand each other perfectly by and by" (p. 129).

The slang use of *ride* for the act of intercourse is at the root of the double-entendres in these passages. Braddon here raises the spectre of sexual cruelty, one which her readers probably perceived, as in an 1867 review in which Mrs. Oliphant identified "horsey" novels as "akin to immoral."[27] Nonetheless, the need for evasion ultimately creates a false and vaguely preposterous situation, for despite all his threats Carmichael does nothing except cut off Vixen's allowance and close her mother's account with her dressmaker.

Fire is another metaphor for sexual passion in *Vixen,* notably in its climactic scene. Confronted by Carmichael after her refusal of Rorie's proposal, told by him that he hates her because she rejected his love, attacked for her "shameful" conduct with Rorie, Vixen is "beside herself with anger."

> She grasped the lamp with both her hands, as if she would have hurled it at her foe. It was a large moon-shaped globe upon a bronze pedestal—a fearful thing to fling at one's adversary. A great wave of blood surged up into the girl's brain. What she was going to do she knew not; but her whole being was convulsed by the passion of that moment. The room reeled before her eyes, the heavy pedestal swayed in her hands, and then she saw the big moon-like globe roll on to the carpet, and after it, and darting beyond it, a stream of liquid fire that ran, and ran quicker than thought toward the open window.
>
> Before she could speak or move the flame had run up the lace curtain like a living thing, swift as the flight of a bird or the gliding motion of a lizard. The wide casement was wreathed with light. They two—Vixen and her foe—seemed to be standing in an atmosphere of fire. (p. 229)

The next day Carmichael refers to this fire when he tells Vixen that she is to be sent to Miss Skipwith:

> "Go and pack your boxes!" cried the captain, angrily. "Do you want to raise the devil that was raised last night? Do you want another conflagration? It might be a worse one this time. I have had a night of fever and unrest."
>
> "Am I to blame for that?"
>
> "Yes, you beautiful fury. It was your image kept me awake. I shall sleep sounder when you are out of this house." (p. 236)

Taken together these two passages illustrate the strengths and weaknesses of Braddon's presentation of sexual passion. Clearly she recognizes sexual obsession and is willing to depict it. Phrase after phrase in the description of the fire scene evokes sexual intercourse, from the symbolic "moon-shaped globe upon a bronze pedestal" to the physical "great wave of blood." Vixen's blood "surge[s]" and her being is "convulsed by the passion of that moment." Carmichael's speech the next day is also suggestive, with its talk of raising the devil and "a night of fever and unrest." Braddon's perception of sexual passion is undercut by conventionality and reticence, but the fire scene succeeds in evoking the passion which it describes despite the conventionality of much of its language. Braddon makes up for the waves of blood and the reeling room with the flame like a lizard and the iconographic quality of the close of the scene when Carmichael and Vixen stand surrounded by the wreath of flame around the casement. There is, however, nothing to compensate for the coyness and artificiality of Carmichael's language the next day. Overwritten though it is, the fire scene is imaginable. What is not imaginable is that anyone in the heat of anger would ask about "conflagrations" or call a woman a "beautiful fury."

The Carmichael/Vixen relationship is alive with the threat of sexual violence which is expressed only in elliptical terms. That relationship also raises questions about the relationship which it replaces, that of Vixen and her father. Vixen's adoration of her father and his fondness of her is succeeded by Vixen's repulsion for Captain Carmichael and his passion for her. *Vixen* presents a dark countervision of the Victorian home. Unfortunately, Braddon retreats from the implications of the Carmichael/Vixen relationship into unbelievable propriety. The threat of rape becomes the cutting off of an allowance.

The falseness of Carmichael's response is epitomized by a passage late in the novel when he sits beside his dying wife "with anger and envy gnawing his heart." He wishes to kill Violet and Rorie but "happily the captain was too cautious a man to be guilty of any overt act of rage or hatred. His rancorous feelings were decently hidden under a gentlemanly iciness of manner, to which no one could take objection" (p. 333). Braddon also hides rancorous feelings under iciness of manner; readers of *Vixen* can object, however, and wish that she had been truer to her own perceptions.

In her sensation novels, Braddon sees through Victorian propriety to a counterworld of feminine rebellion; in *Vixen* she recognizes one of sexual violence and incestuous passion. She dilutes this vision, however, by setting it in a plot of fortuitous errors, weak male characters, and a decorous happy ending. The *Christian Remembrancer's* reviewer of *The Lady's Mile* had regretted the necessity of "outward illogical attention to the decencies of society; a requirement which must exceedingly bore and embarrass any writer who cares for philosophical correctness and the dependence of effects on causes."[28] One wonders to what extent Braddon was bored and embarrassed by *Vixen,* a novel which succumbed to the pressure of other people's prudery and which is therefore less interesting as a finished work of art than for what it reveals about its age.

Notes

1. Louis James, "The Rational Amusement: 'Minor' Fiction and Victorian Studies," *Victorian Studies,* 14 (1970), 195.

2. Richard Altick, "The Literature of an Imminent Democracy," in *1859: Enter-*

ing an Age of Crisis, ed. Philip Appleman et al. (Bloomington: Indiana Univ. Press, 1959), p. 223.

3. A.O.J. Cockshut, *Truth to Life* (London: Collins, 1974), p. 36.

4. Elaine Showalter, *A Literature of Their Own* (Princeton: Princeton Univ. Press, 1977), pp. 163–68.

5. Winifred Hughes, *The Maniac in the Cellar* (Princeton: Princeton Univ. Press, 1980), pp. 120–36.

6. U.G. Knoepflmacher, "The Counterworld of Victorian Fiction and *The Woman in White*," in *The Worlds of Victorian Fiction*, ed. Jerome H. Buckley (Cambridge, Mass.: Harvard Univ. Press, 1975), pp. 351–69.

7. Quoted in Michael Sadleir, *Things Past* (London: Constable, 1944), p. 80.

8. "Youth as Depicted in Modern Fiction," *Christian Remembrancer*, 52 (July 1866), 185.

9. Henry James, "Miss Braddon," *The Nation*, 1 (9 Nov. 1865), 593.

10. H.A. Page [A.H. Japp], "The Morality of Literary Art," *Contemporary Review*, 5 (June 1867), 187.

11. James, "Miss Braddon," p. 594.

12. Mrs. Oliphant, "Novels," *Blackwood's*, 94 (Aug. 1863), 168–69.

13. Ibid., 102 (Sept. 1867), 263.

14. See, for example, [W. Fraser Rae], "Sensation Novelists: Miss Braddon," *North British Review*, 43 (Sept. 1865), 202, and Page [Japp], "Morality of Literary Art," p. 178.

15. Robert Buchanan, "Immorality in Authorship." *Fortnightly Review*, 6 (15 Sept. 1866), 296.

16. All citations of *Vixen* are from Mary Elizabeth Braddon, *Vixen* (New York: Lovel, Coryell, n.d.); with the exception of the change of Captain Winstanley's name to Carmichael and some consolidation of chapters, this edition is identical to the serialized version which appeared in *All the Year Round*.

17. Henry James, "Miss Braddon," p. 593.

18. Clive Holland, "Miss Braddon," *The Bookman*, 42 (July 1912), 157.

19. Michael Sadleir, *Things Past*, p. 80.

20. Michael Sadleir, "Mary Elizabeth Braddon," *Times Literary Supplement* (2 Oct. 1937), p. 711, and *Things Past*, pp. 78–80; Lionel Stevenson, *The English Novel* (Boston: Houghton Mifflin, 1960), p. 355.

21. *Athenaeum*, 73 (1 March 1879), 275.

22. R.F. Littledale, *Academy*, 15 (15 March 1879), 233.

23. *Saturday Review*, 47 (1 March 1879), 280–82.

24. This irony is not limited to sexual matters. For example, the many satiric comments in *Vixen* on class and money are discussed by Robert Lee Wolff, *Sensational Victorian* (New York: Garland, 1979), pp. 278–81.

25. See Wayne Burns, *Charles Reade* (New York: Bookman, 1961), pp. 266–67.

26. See Russell M. Goldfarb, *Sexual Repression and Victorian Literature* (Lewisburg: Bucknell Univ. Press, 1970), pp. 66–81, for some suggestive comments about riding as a metaphor and for an overextended discussion of Browning's poem.

27. Mrs. Oliphant, "Novels," *Blackwood's*, 102 (Sept. 1867), 272.

28. "Youth as Depicted in Modern Fiction," p. 185.

Richard D. McGhee

"Swinburne Planteth, Hardy Watereth": Victorian Views of Pain and Pleasure in Human Sexuality

Tess Durbeyfield, on her way home from her disaster with Alec d'Urberville, encounters an itinerant "Text-painter." He goes about the countryside painting biblical texts "on every wall, gate, and stile" he can find. Tess thinks they are "horrible," "crushing! killing!" "'That's what they are meant to be!' he replied in a trade voice. 'But you should read my hottest ones—them I kips for slums and seaports. They'd make ye wriggle!'"[1] Moralists and puritans of all kinds were capable of deriving pleasure from inflicting pain on the victims of their condemnation, and they could do it in their most professional "trade voice," like Hardy's Text-painter.

In the name of Love, Victorian "Text-painters" condemned love. Both Swinburne and Hardy early discovered that they could not speak the truth of love, in its essential sexuality, without making themselves the targets of many a Text-painter. As artists they had to make their art—and they had to make it true as well as beautiful—and their truth increasingly incorporated the same sexual ambivalences in their critics as their critics condemned in them. When Robert Buchanan calls Swinburne's *Poems and Ballads* of 1866 "prurient trash,"[2] Buchanan confesses his own prurience, and when Mrs. Oliphant accuses Hardy of leadership in "the anti-marriage league,"[3] she articulates one of the major anxieties of her era. Surely one reason Hardy held such deep respect for Swinburne was that Swinburne had been a victim, like himself, of the Victorian Text-painters. Hardy reports that when he visited Swinburne in June 1905, Swinburne "spoke with amusement of a paragraph he had seen in a Scottish paper: 'Swinburne planteth, Hardy watereth, and Satan giveth the increase.'"[4] By that date the two great artists could laugh and condole "with each other on having been the two most abused of living writers."

One of the earliest critics to take general exception to the hostile reception of Hardy was Edmund Gosse, his friend and the biographer of Swinburne; Gosse recognized that Swinburne had "prepared the way for an ultimate appreciation of Mr. Hardy."[5] There have been few critics of either writer to make much of their mutual temperaments and respect for one another's art. D.H. Lawrence had some insight into the significance of their relationship because Lawrence, to an extent, shared in it himself, as Ross C. Murfin has seen in his recent book on the three.[6] But Murfin has left largely unexamined one of the most sensitive but nevertheless essential subjects shared by these three great writers; the subject which Havelock Ellis described as "one of the most difficult problems, and yet one of the most fundamental, in the whole range of sexual psychology." This subject is "the relation of love to pain." Ellis asks, in his landmark study of the subject, "why is it that love inflicts, and even seeks to inflict pain? Why is it that love suffers pain, and even seeks to suffer it?"[7] Swinburne and Hardy do not answer these questions so much as testify to the significance of the experience which gives rise to the questions themselves.

I

Swinburne in his correspondence writes with a healthy sense of decorum that might surprise readers appalled or even bored by his *Poems and Ballads,* First Series. In 1858 he recalls that during one of those glorious sessions, while painting murals for the Oxford Union, he and Edward Jones defended the idea that heaven was "a rose-garden full of stunners." Then "two respectable members of the University" came by to look at the paintings; the young painters heightened their lively debate, for the special sake of the "respectable" audience, with Swinburne and Jones expanding their point that kissing was a "necessity of life" that would be more exquisitely developed in heaven. Swinburne recalls that their listeners "literally fled from the room" (I: 17–18).[8] A "stunner" inspired the young men with visions of heavenly, but fleshly, delight; yet, Swinburne is worried that Morris's marriage to Jane Burden will be a troublesome affair because Jane is a "perfect stunner" who might not adapt very easily to the mundane realities of marriage. Swinburne could also entertain the radical notion of a negative ideal, equally a product of sexual fantasy. He describes a scene in which he and Rossetti read *Justine* together, and their fun echoes that of the group who had such a good time while painting the Oxford Union pictures. Here is the same excitement in exploring the forbidden: Swinburne says "I never laughed so much in my life," and when Rossetti "read out the dissection of the interesting Rosalie and her infant," they filled the "whole house by our screams of laughter" (I: 54).

However, fun though it was to read the story as a comic exaggeration of the trials of sexuality, Swinburne cannot be so enthusiastic in his analysis of De Sade's intellectual, or philosophical, principles.[9] He finds, to his great disappointment, that his "illusion" has been shattered. Just as he feared for Morris when Swinburne learned of his marriage to Jane Burden, Swinburne here records his disillusionment of an ideal image of sexuality. Swinburne says that he "looked for some sharp and subtle analysis of lust—some keen dissection of pain and pleasure," but he did not find it in *Justine*. Swinburne criticizes DeSade for failing to stimulate the sexual imagination: "You have gathered up and arranged in rows all manner of abominations and your work is *fade* after all—flat, flaccid, impotent, misshapen, hung awry." But most of all, De Sade shows himself to be little more than "a Christian ascetic bent on earning the salvation of the soul through the mortification of the flesh."

Swinburne structures his novel of *Lesbia Brandon* around the education of Herbert Seyton ("Bertie"), particularly under the tutorship of one Denham, who applies the birch liberally and often as he seeks to "train the crude mind" of his young ward.[10] Somewhat awkwardly, Swinburne brings in two peripheral characters to establish the extremes of sexual ideals which he uses to define the education of his hero: Attilio Mariani is an Italian patriot in exile, representing "soul almost without body," and Leonora Harley is a "body almost without soul." They are "'*Courtisane manquée, patriote manqué,*' Mr. Linley might have said. The one, I am told by men skilled in the science of erotics, was a failure in their eyes, a discredit to her calling, incompetent to fulfil expectations and respond to desires. The other, I am told by men skilled in the art of politics, was not less imperfect; inadequate to the pressure of the moment, contemptible to all trained statesmen" (p. 352). Each is, then, a victim of extremist values, and each is finally reduced to little importance in Swinburne's world of the novel: "she became a wife, and he a martyr."

The fortunes of other characters in the novel are not much more attractive, however. Denham falls in love with Herbert's sister, Margaret, Lady Wariston, and because he must suppress his very physical desire for her, he perverts his lust into a power to punish her through whipping Bertie: "Silent desire curdled and hardened into poisonous forms; love became acrid in him, and crusted with a bitter stagnant scum of fancies ranker than weeds. Under the mask or under the rose he was passing through quiet stages of perversion" (pp. 207–8). Later, Denham hates "her with all his heart as he loved her with all his senses, he could but punish her through her brother, hurt her through his skin; but at least to do this was to make her own flesh and blood suffer for the pain inflicted on himself" (p. 218). Swinburne thus analyzes the psychology of the sadist as an unsatisfied sexual desire converted into a satisfied will for power. Later, when Denham and Lady Wariston have become lovers, they realize that their relationship can go no further: they have been identified as half-brother and sister, and they are trapped by her marriage to Wariston. Denham announces that he will kill himself, and they embrace in a wildly ecstatic scene of romantic physicality: "she sobbed and sighed with love under her kisses; her fragrant glittering throat trembled, her veins felt fire . . . she clove to him with fluttering body and vibrating hair. So for some moments they took the cruel pleasure left them as their love drew to a close; they grew and hung together for a little, then divided slowly, one weeping" (p. 316).

While the violent loves of Denham and Lady Wariston are the larger portion of the manuscript, the education of Herbert Seyton remains central to the main plan of the narrative, and his education involves Swinburne's analysis of masochism—the analysis, perhaps, which he had hoped to find when he read de Sade and was disappointed. There had been a hint of this interest in *Love's Cross-Currents,* but there the subject was greatly subordinated to the machinations of Lady Midhurst. With Herbert, the issue is introduced by the appearance of Denham as Herbert's tutor; it is elaborated by the sly Linley, who makes it clear to Bertie that he will have to get in shape for the flagellations which will be in store for him at the public schools; and finally it is complicated by Bertie's infatuation with Lesbia Brandon herself, the Sappho of this fiction. The identity that Bertie makes between the pleasures of swimming, the pain of corrective punishment, the excitement of exploring the forbidden, and the death-threat of the sea—all come together in his sensing that the sea is a woman for him: "I think they were right to put a lot of women in the sea: it's like a woman itself: the right place for sirens to come out of, and sing and kill people," Bertie says to Denham (p. 211).

After an outing with his friend Lunsford, Bertie dreams that he is visited by Venus herself. She arrives in an atmosphere that mixes ocean and moonlight: he sees her at first as "the star of Venus, white and flower-like." She descends as a white rose, "with a reddening centre that grew as it descended liker and liker a living mouth; but instead of desire he felt horror and sickness at the sight of it." The noise of the sea increases, sharpening into "a shrill threatening note," and Bertie dreams that he is drowning as the mouth of Venus seems to envelop him: "he woke as the salt froth seemed coming round lips and nostrils and ears, with a sense of sterility and perplexity" (pp. 281–82). This dream is a revelation to the boy that his sexual nature is complicated by a fear of women and a sense of satisfaction from physical punishment. It is surely an anxiety dream that hints, as fully as Swinburne was capable of doing so, that Bertie's masochism is a symptom of his oedipal complex. The boy is afraid of losing his penis, which is what he vaguely realizes in his dream of the flower-mouth symbol of the vagina about to devour him; and he is satisfied to accept physical punishment in lieu of that loss—hence he can feel pleasure in the pain. But, without analysis, Swinburne witnesses to the sexual phenomena which later psychoanalysis has sought to explain.

It is fully predictable, because consistent in the psychology of his sexual development, that Bertie would be attracted to Lesbia Brandon. She is Bertie's "fate," as his sister had realized, but perhaps for reasons that she could not have understood. His environment, including especially his means of education, has perverted Bertie's sexuality into a sterile trap of perpetual dissatisfaction except through corporeal punishment. Bertie, like Meleager in *Atalanta in Calydon*, pursues the very woman he cannot possess, both because she is a manly woman and because her resistance will contribute to his need for punishment. She may even be, for his unconscious needs, the father with whom he needs to identify. In all of this Swinburne has but given the reader raw material, but clear and certain evidence that he could recognize the essential ingredients in neurotic sexual behavior. What further characterizes Swinburne's attitude toward sexuality is his underlying, sometimes unspoken, assumption that all human sexuality is neurotic to some degree, driven as it is to take the extreme shapes of Attilio Mariani ("soul almost without body") or Leonora Harley ("body almost without soul"). These are the poles of attraction, dividing all between, which set up the distorting forces human beings must contend with in Swinburne's milieu.

II

Atalanta in Calydon is constructed upon a narrative which centers on a hunt for a great boar, a prize which Meleager kills and offers to Atalanta in a ritual of courtship—a ritual both bloody and violent.[11] The imagery of the boar-hunt is highly sexual, and the story of the drama makes clear that Meleager's desire for Atalanta is a threat to the sexual tie of Meleager to his mother Althaea, who warns Meleager to abstain from following after "strange loves" (pp. 266–67, 272).[12] The unwillingness of Meleager to subordinate his sexual desire for Atalanta results in his mother's decision to destroy her son. Meleager knows that "there is nothing terribler to men / Than the sweet face of mothers, and the might" (p. 273), but still he is driven by his lust for immediate satisfaction.[13]

Atalanta does not care for the sexual side of life. Rather she is, like Sappho and Lesbia Brandon, not interested in the satisfactions of female sexuality. Althaea knows that her son is doomed to great unhappiness in his pursuit of Atalanta. What Meleager has to learn is what Althaea already knows from experience, that they will be hurt where they are healed (p. 254); Atalanta comes to "heal" the wound caused by the boar, but Atalanta will bring yet more "hurt" to them all. This is a constant cycle of hunting, catching, devouring, resting, and hunting again; it is a cycle of pleasure (somewhat as in Freud's notion of Eros, the life instinct) and pain (as in Freud's notion of the death instinct). In matters of love, the Chorus chants, Aphrodite is "a mother of strife."

The two brothers of Althaea, Plexippus and Toxeus, are indignant and even insulted by the presence of Atalanta on the hunting expedition; they, like Althaea, see her as a sexual contradiction, and if Meleager will pursue her, then he has conspired to turn the sexual relationship upside down. Plexippus and Toxeus share their sister's view of the sexual order as divinely arranged between man the hunter and woman the hunted. They perceive courtship as a conquest of the woman by the man, as a sacrifice of the victim-woman to the aggressor-man. To the view of his uncles, Meleager's pursuit threatens this proper relationship between the sexes, and so they seem to support the position of Althaea, although hers is a more complicated psychological relationship with her son. All would agree, however, with the Chorus when it says that the gods "circled pain about with pleasure, / And girdled pleasure about with pain." This is true on the simple physical level of breaking the hymen of a virgin in the consummation of a marriage: the gods "put moans into the bridal measure / And on the bridal wools a stain" (p. 285). It is also true in an emotional and intellectual sense throughout Swinburne's poetry.

In his later poetic drama, *Erechtheus,* Swinburne continues to set human sexuality in a context of the hunt, where the female is victim and the male is aggressor.[14] However, there is an even greater emphasis upon the mutual entrapment of all in a natural order that requires pain as a part of the definition of all pleasure. The opening of the drama describes how "strange hunters are hard on us, . . . They have staked their nets round the fair young city" (pp. 345–46). The Chorus thus laments the plight of Athens under siege from the sea. Erechtheus has learned from the Pythian Apollo that he must sacrifice his daughter Chthonia in order to hope for the city's rescue. The somber note that runs throughout this drama is the concern that such a price may be too great:

What thanks shall we give that are mixed not and marred with dread
For the price that has ransomed thine own with thine own child's head?
For a taint there cleaves to the people redeemed with blood,
And a plague to the blood-red hand.
The rain shall not cleanse it, the dew nor the sacred flood

. . . .

And a curse [goes up] for a virgin slain.   (p. 408)

This choral song challenges the conventional view that virgins must be sacrificed to the higher order of things, to secure the welfare of the family, of the state, of the gods.[15] The drama makes a tragic point that continuing sacrifice involves an accumulating guilt. Submission to the natural order, as Chthonia's mother Praxithea submits to the pain of her sacrifices, is the only option for a human being trapped by her sexuality: "there is no grief / Great as the joy to be made one in will / With him that is the heart and rule of life" (p. 412).

In the mythic background to this story there is an event which reappears throughout the texture of the poetry. This is the story of Oreithia raped by Boreas, and it is the old woe of Erechtheus's family, because Oreithia too is his daughter by Praxithea. Oreithia was surprised by Boreas, who attacked her as an animal "given over for a spoil unto the strong"; he sprang upon her as a lion might upon a fawn, making her "the spoil of his desire" (pp. 361–62). This child of Erechtheus has been torn from his house by the god of the north wind, and now his city is threatened by the god of the sea. The human community is threatened by all of nature, its own as well as that of its environment. Like another child, Procris, all are "ensnared and ensnaring" (pp. 347–48). The sex between persons is a repetition on the individual, personal level of a relationship which exists on a much larger, cosmic level, for, as Swinburne presents it, the entire universe of human experience can be understood best as a pulsating rhythm of tumescence/detumescence, fecundity/sterility, pleasure/pain, and life/death.

The sacrifice of Chthonia to Apollo-Athena-Poseidon is described as a marriage with death because by this ritual action, mankind hopes to appease nature and at the same time admit the paradoxical truth that life is a marriage with death, with all the mysterious consequences that flow from that essential truth. The killing of the maiden is an orgasm of fulfillment and termination, but it is an embrace of a terrible beauty at the same time. Chthonia is brought as a bride, "a prey for the bridegroom, a flower for the couch of her lord" (p. 372); she is "the new bride" given "to be / A stay to the fetter of the foot of the sea" (pp. 363–64). While the death/marriage of Chtonia is taking place offstage, the Chorus implores Athena to assist their city, and the relationship of the citizens to their city is described as that of children to a mother; furthermore, children are the flowers of the earth, begot by the penetrating sunlight of Apollo upon the quickening soil of the earth. In this Shelleyan, and typical Swinburnean, paean to earth and sun, the creation is a procreation, the primal marriage is a cosmic "wedlock of heaven and of earth," and there is a primal sex act in "the moisture of marriage—the child-bearing dew" that is produced by the union of sun and earth. (pp. 385–88). This song of cosmic marriage and primal sexuality serves to sanctify the ritual sacrifice of Chthonia taking place in the background. There is, then, to continue the metaphor of the drama, a lingering post-coital sadness at the end.

III

Tess Durbeyfield, seen at first in the lovely scene of the May-Day dance, wearing white with a red ribbon in her hair, is a virgin being prepared for sacrifice. Her condescending attitude toward her family notwithstanding, she is very much a Durbeyfield, a woman of the earth, even if there does run in her veins a bit of aristocratic, though fallen, blood. Her blood is passionately red, though her father's discovery has made conscious the bit of blue in her nature as well. When she first meets Alec, he picks ripe strawberries for her and coaxes her to accept one from him. Swinburne himself could not have done a better job of suggesting the luxury of the scene: "she parted her lips and took it in." This is erotic in a very effective way, and it is highly sensual as a scene because Tess is a highly sensual person.[16] She not only parted her lips but she very emphatically "*took it in*" (p. 42; my italics).

The attractiveness of Tess, not only to Alec but to many men—even to Angel Clare—is described this way by a Hardy trying to be scrupulous and at the same time ironic toward his audience: "She had an attribute which amounted to a disadvantage just now; and it was this that caused Alex D'Urberville's eyes to rivet themselves to her. It was a luxuriance of aspect, a fulness of growth, which made her appear more of a woman than she really was. She had inherited the feature from her mother without the quality it denoted" (p. 43). Later, when Joan Durbeyfield is preparing Tess to be as attractive as she can be, she does up Tess's hair, ties it in a pink ribbon, and dresses her in her white frock, imparting "to her developing figure an amplitude which belied her age" (p. 51). Unknowingly, or knowing without understanding, Joan sends Tess as a sacrifice to domestic order, just as Swinburne had Praxithea do with her daughter in *Erechtheus* and Althaea do with her son, though for inverted reasons, in *Atalanta in Calydon*.

When Alec meets Tess on her way back to Trantridge, he immediately begins to assert himself sexually. He attempts "the kiss of mastery," and she resists like "a wild animal." He cracks his whip and races his horse, frightening her into submission. She is entirely unaware of it, but to Alec she is very much a challenge—even perhaps something of a "flirt" (which Angel later, in a pleasing way, accuses her of being to him, p. 206). Alec "rescues" Tess from the fight with drunken field-women on their way home from the dance at Chaseborough, a scene of wildly sexual ambience. The dancers together form "a sort of vegeto-human pollen," and in the haze of "peat and hay," they seem to be "satyrs clasping nymphs—a multiplicity of Pans whirling a multiplicity of Syrinxes; Lotis attempting to elude Priapus, and always failing." [17] This could well be a scene from one of the poems in Swinburne's *Poems and Ballads,* First Series. From Tess's point of view as an outsider, the scene is dangerously attractive and frightening at the same time. Tess attempts to elude Alec, but he succeeds in removing her from the protective constraints of community. He takes her deep into an ancient forest, The Chase, with its druidic oaks and mistletoe, and there he takes her virginity as an ancient priest might have taken away the life of a young girl. [18]

After the rape, Tess has realized something in herself that she cannot accept, cannot repress, and finally cannot deny—her pleasure in her sexuality. [19] She tries to escape her own nature when she leaves Trantridge to return home. At Talbothays Dairy, Tess finds herself in a bower of bliss, a garden of Adonis; she becomes Venus Aphrodite and Eve in one. Her femininity is felt as a liberation but also a prison. She discovers that her three colleagues are in love with Angel, and they share a mutual sense of sexual frustration, even hysteria, for his attention. Hardy thus describes their sleeping-chamber, which

> seems to palpitate with the hopeless passion of the girls. They writhed feverishly under the oppressiveness of an emotion thrust on them by cruel Nature's law—an emotion which they had neither expected nor desired. The incident of the day had fanned the flame that was burning the inside of their hearts out, and the torture was almost more than they could endure. The differences which distinguished them as individuals were abstracted by this passion, and each was but a portion of one organism called sex. (p. 165)

In a very Swinburnean manner, Hardy says that they are being "ecstasiz[ed] . . . to a killing joy." He is serious but he is also ironical, since he can conclude this enraptured scene by observing that while the girls "tossed and turned on their little beds, . . . the cheese-wring dripped monotonously downstairs."

To make sure that Swinburne's view is articulated in his account of love's painful pleasure, Hardy quotes the important line "pleasure girdled about with pain" from *Atalanta in Calydon* when he describes how the four girls looked forward to "four months or so of torturing ecstasy in [Angel's] society" (p. 175). At this same time, Angel declares his love for Tess, and she feels that she has never before "known a time in which the thread of her life was so distinctly twisted of two strands, positive pleasure and positive pain" (p. 199). When Angel "kisse[s] the inside vein of her soft arm," and she feels "her blood driven to her finger-ends, and the cool arms flushed hot" (p. 199). He asks her to marry him, and she wants "to snatch ripe pleasure before the iron teeth of pain could have time to shut upon her," the very fate which Swinburne says is always in store for love and lust (as in "Laus Veneris"). Tess is in "a terror of ecstasy." Her sensuality confesses itself in many ways now during the several occasions when she and Angel are alone: she has "a roguish curl"; he accuses her of being "Miss Flirt"; he uses his whip to pick ripe blackberries for her (thus combining two significant actions of Alec toward Tess earlier), and so she becomes for Angel "a whole sex condensed into one typical form." Hardy says that Tess has been for Angel an "aesthetic, sensuous, pagan pleasure in natural life and lush womanhood."

When Alec reappears, he accuses her of provoking his lust for her and, ironically if not cynically, causing his own spiritual fall from grace—"backsliding." He pursues her, and at one point she strikes him with her gloves, drawing blood in a scene and action that adumbrates the murder scene at the end of the novel.[20] She says to him, when she sees the blood, "Now, punish me! . . . Whip me, crush me; you need not mind those people under the rick! I shall not cry out. Once victim, always victim—that's the law!" (p. 379). Alec is calm throughout. He walks with her, observing "how the little limbs tremble! You are as weak as a bled calf." And then, in the end, they are found living together, after Tess has had to admit to "a consciousness that in a physical sense this man alone was her husband."[21] When Angel sees her again at last, he reflects that Tess "had spiritually ceased to recognize the body before him as hers": it has become merely a corpse, already dead, drifting without connection to mind any longer. What she had denied she has separated in a psychological sense now, so that Tess is already dead long before she is hanged in the last lines of the novel. Before that can happen, however, she is given her honeymoon with Angel Clare after all, but what an ironic honeymoon it is! They get to bed finally, but there is little energy for a bed "along the head of which were carved running figures, apparently Atalanta's race" (p. 446). The symbolic tomb of their earlier wedding night has here reappeared as a bed of sterility, with Tess-Atalanta still in flight from her sexuality, and finally will appear as the altar at Stonehenge, where her sacrifice will be completed.

During their courtship at Talbothays Dairy, in the fecund ambience of that environment, Angel would call Tess by the names of Artemis and Demeter, which she did not like. She insisted he call her simply by her name, Tess (pp. 146–47). And well she should, because as Artemis she would be the virgin huntress who is sister to Apollo and protector of women in childbirth. It was Artemis who sent the boar to ravage Calydon, and it was Artemis who favored Atalanta, a virgin huntress like herself and frigid as well to male sexuality. Hardy knew his Swinburne as well as he knew his classics, although Tess does not know what the allusions mean. She has an instinctive sense of their inappropriateness, or of their ironic appropriateness. She is a huntress now, pursuing Angel Clare, but she is no virgin, which he wants to believe she is; she is no protector of mothers, nor does she know whether she should tell Angel that she has been a mother. And, more deeply ironic, she would shudder at the imaginative incest she might commit as Artemis loving Apollo, since it is as Apollo that she inclines to view Angel (p. 443).

The sexuality of this association becomes clearer, and in a Swinburnean manner, when we consider the significance of the allusion to Demeter. As Demeter to Angel, Tess is the corn-goddess and earth-mother of the ancient pagans, but she is also doomed to wander in search of her daughter Proserpine, who is abducted by Hades into the underworld. More emphatic, if equally ironic, is the fertility implied by the association with the corn-goddess and earth-mother. Several times Hardy identifies Tess with the earth itself, whether in springtime, harvest time, or winter — wandering like Demeter. Once, at her parents' home with the baby, Tess is found working in the fields under "a hazy sunrise in August. . . . The sun, on account of the mist, had a curious sentient, personal look. . . . The luminary was a golden-haired, beaming-faced, mild-eyed, god-like creature, gazing down in the vigor and intentness of youth upon an earth that was brimming with interest for him" (pp. 94–95). Out of the warmth of this scene emerge two significant figures: a mechanical reaper that moves with "a ticking like the love-making of a grasshopper" and the field-women who are "a portion of the field," including the young mother, Tess Durbeyfield. The earth is feminine to the sun's masculinity, and Tess is of the earth. The same relationship abides during the sorrowful winter at Flintcomb-Ash, surrounded by hills like the breasts of Cybele and penetrated by the hard, phallic-shaped flintstones: the "desolate drab" of the fields looked up like a face without features, to confront the "white vacuity" of a sky whose "countenance" had not lineaments: so "these two upper and nether visages confronted each other all day long" in a scene frighteningly empty of human passion. When Tess lies down upon the altar stone at Stonehenge, she is submitting again, almost with full consciousness this time, to the only god who has stayed with her through her trials — the sun, if not Apollo or Angel Clare.

IV

Swinburne's *Poems and Ballads,* First Series,[22] includes many poems obviously sexual in content and often deliberately distasteful to many readers whose sensibilities the poet wished to challenge through mockery, satire, and correction. What Swinburne wished to say, to sing, in such poems as

"Faustine" and "Dolores" is akin to what he had to say in *Atalanta in Caly-don:* that "Aphrodite [is] a mother of strife," and that nature ("the gods") "put moans into the bridal measure," "circled pain about with pleasure."

"Dolores" (p. 154) is a poem of obscene gestures. Mocking prayers to the Holy Mother, Swinburne speaks in adoration of this Lady of Sorrows, whose mother was Libitina and father was Priapus. Because Dolores is also "Tha-lassian" and thus arose "foam-white, from the foam," she has some of the features of Aphrodite herself. She is worshipped as a "rose of the mire," beautiful "joys of the flesh," but "cruel" and capable of making "barren our lives." What she represents for Swinburne's speaker is the possibility for un-restrained pleasure in a life which would otherwise be haunted by guilt and limited by fear of pain. She is the lost possibility for unselfconscious ful-fillment in the flesh—the modern's wistful longing for an imagined pagan, primitive existence. But Swinburne did not believe that the answer to sex-ual frustration and sexual perplexity was easily found by looking to a pagan past for a model of decorum. He knew that whatever could be done to re-lease sex from its bondage to bitterness and sterility, it had to be done with an acknowledgment that Christianity conditioned the circumstances in which all Europeans had to live and solve their problems with sexuality. His speaker in "Dolores" dreams of a time when things were more clearly exposed to the light of understanding, not as now "in a twilight where virtues are vices." He wants her to "redeem us from virtue." Today's lovers are "dried" and "contracted"; they need to be let back into the gardens of Venus, Bacchus, and Priapus, where there is hope for real virtue out of what the smug and fearful call vice.

The knight who speaks the lines of "Laus Veneris" (p. 11) has chosen his life of devotion to sensuality, unlike Faustine who was doomed to hers. For the knight, Venus is his "soul's body," and so in her he finds the iden-tity he has been denied by a Christian culture. He has learned to realize that his hunger for Venus is essential to his identity, exactly as his need for food is necessary for his life. It should be no shame for him to admit that he wants to "eat" her, to "devour" her, to hurt her in loving her just as he is hurt in being loved by her:

> There is a feverish famine in my veins;
> Below her bosom, where a crushed grape stains
> The white and blue, there my lips caught and clove
> An hour since, and what mark of me remains?   (p. 17)

The consummation of his sexuality is like the achievement of any function of his being: it is temporary and will subside to begin all over again, or it will fade away into nonexistence altogether.

The frequency with which Swinburne describes sexual relationships as experiences in eating, devouring, consuming suggests that he may be punning on the importance of Christian sacrament of Holy Eucharist. At the same time, he employs such language because he recognizes the ego-instinct for consuming that expresses itself in sexual relationships. Swinburne did not need modern psychoanalysis to point out connections between the erotic zones of the body. All of his lovers want to eat one another, and to enjoy the experience of giving pain to their beloved, but none perhaps so intensely as Sappho in the powerful poem called "Anactoria."[23] At one point Sappho cries out,

> That I could drink thy veins as wine, and eat
> Thy breast like honey! that from face to feet
> Thy body were abolished and consumed,
> And in my flesh thy very flesh entombed!   (p. 60)

She wants to crush the life out of Anactoria, to delight in her pain, and die with her in an orgiastic mixture of their blood (p. 61).

Lest this seem cruel, Sappho says, she is not as cruel as she would be if she "might be crueller than God," who has ordained through His mysteries "the cruelty of things" (p. 62). For Sappho, there is no more effective a way to express the intensity of her desire than through this language of pain and hunger. Ironically, both she and Swinburne imply that if people love God so intensely as they profess to do, then they must love to be hurt and suffer from His demonstrably sadistic attentions. Therefore, if one is to love perfectly, to love as would God, then one must refine methods of divine cruelty. In the nature of things may be this cruelty, but behind the myth, or the face of the myth, Sappho acknowledges that one's perception of nature is a projection of one's own state of mind. Like Hardy's Tess, Sappho sees reality as a continuous sexual relationship between the human and natural environments.

Swinburne's interest in the lesbian relationship of Sappho and Anactoria is but a variation of his interest in the full range of possibilities in the combinations of human sexuality. The various traps of sex intrigue the poet, a point amply illustrated by the variety of ways he explores sexuality in *Poems and Ballads*, First Series. While the "normal" heterosexual relationship is fraught with difficulties, from nature and from culture, even more difficult are those sexual relationships which are "perverse" when defined against the cultural norm. Perverse sexuality attracts the student of the subject, such as Swinburne is, because it heightens and focuses particular elements of all sexual experience in ways that would not easily be noticed in the socially approved modes. If one extreme of the sexual norm is the male ego striving to dominate and consume the female ego, and at the other extreme the female ego eagerly trying to do the same, then there is a similar set of extremes in the sexual abnormal. In this case, we may gather from Swinburne's poems, there will be the woman-in-the-man, or the man-in-the-woman at one extreme (either variation); and at the other extreme will be the both-at-once, or hermaphrodite in the literal, physical sense. Swinburne's hermaphrodite is both symbol and type. As symbol, this person represents the ambivalence that underlies all things of value in human existence; here abide the contraries always in opposition so long as they endure. As a type, the hermaphrodite *is* the condition of sexuality in every human being, where male and female struggle for domination. The potential for either exists in every person, and culture as much as nature determines which will be realized. The hermaphrodite, then, as a type is also a symbol because the person so endowed is both complete and incomplete at the same time—a symbol of the potential unrealized. Sexuality is identity, finally, for Swinburne in his poetry.

V

In his poem, "The Sleep-Worker" (p. 121), Thomas Hardy impatiently asks "Mother" nature when she will wake up to the perversities of "Life," to the "Strange orchestras of victim-shriek and song, / And curious blends of ache and ecstasy?"[24] Although the complaint, the poem itself, includes a wish for either apocalyptic annihilation of pain and evil or a mild adjustment and healing, Hardy does not shrink from recognizing that the song may be more powerful because it is related to the shriek and that the ecstasy can be known only because of the ache. This awareness is less often expressed so obviously and directly querulous as in "The Sleep-Worker." It is more likely to be expressed as a complication of feeling conditioned by time. That is, Hardy's attitude toward the pleasure and pain of sexuality is shaped by his strong sense of the passage of time. It is rare to find a poem by Hardy that celebrates the present pleasure of joy in sex; it is often that one may find his poetry brooding over present pain from old pleasures or the strange pleasures of remembered pains.[25] Love and lust are intimately akin, and because Hardy does not deny this kinship, his love poetry is the more interesting because he frequently explores the vagaries of lust in it.

In "A Practical Woman" (p. 881), Hardy describes sex without pain or pleasure when he describes the woman who searched for a man who could do her the service of providing her with "a blooming boy"—she found one and "used him till he'd done his job." This sanely utilitarian approach to sex, as a means to a specific end that produces pleasure in consequence, is implied in the humorously ironic dialect poem of "The Ruined Maid" (p. 158), where Melia has prospered because she has been "ruined."[26] This poem not only confesses what many of Hardy's contemporaries knew but would not admit; it also hints that the emotional illness of much "home-life" could be cured if wives were more often "ruined" like Melia—at least that they be sexually satisfied and not suffer from many "megrims or melancho-ly." There is present pleasure in Melia's profit from sex, even though the poem only hints that there is pleasure in the act itself.

Nearly always in Hardy's poems a price of some kind of pain must be paid for whatever profit of pleasure there is in one's sexuality. "The Dark-Eyed Gentleman" (p. 243) is a statement also by a "practical" woman, although it has taken her some years of pain since her sexual pleasure to recognize how practical her sexuality has been for her. She recalls how she paused from her work to tie up her garter when along came a "dark-eyed gentleman" to see her so embarrassed; she, in her modesty, turned "rose-red," but she let him tie up her garter for her. Tying up her garter was, of course, an act of seduction in the ritual of her mating with the man, but as far as Hardy's readers are concerned, tying up the garter is practically a figure of speech for the most intimate form the sexual relationship can take. It led, first, to her pleasure, then pain of separation from the man, but finally to the joy of her pleasure in the son it produced. The man's name she never knew—it was "his nature" that she valued, "and all that it brought."

The bitterness of her loss when she separated from her lover was, in retrospect, a small price for the woman to pay in "The Dark-Eyed Gentleman." She does not dwell on the pain as do so many of Hardy's people in his poems. One of these, "On the Doorstep" (p. 944), describes a melodramatic scene of a wife who has been cast out by her husband, apparently beaten by him as well, when her father arrives to ask, "He at it again?" When her husband appears, the father strikes him and the woman cries out that she hates her father for interfering; she exclaims to her husband, who may be dead, that he can "do as you will" to her. This poem, otherwise not very accomplished, peeks at what seems to have been an all too common sight in Victorian England—the woman's fierce loyalty to the husband, or lover, who beats her. That there might be some pleasure in her pain is possible, even in this poem, but it is more clearly so in the otherwise curious "Circus-Rider to Ringmaster" (p. 708). This poem is spoken by a woman to her lover; their relationship has been, literally, that of a rider to ringmaster, but it is also a relationship of dark sensuality. She tells her lover that if he should one day be tempted to forget her, he should "trace the tan-laid track you'd whip me round in / On the cantering roan." The presence of the whip, as in *Tess of the d'Urbervilles*, discreetly describes Hardy's mild fascination with what wildly excited Swinburne—the pleasures of flagellation. Of course, here the object of the whipping is the horse and not the rider, but it would be simply obtuse of a reader not to recognize the importance of the whip to the mastery of the woman.

Sometimes Hardy's characters will express a present pleasure in the joy of sex, but reveal, or have revealed, an internal center of perversity. This might be in such a form that it would strike a twentieth-century reader as nothing but healthy, as "In the Nuptial Chamber," where the bride springs up in the bed, hearing the sounds of music—"that mastering tune!" (p. 420). Music and dancing are for Hardy virtually synonyms for sexual behavior, and in a poem like this one, they are explicitly identified. The bride, however, reveals to her new husband that the music she hears is a reminder of her "old Love" who waltzed with her in an earlier time. This memory and her confession of it lead, in the end, to a more startling admission, that when she is embracing her husband she does thrill from the act, but it is "really" her old Love she is embracing in her fantasy.

Not all of Hardy's brides are able or willing to make use of such a fantasy to control their wills into wifely submission. "A Conversation at Dawn" (p. 366) occurs between a bride and groom during their honeymoon, and in this conversation the woman learns to "yield in silence" to her husband's mastery. He uses the occasion to teach her that he is "a practical man" who will not hesitate to use brute force in asserting his authority with her. The wife uncovers secret within secret to her new husband; they are, from the conventional point of view, sexual horrors, because, she finally confesses, she carries a child by a former lover. Her husband, in bitter irony, observes that she "raise[s] the veil by degrees," but he surprises her by saying that he will "father the child." In truth, he seems to enjoy what she meant as pain because he finds that he may use his knowledge of her as a means of his power and mastery over her. The story is a variation of the relationship between Phillotson and Sue Bridehead in *Jude the Obscure*.

Even when marriage seems to bring happiness and beautiful children out of sexual satisfaction, it can be agonizingly painful *because* it is so successful. This mysterious mix of life's passions is formulated in the story of "San Sebastian" (p. 21) where the veteran of that battle explains why he is so unhappy when he watches his beautiful seventeen-year-old daughter dance "round a Hintock maypole." She is a forceful reminder of his rape of a girl about her age during the battle of San Sebastian. Out of that violence and sexual passion has come this "punishment" in his dear daughter, the child of his flesh and conscience. His love for her, as for her mother, is a pleasure so mixed with pain that he cannot bear to witness their cheerful happiness— he must take long walks away from his home to escape them. When Jenny's conscience is aroused in "The Dance at the Phoenix" (p. 43), she also realizes it is a punishment for sexual pleasure, although it is a pleasure of the head more than of the loins. She leaves her husband's bed to join in the revelry of the cavalry, where her dancing is a reliving of her youthful pleasures (when her "life had hardly been / A life of modesty"); after she returns from the dance, Jenny experiences both physical and moral pain—"shoots of agony" and "inner mischief." She dies of guilt and cardiac arrest.

The parson in "The Collector Cleans His Picture" (p. 617) discovers that the "strange picture" he cleans is a picture of himself—a picture of his sexual lusts, hidden and repressed until they express themselves through his uncontrollable hunger for the woman in the painting. She seems to emerge from the canvas in "the guise of the ranker Venus, / Named of some Astarte, of some Cotytto." He grows ecstatic in his response to this discovery, behaving like some character out of Swinburne's *Poems and Ballads*. He notices the curving outline of her body, its "fair flesh," and he kneels before it to kiss the picture, "drunk with the lure of love's inhibited dreamings." But like so many other of Hardy's characters, he is punished for his pleasure, however perverse, with a pain equally perverse—the picture of Venus turns into a picture of "a hag." This happens at that critical time for sex in Hardy's world, the dawn, when she points her finger at the parson in a "lashing lesson" of condemnation for "the lusts of a lifetime!"

"The Chapel-Organist" (p. 633) is another story of perversion and sexual power that gets its socially approved expression through art. The organist says that she craves "minstrelsy more than lovers," but both will prove her undoing because she must play the organ and she must have lovers. In the world of Victoria, as Hardy represents it here, both desires cannot be satisfied at once. She is so attractive and so sensual in appearance that the church members are embarrassed: "'A handsome girl,' . . . / But—too much sex in her build." What is noticed is the heaviness of her eyelids (a sure sign of sensuality for Swinburne's characters too), and the amplitude of her bosom (the same sign that undoes Tess Durbeyfield). The organist hints that she must sell herself to earn the money to pay her way back and forth to play the organ, an ironic turn of events since she has been forced to this by the congregation's unwillingness to continue her stipend. The poem is not only a satirical picture of Victorian prurience and prudishness; it is also an exploration of the relationship of art and sexuality, of their mutual possessiveness in the artist, and of the sterility or death or both that come in the end. This is a view that Swinburne would have found quite compatible with his own.

VI

Jude Fawley, like Tess, early discovers that he is a sexual being. He is exhilarated, though puzzled, by this "strongest passion known to humanity" (p. iv).[27] Hardy compares the strength of this passion to the violence of a schoolmaster who seizes a boy by the collar, compelling him to move with little regard for "reason or will." The key word here is in the *violence* as much as in the *compulsion* (p. 45). The analogy repeats the essential meaning of an early experience in Jude's life, when he was punished for allowing rooks to eat in the field he was supposed to be protecting. The farmer seized the boy, swung him like "a hooked fish swinging to land," and beat Jude rhythmically as he remonstrated with him for his delinquency (p. 11). This experience of punishment for his sympathy with the hungry animals is one of the complicating elements in Jude's life of discovering that pain is the price he must pay for his love and sympathy with life. He seeks to relieve suffering, to give himself to others, but he seems only to bring on more pain for himself and increase that of others as well.

After the farmer let him go, Jude ran home across a pasture where "he beheld scores of coupled earthworms lying half their length on the surface of the damp ground" (p. 12). Jude recognizes that it would be impossible to move through them "in regular steps without crushing some of them at each tread," and so he "picked his way on tiptoe among the earthworms, without killing a single one." If he were god or society or nature, he would leave animals free to couple like these earthworms without fear of being crushed. After much frustrating experience to couple himself, Jude asks later if it is possible to do as an adult what he did here as a child: to follow inclinations "which do me and nobody else any harm, and actually give pleasure to those I love best" (p. 388).

Somebody or something, both within individuals and outside them, cannot pick a way through human coupling without crushing people. Indeed, at one point Jude wonders if the crushing might not even be a part of some efficient plan: frustrated in all his ambitions, for education and for sexual happiness, Jude asks "Is it that the women are to blame; or is it the artificial system of things, under which the normal sex-impulses are turned into devilish domestic gins and springes to noose and hold back those who want to progress?" (p. 257). By the end of the novel, just before all of his ambition has been defeated and his spirit nearly destroyed, Jude exclaims at Sue Bridehead that she is on the verge of self-hallucination when she says that "it is no use fighting against God!" Jude reminds her of what she has always understood and what he is only beginning to understand: "It is only against man and senseless circumstance," not God, that they fight and must continue to fight. While his own education in sexuality has been responsible for some of his difficulties in learning to deal with it, Jude gradually overcomes the temptation, into which Sue falls at the end, to submit to the pains of love as proper punishment for yielding to the claims of the flesh.

That human sexuality is beastly is a view that Jude has to accommodate when he is struck by the pig's pizzle and awakened rudely from his daydreams of Christminster (pp. 38–43). Arabella is a pig-woman in more than one sense, but she is a forceful woman, however narrow her veins of life might be. It is no surprise to learn that D.H. Lawrence felt in her character some of the healthy life-force that he vainly looked for in modern sex experience. Arabella is vigorous, but she is coarse, as all her behavior reveals again and again: her frankly sensual and obscene way of calling Jude's attention to her, her employment of the "trap" to get him as her husband, her role in the pig-killing, her getting him drunk so that he will marry her again, and in the end her cruel treatment during and after his death.[28] She is the very Aphrodite that Swinburne calls mother of strife and mother of death. While she has no illusions about the central importance of sex in human life, neither does Arabella have any ideals of redeeming value. She is the dark unconscious and selfish ego-instinct that rages through all animal sexuality. Her one deference to social order, and it is a deference of little fundamental importance to Arabella, is her recognition that marriage is important. She does not hesitate to use marriage as a weapon of her instinct, as she admits to Sue: "Life with a man is more business-like after [marriage], and money matters work better. . . . you can get the law to protect you" (p. 318). While Sue's own view of sex is much different and more complicated, Sue nevertheless recognizes this same importance in marriage to many women. She tells Jude that "fewer women like marriage than you suppose, only they enter into it for the dignity it is assumed to confer, and the social advantages it gains them sometimes" (p. 307). Jude wants marriage with Sue to establish his social claim on her affections; she resists because she does not want any of the values from it that Arabella recognizes, and she wants her freedom to deny herself to Jude.

Arabella is Venus to Jude's Tannhäuser. He is absorbed in her power, is disenchanted and separated from it, liberated from it for a while, but in the end is lured back, into it as his last significant act in life. The conclusion is not a revelry, nor even a conscious choice to accept damnation in return for sexual ecstasy, as it was for Swinburne's knight in "Laus Veneris." But back to her he goes, and under her villainous influence he dies. The novel cannot quite convict Arabella, however, for this miserable end to the life of Jude Fawley. Arabella is almost without personal guilt in anything she does; she is little more than a temporary manifestation of eros. She is in a frightening way exactly the right person for Jude, just as Alec D'Urberville is the right person for Tess: both Arabella and Alec satisfy a part of the natures of their lovers, a part which their lovers do not understand, misinterpret, and to some extent attempt to deny in themselves. This last is not so true of Jude as of Tess, but certainly Jude quite as much as Tess does not know how to deal with his sexual urges. His ignorance is a reason for his fatality. Jude goes beyond Tess in perverting his identity by his dream of intellectual distinction. He has had his head turned by Phillotson, by his lonely and undisciplined reveries, and by his unguided (if not misguided) ambitions; he lets the dream precede the experience and that seems to ensure a certain degree of misapprehension and misunderstanding of the meanings of his experience.

Arabella would, and does, think Jude is "a tender fool" because he does not understand how to deal with the world as a place of pain as well as pleasure. He is attracted to Sue Bridehead for precisely this reason of tenderness in his sensibility. He sees her first in a photograph in which she seems to be surrounded by "the rays of a halo." When he meets her, he discovers that she has a mind and that she uses it in vigorous and independent ways that excite his intellectual curiosity; she also has a beautiful and appealing body. Thus Sue Bridehead seems to be all that Arabella was—and more. But, as Sue will later and in misery tell Mrs. Edlin, "this pretty body of mine has been the ruin of me" (p. 470). Because Sue has the physical attractiveness of Arabella (and perhaps more so), she would seem to be a much more compatible sex partner for Jude than Arabella, who has absolutely no sympathy for his intellectual interests. But the appearance is deceiving, because Sue Bridehead is frigid, and that is something that Jude simply cannot grasp. It drives him to distraction and finally to death.

Sue Bridehead is certainly an interesting literary character, and her special, even perverse, sexual nature marks an advance in literary analysis of human sexuality.[29] She is an even more advanced "modern" woman than Tess was supposed to be.[30] In fact, Tess seems quite old fashioned in many ways when compared with Sue Bridehead, who had the opportunities for reading and thinking that Tess never knew. More interesting in Sue is the nature of her sexuality as a form of the perversities that both Hardy and Swinburne found so fascinating. Hardy speculates that Sue's sexual frigidity might be, as Lesbia Brandon's and Atalanta's are, the result of a lesbian propensity. Sue tells Jude enough about herself before they become lovers that Jude should have been well warned. She says that she has "no fear of men, as such, nor of their books. I have mixed with them—one or two of them particularly—almost as one of their own sex" (p. 173). She has lived for fifteen months in London with a young undergraduate who killed himself out of sexual frustration. Jude can only admire her for her protection of her virginity, but Sue goes on to say that she has been described as "cold-natured,—sexless," and that should have settled the issue for both Sue and Jude.

When Arabella comes back into Jude's life, Sue finally gives her body to him. After recognizing the sexual threat of Arabella, Sue is "in painful tension," and then she pleads with Jude, flinging her arms around his neck, saying "I am not a cold-natured, sexless creature, am I, for keeping you at such a distance? . . . I do belong to you, don't I? I give in!" (p. 315). After this, Jude and Sue have two children and she is carrying another during the last section of the book; they have as well in their care the child of Jude and Arabella, the strange creature "Father Time," as they call him. And it is Sue's inability to deal with Father Time's queries about her forthcoming child (he has a Malthusian cast that echoes Tess's about her mother's over-production), that leads to the great catastrophe of the novel—the deaths of the children. Sue cannot explain the "facts of life" to the little boy, and so she feels responsible for the deaths. It is of course ironic that she should be the one to try to explain birth and the sexual process, but it is quite appropriate that her failures should be the cause for so much death and suffering, since her sterile conception of sex, emotionally and intellectually at least, must conclude in death. Sue cannot bear the final strain of her nature and her responsibility. She becomes a religious neurotic, searching for the punishment to her body that Tess had felt when she sacrificed it to Alec at the end of her novel.

Sue goes back to Phillotson and sacrifices her body to the most hideous pain she can appreciate, to the sexual privilege her husband may rightfully claim under all social conventions of marriage—the very privilege she would never allow to Jude. When she returns to Phillotson, just before their remarriage, Sue feels "her flesh quivering under the touch of his lips" (p. 433). Then, after their remarriage, she continues to withhold her body from Phillotson as long as she can until, after a meeting with Jude, she goes to her husband and makes the ultimate sacrifice, clinching her teeth to keep from screaming (p. 474). Mrs. Edlin has watched Sue going to her husband's bedroom, and she observes that "weddings be funerals 'a b'lieve nowadays." What Phillotson's attitude toward his now penitent wife will be is a matter that Hardy suggests with some trepidation. Gillingham, a friend of Phillotson, fears that Phillotson will be "more orthodoxly cruel to her than he had erstwhile been informally and perversely kind" (pp. 436–37). As Sue prepares to go into her husband's bedroom, Mrs. Edlin recalls a strange tale of a time "when the saints were upon the earth [and] devils used to take husbands' forms o'nights, and get poor women into all sorts of trouble" (pp. 470–71). The door closes with the sound of doom as Sue is carried to her husband's bed, a place of pain and terror for this "sexless" creature. And it is not much better for Jude, thrown back into the devouring arms of Arabella. Sexuality may not be fate, perhaps, in the world of Hardy's novels, but it is certainly a force that drives with the insistence of fate.

VII

In 1905—the same year that Swinburne quoted the Scottish paper to Hardy, that "Swinburne planteth, Hardy watereth, and Satan giveth the increase"—Havelock Ellis published another installment in the major work of his career, *Studies in the Psychology of Sex*, completed in 1910. Ellis could have had every right to think he was the very "Satan" who "giveth the increase" after Swinburne planted and Hardy watered. In the foreword to his reissue of the *Studies* in 1936, Ellis narrates the difficult and harrowing time he had before his work could be brought before the public without legal interference, for in 1898 when Ellis had first sought publication, George Bedborough was prosecuted for selling the work on the charge that he had sold "a wicked, bawdy, and scandalous and obscene book" (p. xvii). Havelock Ellis was one of Thomas Hardy's earliest and most vigorous admirers; he published a long essay on "Thomas Hardy's Novels" in the *Westminster Review* in 1883 and he later came to the defense of *Jude the Obscure* during the height of the critical outcry against that novel. Ellis praised Hardy for recognizing that "love is the chief business of life" and for devoting "himself so frankly to the rendering of its devious ways."[31]

Ellis gives a long section of his second volume to a discussion of "Love and Pain," in which he attempts to come to terms with "one of the great mysteries of love" (p. 66). Like Swinburne, Ellis concludes from his observations that "the masochistic tendency may be said to be fairly common," and he believes that the "normal and typical woman" delights "in suffering pain" (pp. 103, 112). Hardy could concur, and in concurring did employ what Ellis calls "the love-bite" to suggest "that perverse impulse which has been commonly called sadism" (p. 104). The motif of lips, kissing, and blood in Hardy's works, especially in *Tess of the D'Urbervilles,* and throughout Swinburne's early poetry, could have been cited as additional evidence of his point if Ellis had needed it for his argument. But he did not need additional evidence – he has amassed, in characteristic manner, an overwhelming body of textual authority for his thesis.

He does the same for that favorite Swinburnean subject, flagellation. Ellis insists that "it is perfectly easy and natural for an interest in the subject to arise in an innocent and even normal child, and thus to furnish a germ round which, temporarily at all events, sexual ideas may crystallize" (p. 129). He goes on to maintain that "whatever the precise origin of sexual flagellation in Europe, there can be no doubt that it soon became extremely common, and so it remains at the present day" and "that sexual flagellation is the most frequent of all sexual perversions in England" (pp. 130–31).[32] Ellis's own attempts to explain how pain can be a "tonic" to human sexuality are largely puzzled analogies between human and animal courtship rituals calling for male dominance of female victims, and he does not do much to illuminate the dark mystery of the subject.[33] But even though his answers are not sophisticated, his courage in proposing the questions is, like Swinburne's and Hardy's, admirable, sometimes enlightening, and always interesting as a voice from that troubled era.[34] He sounds at times like Swinburne himself, as when he says, "In algolagnia, as in music, it is not cruelty that is sought; it is the joy of being plunged among the waves of that great primitive ocean of emotions which underlies the variegated world of our everyday lives, and pain . . . is merely the channel by which that ocean is reached" (pp. 184–85).

Notes

1. Thomas Hardy, *Tess of the D'Urbervilles: A Pure Woman Faithfully Presented* (New York: Harper, 1919). Page numbers in parentheses are references to this text.

2. Robert Buchanan's unsigned review of *Poems and Ballads,* in *Athenaeum,* 4 Aug. 1866; rpt. in *Swinburne: The Critical Heritage,* ed. Clyde K. Hyder (New York: Barnes & Noble, 1970), pp. 30 34. This quotation is from p. 32.

3. Mrs. Oliphant, "The Anti-Marriage League," *Blackwood's Magazine,* 49 (Jan. 1896), 135–49; rpt. in *Thomas Hardy: The Critical Heritage,* ed. R.G. Cox (London: Routledge & Kegan Paul, 1970), pp. 256 62.

4. Florence Emily Hardy, *The Life of Thomas Hardy* (New York: St. Martin's Press, 1962), p. 325.

5. "Mr. Hardy's Lyrical Poems," *Edinburgh Review,* 207 (April 1918), 272; rpt. in *Thomas Hardy: The Critical Heritage,* pp. 444–63. This quotation in from p. 445.

6. "Study of Thomas Hardy," in *Phoenix: The Posthumous Papers of D.H. Lawrence,* ed. Edward D. McDonald (New York: Viking Press, 1936); see especially pp. 478–79. The title of Murfin's book indicates the main interest of his study, *Swinburne, Hardy, and Lawrence and the Burdens of Belief* (Chicago: Univ. of Chicago Press, 1978).

7. Havelock Ellis, *Studies in the Psychology of Sex,* I (New York: Random House, 1942); from the "Foreword," p. xxiii, and *Part Two,* "Love and Pain," p. 66.

8. *The Swinburne Letters,* ed. Cecil Y. Lang (New Haven: Yale Univ. Press). Vol. 1: 1854–1869; Vol. 2: 1869–1875 (1959); Vol. 3: 1875–1877; Vol. 4: 1877–1882 (1960); Vol. 5: 1883–1890; Vol. 6: 1890–1909 (1962). Volume numbers and page numbers are cited in parentheses in the text.

9. See the essay by Julian Baird, "Swinburne, Sade, and Blake: The Pleasure-Pain Paradox," *Victorian Poetry,* 9 (Spring-Summer 1971), 49–75.

10. *The Novels of A.C. Swinburne: Love's Cross-Currents* and *Lesbia Brandon,* introd. by Edmund Wilson (New York: Farrar, Straus and Cudahy, 1962). Page numbers in parentheses are references to this text.

11. *The Poems of Algernon Charles Swinburne,* IV (London: Chatto and Windus, 1911). Page numbers for passages from *Atalanta in Calydon* are references to this text.

12. See Richard Matthews' essay, "Heart's Love and Heart's Division: The Quest for Unity in *Atalanta in Calydon,*" *Victorian Poetry,* 9 (Spring–Summer 1971), 35–48.

13. See John O. Jordan's essay, "The Sweet Face of Mothers: Psychological Patterns in *Atalanta in Calydon,*" Victorian Poetry, 11 (Summer 1973), 101–14.

14. *The Poems of Algernon Charles Swinburne,* IV (London: Chatto and Windus, 1911). Page numbers for *Erechtheus* are references to this text.

15. Eric Trudgill has an interesting discussion of this subject in his *Madonnas and Magdalens: The Origins and Development of Victorian Sexual Attitudes* (London: Heinemann, 1976), pp. 56–64, "The Necessary Ordeal."

16. Irving Howe's analysis follows this approach in his *Thomas Hardy* (1967). Portions reprinted in the Norton Critical Edition of *Tess of the D'Urbervilles,* ed. Scott Elledge, 2nd ed. (New York: Norton, 1978), 439–55; see especially p. 445.

17. This passage has been omitted from the Harper & Brothers text of 1919. It may be found in the Norton Critical Edition, p. 53.

18. For an emphasis on this point, see Geoffrey Thurley, *The Psychology of Hardy's Novels: The Nervous and the Statuesque* (St. Lucia, Queensland: Univ. of Queensland Press, 1975), p. 164.

19. Thurley says that "it is in her 'sensuality' that we shall find the meaning of Tess," p. 152.

20. Tony Tanner discusses the point at length in his essay, "Colour and Movement in *Tess of the D'Urbervilles,*" *Critical Quarterly,* 10 (Autumn 1968), rpt. in *Hardy: The Tragic Novels,* ed. R.P. Draper (London: Macmillan, 1975), pp. 182–208.

21. Omitted from the Harper & Brothers text of 1919; see the Norton Critical Edition, p. 297. As Perry Meisel points out, "Tess's return to Alec is in accord with the finally amoral 'naturalistic premise' of the book, as symbolized by the earth." See *Thomas Hardy: The Return of the Repressed, A Study of the Major Fiction* (New Haven: Yale Univ. Press, 1972), p. 134.

22. *The Poems of Algernon Charles Swinburne,* I (London: Chatto and Windus, 1911). Page numbers for passages from *Poems and Ballads, First Series* are references to this text.

23. See the essay by David A. Cook, "The Content and Meaning of Swinburne's 'Anactoria,'" *Victorian Poetry,* 9 (Spring–Summer 1971), 77–93.

24. *The Complete Poems of Thomas Hardy,* ed. James Gibson (New York: Macmillan, 1976). Page numbers in parentheses are references to this text.

25. James Richardson has a clever analysis of this feature in *Thomas Hardy: The Poetry of Necessity* (Chicago: Univ. of Chicago Press, 1971).

26. Trugdill narrates the "fortunes of the Magdalen" in his book. G.B. Shaw makes the subject into the drama of *Mrs. Warren's Profession.*

27. Thomas Hardy, *Jude the Obscure* (New York: Harper, 1923). Page numbers in parentheses are references to this text.

28. Thurley makes a telling analysis of "the harridan side of animal sexuality" in the character of Arabella, pp. 188–89.

29. Thurley goes so far as to say that some of the scenes describing Sue's sexual complications are "revolutionary in literature," p. 196.

30. Irving Howe argues that *Jude* is above all things a modern novel because it is "a vision of modern deracination," and Sue Bridehead's deracination is one of the most modern forms it describes: "she is promethean in mind but masochist in character"; *Thomas Hardy* (1967). Portions reprinted in the Norton Critical Edition of *Jude the Obscure,* ed. Norman Page (New York: Norton, 1973), pp. 395–406; see especially p. 403.

31. "Thomas Hardy's Novels," *Westminster Review,* 119 (NS 63) (April 1883), 334–64. Rpt. in *Thomas Hardy: The Critical Heritage,* ed. R.G. Cox (London: Routledge & Kegan Paul, 1970), pp. 103–32. The quotation is from p. 125.

32. Ronald Pearsall narrates other accounts to document this observation. *Public*

Purity, Private Shame: Victorian Sexual Hypocrisy Exposed (London: Weidenfeld and Nicolson, 1976); see especially pp. 169–81.

33. As Phyllis Grosskurth puts it, Ellis's study is "a thoroughly Victorian treatment of female sexuality." *Havelock Ellis: A Biography* (New York: Knopf, 1980), p. 219.

34. Fraser Harrison reviews the work of Ellis as "an Unprejudiced Statement of the Precise Facts," *The Dark Angel*, pp. 98–106. Also, see Grosskurth, pp. 220–25.

Susan Beegel

Bathsheba's Lovers:
Male Sexuality in
Far from the Madding Crowd

In 1875 an anonymous author for *The Saturday Review* faced the problem of briefly summarizing for his readers the plot of *Far from the Madding Crowd*. He described the story as follows: "'Bathsheba and her Lovers' the novel might have been called (except that its own title is very much better), and the story consists in contrasting the three lovers in their respective attitudes towards the heroine."[1] Such reduction of a complex novel's plot is possible precisely because that plot is so obviously archetypal. How many of our myths and fairy tales are stories of an unusual, beautiful woman courted by three men? And how many of our culture's greatest literary masterpieces (*The Merchant of Venice* and *Portrait of a Lady* immediately come to mind) revolve around this always interesting romantic situation?

The critical problem of describing the novel's ending is far more complex. When, at the conclusion of *Far from the Madding Crowd*, Bathsheba weds Gabriel Oak, can we safely say that hero and heroine live happily ever after? Or do we regretfully admit that Bathsheba, despoiled by experience, makes a pragmatic, perhaps economic marriage; that she and Oak will live an undisturbed but uninteresting existence ever after? In other words, is this marriage the triumphant conclusion to a book that advocates a new, even Lawrentian, kind of love[2]—one based on equality of the sexes and destined to survive the exigencies of the modern world? Or is *Far from the Madding Crowd* about the inferiority of passionate sexuality to utilitarian reason, making Bathsheba's marriage a kind of "settling for less" and a fitting conclusion to a tragedy of reduced expectations?

Critical tradition almost unanimously supports a tragic reading of the novel. Henry James was disappointed by Bathsheba's union with Gabriel, who was, in James's opinion, "much too good for her."[3] J. Hillis Miller writes that the "happy" ending of *Far from the Madding Crowd* is in reality only "the lovers' acceptance of the gap between them. . . . Bathsheba Everdene and Gabriel Oak have outlived the time when they might have sought the bliss of full union with another person."[4] Perry Meisel feels that Bathsheba "remains morally infected, even with the apparent reestablishment of peace and order by marriage at the end of the novel," and that the marriage resists "the deepest impulses" of this early work.[5] Indeed, those critics who concede that *Far from the Madding Crowd* has a true "happy" ending take pains to point out that same ending's departure from the sexual pessimism expressed in the body of the novel and from the tragic endings of Hardy's mature work. Normally the anomalous ending of *Far from the Madding Crowd* is ascribed to Hardy's own marriage, approaching as he hastily concluded the novel and prompting an uncharacteristic optimism.[6]

Of course critical controversy about the novel's ending is controversy about the nature of the novel itself. In the final paragraph of chapter 56, "After All," the narrator himself tells us what he thinks of Gabriel and Bathsheba's impending marriage:

> He accompanied her up the hill, explaining to her the details of his forthcoming tenure of the other farm. They spoke very little of their mutual feelings; pretty phrases and warm expressions being probably unnecessary between such tried friends. Theirs was that substantial affection which arises (if any arises at all) when the two who are thrown together begin first by knowing the rougher sides of each other's character, and not the best till further on, the romance growing up in the interstices of a mass of hard prosaic reality. This good-fellowship—*camaraderie*—usually occurring through similarity of pursuits, is unfortunately seldom superadded to love between the sexes, because men and women associate, not in their labours, but in their pleasures merely. Where, however, happy circumstance permits its development, the compounded feeling proves itself to be the only love which is strong as death—that love which many waters cannot quench, nor the floods drown, beside which the passion usually called by the name is evanescent as steam.[7]

Many things about this passage have a disappointing ring for the person of Romantic sensibility. The impassioned speeches of *Wuthering Heights*, say, are missing here: the newly betrothed lovers discuss farming. We find a "mass of hard prosaic reality" at the very center of the passage; romance only grows up in its "interstices," like some sort of lichen growing in the crevices of a rock—not a very lovely or luxuriant plant, but, if you will excuse the pun, a hardy one. The narrator defines "good fellowship" and "*camaraderie*" as the qualities which give this rock-lichen love its strength, qualities perhaps less interesting than the passion Hardy says this love is stronger than.

Nor is the passage without Hardy's characteristic sexual pessimism. Pretty speeches are only "*probably* unnecessary" between lovers who are "tried friends." Gabriel and Bathsheba's "*camaraderie*" is "*seldom* superadded to love between the sexes," a "substantial affection" which, although it has arisen between them, usually does not arise at all. Yet it must be noted that the sexual pessimism of *Far from the Madding Crowd* is only pessimism. Hardy laments the rarity of the marriage he describes, but he has not yet embraced the nihilism that would deny its possibility.

I want to propose an alternative to the critical tradition which reads *Far from the Madding Crowd* as a tragedy of reduced expectations. Our readings of Hardy's later works have distorted our appreciation of *Far from the Madding Crowd's* text. It is time to stop reading the novel as a failed tragedy, as a tragic novel botched by a "happy" ending like that imposed on *The Return of the Native* by publishers. Instead, we should sharpen our reading of the mature tragedy, the fulfillment of Hardy's early pessimism, by appreciating *Far from the Madding Crowd's* early, though fragile, optimism. It is the novelist's fullest treatment of a rare, ideal love, written when Hardy, on the brink of his first marriage, still believed in both the existence of such love and the possibility of fulfilling it. Such a reading only strengthens the poignancy of the later novels. True cynicism proceeds from disillusionment, and we cannot fully appreciate the tragedy of doubt or disbelief without embracing the faith (or at least the faint hope) which preceded them.

In the passage quoted above, Hardy tells us that Gabriel and Bathsheba's love is not only stronger than passion, but stronger than death. This triumph over death is the stuff of comedy, not tragedy, and a comic reading of the novel depends on the truth of the narrator's claim. It is a substantial claim, and deserves careful consideration. Towards that end, we must return to the story an early critic called "Bathsheba and her Lovers," and give the three suitors and "their respective attitudes towards the heroine" the thorough comparison the novel's archetypal plot demands.

Bathsheba's most passionate lovers, Boldwood and Troy, are the purveyors of death in this novel. The intensity of Boldwood's jealousy more than once leaves Bathsheba frightened for her own life. Small wonder she is not interested in reading *Othello* when Liddy suggests it. The marriage Boldwood offers her is one of entombment, of suffocation. In fact, Boldwood proposes to Bathsheba by promising her that she will never have to step outdoors again. Bathsheba accepts his last proposal because she is hounded, because she feels guilty, and because her marriage to Troy has caused her to lose faith in the possibility of love. Such a marriage would be a living death for Bathsheba, and a true tragedy of reduced expectations.

It is after Bathsheba's acceptance that the incipient deadliness of Boldwood's passion bursts forth. He murders Troy and must be prevented from shooting himself. In Boldwood's case, passion and morbidity are clearly aligned. His idealized love for Bathsheba is a love which insists on exclusive possession of its object. He wants to lock her away from the rest of the world to be placed on a pedestal, ornamented, and worshipped. This is not love at all, but an insane amalgam of homicidal and suicidal impulses. Moreover, it is a reactionary passion. He is an old and old-fashioned landowner who seeks to turn a modern businesswoman back into a household goddess. There is a kind of bewildered, pathetic regresssiveness about Boldwood, a desire to stop the earth from turning and the clocks from ticking. Boldwood is a character who cannot adapt to change and who is finally broken by it. His chief desire is to bring himself and his love into a deathlike condition of stasis.

Sergeant Troy's brand of death-dealing passion is superficially different from Boldwood's reactionary, frigid idolatry. Troy is hotly sexual, but his lust, like Boldwood's idealizing passion, is an agent of death. His affair with Fanny Robin leaves a dead mother and a stillborn child; his marriage to Bathsheba results in his own death. If Hardy uses Boldwood to expose the essential morbidity of the Victorian male's sentimental woman-worship, he uses Troy to expose the equivalent morbidity of that other-annihilating, self-consuming love exalted by Emily Brontë in her treatment of Cathy and Heathcliff. But Troy is no Heathcliff, although equally destructive. Troy lacks the dimension of a Byronic hero. While a rebel against conventional morality, Troy lacks Heathcliff's Romantic capacity for deep feeling and abiding love. Troy is a false front of words and red uniform, a cardboard cutout of a Byronic hero and therefore a criticism of the Romantic affinity for outlaw heroes and demon lovers.

Troy nevertheless possesses all the sexual magnetism of a Heathcliff. Bathsheba is hooked, both literally and figuratively, from the moment her skirt catches on the sergeant's spurs. She is trapped and, significantly enough, cannot escape without either tearing her skirt off or waiting until he pleases to release her. It is Bathsheba who initiates the novel's most explicit sexual encounter by begging Troy to perform the sword-exercise for her — not with a walking-stick, mind you, but with a real sword. The appointment is made in whispers, with many blushing protests, and Bathsheba arrives panting and trembling at the site of the rendez-vous, the hollow amid the ferns. Keeping in mind those useful concepts of phallic symbol and feminine space,[8] let us have a close look at the sword-play in the fernpit.

Troy exhibits the different sorts of cuts, and Bathsheba is much impressed. "How murderous and bloodthirsty!" she exclaims. The foreplay over with, Troy then proposes a more exciting game.

> "They are rather deathy. Now I'll be more interesting, and let you see some loose play—giving all the cuts and points, infantry and cavalry, quicker than lightning, and as promiscuously—with just enough rule to regulate instinct and yet not to fetter it. You are my antagonist, with this difference from real warfare, that I shall miss you every time by one hair's breadth, or perhaps two. Mind you don't flinch, whatever you do."
>
> . . . He flourished the sword by way of introduction number two, and the next thing of which she was conscious was that the point and blade of the sword were darting with a gleam towards her left side, just above her hip; then of their reappearance on her right side, emerging as it were from between her ribs, having apparently passed through her body. The third item of consciousness was that of seeing the same sword, perfectly clean and free from blood held vertically in Troy's hand (in the position technically called "recover swords.") All was as quick as electricity.
>
> "Oh!" she cried out in affright, pressing her hand to her side. "Have you run me through?—no, you have not! Whatever have you done?"   (p. 210)

At this juncture, Bathsheba becomes frightened, and Troy only gains permission to proceed by lying, telling her that the sword is not really sharp. We then proceed to the scene's climax, in the sexual as well as literary sense, for if "motion and light destroy the materiality of bodies,"[9] so does orgasm:

> In an instant the atmosphere were transformed to Bathsheba's eyes. Beams of light caught from the low sun's rays, above, around, in front of her, well-nigh shut out earth and heaven—all emitted in the marvelous evolutions of Troy's reflecting blade, which seemed everywhere at once, and yet nowhere specially. These circling gleams were accompanied by a keen rush that was almost a whistling—also springing from all sides of her at once. In short, she was enclosed in a firmament of light, and of sharp hisses, resembling a sky-full of meteors close at hand.   (p. 211)

This chapter is obviously a brilliantly written paradigm of sexual intercourse. No wonder Bathsheba feels as if "she had sinned a great sin" when Troy finally kisses her and departs. But what does the sword-exercise tell us about the nature of sexual passion? In Troy's own words, it is "rather deathy." The iridescent, world-obscuring blur of the sword in the air and the fresh luxuriance of the fern-pit are undeniably sensual and attractive. But the scene's real excitement depends on the sword's capacity to deal death. The lovers are arrayed as antagonists in a mortal combat. Bathsheba flirts with death by standing still for Troy—at first unknowingly, and then willingly, as he lops off a lock of her hair and splits a caterpillar on her breast. Twice Bathsheba believes he has murdered her by penetrating her with the blade; and Troy exerts all his skill to bring her as near to death as possible without actually killing her.

It is the sword-exercise which wins Bathsheba's love, but her love is also "rather deathly." It is self-destructive, a desertion of will. Hardy writes, "Bathsheba loved Troy in the way that only self-reliant women love when they abandon their self-reliance. When a strong woman recklessly throws away her strength she is worse than a weak woman who never had any strength to throw away. One source of her inadequacy is the novelty of the situation. She has never had practice in making the best of such a condition. Weakness is doubly weak by being new" (p. 214). Bathsheba's love for Troy is a love which embraces helplessness; his feeling for her one which exults in the powerlessness of its victim. Although Bathsheba is weakened by her love, her strength is not entirely dissipated, for she remains the head of the household, whom the unemployed Troy must pester for pocket money. He finds the situation unendurable, and it seems to typify the sexual power struggle of their marriage. Throughout the book, Troy both fears and resents Bathsheba's proud independence of character.

The essential morbidity of their relationship is dramatized when the corpses of Fanny Robin and her child are laid out in Bathsheba's parlor. Bathsheba recognizes Fanny as Troy's lover, and is immediately consumed with jealousy for the dead woman. Bathsheba believes her rival has eclipsed her in Troy's eyes through the simple expedient of dying, and she is right. When Troy comes in, he kisses Fanny with all the affection he is capable of, spurning Bathsheba's pleas to kiss her too. Troy's passion smacks of necrophilia, for his ideal woman is a dead woman. He announces this fact to Bathsheba: "'Ah! don't taunt me, madam. This woman is more to me, dead as she is, than ever you were, or are, or can be. . . .' He turned to Fanny then. 'But never mind, darling,' he said; 'in the sight of Heaven you are my very, very wife!'" (p. 345). Bathsheba contemplates suicide twice in this scene: once, as a means of successfully competing with Fanny for Troy's love; the second time as a means of escaping the degradation of continuing in his presence. Bathsheba and Fanny have exchanged places. The servant girl, by dying, has become Troy's accepted, legitimate wife; the wife remains behind as the soiled and ruined lover.

Bathsheba flies from Troy and hides herself in that same fern-pit where the sword-exercise took place, but the season has changed and the brake of fern "is now withering fast." Contact with Troy has turned the novel's feminine space, and Bathsheba's perception of her own sexuality, into a "loathsome, malignant thing."

> There was an opening towards the east, and the glow from the as yet unrisen sun attracted her eyes thither. From her feet, and between the beautiful yellowing ferns with their feathery arms, the ground sloped downwards to a hollow, in which was a species of swamp, dotted with fungi. A morning mist hung over it now—a fulsome yet magnificent silvery veil, full of light from the sun, yet semi-opaque—the hedge behind it being in some measure hidden by its hazy luminousness. Up the sides of this depression grew sheaves of the common rush, and here and there a peculiar species of flag, the blades of which glistened in the emerging sun, like scythes. But the general aspect of the swamp was malignant. From its moist and poisonous coat seemed to be exhaled the essences of evil things in the earth, and in the waters under the earth. The fungi grew in all manner of positions from rotting leaves and tree stumps, some exhibiting to her listless gaze their clammy tops, others their oozing gills. Some were marked with great splotches, red as arterial blood, others were saffron yellow, and others tall and attenuated, with stems like macaroni. Some were leathery and of richest browns. The hollow seemed a nursery of pestilences small and great, in the immediate neighborhood of comfort and health, and Bathsheba arose with a tremor at the thought of having passed the night on the brink of so dismal a place.   (pp. 347–48)

The site of the novel's most explicit sexual encounter has been despoiled. Troy's once dazzling scarlet and brass are, as many have pointed out, echoed in the blood and saffron of the fungi.[10] His sword, exchanged for a less romantic instrument perenially allied with death's harvest, is recalled by the scythe-like blades of flag. The morning mist that silvers and beautifies the scene asks us to remember the *aurora militaris* produced by Troy's blade but reveals its deceptive and impermanent beauty. Morning mist, like passion, the evanescent steam of the novel's conclusion, must rise and evaporate before the sun,[11] unveiling the face of reality.

As a reading of the second fern-pit sequence shows, Fanny's death has destroyed the sexual metaphor that originally surrounded Troy and made him glamorous. A dark tower surmounted by a hideous gurgoyle now replaces the gleaming blade, and the chapter titled "The Gurgoyle: Its Doings" is a metaphor for sexual intercourse far more sinister than the sword-exercise. I want to look closely at some passages in this chapter, but before I do, let me mention that "gurgoyle" does not precisely mean a mythical beast carved in stone. The word is derived from Old French "*gargouille*," meaning "throat," and literally means a "hideous spout," which may take either human or animal form. All of which, combined with a tower taller than it is wide and a certain tendency on Hardy's part to overuse the word "erect," is my justification for giving this chapter a sexual reading. The gurgoyle:

> The tower of Weatherbury Church was a square erection of fourteenth-century date, having two stone gurgoyles on each of the four faces of its parapet. Of these eight carved protuberances only two at this time continued to serve the purpose of their erection—that of spouting the water from the lead roof within.
>
> . . . only that at the south-eastern corner concerns the story. It was too human to be called like a dragon, too impish to be like a man, too animal to be like a fiend, and not enough like a bird to be like a griffin. This horrible stone entity was fashioned as if covered with a wrinkled hide; it had short, erect ears, eyes starting from their sockets, and its fingers and hands were seizing the corners of its mouth, which they thus seemed to pull open to give free passage to the water it vomited. The lower row of teeth was quite washed away, though the upper still remained. Here and thus, jutting a couple of feet from the wall against which its feet rested as a support, the creature had for four hundred years laughed at the surrounding landscape, voicelessly in dry weather, and in wet with a gurgling and snorting sound.
>
> Troy slept on in the porch, and the rain increased outside. Presently the gurgoyle spat. In due time a small stream began to trickle through the seventy feet of aerial space between its mouth and the ground, which the water-drops smote like duckshot in their accelerated velocity. The stream thickened in substance, and increased in power, gradually spouting further and yet further from the side of the tower. When the rain fell in a steady and ceaseless torrent the rain dashed downward in volumes.
>
> We follow its course to the ground at this point of time. The end of the liquid parabola has come forward from the wall, has advanced over the plinth mouldings, over a heap of stones, over the middle border, into the midst of Fanny Robin's grave. (pp. 360–61)

The gurgoyle chapter represents male sexuality as a malignant, destructive outpouring, and its female receptacle as a grave. Troy's nearest approach to love is the sentiment which compels him to plant Fanny's grave with spring flowers. This sentimentality is too weak to withstand a pestilential torrent of passion, and Troy has been too weak to refrain from ruining Fanny.

> The persistent torrent from the gurgoyle's jaws directed all its vengeance into the grave. The rich tawny mould was stirred into motion, and boiled like chocolate. The water accumulated and washed deeper down, and the roar of the pool thus formed spread into the night as the head and chief among other noises of the kind created by the deluging rain. The flowers so carefully planted by Fanny's repentant lover began to move and writhe in their bed. The winter-violets turned slowly upside down, and became a mere mat of mud. Soon the snowdrop and other bulbs danced in the boiling mass like ingredients in a cauldron. Plants of the tufted species were loosened, rose to the surface, and floated off.   (p. 362)

The fragile flowers of sentiment are easily overturned, and their roots are ugly ones. Troy's feeling for Fanny, perhaps because of the ugliness of its origins, is also easily uprooted, and he retreats from her despoiled grave.

Hardy spoke of Gabriel and Bathsheba's love as "a love . . . strong as death—that love which many waters cannot quench, nor the floods drown." We've reviewed the loves of Boldwood and Troy for Bathsheba Everdene, and find that the emotions these men call love are variously idolatry, lust, and sentiment. There is no question of whether such loves are weaker or stronger than death: Boldwood and Troy are agents of death; their passions destroy them and others as well. In Troy's case, his love for Fanny is quickly quenched by a flood, and the origin of that flood is his own morbid sexuality.

I turn to Gabriel with a sense of relief. Compared with the passions of Boldwood and Troy, the idea of "*camaraderie*" and "good fellowship" between the sexes seems enormously refreshing. If we are still disappointed, perhaps it is because we associate "*camaraderie*" and "good fellowship" with Platonic love, and Platonic love with asexuality. A complete relationship between a man and a woman must include healthy sexuality, and when this is lacking we are disappointed. For Bathsheba, scarred by her encounters with Boldwood and Troy, to settle for a Platonic, indifferently sexual union, would be a tragedy of reduced expectations indeed.

Our reading of the novel, then, and particularly our reading of its conclusion, depends on Gabriel Oak's sexuality. Whether the book's conclusion is triumphant or anticlimactic hinges on Gabriel's adequacy as a lover. It is because I see in Gabriel a potent, life-affirming sexuality that I read *Far from the Madding Crowd* as a *Paradise Regain'd* rather than a *Paradise Lost*.

Gabriel, like Troy, comes equipped with phallic instruments.[12] Whereas Troy's are the sword and gurgoyle, Gabriel's are the sheep shears, trochar, marking iron, ricking rod, and flute. Let's look at a passage in which Gabriel shears a sheep:

> Bathsheba, after throwing a glance here, a caution there, and lecturing one of the younger operators who had allowed his last finished sheep to go off among the flock without re-stamping it with her initials, came again to Gabriel, as he put down the luncheon to drag a frightened ewe to his shear-station, flinging it over upon its back with a dextrous twist of the arm. He lopped off the tresses about its head, and opened up the neck and collar, his mistress quietly looking on.
>
> "She blushes at the insult," murmured Bathsheba, watching the pink flush which arose and overspread the neck and shoulders of the ewe where they were left bare by the clicking shears—a flush which was enviable, for its delicacy, by many queens of coteries, and would have been creditable, for its promptness, to any woman in the world.
>
> Poor Gabriel's soul was fed with a luxury of content by having her over him, her eyes critically regarding his skilful shears, which apparently were going to gather up a piece of flesh at every close, and yet never did so. Like Guildenstern, Oak was happy in that he was not over happy. He had no wish to converse with her: that his bright lady and himself formed one group, exclusively their own, and containing no others in the world, was enough.
>
> So the chatter was all on her side. There is a loquacity that tells nothing, which was Bathsheba's; and there is a silence which says much: that was Gabriel's. Full of this dim and temperate bliss he went on to fling the ewe over upon her other side, covering her head with his knee, gradually running the shears line after line round her dewlap, thence about her flank and back, and finishing over the tail.
>
> "Well done, and done quickly!" said Bathsheba, looking at her watch as the last snip resounded.
>
> "How long, miss?" said Gabriel, wiping his brow.
>
> "Three and twenty minutes and a half since you took the first lock from its forehead. It is the first time that I have ever seen it done in less than half an hour."
>
> The clean, sleek creature arose from its fleece—how perfectly like Aphrodite rising from the foam should have been seen to be

realized—looking startled and shy at the loss of its garment, which lay on the floor in one soft cloud, united throughout, the portion visible being the inner surface only, which, never before exposed, was white as snow, and without flaw or blemish of the minutest kind.   (pp. 167–68)

Again the sexual metaphor is clear. Gabriel flings the ewe over on her back and opens her neck and collar as if she were a woman and he were undressing her. The sheep even blushes. But more important are the parallels between the sheep-shearing and the sword-exercise. Both are sexual displays intended to impress Bathsheba with the performer's prowess. Gabriel is plainly showing off; with Bathsheba's eyes "critically regarding his skilful shears," he clips the ewe faster than his mistress has ever seen it done before. The object of sheep-shearing and sword-exercise is also the same—to shave a body as closely and as quickly as possible without cutting it. Gabriel even lops off the ewe's tresses, to correspond with Troy's cutting a curl from Bathsheba's head. Both men are clearly masters of their respective instruments.

There the similarity between the two incidents ends. Unlike the sword-exercise, the sheep-shearing is neither deathy nor ultimately despoiling. Instead, the images are of birth, renewal, and cleansing. The newly shorn sheep rising from its fleece is described as Aphrodite, the newborn and naked goddess of love, rising from the sea. The fleece is snow-white, Gabriel having cut until he reached the inner, pure wool, and leaving the soiled side against the floor. The wool reverses the motion of the flowers on Fanny's grave. Whereas Troy overturns things to reveal their dirty undersides, Gabriel overturns them to reveal their inner purity.

The idea of describing a shorn sheep, a ridiculous object if ever there was one, as Aphrodite, is certainly at least mildly amusing. Gabriel generates much of the comedy in this book, while Troy generates only tragedy. Gabriel is a bringer of life and liveliness (one thinks of him standing in the tavern door with newborn lambs slung over his shoulders), while Bathsheba's other suitors are purveyors of death. Often Gabriel's phallic instruments are instruments of salvation, objects which change death into life. I think particularly of the trochar, the tool for sticking bloated sheep. Shortly after Bathsheba has dismissed Gabriel for criticizing her flirtation with Boldwood, her sheep break through a fence and "blast" themselves on young clover. There is comic force to the passage in which her men inform her that she must send for Gabriel Oak to save her flock:

"There's only one way of saving them," said Tall.
"What way? Tell me quick!"
"They must be pierced in the side with a thing made on purpose."

"Can you do it? Can I?"

"No, ma'am. We can't, nor you neither. It must be done in a particular spot. If ye go to the right or the left but an inch you stab the ewe and kill her. Not even a shepherd can do it, as a rule."

"Then they must die," she said in a resigned tone.

"Only one man in the neighborhood knows the way," said Joseph, now just come up. "He could cure 'em all if he were here."

"Who is he? Let's get him!"

"Shepherd Oak," said Matthew. "Ah, he's a clever man in talents!"

"Ah, that he is so!" said Joseph Poorgrass.

"True—he's the man," said Laban Tall.

"How dare you name that man in my presence!" she said excitedly. "I told you never to allude to him, nor shall you if you stay with me. Ah!" she added, brightening, "Farmer Boldwood knows."

"O no, ma'am," said Matthew. "Two of his store ewes got into some vetches t'other day, and were just like these. He sent a man on horseback here posthaste for Gable, and Gable went and saved 'em. Farmer Boldwood hev got the thing they do it with. 'Tis a holler pipe, with a sharp pricker inside. Isn't it Joseph?"   (p. 157)

Bathsheba's blind questions and false starts pile up until they lend melodramatic force to the recognition that Gabriel Oak alone can do the job. Not only is Gabriel the only man who can save the sheep, but also the only man who can wield the dangerous trochar without killing the sheep with the instrument itself. If the sheep-shearing business in the barn does not convince us that Gabriel possesses a strong, life-affirming sexuality, then the trochar passage must. Gabriel comes equipped with his own trochar (he doesn't have to borrow Farmer Boldwood's after all) and performs the operation out of love for Bathsheba. His act of salvation is successful; he saves most of Bathsheba's flock, restoring the half-dead sheep to life with the trochar.

Gabriel's phallic instruments, the sheep shears and trochar, are literally tools. Boldwood and Troy are characterized by implements of destruction (rifles and swords) and ornamentation (walking sticks and gurgoyles). Gabriel's instruments of salvation are the tools of his trade. His sexuality is inseparable from his work. This is scarcely surprising, since *Far from the Madding Crowd* elevates work to the status of religion. The farmer's work in this novel is a procreative process—he or she joins with others to cause the flocks to multiply and the earth to bear fruit.

Hardy describes the shearing-barn as resembling a church. The description is one of the novel's most moving passages; Hardy makes the barn a symbol of an eternal purpose not subject to the fluctuating, transient demands of church and state. The barn is, in fact, superior to a church, and its description an interesting contrast with the description of the gurgoyle-topped Weatherbury church.

> One could say about this barn, what could hardly be said of either the church or the castle, akin to it in age and style, that the purpose which had dictated its original erection was the same with that to which it was still applied. Unlike and superior to either of these two typical remnants of medievalism, the old barn embodied practices which had suffered no mutilation at the hands of time. Here at least the spirit of the ancient builders was at one with the spirit of the modern beholder. Standing before this abraded pile, the eye regarded its present usage, the mind dwelt upon its past history, with a satisfied sense of functional continuity throughout — a feeling almost of gratitude, and quite of pride, at the permanence of the idea which had heaped it up. The fact that four centuries had neither proved it to be founded on a mistake, nor given rise to any reaction that had battered it down, invested this simple grey effort of old minds with a repose, if not a grandeur, which too curious reflection was apt to disturb in its military and ecclesiastical compeers. For once medievalism and modernism had a common standpoint. The lanceolate windows, the time-eaten archstones and chamfers, the orientation of the axis, the misty chestnut work of the rafters, referred to no exploded fortifying art or worn-out religious creed. The defence and salvation of the body by daily bread is still a study, a religion, and a desire.
>
> To-day the large side doors were thrown open towards the sun to admit a bountiful light to the immediate spot of the shearers' operations, which was the wood threshing-floor in the centre, formed of thick oak, black with age and polished by the beating of flails for many generations, till it had grown as slippery and as rich in hue as the state-room floors of an Elizabethan mansion. Here the shearers knelt, the sun slanting in upon their bleached shirts, tanned arms, and the polished shears they flourished, causing these to bristle with a thousand rays strong enough to blind a weak-eyed man. Beneath them a captive sheep lay panting, quickening its pants as misgiving merged in terror, till it quivered like the hot landscape outside. (pp. 164-65)

One of the shearers kneeling to his work in this barn-church is Gabriel, and the Aphrodite passage follows almost immediately. Shepherd Oak appears as the high priest of both love and work. Certainly he understands the intimate connection between the two, and finds a species of fulfillment in working for his beloved. The moment when Gabriel turns the lambs he has rescued into living love-tokens is only one example: "Oak took from his illimitable pockets a marking iron, dipped it into the pot, and imprinted on the buttocks of the infant sheep the initials of her he delighted to muse on—'B.E.,' which signified to all the region round that henceforth the lambs belonged to Farmer Bathsheba Everdene, and to no one else" (p. 127).

The relationships between love, death, sex, work, and religion are dramatized in a serious and complicated way in the chapter titled "The Storm." The thunderstorm which threatens Bathsheba's ricks is apocalyptic in its dimensions. There are seven flashes of lightning, each one numbered and accompanied by images of death and demonism. One flash crosses the sky like a flapping of phosphorescent wings, another gleams in the heavens like a mailed army, another breaks with the spring of a serpent and the shout of a fiend. Naturally the seventh flash, like the opening of the seventh seal, is the final and climactic one:

> Heaven opened then, indeed. The flash was almost too novel for its inexpressibly dangerous nature to be at once realized, and they could only comprehend the magnificence of its beauty. It sprang from east, west, north, and south, and was a perfect dance of death. The forms of skeletons appeared in the air, shaped with blue fire for bones—dancing, leaping, striding, racing around, and mingling together in unparalleled confusion. With these were intertwined undulating snakes of green, and behind these was a broad mass of lesser light. Simultaneously there came from every part of the tumbling sky what may be called a shout; since, though no shout ever came near it, it was more of the nature of a shout than of anything else earthly. (p. 287)

This apocalyptic storm is an impressive example of that "blind force which drives all things"[13] in Hardy's world. As J. Hillis Miller has pointed out, "sexual passion is the chief way in which Hardy's characters participate in the impulsions of this force."[14] The dangerous flashing of Troy's sword is only a miniaturization of this grand electric "*aurora militaris*" of malignant nature.

Gabriel has recognized the unpredictable deadliness of nature ever since his overzealous dog drove his flock into the chalk-pit. It is Gabriel who reads the signs of the approaching rain of death, and Gabriel who opposes himself to the fury of the universe. He risks his life against the storm because there is "important and urgent labour" to be done. The ricks must be covered, or the harvest will be lost. Gabriel's labor is two-fold. First, it is a labor of love: he has sworn to help to his last effort the woman he loves. Second, it is labor in the procreative sense. Gabriel is a kind of midwife to nature. He brings the lambs safely into the world, and here he is concerned with the bringing forth of the harvest. Again, Gabriel appears as a savior. He is not interested in the monetary value of the ricks, but endeavors to save them because they are Bathsheba's, and because they are food for man and beast, nourishment and employment for his little community. Gabriel emerges in the storm chapter as a defender of love and life, fragile things in a death-dealing universe.

The instrument Gabriel opposes against the storm is another phallic tool, "his ricking-rod, or poniard, as it was indifferently called—a long iron lance, polished by handling" (pp. 284-85). The rod is stuck among the sheaves in the stack to support them against the wind. Ungrounded, Gabriel's rod jeopardizes his life by attracting lightning. In this condition, it conducts deadly electricity from the sky—the kind of sinister sexual energy that characterizes Troy. Gabriel, however, wishes to proceed with his work in safety. He grounds the ricking rod with a chain, turning it into an "extemporized lightning-conductor" (p. 285), and this foresight ultimately saves both his life and Bathsheba's: "In the meantime one of the grisly forms had alighted upon the point of Gabriel's rod, to run invisibly down it, down the chain, and into the earth. Gabriel was almost blinded, and he could feel Bathsheba's warm arm tremble in his hand—a sensation novel and thrilling enough; but love, life, everything human, seemed small and trifling in such close juxtaposition with an infuriated universe" (p. 287). Gabriel clasps Bathsheba to preserve her from the lightning. Gabriel is grounded by the ricking-rod, and Bathsheba is grounded by Gabriel's embrace. Their union is not without a sexual dimension—Gabriel is acutely aware of Bathsheba's trembling, and this moment constitutes their only physical contact in the novel—but grounded by love and reason, Gabriel's sexual energy brings life in defiance of the infuriated universe. The grounded ricking rod is an emblem of an heroic sexuality opposed to Troy's unfettered passion. The rod directs destructive natural energies to serve the demands of life and love, to work "the defence and salvation of the body."

The storm causes Bathsheba to turn to Gabriel for the first time. She confesses to him her shame at having married Troy, whose drunken irresponsibility has so nearly destroyed her farm and the community's livelihood. She confesses too, the circumstances of coercion surrounding her marriage, her appreciation for Oak's devotion, and her fear lest he be injured in the storm. Some recognition of Oak's worth has taken place in Bathsheba, perhaps in that blinding moment on the haystack. Love brings her to her shepherd-lover with confidence and concern, causes her "to speak to him more warmly [tonight] than she ever had done whilst unmarried and free to speak as warmly as she chose" (p. 291).

If we recall the passage describing Gabriel and Bathsheba's marriage, we'll recall that the "good fellowship" between the sexes Hardy believed essential to a love stronger than death arises only when the sexes associate in their labors as well as in their pleasures. Naturally any work of procreation requires the participation of both sexes. Bathsheba frequently works with Gabriel (none of her other suitors will work with her or even for her): she leaves the house to help Gabriel protect the ricks against the storm; she sings while he plays the flute; and, most significantly, she works with him to repair Fanny Robin's grave. Gabriel refills the hollowed grave, a feminine space previously emptied by the novel's second big storm, and Bathsheba restores the space to loveliness by replanting the uprooted flowers. Gabriel and Bathsheba's combined and harmonious labors oppose themselves to the gurgoyle's deathy sexuality. Like an ungrounded ricking rod, the gurgoyle has been a conduit for destructive natural energies. When the couple's work together is ended, however, the gurgoyle's stream has been permanently rerouted.

Since Gabriel's attendant phallic symbols are tools, and since the sexes are expected to work together in Hardy's revisionary sort of love, Bathsheba sometimes gets to handle the symbols right along with Gabriel—although like most men he is a bit grouchy and superior when a woman gets hold of his tools. Perhaps *Far from the Madding Crowd's* most extraordinary love passage is the one in which the two grind shears together.

> . . . Oak stood somewhat as Eros is represented when in the act of sharpening his arrows: his figure slightly bent, the weight of his body thrown over on the shears, and his head balanced sideways, with a critical compression and contraction of the eyelids to crown the attitude.
>
> His mistress came up . . . then she said—
>
> " . . . I'll turn the winch of the grindstone. I want to speak to you, Gabriel."
>
> . . . Bathsheba turned the winch, and Gabriel applied the shears.
>
> The peculiar motion involved in turning a wheel has a wonderful tendency to benumb the mind. It is a sort of attenuated variety of Ixion's punishment, and contributes a dismal chapter to the history of gaols. The brain gets muddled, the head grows heavy, and the body's centre of gravity seems to settle by degrees in a leaden lump somewhere between the eyebrows and the crown. Bathsheba felt the unpleasant symptoms after two or three dozen turns.

"Will you turn, Gabriel, and let me hold the shears?" she said. "My head is in a whirl, and I can't talk."

Gabriel turned. Bathsheba then began, with some awkwardness, allowing her thoughts to stray occasionally from her story to attend to the shears, which required a little nicety in sharpening.

" . . . You don't hold the shears right, miss — I knew you wouldn't know the way — hold like this."

He relinquished the winch, and enclosing her two hands completely in his own (taking each as we sometimes take a child's hand in teaching him to write), grasped the shears with her. "Incline the edge so," he said.

Hands and shears were inclined to suit the words, and held thus for a peculiarly long time by the instructor as he spoke.

"That will do," exclaimed Bathsheba. "Loose my hands. I won't have them held! Turn the winch." (pp. 150–51)

Bathsheba's other, death-purveying suitors are idle men, and share no work with her. Boldwood is a gentleman-farmer. His hirelings do his work for him, and eventually he must hire Gabriel Oak to manage his land. Boldwood resents Bathsheba's working as bailiff on her own farm — he proposes to make her an idle lady. One of her reasons for rejecting his first proposal is the pleasure she still takes in farming. Similarly, Troy begins as a soldier who has never fought. His courtship of Bathsheba is deceitful — he pretends to be a man who enjoys farm labour. Troy hives the bees, plays at haymaking, and tells Bathsheba that he loves to work for her. In short, to win Bathsheba, Troy pretends to be like Gabriel. But Troy is a man of words rather than action, his interest in work is purely verbal. After the wedding, Troy settles down to live in idleness off Bathsheba's earnings, and his pursuit of pleasure in the form of gambling nearly destroys the farm.

Both Boldwood and Troy fail the test of the apocalyptic storm. Boldwood fails through a kind of despairing apathy. He is aware of the approaching thunderstorm, but he does not lift a hand to save his ricks, and will not even order his men to work. Boldwood's behavior in the storm illustrates his fundamental self-destructiveness. Troy fails through an other-destructive negligence. He persists in making Bathsheba's workers drunk at the harvest-home supper, and presides over their revels like a demon in his red coat. The debauchery takes place in the shearing barn, and Troy's drunken desecration of work's temple almost seems to bring on the storm in the first place. In any event, Troy makes the storm doubly dangerous to Gabriel and Bathsheba by depriving them of their assistants.

Troy is not the man, and Boldwood is not the man, but Gabriel *is* the man. Bathsheba proceeds through a series of mistaken identities which culminates in the recognition of a hero. The brief passage in which she questions her men and learns that only Gabriel can save her sheep is a paradigm for the plot of *Far from the Madding Crowd,* or "Bathsheba and her Lovers." "Can you do it? Can I do it? Can Farmer Boldwood do it? No, only one man can do it—Shepherd Oak." This kind of series of mistaken identities is commonly used in our culture to dramatize the entrance of a hero. And although Oak is rewarded fairy-tale fashion with the hand of the princess and a kingdom (Boldwood's farm) to rule, Hardy undoubtedly derived the pattern from the archetypal Biblical story in which the Lord tries many men, and finds all wanting but one. Given Hardy's affinity for the Old Testament stories about David, one thinks particularly of Samuel's consecutive rejection of each of Jesse's seven sons, until the eighth is sent for and revealed as God's choice for the future king of Israel:

> And Samuel said unto Jesse, Are here all *thy* children? And he said, there remaineth yet the youngest, and behold, he keepeth the sheep. And Samuel said unto Jesse, Send and fetch him: for we will not sit down until he come hither.
> And he sent, and brought him in. Now he *was* ruddy, *and withal of a beautiful countenance, and goodly to look to.* And the Lord said arise, anoint him: for this *is* he. (I Sam. 16:11-12)

Gabriel is a true hero, and his marriage to Bathsheba a truly happy ending to the novel. *Far from the Madding Crowd* is no tragedy of reduced expectations, but a comic triumph of good over evil, and life over death. Let's return once more to the paragraph with which we began:

> He accompanied her up the hill, explaining to her the details of his forthcoming tenure of the other farm. They spoke very little of their mutual feelings; pretty phrases and warm expressions being probably unnecessary between such tried friends. Theirs was that substantial affection which arises (if any arises at all) when the two who are thrown together begin first by knowing the rougher sides of each other's character, and not the best til further on, the romance growing up in the interstices of a mass of hard prosaic reality. This good-fellowship—*camaraderie*—usually occurring through similarity of pursuits, is unfortunately seldom superadded to love between the sexes, because men and women associate, not in their labours, but in their pleasures merely. Where, however, happy circumstance permits its development, the compounded feeling proves itself to be the only love which is strong as death—that love which many waters cannot quench, nor

the floods drown, beside which the passion usually called by the name is evanescent as steam.   (pp. 456–57)

If the lovers talk about farming, it is because work is the language of love in this novel. All other language is unreliable: Troy lies; Boldwood speaks in clichés. The good fellowship between the sexes which grows out of shared work is not asexual at all, because work in this novel is a common labor of procreation – of bringing food from the earth, of standing between man and death. Beside it all other passions are deadly and sterile. Hardy tells us that this kind of love grows in the crevices of hard prosaic reality. The lichen metaphor works well here, for the lichen is not a plant at all, but a symbiotic relationship between fungi and algae. It is a community of organisms mutually dependent on one another for the defense and salvation of the body. It is stronger than death. It does not wither or change with the seasons. It is not easily uprooted. If we still find it unlovely, we can compare it to the withering fern-pit and the uprooted flowers on Fanny's grave. And if we still doubt the beauty of such a love, we can consider its restorative powers. Gabriel's love rejuvenates Bathsheba; it is "as though a rose should shut and be a bud again" (p. 462). It is a love which converts instruments of death (trumpet and cannon) to instruments of community rejoicing. And that restorative power is the result of passion fettered by reason, and is the miracle of Gabriel's rod.

Notes

1. [Unsigned review] *Saturday Review,* 9 Jan. 1875, in *Thomas Hardy: The Critical Heritage,* ed. R.G. Cox (London: Routledge and Kegan Paul, 1970), pp. 43–44.

2. D.H. Lawrence's interest in and affinity for the Victorian novelist are made plain in the chapter of *Phoenix* titled "A Study of Thomas Hardy."

3. Henry James, *Nation,* 24 Dec. 1874, in Cox, *Thomas Hardy,* p. 30.

4. J. Hillis Miller, *Thomas Hardy: Distance and Desire* (Cambridge, Mass.: Belknap Press, 1970), p. 154.

5. Perry Meisel, *Thomas Hardy: The Return of the Repressed, A Study of the Major Fiction* (New Haven: Yale Univ. Press, 1972), pp. 45–52.

6. J.I.M. Stewart, *Thomas Hardy: A Critical Biography* (New York: Dodd, Mead, 1971), p. 89.

7. Thomas Hardy, *Far from the Madding Crowd* (London: Macmillan, 1922), pp. 456–57. R.L. Purdy, in his *Thomas Hardy: A Bibliographical Study* (London: Oxford Univ. Press, 1954), calls this "in every sense the definitive edition of Hardy's work and the last authority in questions of text." All page references in parentheses refer to this edition, a late reprint of the so-called Wessex edition, containing the slight revisions and corrections made in 1919 and 1920.

8. It is customary today to flinch away from those useful concepts of phallic sym-

bol and feminine space. "Freudian fiddle-faddle," I believe Carlos Baker calls them. But no one reading the sword-in-the-fern-pit sequence of *Far from the Madding Crowd* can doubt that Hardy was quite conscious of the sexual metaphor in his chosen images. Nor can anyone who has read Thomas Moser's lively thoughts on pokers and pistols, doors and graves in *Wuthering Heights* deny the illumination such an approach can shed on a work in which the sexual meaning is probably unconscious.

9. I am indebted to J.I.M. Stewart (*Thomas Hardy*, p. 86), for this assertion of Futurist art's apt application to the effect produced by Sergeant Troy's blade in the sunlight.

10. Penelope Vigar, *The Novels of Thomas Hardy: Illusion and Reality* (London: Athlone Press, 1974), 108.

11. We recall the novel's first paragraph: "When Farmer Oak smiled, the corners of his mouth spread until they were within an unimportant distance of his ears, his eyes were reduced to chinks, and diverging wrinkles appeared around them, extending upon his countenance like the rays in a rudimentary sketch of the rising sun" (p. 1).

12. I apologize for ignoring Boldwood in this respect, but since, as Troy sadistically points out, the gentleman-farmer never attains possession of Bathsheba, his sexuality is less important to our study than that of his more powerful rivals. Hardy himself devotes most of his energy to developing parallels between Gabriel and Troy in which Boldwood does not participate. However, if we were to assign phallic instruments to Boldwood, I suppose they would be the cane and the rifle, signifying the crippled, murderous nature of his love.

13. Miller, *Thomas Hardy*, 209.

14. Ibid.

Michael Slater

The Bachelor's Pocket Book for 1851

In his lively and wide-ranging study of Victorian sexuality, *The Worm in the Bud* (1969), Ronald Pearsall gives an account of some of the handbooks available to would-be men-about-town, the young gentlemen up from the country anxious to taste the delights and dissipations of big-city life. Such guide books had existed before the nineteenth century, but these were often little more than lists of ladies of easy virtue with addresses and prices: *Harris's List of Covent Garden Ladies,* for instance, published at intervals during the last decades of the eighteenth century.[1] But, with the growth of Victorian London and easier access to it provided by the developing railway system, together with the ever-increasing variety of entertainments on offer, more comprehensive guides to metropolitan pleasures were required. Thus *The Swell's Night Guide* (1841 and into its twentieth edition by 1846) gave details of "Paphian beauties" and "Fancy Ladies and their Penchants," but described also "The Saloons . . . The Chaffing Cribs [drinking rooms with professional comedians]; the Introducing Houses [brothels]; the Singing and Lushing [drinking] Cribs; the Comical Clubs &c &c." Two standard features of such books would seem to have been the promise to instruct "yokels" how to avoid being fleeced and a few pages giving such medical information as might seem most immediately relevant to the would-be sampler of "Paphian" delights. *The Yokel's Preceptor* (1855?) offered "a regular and Curious Show-Up of the Rigs and Doings of the Flash Cribs in This Great Metropolis . . . By which the Flat is put Awake to all the Plans adopted to Feather a Green Bird, and let him into the Most Important Secrets." Pearsall, in the study mentioned above, quotes an advertisement for a book called *Hints to Men About Town* which promises, besides "a notice of the celebrated seraglios," some "hints to 'yokels' to prevent them being kidded, grabbed and flabbergasted, and eased of their tin" as well as "hints to prevent infection, remedies to cure, and a fund of useful information by a sporting surgeon."

The market for this kind of book must have received a tremendous boost with the influx of more than 4 million visitors to the Great Exhibition of 1851, a substantial number of whom would have been anxious to complete their education in "the Great Metropolis" before they departed. One of those who sought to exploit this situation was the print and bookseller William Ward, who ran a "Parisian Depository" (what today we, more brutally direct, would call a Sex Shop) at 67 Strand with a second establishment at 181 Fleet Street, next door to yet another Repository run by a William Edwards. Ward's publication, *The Bachelor's Pocket Book for 1851,* was a good vehicle for advertising some of his other wares too, such as French letters ("also known by the term of French Gloves, Cundums, etc.") and his Reviripogenitive Medicated Cordial for "seminal weakness." The merits of the latter item (price one guinea) are testified to by an anonymous specialist on "the generative organs" who proclaims a distaste for "the ordinary quack medicines of the day," but asserts that the Cordial is infallibly efficacious in a wide variety of circumstances "where involuntary emissions have been frequent; . . . where . . . erection has been unknown for years; also, where flagellation has proved insufficient to produce transitory enjoyment (and when produced by these means, the consequences are destructive to age), where sterility has embittered domestic happiness, and where the hymeneal pair have indulged inordinately." (The casual reference to flagellation as a commonly used sexual stimulus is interesting.)

A (somewhat battered) copy of Ward's *Pocket Book* has recently come into my possession and, although Mr. Pearsall's book includes some quotations from it, a fuller description of its contents may be found of interest. *The Bachelor's Pocket Book* consists of 150 pages with ten full-page engravings and an engraved title-page. It is bound in soft red leather and designed literally as a pocket book. The frontispiece, entitled "The Opera" shows a pirouetting ballerina and the engraved title-page has a design strikingly similar to Phiz's designs for the monthly-part covers of Dickens's novels in their serial form. At the bottom of the page in the center we see the back of a Pickwickian-looking figure in top-boots who, his arms raised in astonishment, seems to be gazing up to the top of the page where two (very female) angels are supporting a model of the Crystal Palace. To the left and right of the Pickwickian figure railway trains crammed with people are arriving and on either side of the page energetic little figures are being swept up, in two columns, towards the Crystal Palace. These figures include a Red Indian, a Chinaman (wearing a teapot), an American ("From Pensylvania" his hat informs us), Mr. Punch, and a young lady in a see-through skirt holding a sign which identifies her as the representative of "Fine Arts." The full title appears on the next page: *The Bachelor's Pocket Book; or Man of Pleasure's Night Guide to All that is Worth Seeing in "This Little Village," forming the Most Complete Directory to Casinos, Saloons, Theatres, Concerts, Night-houses, &c.*

The unnamed editor supplies a flowery little preface, complete with a monitory Shakespearian epigraph ("Let us teach ourselves that honourable / Stop, not to out-sport discretion"). The "courteous reader" is begged not to read the book

> as the beacon-light to the fatal quicksands of pleasure and dissipation, but rather as the good genius of pleasure's gay *parterre,* conducting the enchanted visitor to those bowers where bloom the fairest yet innoxious flowers—to those fountains where flow the purest waters—and to temples where the voice of the lute is sweetly heard stealing o'er the senses like fairy songs upon the evening air.

Without pausing to speculate on the frequency with which lutes were to be met with in Victorian brothels, we turn the page and find that elaborate imagery has been abandoned in the interests of some man-to-man plain speaking: "Depend upon it, Reader, there are very few persons who really know how to enjoy themselves. When I say enjoy themselves, I mean with the least expense to our constitution or our pocket. . . . " From this the writer seeks to soar upwards again on the wings of some sub-Chesterfieldian sentiments—" . . . since, to indulge moderately in the gai[e]ties of life forms, in some measure, a CORRECT portion of the education of the man of the world, it then becomes highly important that at least he should know how and where to pass his novitiate in town"—only to sink abruptly into some very commonplace similes: "I trust the Reader will bear in mind this *trite* axiom—to skim the surface of pleasure like a swallow, and not plump in like a goose."

The next twenty-five pages offer lists of dance-halls, theatres, pleasure-gardens, billiard rooms, oyster and supper rooms, "concerts" (drinking places where professional singers were engaged, their repertoire being mainly comic songs), "sporting houses" (pubs run by retired sporting characters, many of them offering tuition in sparring[2]), saloons, wine rooms, and so on. In the case of some entries there is a strong flavor of paid advertisement. Thus, "Mr. Laurent's Grand Casino" at the Argyll Rooms in Great Windmill Street is the only dance-hall listed (an engraving shows couples bounding about in the execution of what appears to be a polka) and "this really unequalled Temple of the Muses," as it is called, is lavishly praised—"so recherché and fashionable, that it may be truly designated THE FIRST CASINO IN EUROPE"—whilst Mr. Laurent himself is found to be nothing less than "soul-inspiring."[3] Follit's Cigar Stores at 219 Oxford Street would seem to be another case in point. No other such stores are listed (though the cigars obtainable at "the renowned, the luxurious Simpson's" Grand Divan in the Strand are highly praised) and Mr. Follit is described as an "out-and-out good fellow, and on no account must our country brethren leave town without visiting these stores."

Throughout the text of this part of the book little sketches are scattered, all tending to evoke a sexy atmosphere of casual flirtations or even downright pick-ups. The brief description of Vauxhall pleasure-gardens, for example, informs the reader that "the beautiful Italian walk" is "notorious for the amours of former Royalty" and the accompanying sketch shows a young swell passing and turning towards a demure-looking young woman who seems to be fully conscious of his interest. At the Swan in Hungerford Market, the reader is told, he can hear at eight o'clock every evening (admission three pence) "some pretty songs from 'pretty petticoats'" and the accompanying little sketch shows a very décolletée young lady in a tight bodice and a short ballet dress trilling away on a platform. A cheroot-smoking beauty sprawls sexily on a couch above the description of the Victoria Saloon (also known as Jessop's) in Catherine Street, Strand, where "may be found all the most nobby ladies in town . . . and also some of the right sort of swells"; an admission charge of one shilling helps to keep the company "select."

Several of the wine rooms and public houses are specifically mentioned as places where prostitutes ("Cyprian dames" – both "Paphian" and "Cyprian" were epithets of Venus, of course) may be found. The Old Bell in Wellington Street, Strand, is situated "at the corner of Exeter Street, the abode of many first-rate women"; the White Hart in the Strand is "frequented by every class of Cyprian, from the Jessopites, down to the lowest class of girls"; and so on. One old coaching-inn in the City, the Cross Keys in Gracechurch Street, is recommended as one of the best "accommodation houses": "Private rooms can be had here either by day or night; the charge for a sleeping room for self and lady is 4s, but for a short visit the mere calling for wine is deemed sufficient."[4] One wonders how many others of the once great coaching-inns, by then fallen on evil days, contrived to keep going in this rather dubious fashion.[5]

Four and a half pages, by far the longest entry, are devoted to Nicholson's "Justice Tavern" in Bow Street and, again, one suspects that there may be some paid-for puffing going on. However, Nicholson was such a prominent figure in London "flash" circles[6] and his unique entertainment so notorious that to have ignored him or skimped the description of his "Judge and Jury Show" would have reflected very poorly on such a compilation as the *Bachelor's Pocket Book*.

Renton Nicholson (1809–61) had made his reputation editing a scandal-sheet called *The Town* from 1837 to 1840. He established his "Judge and Jury" show at the Garrick's Head in Bow Street in 1841. Dressed in Judge's robes and styling himself "the Lord Chief Baron," Nicholson, supported by two lieutenants acting as counsel for the prosecution and the defense and with a jury drawn from the public, presided over a series of mock trials. Henry Vizetelly disapprovingly recalled many years later: "Recent divorce cases, with variations and additions, or mock trials of a similar nature, liberally interspersed with indelicate innuendoes or *double entendres* of exceptional grossness formed the stock proceedings." The audience, said Vizetelly, was mainly composed of "men about town, city clerks of all kinds, betting men and provincials ambitious of initiation into the shady side of London life."[7] By 1851 Nicholson had added "poses plastiques" and "tableaux vivants" (girls posing in flesh-coloured tights) to his show[8] but these attractions are, oddly, not mentioned in the *Bachelor's Pocket Book*, which concentrates on praising Nicholson himself (his "head, craniologically considered, exhibits great power in the perceptives, it has also the bumps of benevolence and veneration") and on convincing the reader that the parlor of the Justice Tavern is where he should aspire to be if he has any pretensions to being "one of the right sort":

> The room at night boasts the occupancy of leading men about town in the literary, corinthian, and sporting worlds, who may be seen until
> "Phoebus opes the gates of day"
> doing their weed, and sipping their *frigidum sine* with infinite *gout.*

The central section of the book, entitled "Paphian Bowers" is a series of descriptions (with portraits) of twenty "Cyprians." The reader is told in a general preamble that "a thoroughbred Londoner" has no difficulty in picking out a Cyprian's abode from a whole street of houses: he looks for "the door being left ajar, or the window blinds within being drawn down, and mostly large heavy-looking curtains." More precise signs are helpfully given for finding a number of the individual women subsequently listed, however: "Two Birds hanging in Parlour Window," "Amber Curtains to Windows," "A grey parrot in window," and so on.

A feature of these descriptions that seems to be carried on from the eighteenth-century *Harris's Lists* is the prefacing of each one with a little verse epigraph, and it is curious that the highest price mentioned (£5) is the same as that of sixty or seventy years before.[9] Great emphasis is laid upon how little the women described drink or swear and of course they are represented as participating very fully in the enjoyment of sexual pleasures. Jane Fowler, for example, of Church Street, Soho,

has a peculiar method of disrobing, and possesses excellent tact in
managing a charming repulse to the eager advances of a vigorous
gallant [this would seem to involve much work for the elbow,
judging by the accompanying sketch of Miss F. at work] for the
purpose of enhancing the enjoyment, which she well understands
how to take a share of[10]

while her near neighbour, Miss Godlington of Dean Street, Soho, forsook
an adoring husband and a respectable marriage to "taste the sweets of love
blended with variety" and "in bed will give you such evincing proofs of her
attachment to love's games, that although you leave a sovereign behind, you
will be frequently tempted to renew your visit."

Breast-fetishists seem to be especially well catered for in this particular
Ladies' Directory. They may be tempted to expend a guinea in the enjoyment of the "sister hills" of young Anna Merton, described as "prominent,
firm, and elastic, and from their extensive size must have driven the ruby
current through the Cyprian channel at a very early period." Or, for the
same price, there are available the "twin hillocks of delight" belonging to
another eighteen year old, Miss M. Jackson; these are "redundantly stocked
with lactiferous tubes, and swell prominently rich with love's choicest sweets,
forming for the head two pillows of the softest down" (the accompanying
sketch shows one of Miss Jackson's clients reclining in her lap and apparently
transfixed by the proximity of her bared right breast). For two pounds more
the connoisseur could enjoy the splendors of the majestic Maria Bolton,
"nearly six foot high . . . and . . . exceedingly well proportioned." Her breasts
(to which the accompanying sketch, showing Maria naked in bed, does full
justice) are "remarkably firm, plump, and white, and in their rise and fall
paint the exuberance of the soil in the most expressive terms."[11] A more
fastidious taste might, however, prefer the small breasts of Mrs. Woolford,
"as plump and hard as an untouched virgin's," especially as they are allied
with "an unusual share of vivacity" and a leg and thigh that are "the most
perfect pieces of work nature ever formed!" But to gain access to this paragon
will cost no less than "five sovs."

More eccentric tastes would seem to be provided for by such ladies as
Mrs. Harding of Sheppard Street, Oxford Street, who numbers among her
clients a certain doctor who pays five pounds for the pleasure of combing
her "flowing tresses" with "a tortoiseshell comb, which he always carries
about with him for that purpose," or Miss Alice Grey of New Street, Port-
land Road who "frequently performs the rites of the love-inspiring queen
according to the *equestrian* order, in which style she is said to be perfect
in her paces, having studied under a professed riding master, who has taught

MISS GODLINGTON,
DEAN STREET, SOHO.

Give me a life of luscious love,
  Free from a husband's rig'rous sway,
Thro' ev'ry scene of bliss to rove,
  And ne'er be tied to cursed *obey.*

This genuine daughter of mirth and jollity is a native of Plymouth. Good natural parts, improved by a genteel education, make her quite the chatty, witty, and agreeable companion. She passed "the spring tide of life" without much of the "fuel of love," and, much against her inclination, tied the nuptial knot at the ripe age of nineteen, enjoying for some time a kind of negative happiness, as her feelings would never permit her to return her husband an equal share of fondness. He seemed to love her to distraction, which not only served to entirely root out the small affection that once had taken place, but brought on an entire contempt and hate, and without much hesitation she was easily prevailed on to leave her fond spouse, and taste the sweets of love blended with variety. She is ever lively, merry, and cheerful; and in bed will give you such evincing proofs of her attachment to love's games, that although you leave a sovereign behind, you will be frequently tempted to renew your visit.

MISS REBECCA LEE,
GEORGE STREET, ADELPHI.

(Lives on the first floor of the third house on the right hand.)

———

" Now, by my hood, a Gentile and no Jew."

———

This lady is commonly called " the agreeable Jewess," for what reason those who have seen the lady can only determine ; for she has not the covetousness or artifice which attends all the followers of Moses ; nor, like them, is distinguished among her neighbours for " despoiling them of their jewels of silver and their jewels of gold." It may, perhaps, be accounted for upon other principles : for though she is genteely made, and has a very good face, yet a fine black eye and black hair make her look not unlike to one of the daughters of Abraham. Her mouth is small, and looks like Suckling's girl in the song of the wedding whose nether lip

" Look'd as if some bee had stung it newly."

Her conversation is pleasing, she drinks little, and swears seldom; so that, as times go, she is a very desirable companion.

MISS MARIA BOLTON,
SLOANE STREET, CHELSEA.
(A small white house.)

———

"Endless joys are in that haven of bliss—
A thousand cupids dance upon her smiles,
Young bathing graces wanton in her eyes,
Melt in her looks, and pant upon her breasts;
Each word is gentle as a western breeze
That fans the infant bosom of the spring,
And every sigh more fragrant than the morn."

To all lovers of elegance and taste we recommend this Cyprian fair, who is a native of Paris, and although at present in tolerable good keeping, she dispenses her favours very liberally abroad to any one who has courage to advance with three quid in his cly. Being nearly six feet high, she makes a stately appearance, and is exceedingly well proportioned; her breasts are remarkably firm, plump, and white, and in their her the *menage* in the highest perfection. For these lessons which she daily and nightly gives, she expects two or three cooters [pounds] at least." The illustration shows Miss Grey, fully clad but showing a great deal of leg, mounted astride a poetic-looking gentleman leaning easily upon his elbow and gazing rather soulfully up into her severe countenance.[12] It is both the naughtiest and the most comical illustration in the book.

The obscene double entendres sprinkled through these descriptions and carefully italicised so that they shall not escape the reader's notice seem to be a standard feature in such publications, and this should not surprise us when we remember the Victorian passion for punning, that art of which Thomas Hood was the greatest exponent. In the *Bachelor's Pocket Book* it is so rife as to be in some cases only partially comprehensible today. One can see the joke about the melodious Miss Parks's satisfactory employment of her tongue and voice in duets ("She performs her part with admirable skill and dexterity, and in such cases chooses the *lowest* part")[13] and also about the advantage of Miss Moriella's having been trained as a clear-starcher ("few ladies . . . are better qualified to get up *small things* to the *highest* perfection"), but one may become a little bemused about what exactly is going on in the following passage about Mrs. De Lainier ("a first-rate Thais . . . in good keeping by a Count, whose name she has now taken"):

> . . . Mrs. D. is a great frequenter of auctions, and being a particular admirer of old china, she, upon these occasions, makes acquaintance with some connoisseur, whom she desires to bid for her; the consequence is, the lot is entered in his name, and to prevent giving him farther trouble, she takes it home in her carriage. . . . Her sideboard of plate is said to be very valuable, as she occasionally increases it at sales by her uncommon *adroitness* in forming good connections in a hurry. We think Mrs. D-'s intrigues may afford some useful hints to the frail sisterhood in her elevated line.

In one case, that of Miss Walbeck of William Street, King's Cross, the double entendre is reinforced by a picture. Miss Walbeck has been training for the stage, we read, "and is exceedingly fond of taking *male parts*"; the accompanying sketch shows her in chemise, top hat and men's trousers leaning rakishly against a table with a wine bottle on it and holding a whip. This last detail may be connected with the information that "she has a piece of the termagant about her." Swinburne, one suspects, would have been most interested in this lady.

The list of individual women is followed by a shorter list of "French Introducing Houses" or brothels where "importers of French mutton, lamb and chicken set up their shambles." The brutal abattoir metaphor is relentlessly pursued in the description of the first of them, Madame Audray's "Establishment for Young Ladies" in Church Street, Soho, and also at Fulham:

> This abbess has just put the kipehook on all other purveyors of the French flesh market. She does not keep her meat too long on the hooks, though she will have her price; but nothing is allowed to get stale here. You may have your meat dressed to your own liking, and there is no need of cutting twice from one joint; and if it suits your taste, you may kill your own lamb or mutton, for her flock is in prime condition, and always ready for sticking. When any of them are *fried* they are turned out to grass, and sent to the hammer, or disposed of by private contract, but never bought in again; consequently, the rot, bots, glanders, and other diseases incidental to cattle, are not generally known here, though there are instances of the awful enemy lodging itself here through some private jobbing in overtime.

Three other brothels run by Frenchwomen are then described with equally plentiful use of "flash lingo" and double entendre. Madame Lemercier's "Seminary for Young Ladies" in the Wandsworth Road was well placed, it is noted, to catch prosperous clients "as they return from business in town" and the name of the house, The Priory, stimulates the writer to some obvious facetiousness: "The nuns of this convent can chaunt a tidy stave, grind the piano—and that is not the only slum [thing] they can grind." Complicated jokes, heavy with innuendo, about playing cribbage and billiards follow and the reader is warned to be alert to "the downments of this donna and her kinchin" to avoid being cheated. Madame Lemercier's "town depot" in Villiers Street, Strand, can be found by looking for a zinc plate advertising "Professor of the Pianoforte and the Guitar." For Madame Jacot of Albion Place, Walworth Road, the writer chooses first a cavalry metaphor ("being an old trooper herself, she understands the art of mounting, which she teaches with considerable success, and is rough-rider in her own establishment") and then one about French grammar lessons ("the conjugation of the verbs is reduced and rendered easy by copulative conjunction, tense, number, and gender indiscriminately accepted"). Lastly, there is Madame Maurin, Stay and Corset Maker, of York Place, Waterloo Road, whose enterprise in using the same labor force to run a respectable business by day and a brothel by night is dubbed by the writer "about the neatest stitch we have tumbled to." She is also commended for supplying free medical attention for any "contagion imbibed at her quarters," although the results of this do not always seem to have been very satisfactory: of the two sufferers mentioned by the writer as having benefited from Madame Maurin's doctor "one . . . lost his nose and the other had a silver plate in his mouth."

All of the French Madames are praised by the writer for having "much improved the breed and condition of the native flag-trampers, as also the manners and treatment of the British bawds to their wretched labourers." Thus, Mother Willit of Gerrard Street, who used to be a tyrant to her girls "has now turned to the pious dodge, and calls them her *darters,* her *chickens,* and *kids.*" Mother Willit's is the only individual speaking voice we hear throughout this whole guide to the seamier side of London, and the quotation from her dilating upon her own professional pride has a marvellous air of salty authenticity: "'So help her kidneys, she *al'us* turned her gals out with a clean a—e and a good tog; and as she turned 'em out, she did'nt care who turned 'em up, 'cause 'em vos as clean as a smelt and as fresh as a daisy—she vould'nt have a speck'd 'un if she know'd it.'"

This brief snatch of actual speech is a good deal more convincing than much of the thirty-eight pages of vocabulary, entitled "The Modern Flash Dictionary," that follow the section on brothels. This Flash Dictionary seems to contain rather a high proportion of obsolete slang taken from eighteenth-century sources, as does the list of "The Sixty Orders of Prime Coves" that follows it. This list includes "Cloak twitchers," for example—that is, thieves who steal cloaks by twitching them off people's backs—yet the *New Canting Dictionary* of 1725 commented that this practice was dying out as cloaks were no longer worn much. Nor can many highwaymen have been active in 1851, yet we find "rum prad" (a highwayman's horse) listed in the Flash Dictionary.

This section of the *Pocket Book* is followed by Ward's advertisement for his French letters and then "Certain Prescriptions important to the Health of the Man of Pleasure, with hints how and when to use them." Various venereal diseases are discussed and treatment for them suggested, with much emphasis on chewing "gum arabic" and drinking linseed tea, but nothing at all is said about syphilis, which is strange in view of Pearsall's comment that "For many medical men syphilis *was* venereal disease."[14]

After this medical section the *Pocket Book* concludes in more conventional vein with a list of the 1851 racing fixtures together with a bit of history about the Derby, the Oaks, and the St. Leger; a brief description of the projected Crystal Palace ("Neither oriental fancy or poetic imagining has bodied forth a more wondrous structure than this Fairy Hall"); a Calendar for 1851, noting various anniversaries; lists of the Royal Family, European sovereigns and Government ministers; and other standard diary information.

The Bachelor's Pocket Book is a fascinating document in its own right, but for the student of Victorian literature it has a particular interest in that it provides a vivid glimpse of that disreputable underworld of the London of the day that the great novelists could only hint at when describing the careers of their young men about town. In a famous passage of his preface to *Pendennis* (1850) Thackeray remarks that "even the gentlemen of our age" cannot be shown by the novelist "as they are with the notorious foibles and selfishness of their lives and education." Rounding on his lady readers, he says, "You will not hear—it is best to know it—what moves in the real world, what passes in society, in the clubs, colleges, mess-rooms,—what is the life and talk of your sons." Since it is clear, from the fiction of Thackeray himself, that there was no interdiction on the mention of gambling, drinking, and general riotous behavior by young men about town, it would seem that the "notorious foibles and selfishness" he is alluding to here must refer to sexual escapades, the sort for which such compilations as *The Bachelor's Pocket Book* were intended as a useful vade mecum (one feels Pendennis's "swell" young friend Mr. Harry Foker must have invested in a copy).

As the *Pocket Book* makes clear, the center for all the various louche activities to which it offers a guide was the area along the Strand and the roads leading off the Strand to Covent Garden, so references in fiction to young men disporting themselves in Covent Garden would surely have suggested to the more sophisticated readers pleasures of a very dubious kind indeed. This is the context into which we should set Steerforth in *David Copperfield* when he tells David that he has arranged to meet his friends Granger and Markham at a hotel in Covent Garden. It was for such young men about town as Steerforth and his friends (or, in *Great Expectations*, Startop and Bentley Drummle) that books like *The Bachelor's Pocket Book* were produced. Thus Dickens could suggest to such readers a far wider range of dissipation than Pip could state when he describes "The Finches of the Grove," that hedonistic club of young bachelors: "The Finches spent their money foolishly (the Hotel we dined at was in Covent-garden) —."

Notes

1. In *A Long Time Burning: The History of Literary Censorship in England* (London: Routledge and Kegan Paul, 1969), Donald Thomas quotes (pp. 381–84) some descriptions of "Covent Garden Ladies" from *Harris's List* for 1788 and 1793.

2. We may recall that the Game Chicken, Mr. Toot's sparring instructor in Dickens's *Dombey and Son*, intends going in for "the public line" (i.e., to keep a public house) when he abandons his pupil in disgust at his lack of "pluck" (ch. 56).

3. Dickens refers to the Argyll Rooms in a letter written on 22 April 1856 to Wilkie Collins from Paris: "On Saturday night I paid three francs at the door of that place where we saw the wrestling, and went in, at 11 o'clock, to a Ball. Much the same as our own National Argyll Rooms. Some pretty faces, but all of two classes—wicked and coldly calculating, or haggard and wretched in their worn beauty." See *Letters of Charles Dickens*, ed. Walter Dexter (Bloomsbury: Nonsuch Press, 1938), II, 763. No doubt it is to the Argyll Rooms, too, that he refers in a letter of 16 August

1855 to Lord Lyttleton when he writes: "When the custom [of prostitutes plying their trade] began to die out of our London theatres, a certain Dancing Establishment arose (I mean a Ball Room) which great numbers of women regularly frequent. Great order is observed there, but it is understood to be a place where this allurement is always found, and to which few resort for anything else." See *Catalogue of the Lyttleton Papers*, (London: Sotheby's, 12 Dec. 1978), p. 173.

4. Pearsall comments that "the mere calling for wine" was probably a costly business; he points out that at Kate Hamilton's famous Night-house a bottle of Moselle cost 12 shillings. See *The Worm in the Bud* (Toronto: Macmillan, 1969), p. 320.

5. We may feel reasonably certain that this particular development as regards the old coaching inns would *not* have figured in the article that Dickens suggested in 1856 to his sub-editor W.H. Wills might be written for his magazine *Household Words*: "For a light article, suppose Thomas went round . . . to a number of the old coaching houses, and were to tell us what they are about now. . . . " See *Letters of Charles Dickens*, II, 726.

6. The 1846 edition of *The Swell's Night Guide* was advertised as "Revised and carefully corrected by the Lord Chief Baron [i.e., Nicholson]"; see the title page reproduced in Peter Fryer's *The Man of Pleasure's Companion: A Nineteenth-Century Anthology of Amorous Entertainment* (London, 1968).

7. Henry Vizetelly, *Glances Back Through Seventy Years* (London, 1893), I, 169.

8. "Renton Nicholson," *Dictionary of National Biography*, 1937–38 ed. XIV, 470–71.

9. See Thomas, *A Long Time Burning*, p. 382, where it is stated that the prices given in *Harris's List* range from 5 shillings to £5, but are usually in the £1–£2 range.

10. Miss Fowler seems not to have confined the exercise of her talent for titillation to the bedroom: "When stepping into a cab or coach, she makes the most of her leg; and in an omnibus she generally sets fire to all the male passengers, so that you see them fidgeting and adjusting their rebellious members the remainder of the journey."

11. Pearsall, *Worm in the Bud*, p. 322, speculates that "soil" here may be a misprint for "soul," which seems very plausible.

12. The epigraph from Samuel Butler's *Hudibras* preceding the description of Miss Grey seems a particularly curiously-chosen one, hardly calculated to encourage customers: "For 'tis vain to guess / At women by appearances: / They paint and patch their imperfections / Of intellectual complexions, / And daub their tempers o'er with washes / As artificial as their faces."

13. Miss Parks, being able to speak French, was, according to her description in the *Pocket Book*, much sought after by "foreigners of distinction" (whom she seems to have been inclined to fleece), though she "will not refuse five pounds from a British hand."

14. Pearsall quotes a Dr. Spencer Thomson writing on the subject in 1856 and comments further, "Morbid fear of syphilis was so widespread as to give currency to its own name—syphilophobia." See *Worm in the Bud*, p. 286.

Geoffrey Carter

Sexuality and the Victorian Artist: Dickens and Swinburne

An unusual number of the great Victorians seem to have had alarming sexual dysfunctions. Carlyle, the morning after his wedding, is supposed to
have "torn to pieces the flower garden at Comely Bank in a fit of ungovernable rage," and Jane Welsh Carlyle's nervous hypochondria is allegedly
related to his impotence;[1] Ruskin's marriage of seven years was unconsum-
mated and later in life he fell tragically in love with a mere child; Lewis
Carroll liked to photograph unclothed little girls; Swinburne wrote some
of the most erotic poems in the language and yet was apparently able to
achieve sexual gratification only by paying prostitutes to whip him. Dickens'
sexual life seems to have been relatively normal, but there is a striking dispar-
ity between the melodramatic horror with which in his novels he refers to
any kind of non-marital sex, and his own behavior in publicly renouncing
his wife, and later setting up an actress in a cottage.

Steven Marcus, in a book about Victorian pornography, has enabled us
to understand this state of affairs somewhat.[2] The thesis of his first chapter
is that in the 1870s the writings about sexuality of intelligent, well-qualified
professional men are as much distorted by fantasy, wishful thinking, and
unexamined myth as the pornography of the day and that these works are,
therefore, at about the same intellectual level as the pornography. Marcus
shows how an intelligent and humane man of science was able to believe
that a healthy, active child never has a sexual thought or feeling; that masturbation is deviant behavior and a frequent cause of insanity or worse; that
overindulgence by a married man has the same ill effect as masturbation;
that most women do not have any kind of sexual feeling; and that a modest
married woman will, of course, submit to her husband but seldom desire
sexual gratification herself. Earnest middle-class Victorian men, anxious to

live cleanly, were assured that they were morally accountable for sexual dreams since dreams reflect daytime preoccupations. Such views were held in the face of overwhelming evidence against them, and we can easily imagine the desperation they must have caused. A tragically precarious purity was paradoxically seen as the norm achievable by anyone.

Warned by Marcus, we should be safe from any temptation to patronize the Victorians on grounds of their naiveté or reticence in dealing with sexual matters: it is not, after all, to our credit that we were born after, instead of before, the Freudian upheaval. But by the same token, we should acknowledge the merit of any Victorian writer who was able to confront unflinchingly the problems of sexuality. And Swinburne was such a writer.

Our mental set when we approach an author helps to determine our responses to him. In some ways our attitudes to Dickens and Swinburne are Victorian to this day, for when we read Dickens our mental set might be something like, "Expect great genius"; but when we read Swinburne our mental set might be more like, "Expect something scandalous, erotic, masochistic, adolescent and 'merely the hallucination of meaning.'" [3] This state of affairs makes it easy to overpraise Dickens, who in certain respects cannot, of course, be praised enough; and very difficult to see Swinburne clearly —especially if one has loosely accepted text-book generalizations about "art for art's sake" and "decadence." But moving from the very worst parts of Dickens to the best things in Swinburne's marvelous decade, the 1860s, one can see that in certain cultural situations decadence is healthier than orthodoxy and is therefore not really decadence at all, and that one of the things "art for art's sake" means is "art for *truth's* sake, at all costs." In certain respects, then, Dickens is more indecent than Swinburne; or perhaps we should say rather that while Dickens is sometimes indecent, Swinburne in his serious works never is.

Where do we get our "mental set" in approaching Swinburne? In part from the literary gossip we all love. Who does not relish the story that is told about Swinburne's apparent impotence? D.G. Rossetti, we are told, upset that the author of *Poems and Ballads,* which were denounced for their eroticism, had not slept with a woman, paid a female circus rider ten pounds to seduce him. She went to live with Swinburne, had no success, returned Rossetti his ten pounds, and remarked that she could not bring him up to scratch or make him understand that "biting was no use." [4] Somehow it is easy to remember, while reading Swinburne, that he was a masochist, whereas while reading Dickens it is with a jolt that we recollect that this man had an affair with an actress much younger than himself and thus was technically an adulterer. [5]

In Swinburne's case, however, a great work of scholarship has reinforced the gossip. Mario Praz, in his book, *The Romantic Agony,* a survey of Satanism, *femmes fatales*, and sadism in nineteenth-century literature,[6] devotes many pages to Swinburne, including an appendix entitled "Swinburne and the *vice anglaise*." De Sadean and masochistic elements in Swinburne are given very free play. There is only one reference to Dickens in the book, where it is remarked with ironic surprise that Lafourcade, the major Swinburne scholar of the century, once wrote an article on sado-masochism in *Nicholas Nickleby*.[7] I propose in what follows to redress the balance a little: to suggest that there is a great deal more sadism and related perversities in Dickens than might have been supposed,[8] and to suggest that Swinburne is not nearly so simply a writer of sadistic and masochistic inclinations as Praz has led us to believe.

In his preface to *Pickwick Papers*, Dickens promised that nothing therein would bring a blush to the most delicate cheek, and throughout his novels he observed that principle. How is it then that he often makes us, twentieth-century adults, squirm?

Esther Summerson, in *Bleak House*, for instance has found very few defenders even among Dickensians. Those with a low squirm threshold start squirming the moment she begins deprecating herself at her first entry; but surely even the toughest readers squirm when, on Ada and Richard's wedding-night, Esther cannot resist going to stare at their lighted windows and then, once there, cannot resist entering the building, which is otherwise in darkness, and stealing up the staircase to their apartment door. She tells us, "I listened for a few moments; and in the rusty rotting silence of the house, believed I could hear the murmur of their young voices. I put my lips to the hearse-like panel of the door as a kiss for my dear."[9] This has to make a modern reader feel very uncomfortable: Esther is listening, tip-toe, outside the wedding chamber on the wedding night! At the best, this is a grotesque interference in other people's privacy; at the worst, it is voyeurism masquerading as selfless love.

Another moment in *Bleak House* that makes us uneasy is the reunion of Esther and Ada after Esther's convalescence from smallpox. Dickens indulges Esther's sickness and gives it the amount of space he does because he knows that the romance of sickness and convalescence is good box office. But, by means of it, he is also enabled to render the relationship between Esther and Ada more exquisite. As soon as Esther realizes that her maid, Charlie, has smallpox, her "darling," Ada, is rigorously excluded from her presence although "at first she came very often to the door, and called to me; and even reproached me with sobs and tears" (p. 333; ch. 31). Forty pages later we are told, "I had heard my Ada crying at the door, day and night; I had heard her calling to me, that I was cruel, and did not love her" (p. 371; ch. 35). Even when Esther is perfectly well again she still refuses to see Ada, although, as Jarndyce remarks, it is at "the price of tears down stairs"

(p. 375; ch. 35), a remark to which the normally tender-hearted Esther omits to respond. A week or so after this, when Esther holds long talks with Ada, from behind the window curtain, without looking at her, though it would have been easy to do so without being seen (p. 376), we begin to feel that her behavior is as absurd as that of Gulliver returned from the land of the Houyhnhnms. Weeks after this, Esther has coyly removed herself to another house and only then is Ada finally allowed to come to see her. A whole page is devoted to Esther's hysterical excitement at the prospect of reunion; when she hears Ada is coming, she withdraws again, runs upstairs, and hides behind a door, just as Dora hides away from David Copperfield. And finally, "O how happy I was, down upon the floor, with my sweet beautiful girl down upon the floor too, holding my scarred face to her lovely cheek, bathing it with tears and kisses, rocking me to and fro like a child, calling me by every tender name that she could think of, and pressing me to her faithful heart" (p. 392; ch. 36). What upsets us here, perhaps, is that in the guise of portraying an innocent girl's sisterly altruism, Dickens is, in fact, titilating us with a scene of sexual hysteria, set up by weeks of subtly sadistic postponement of gratification.

Esther Summerson's apparent annihilation of self leads, as we might expect, to behavior that we find disgusting but for which she is full of self-congratulation. Is this a case of Dickens' intuitive genius painting the case correctly although making the wrong judgments on it? It would seem so. For the view of Esther just presented is corroborated by Dickens' portrayal of two characters in *Little Dorrit* who are neat inversions of Esther Summerson. All the hostility she has successfully translated into sweetness, they express violently. Tattycoram, the Meagles' unhappy maid, and Miss Wade, her rescuer, are, like Esther, bastards, and, like Esther, have been brought up by stand-ins for their real parents. But unlike Esther, they are not models of selfless, all-nurturing love; rather they are full of passionate hatred of those who attempt to be good to them. Whereas Esther, with an unconvincing unawareness of her own niceness, assumes that there is a conspiracy on other people's part to make her happy, Tattycoram and Miss Wade suffer from paranoia and interpret everything that is done around them as designed to hurt them. In Miss Wade, Esther's latent sadistic lesbianism is made overt. Tattycoram, the rebellious maid whom she persuades to come and live with her, is always seen as a sexual object. When she first draws Miss Wade's attention, she is weeping on her bedroom floor: "her rich black hair was all about her face, her face was flushed and hot, and as she sobbed and raged, she plucked at her lips with an unsparing hand . . . her neck freshly discolored with great scarlet blotches." [10] Miss Wade stands looking at her "with a strange attentive smile" (we are told elsewhere that she has a "cruel mouth") and "with her hand upon her own bosom . . . as one afflicted with a dis-eased part might curiously watch the dissection and exposition of an analo-gous case" (p. 65). The motifs of dishevelled hair and self-inflicted injury are repeated in the other major scene in which they appear together when Meagles tries to persuade his former maid Tattycoram to leave Miss Wade. He warns Tattycoram that Miss Wade might be "a woman, who from what-ever cause, has a perverted delight in making a woman as wretched as she is" and adds "for I am old enough to have heard of such." In reply Miss Wade, who has already "laid her hand protectingly on the girl's neck for a moment," now puts her arm about Tattycoram's waist "as if she took pos-session of her for evermore" (p. 379; bk. 1, ch. 27). Here Dickens seems to be referring to lesbianism as clearly as he was able to.[11]

All this shows how skillfully Dickens can suggest the forbidden topics while observing, more or less, Victorian proprieties; but, unfortunately, we feel that his judgments are all wrong. In her autobiography, "The history of a Self-Tormenter" (bk. 2, ch. 21), Miss Wade clearly reveals herself as para-noid; but the case against the Meagles' treatment of Tattycoram is sound. They do patronize her; they have given her a ridiculous name that sets her apart from the family, and she is thoughtlessly neglected as a person. Meagles' response to her quite natural emotional turbulence is to bid her count to twenty-five, his explanation of such turbulence—an explanation which un-fortunately Dickens seems to endorse—being that it must be a reflection of the passion of the mother who was able to conceive her illicitly (p. 370; bk. 1, ch. 27). (This comes close to endorsing the view of the aunt that reared Esther Summerson who regards bastards as themselves criminal.) At the end of the novel the passionate Tattycoram comes submissively and lovingly home, promising to count to twenty-five whenever she feels her temper ris-ing in the future, a denouement that is totally unconvincing. Dickens' point seems to be that Tattycoram and Miss Wade should become Esther Sum-mersons if they possibly can; and that Tattycoram comes home to be an Esther Summerson. I much prefer not only the tempestuous Tattycoram to the tame one, but also both Tattycoram and Miss Wade to Esther Summerson—and find myself murmuring with Blake, "Expect poison from standing water," or with Swinburne and the Marquis de Sade, "Virtue is essentially sterile."[12]

We realize that there is a radical inconsistency in Dickens's presentation of Esther Summerson; indeed, we are made to feel that her aunt's Calvinis-tic terrorising of her is evil when the aunt says sternly, "Submission, self-denial, diligent work are the preparatives for a life begun with such a shadow [as that of bastardy] on it" (p. 13; bk. 1, ch. 3). But this is an accurate pre-diction of the way Esther lives: she totally submits to and internalizes the aggressor's view of her. It is never questioned, for instance, by herself or anyone else, that she should be the housekeeper at Bleak House and that she shall be wonderfully good at it. Dickens condemns the harsh moralizing about bastards but then implicitly endorses it.

We find, then, in Dickens, the popular author of the day, the scandalous subject of lesbianism that so shocked the first readers of Swinburne's *Poems and Ballads;* but Dickens was able to get away with it because he was master of the rhetoric of unctuous puritanism, whereas Swinburne insisted on inverting it.[13] It is one of the paradoxes of the Victorian period that one could get away with more then than one can now as long as one's language was appropriately pious. No man nowadays, for instance, would risk asking his lady friends if he could photograph their young daughters in the nude, but Lewis Carroll could and did; and his delicacy in the matter could be defended by quoting him as follows: "If I had the loveliest child in the world to draw or photograph, and found she had a modest shrinking (however slight, and however easily overcome) from being taken nude, I should feel it was a solemn duty owed to God to drop the request *altogether.*"[14] Well might Swinburne say, *"Ma corruption rougirait de leur pudeur."*[15] Carroll's remark, no less disturbing for being probably quite sincere, enables us to understand better the context of Swinburne's own fierce anti-theism.

We do not have to look far into Dickens to find another Swinburnean topic, the *femme fatale;* in Dickens, however, the proud, cold beauty who has sinned and is potentially destructive is tortured with relish rather than masochistically submitted to. Lady Dedlock of *Bleak House,* for instance, is beautiful, proud, a leader of the fashionable world, and exalted well beyond the reach of ordinary mortals, who can only stare from afar or console themselves by purchasing the Galaxy Gallery of British Beauty. Yet in the course of the novel she is made to submit to two men, Guppy and Tulkinghorn, and to visit the most noisome spot in London twice, the second time to die there in rags. Guppy, the shy and awkward unsuccessful suitor of Esther Summerson, is able to force Lady Dedlock to give him audience in spite of her loftiness. She has the fascinating deadliness of a *femme fatale,* for when it appears that Guppy possesses dangerous information, her "beautiful eyes" look at him in a way that would have made his life worth little had these been days "when ladies lived in strongholds and had unscrupulous attendants within call" (p. 309; ch. 29). When he again comes to see her to admit that he had no such information he "is put at disadvantage by the splendour and beauty of her appearance. She knows its influence perfectly; has studied it too well to miss a grain of its effect on any one . . . she looks at him steadily and coldly" (p. 357; ch. 33).

Proud and deadly as she is, however, Lady Dedlock has to succumb to the sadistic lawyer, Tulkinghorn, who is described by another character as "a slow-torturing kind of man" who "won't hold off and won't come on"

(p. 487; ch. 47)—in short, a sadistic tease. Throughout the novel his stealthy approach to Lady Dedlock is one of its more sinister elements. Dickens deliberately buries Tulkinghorn's motives in a Romantic gloom but suggests that perhaps "her beauty, and all the state and brilliancy surrounding her, only gives him the greater zest for what he is set upon" and that he is "cold and cruel" (p. 306; ch. 29). He triumphs when, after his final sadistic maneuver, she is forced to come to his bedroom. Dickens indicates subtly but unmistakably that his triumph is a sexual one. Although a man "severely and strictly self-repressed" and imperturbably emotionless throughout the book to this point, we are told that now "the blood has not flushed into his face so suddenly and redly for many a long year" as when he realizes that Lady Dedlock has come to his room, for now "he has conquered her." This unmistakably suggests sexual tumescence, the more so since Tulkinghorn has always been associated with the color black hitherto. When she walks toward the parapet beyond the window he follows her with a lover's "jealous glance," as he momentarily fears that she will elude him by throwing herself from it (pp. 436, 439; ch. 12). Henceforth, he has total power over her; the moment she makes a move without consulting him, he punishes her by the gloating insolence with which he lets her know that he is going to destroy her when he chooses—and, of course, he will not tell her exactly when.

Dickens' presentation of Tulkinghorn, the phallic overtones of whose name will not have escaped us, is an excellent study in perverted sexuality. But what is upsetting about it is our suspicion that Dickens as well as Tulkinghorn enjoys torturing the proud, inaccessible, rejecting woman; and that Dickens, always vulnerable on class grounds, and too proud to meet Queen Victoria when invited to do so while he was still in stage paint, finds a self-parodying alter ego in the Guppy, who manages in spite of his fatuousness, to require an audience from her. It is the hypocritical and sadistic puritanism of the society Lady Dedlock finds herself in that enables Tulkinghorn to have such power over her. She is guilty only of having a child by her lover before marrying Sir Leicester. But, as Tulkinghorn brutally reminds her, all he has to do is publish this to the world and "the wall chalking and the street-crying would come on directly" (p. 440; ch. 41). In the two scenes in which he triumphs over her the reader feels that, for dignity's sake, she should show him to the door and that her enduring him is indecent. Dickens and Tulkinghorn are able to make her go through with it because she has internalized society's verdict on herself much as her daughter, Esther Summerson, has. She admits that for a decent girl to have been her maid even for a moment is likely to disqualify her for a middle-class marriage, even to the son of Rouncewell, the eminently humane and wise ironmaster. Her submission to Tulkinghorn is functionless, for it does not make, and could not have made, any difference to the outcome; there is, therefore, no reason why she should not go straight to Sir Leicester. Eventually she condemns herself to death by exposure: Dickens and she seem to agree that what she has done deserves death. There is unfortunately no hint that Dickens disapproves of her internalization and acting out of so harsh a judgment.

The death that Dickens gives to Lady Dedlock is a terrible surrender to the myth that a fallen woman had better die than live. Swinburne, posing as a French critic shocked at English ways, exposed this myth ironically with reference to Shelly's heroine, Beatrice Cenci, the unfortunate victim of her father's lust: "[Shelley] has been reproached," Swinburne writes (and I am translating his excellent French), "for having made spring from Beatrice's lips, in the fifth act, this monstrous cry: 'I want to live!' A woman they maintain who has undergone what this young girl has undergone could only want to die." [16] There is no reason to suppose he would have been any less caustic with Dickens' handling of Lady Dedlock.

In *Bleak House*, then, the healthy sexual passion – that between Captain Hawdon and Lady Dedlock, does not appear, or only appears for moral condemnation. The perverted unhealthy passion of Tulkinghorn does appear and is an important part of the novel. Other relationships that would normally be sexual – those between Ada and Richard, Esther and Woodcourt, Caddy and Turveydrop – do not differ, as shown, from sexless companionship. The paradox is that in Dickens healthy sexuality is not dramatised or is mentioned only to be condemned, whereas perverse sexuality is extensively dramatised. Dickens the novelist, therefore, self-righteously and puritanically condemns illicit passion, but at the same time fills his novels with just the illicit titillation such puritanism helps to foster.

Acute as Dickens intuitively is about distorted sexuality, he has little capacity for perceiving the ambivalence of normal relationships; for instance, those between parents and children. Often when Dickens writes about the filial relationship, an element of fantasy appears to float in. Again and again the parent is given or offered total love, all-suffering and all-sufficing, unquestioned and always available regardless of what characteristics the parents show or whether the parents even want such love. What King Lear wanted and what Cordelia denied him, and what Goneril and Reagan falsely professed – parents in Dickens tend to get, unearned and unasked for. Florence Dombey throws herself at the stoney bosom of Mr. Dombey again and again, no matter how often she is rejected; Little Dorrit still nurtures Mr. Dorrit uncomplainingly however transcendent his mean self-regard and disregard of her become. Lucy Manette in *A Tale of Two Cities* heroically and instantly devotes the rest of her life to loving and protecting a father she has never seen before who has just been released from the Bastille; her suitor assures him that she will go on loving him, the father, for ever "with all the love and reliancy of infancy" although she is grown up, and that she clings to him with "the hands of baby, girl and woman." The father, Dr. Manette, once released from prison, steps instantly into the dream world Lear infantilely demands and does not get. (The reunion of Lucy and Manette seems to be, in fact, a debased version of the reunion of Lear and Cordelia.)

To judge from these instances, a child cannot be too filial for Dickens. At times he takes this fantasy a step further and seems to contemplate a sexless marriage between "father" and daughter. Such is the reader's protest against the union of Annie Strong and Dr. Strong, the white-haired, cherubic old dictionary maker in *David Copperfield*, and the contemplated union of Jarndyce and Esther Summerson that looms balefully for a while in *Bleak House*. Of course, no modern writer has been likely to do this kind of thing since Freud pointed out that men have to overcome the deference for women that stems from their deference for mother and sister (and, he might have added daughter) before they can love maturely.[17] In these instances, Dickens is not in the least hinting at incest, though this is the basis of the modern reader's resistance; rather he is a victim of his age's ideas about purity, or, at the least, chooses to appear so.

We find in Dickens, then, what we find in the society at large: much distorted sexuality, much moral condemnation of relatively minor deviations from the established sexual mores, and a determination to believe in false stereotypes of impossible purity as the standard for normal healthy people. Dickens thus ran no risk of offending public taste. It was far otherwise with Swinburne; Carlyle accused him of "sit[ting] in a cess pool, and adding to it" (*Letters*, II, 276 n.).[18] Another critic remarked that "he deserves credit for the audacious courage with which he has revealed to the world a mind all aflame with the feverish carnality of a schoolboy over the dirtiest passages in Lemprière [i.e., classical mythology]."[19]

How was it, indeed, that Swinburne came to be sitting in a cesspool? He had a representative mid-Victorian boyhood. His father was a High Church disciplinarian, quite as severe as the Calvinistic terrorisers of children in Dickens' novels, if, as is likely, the brutal Captain Harewood, in Swinburne's novel *Love's Cross Currents*, was modeled on his father. As a devout Protestant, the eighteen-year-old Swinburne wrote home from Cologne that he was so distressed at not being able to join Catholics in the prayer in a church one day that he "could have sat down and cried" (*Letters*, I, 4). Into his twenties he looked to Carlyle as a guide and teacher.[20] But by the age of twenty-eight, and probably much earlier, he had reached a position of advanced cultural relativism: he writes in a letter, "if people had read the classics, not to speak of the moderns very often, they must see that many qualities called virtues and vices depend on time, climate and temperament" (*Letters*, I, 137–38).

How had such a remarkable transition been effected? I think the answer has to do with two factors: the culture as Swinburne found it and his enormously wide reading. Swinburne grew up in a most remarkably dichotomized society, so dichotomized as to present any well-to-do- young man with the problem of reconciling the endless sermonising, the churchiness and the moral earnestness of the time with the apparently unparalleled development of the underworld of prostitution and commercialized sexual opportunities. It really does seem, for instance, that the more little girls were idealized, the more child-prostitution flourished. (It is jolting to see a Victorian pin-up of a ten year old girl, posed seductively: the world such pin-ups represent seems, indeed, beyond the flood.) Such a dichotomy is quite sufficient to pose any young man, but for Swinburne, aware of his sexual deviance, the dichotomy would be felt in a very acute form: he could either adopt the orthodox view of himself and suffer immeasurably, or regard it as an illusion. To the solution of the problem he brought the most precocious and cosmopolitan reading of literature of any creative writer of his time. He was a pioneering specialist in the Jacobean theater; he was probably better read in French literature than any other English poet has ever been and, unlike most of his contemporary critics of English literature, he took French literature completely seriously. Unlike Arnold he did not choose those minor French writers that suited his temperament, but read with passionate appreciation Balzac, Stendhal, Baudelaire, and Hugo, all considered more or less dangerous or immoral in England at that time. At some time or other Swinburne, it seems to me, must have started consciously seeking out literature that was as un-Victorian as possible; and certainly the Jacobeans, Blake, and the French must have been useful to him.

A remarkable feature of Swinburne's literary biography is the role the Marquis de Sade played in his imaginative life *before* he had read him. He seems to have known Janin's famous remark that de Sade would drive curates and curates' pupils to madness and death, and found this danger seductive.[21] In October 1861 Swinburne wrote to Monckton Milnes (later Lord Houghton), the editor of Keats and possessor of one of the best libraries of pornography in Europe, to remind him of his promise that Swinburne was one day to "look upon the mystic pages of the martyred marquis de Sade" (*Letters*, I, 46). A little later, apparently, Swinburne wrote a remarkable French poem about de Sade in the style of Victor Hugo, "Charenton" (*Letters*, I, 46 n.). Not until August 1862 was Swinburne able to write to Milnes his opinion of de Sade's *Justine*. He was deeply disappointed. He had looked for "some sharp and subtle analysis of lust—some keen dissection of pain and pleasure" (*Letters*, I, 54) but found only ludicrous arithmetical accumulations of merely physical events. He also looked forward to a discovery of

novel and recondite areas of the perverse but has to complain that there is nothing in de Sade that children have not "said, heard of, thought of, dreamed of, done, been tempted to do" (*Letters*, I, 56).

But Swinburne's disappointment went much deeper than this I think. He had expected some kind of metaphysical enlightenment. He was familiar with an intriguing remark of Dumas who had said, "Le marquis de Sade, voluptueux étrange! poursuit l'idéal de l'ésprit infini dans la torture de la matière bornée" (*Letters*, I, 55). This sort of preview had clearly raised Swinburne's hopes very high. In his disappointment he apostrophizes de Sade: "it is only too easy to pile up horrors, Marquis," writes Swinburne, now "show us how and why these things are as they are . . . you never do this once!" (*Letters*, I, 55).

"Charenton," the French poem celebrating de Sade that Swinburne wrote before he had read a word of de Sade, is of great interest, for it makes still clearer what Swinburne wanted from him. In this poem de Sade appears as the personification of all the sexual desires that society forbids and Swinburne evokes them at length by a clever imitation of the rhetoric of Victor Hugo (from whom Swinburne's interest in the poetry of atrocity probably derives).[22] He sees de Sade as one whom neither desire, nor man, nor God, nor frightful Virtue ("l'affreuse Vertu"), a gouge to the ulcerated heart, can hurt; de Sade looks on everything but is never dazzled.[23] Swinburne revered and admired the Marquis de Sade before having read him because he imagined that de Sade had freed himself from life's suffering by having gone into all the forbidden experiences and habituated himself to them. As a precocious undergraduate Swinburne had seen the Jacobean poet Webster in this way. Of the speech "Mine eyes dazzle: she died young" from *The Duchess of Malfi* he writes: "There is some thing in the man's clear, sad insight into sorrow and sin, which makes one shrink. The eyes that had seen this, how did they look on the common day? The ears that had taken those few quiet brief words, how did they listen to the usual conversation of men? . . . Is there no retribution for the poet who has gone so deep into the dark places where the sun is silent?"[24] What Swinburne felt about Webster seems to have informed his poem about de Sade.

One reason for Swinburne's attraction to de Sade (there are others, of course) is his desire to go "into the dark places where the sun is silent." Like de Sade—and Freud—Swinburne wanted to look on everything and not be dazzled; he wanted to give himself a training in thinking and contemplating the unthinkable. With Freud, he felt that that is the closest one can come to freedom from the suffering that is inherent in life.

In his most notorious poems, "Anactoria" and "Dolores," for instance, he can be seen as supplying the gap created by his disappointment in de Sade

—he provides us with a subtle psychology of lust and at the same time deals movingly with the question of how and why such things as he describes are as they are.

"Anactoria" is a monologue of 300 lines spoken by Sappho to a girl she loves. About one sixth of it consists of exquisitely phrased torments that Sappho would like to impose on Anactoria, but nevertheless the poem has more in common with Aeschylus, Swinburne's most revered model, than with de Sade—in general, in reading the early Swinburne a reader will go far less wrong approaching him as if he were Aeschylus than as if he were de Sade.[25] For "Anactoria" is a tragic poem. Sappho's envisioned cruelties are not merely sadistic; they express her hurt and anger towards an unfaithful and reluctant love and, further, in their very exquisiteness, they convey despair at being the involuntary vehicle of a futile lust which is driven to seek in ever greater refinements an ultimate gratification which is always retreating; or, as Dumas puts it, to seek infinite mind in limited matter. In the course of the poem Swinburne manages to universalize the psychology of lust much as Wordsworth does the psychology of the mind's interaction with Nature in "Tintern Abbey" and is no less concerned than Wordsworth with "the burthen of the mystery"—in Swinburne's phrase, "the mystery of the cruelty of things." The torments imagined (and only imagined) for Anactoria become metaphors for universal suffering. "Anactoria" is written in heroic couplets and at times sounds like Pope: for instance, the concision ("their" anticipates its referent, "lips") and the diction of: "Yea, though their alien kisses do me wrong, Sweeter thy lips than mine with all their song" (p. 61). In this poem Swinburne is at times urbanely yet movingly elegiac in a way reminiscent of the Pope of "Elegy to the Memory of an Unfortunate Lady"; and the violence and suddenness of Sappho's shifts in mood remind us of Pope's "Eloisa to Abelard," for Swinburne too is dealing with the ultimate anguish and despair of a lover. Sappho, in her wounded pride, alternates between acknowledging her inferiority to Anactoria in spite of her poetic gifts and triumphant assertion of her own immortality over Anactoria's transience. But ultimately her awareness of her greatness as a poet does not assuage her suffering, and the close is tragic:

> Alas, that neither moon nor snow nor dew
> Nor all cold things can purge me wholly through,
> Assuage me nor allay me nor appease,
> Till supreme sleep shall bring me bloodless ease;
> Till time wax faint in all his periods;
> Till fate undo the bondage of the gods,
> And lay, to slake and satiate me all through,

> Lotus and Lethe on my lips like dew,
> And shed around and over and under me
> Thick darkness and the insuperable sea.　(p. 66)

We notice here the felicity and unexpectedness of "bloodless," a pun in which "blood" has, besides its obvious sense, the Shakespearean-Jacobean connotations of "hot blood" (passion) that cannot be "allayed" or cooled. The splendid last line in context suggests, in addition to the oblivion of death, the troubled confusion in which Sappho has lived and the submission to the necessities of her nature that has been imposed on her.

Swinburne, as urbane a writer as Nabokov, with whom he has much in common, in this poem takes as his subject matter a sexual perversion and fashions it into a work of art that is beautiful in itself, like *Lolita,* and which touches on the horror, and the frustration and the transience of life in a way that is strangely moving; like *Lolita,* too, it is at the same time a gauntlet thrown down to the Philistines. Dickens, by comparison one might say, intends his Miss Wade, his lesbian, to be tragic but writes merely an oversimplified case history, although a very intuitive one; and allows conventional morality to gravely distort his treatment of Tattycoram and Esther Summerson.

If "Anactoria" can be seen as Swinburne's "Tintern Abbey," "Dolores," another notorious poem, can be seen as a much extended Keatsian ode; in it, stanza by stanza, and from different exploratory perspectives, Swinburne looks at one perplexing object, Dolores, Our Lady of Pain, a *femme fatale* made over into an alternative Madonna. Dolores, like Keats' Melancholy, is set up as a goddess within a shrine, into the inner sanctum of which it is a privilege to have been admitted; and she too is a goddess whose devotees have been initiated into the mystery of the interconnection of pain and pleasure which the poem delicately explores. The poisonous queen, the sterile Dolores, is resorted to only as a retreat from the cruelty of life, for which the poem is thus a metaphor. Brooding on Dolores, Swinburne evokes the sufferings of the gladiator and the Christian martyrs as Hugo does in his poem on Roman decadence.[26] By referring without passing judgment to the days when "gardens were lit with live torches" of burning Christians, Swinburne undoubtedly meant to be outrageous to his immediate audience; but he is raising the problem of those cultures in which the state has institutionalized the most terrible kinds of sadism. The historical perspective universalizes the problem in a disturbing way; what are we to make of man—and of ourselves—given that such things happen?

How does "Dolores" compare with Dickens' treatment of the strange bondage of Tulkinghorn to Lady Dedlock and of Lady Dedlock to Tulkinghorn? It is on the whole too easy to feel that we could never be like Tulkinghorn;

but in "Dolores" Swinburne's subtle psychology of lust makes us feel the fascination of the *femme fatale* and of those parts of Gibbon that every reader reads with increased attention. Swinburne is intimating the presence of the sado-masochistic syndrome within any personality, as Dickens, endorsing the orthodoxy of purity, could not. At the same time, Dickens as a best seller depends on such secret sympathies with cruelty and submission as Swinburne lays bare.

How was it that *Poems and Ballads* was found to be so shocking? It was because Swinburne had dared to do what he says Shakespeare does in *Measure for Measure*, "grapple with the most terrible of energies and passions."[27] But he did so while totally refraining from judgment, the language of moral outrage or melodramatic denunciation. It was in a way dishonest of the Victorians to be shocked at *Poems and Ballads* because much of the subject matter is to be found in the vastly popular Dickens.

The tragedy *Atlanta in Calydon* is Swinburne's masterpiece and one of the best long poems of the Victorian period, and yet it is very little read in comparison to *In Memoriam* or *The Ring and the Book*—partly, perhaps, because critics like T.S. Eliot and F.R. Leavis dismiss it without having read it, as far as one can tell.[28] Some critics that do read it, such as Praz, seem to assume that a masochist is always a masochist even when he writes a tragedy. Yet *Atalanta*, besides being a dazzling imitation and lyrically beautiful, is a penetrating study of "a match of passions to the death between a mother and a son" (Swinburne's formulation of the theme of *Coriolanus*).[29] Althaea, the mother, kills her son because she cannot stand to see herself displaced in her son's affections by a strange girl. Meleager is unable to free himself from the terrible rooted love that "burns" between himself and his mother while at the same time he suffers from an unrequited passion for Atalanta. Atalanta has chosen a celibate life, but the cost is considerable and she yearns for motherhood. Finding herself a murderer of her own son Althaea yearns for the days before puberty. For each of these characters sexuality is, in different ways, a scourge; and, in a chorus, the fall of man is identified with the birth of Venus. With marvelous insight Swinburne shows us how two people, a mother and son, bitterly at odds, goad each other even while appearing to be talking about matters totally unrelated to their division. As their altercation proceeds each produces elaborate rhetorical structures in a futile attempt to prevail over the other. The best speech in the play, perhaps, comes after Meleager, the son, has succeeded in hurting his mother more than she was able to hurt him, and by winning he loses, for her vulnerability is far more potent than her arguments when she retorts:

> there is nothing stabile in the world
> But the gods break it; yet not less, fair son,

If but one thing be stronger, if one endure,
Surely the bitter and the rooted love
That burns between us, going from me to thee,
Shall more endure than all things. What dost thou,
Following strange loves? why wilt thou kill mine heart?[30]

More than three hundred lines of taut conflict suddenly produce this moment in which the truth slips out, "What dost thou, / Following strange loves? why wilt thou kill mine heart?" That the mind's censorship should so slip shows us how vulnerable Althaea has become — and it is the perception of her vulnerability that draws submission from Meleager: "there is nothing terribler to men / Than the sweet face of mothers, and the might" (p. 273).

Althaea wins here in a way she could not have intended; but when Meleager later inadvertently shows that he still prefers Atalanta to her, she kills him. In his last lines Meleager says that it does not dishonor him to die for Atalanta; rather, it honors him. Praz takes this to be the masochist's submission to a *femme fatale*. But in the first place, Atalanta is not a *femme fatale*, and, in the second, the dramatic point of this speech in context is that it is a needle in Althaea's heart, a final assertion of his love of Atalanta.

Ruskin said that in Atalanta there are conceptions of purity beyond anything that so strong a man ever wrote (*Letters*, I, 184) — an interesting judgment. For Swinburne has seen that innocence is only something that is yearned for amid the complexity of suffering that real life involves. The death wish he sometimes expresses is really an expression of the desire to have the burden of sexuality taken off him; but in the foreground always is the recognition that Aphrodite is indeed a terrible, destructive, and inescapable goddess. As Marcus shows in *The Other Victorians*, most Victorians thought so too, but in public the sentiment only got itself expressed in a furtive and clandestine way.

In *Atalanta in Calydon* Swinburne shows his ability to perceive and dramatize ambivalence in the parent-child relationship beyond anything Dickens could have done, because in order to do so in the Victorian period, one had to step decisively outside of the framework of accepted ideas about parents and children, a mythology based on ideals of what ought to be rather than what is.[31]

Dickens was, of course, a much greater genius than Swinburne; but for certain Victorians, Swinburne was a necessary author in ways that Dickens could never have been. Two of them are of especial interest. Ruskin, as a child the victim of Evangelical disciplinarians and a mother so interferingly overprotective as later to accompany him to college, was tragically awry in his own sexual development, yet writes movingly, in a letter to Swinburne: "God made you . . . and you are very wonderful and beautiful. To me your work may be dreadful or deadly – it may be in a deeper sense, or in certain relations, *helpful* and *medicinal*" (*Letters*, I, 182; italics added). The other, D.H. Lawrence wrote, at the time of *Women in Love*, "Swinburne is a great revealer, very great. . . . He is the last fiery spirit among us . . . How wicked the world has been to jeer at his physical appearance . . . There is more powerful rushing flame of life in him than in all the heroes rolled together."[32]

The England of the mid-Victorian period needed, and was lucky to get, its *Poems and Ballads* and *Atalanta in Calydon*, as America in the 1950s perhaps needed, and was lucky enough to get, its *Lolita*. We need these works for their inherent beauty, but also for test cases whenever the claim that art must be moral gets too insistent – and whenever the question of whether there is an inherently wholesome or unwholesome subject matter for art comes up.

Notes

1. James A. Froude, *My Relations with Carlyle* (London: Longman's, 1903), p. 23.

2. Steven Marcus, *The Other Victorians: A Study of Sexuality and Pornography in Mid-Nineteenth-Century England* (New York: Basic Books, 1966).

3. The phrase "merely the hallucination of a meaning" is T.S. Eliot's, in *Selected Essays* (London: Faber and Faber, 1932), p. 327. Jerome J. McGann's distinguished *Swinburne: an Experiment in Criticism* (Chicago: Univ. of Chicago Press, 1972), a work remarkable for its subtle empathy with Swinburne, has done much to demolish the slanders of readers such as Eliot.

4. See Edmund Gosse's account printed in *The Swinburne Letters*, ed. Cecil Y. Lang (New Haven: Yale Univ. Press, 1959), VI, 246–47; hereafter cited as *Letters*. Lang remarks that "it is impossible to separate fact from fancy in the romance of Swinburne and Adah Isaacs Menken" and that the only two established *facts* are that she was born and that Swinburne wrote in a letter to a friend that she was "most loveable as a friend as well as a mistress" (ibid., I, 276n.).

5. See Ada Nisbet's survey of the evidence in *Dickens and Ellen Ternan* (Berkeley: Univ. of California Press, 1952). Dickens met Ellen Ternan before the separation from his wife and their closer relationship seems to date from after the separation, but the marriage had not been annulled.

6. Mario Praz, *The Romantic Agony*, trans. Angus Davidson, 2d ed. (1951; rpt. London: Oxford Univ. Press, 1970).

7. Praz, p. 455 n.

8. See also Jared Wenger, "Character-Types of Scott, Balzac Dickens and Zola," *PMLA*, 62 (1947), 224–25.

9. Charles Dickens, *Bleak House* (Boston: Houghton Mifflin, 1956), p. 530; ch. 51. References in the text will be to this edition.

10. Charles Dickens, *Little Dorrit*, ed. John Holloway (Harmondsworth, Eng.: Penguin Books, 1967), p. 64; bk. 1, ch. 2. References in the text will be to this edition.

11. John Wain points this out in his *"Little Dorrit"* in *Dickens and the Twentieth Century,* ed. John Gross and Gabriel Pearson (London: Routledge and Kegan Paul, 1962), p. 180.

12. Ruskin once advised Swinburne not to publish *Poems and Ballads:* "The world does not want more imaginary tragedy than it possesses and I think every man of intellectual power should now devote himself to overthrowing its idols and leading the way to healthy conceptions and healthy work. I should be sorry that you publish these poems, for I think they would win you a dark reputation, and take away from your future power of teaching and delighting" (*Letters,* I, 85–86n.). Swinburne's response to this, in a letter to William Michael Rossetti, was, "I cannot understand [Ruskin's] combining philanthropic morality with such exquisite sense of what is right and good in things far higher than any matter of right and wrong selon les reveurs. Yet I refrained from citing Justine—'La vertu, ma chère J., est une chose essentiellement stérile, impuissante, bornée, tandis que le vice fait germer et fleurir" (*Letters,* I, 86). Swinburne was hard at work on Blake at this time.

13. Swinburne complained of the dichotomized responses of Victorians to literature: "It is really very odd that people (friendly or unfriendly) will not let one be an artist, but must needs make one out a parson or a pimp" (*Letters,* I, 193). Dickens, when dealing with a Little Emily, or a Lady Dedlock, settles for being a parson.

14. Helmut Gernsheim introduces this extract from a letter of Carrol's as "demonstrat[ing] his delicacy in this matter." See *Lewis Carrol—Photographer* (London: Max Parrish, 1950), excerpted in *Alice in Wonderland,* ed. Donald J. Gray (New York: Norton, 1971), p. 290.

15. "Notes on Poems and Reviews," rpt. in *Swinburne Replies,* ed. Clyde Kenneth Hyder (Syracuse: Syracuse Univ. Press, 1966), p. 19.

16. "On a reproché au poète d'avoir fait jaillir des lèvres de Béatrice, au cinquième acte, ce cri monstrueux: Je veux vivre. Une femme, a-t-on dit, qui a subi ce qu'avait subi cette jeune fille, ne saurer désirer que la mort." See "Les Cenci," in *The Complete Works of Algernon Charles Swinburne,* ed. Edmund Gosse and T.J. Wise, (London: Heinemann, 1925–27), XV, 322; hereafter cited as *Complete Works.* Swinburne's choice of French for this essay is itself, of course, a satiric device for emphasizing the stuffy parochialism of the England of his day.

17. See "The Most Prevalent Form of Degradation in Erotic Life," in Sigmund Freud, *Sexuality and the Psychology of Love,* ed. Philip Rieff (New York: Collier, 1963), pp. 58–70. Freud seems to explain why for some readers the match between David Copperfield and Agnes, who throughout the novel has been thought of by David as a "sister" and associated with light coming through church windows, is so repugnant.

18. Lang quotes Carlyle as a gloss to Swinburne's angry response to the remark in *Letters;* cf. D.A. Wilson and D.W. MacArthur, *Carlyle in Old Age, 1865–1881* (New York, 1934), pp. 137–38.

19. John Morley, "Mr. Swinburne's New Poems: *Poems and Ballads,*" in *Victorian Poetry and Poetics,* ed. Walter E. Houghton and G. Robert Stange, 2d ed. (Boston: Houghton Mifflin, 1968), p. 880.

20. "I must confess that my own belief in the prophet of Craigenputtock as an

inspired guide and teacher did not long survive the expiration of my teens." See "Recollections of Professor Jowett," in Swinburne's *Complete Works*, XV, 245.

21. In his report to Milnes after his first reading of *Justine* Swinburne says, "You see that whether it drives curates and curates' pupils to madness and death or not (Janin says it does – and Janin has the lips that cannot lie) it has done decidedly little damage to my brain or nerves" (*Letters*, I, 57). For Janin on de Sade see Praz, *Romantic Agony*, pp. 126–30.

22. Cecil Y. Lang prints "Charenton" in his *New Writings by Swinburne* (Syracuse: Syracuse Univ. Press, 1964), pp. 7–10, dates it precisely and points out many parallels with Hugo (pp. 178–80). He does not point out, however, the similarity in subject matter between Hugo in a certain mood and the Swinburne who evokes the atrocities of ancient Rome. For instance, when Swinburne read the following he must have realized how different Hugo was from any contemporary writer in England:

> Le boue et l'or régnaient. Dans les cachots profonds
> Les bourreaux' s'accouplaient à des martyres mortes.
> Rome horrible chantait. Parfois, devant ses portes,
> Quelque Crassus, vainqueur d'esclaves et de rois,
> Plantait le grand chemin de vaincus mis en croix;
> Et, quand Catulle, amant que notre extase écoute,
> Errait avec Délie, aux deux bords de la route,
> Six milles arbres humains saignaient sur leurs amours.
> ("Decadence de Rome," ll. 18–25
> from *La Légende des Siècles*)

As Swinburne later does in "Charenton," Hugo makes brief epigrammatic references to legendary figures of the ancient world in order to evoke exotic and forbidden experiences: "Messaline en riant se mettait toute nue, / Et sur le lit public, lascive, se couchait" (ll. 28–29). Like Hugo, Swinburne tries to bring back to life, by the felicity of his rhetoric, the extravagant passions of the ancient world, "Tout ce grand siècle éteint qui n'est qu'un brouillard pâle" ("Charenton," l.19). "Décadence de Rome" was published in 1859; when the entire collection of *La Légende des Siècles* was published in 1883, Swinburne said, "the greatest work of the century is now at length complete" (*Complete Works*, XIII, 112).

23.   On sentait, à le voir rire et songer, que rien,
> Ni le Désir dont l'oeil éblouissant étonne,
> Ni l'Homme qui rugit, ni Dieu qui trompe et tonne,
> Ni l'affreuse Vertu, gouge au coeur ulcéré,
> N'aurait su mettre un pli sur ce front vénéré,
> . . . .
> Il vit tout, mais jamais il ne fut ébloui.
> "Charenton," ll. 10–14, 70.

24. "The Early English Dramatists," in Lang, *New Writings*, p. 38. Swinburne continues, "too much honour cannot be given to the brave clear intellect, the earnest and fearless heart of such writers as these" (p. 39).

25. Swinburne saw Tennyson as the dominant poet of his time (. . . "Tennyson, into whose church we were all in my time born and baptized" [*Letters*, I, 97]) but also as the poet who had made the idyll the dominant form (so that "with English versifiers now, the idyllic form is alone in favor" ["Notes on Poems and Reviews," *Swinburne Replies*, p. 31]). He criticizes *The Idylls of the King* severely for failing to be Aeschylean: "the story as it stood of old had in it something almost of Hellenic dignity and significance . . . as in the great Greek legends" but Tennyson has emasculated it by suppressing the root of the evil, the incest between Arthur and his half-sister and so reduced it to "a case for the divorce court" which is the equivalent to omitting the sacrifice of Iphigeneia from the *Oresteia* ("Under the Microscope," *Swinburne Replies*, pp. 57, 58). The second epigraph for *Atalanta* is from Aeschylus and in his letters Swinburne boasts that "it is pure Greek, and the first poem of its sort in modern times, combining lyric and dramatic work on the old principle" (*Letters*, I, 115). Swinburne sees Aeschylus as a supreme genius who ranks with Michelangelo and Shakespeare and in a passage in which he tries to express his sense of the greatness of these three his diction strongly reminds us of "Anactoria" as well as *Atalanta* ("Notes on Designs of the Old Masters at Florence," *Complete Works*, XV, 158). Of the writing of *Erechtheus* he says, "it must always be . . . evident that I am, in this line of work, above all things a disciple of Aeschylus . . . I am more than ever convinced that all great Greek subjects, historic or mythical, national or spiritual are of universal and lasting import, in a sense and to a degree in which this can be said of no others, ancient or modern" (*Letters*, III, 55–56).

26. See note 22 above.

27. "A Study of Shakespeare," *Complete Works*, XI, 28.

28. T.S. Eliot does say "we should like to have the *Atalanta* entire" but is still able to claim within a page or two that the choruses do not have "even the significance of commonplace" and that in Swinburne generally "the meaning is the hallucination of meaning" (*Selected Essays*, pp. 323, 326, 327). F.R. Leavis calls the chorus, "When the hounds of spring are on the winter's traces," Swinburne's "best-known piece" without any apparent awareness that it is a small fragment of a first-rate long work and bases a sweeping judgment of Swinburne on an analysis of the first stanza only. See F.R. Leavis, *Revaluation, Tradition and Development in English Poetry* (London: Chatto and Windus, 1936), pp. 238–40.

29. "A Study of Shakespeare," *Complete Works*, XI, 134.

30. *The Poems of Algernon Charles Swinburne* (London: Chatto and Windus, 1904), IV, 272.

31. It is enlightening to compare the idealization of mothers in *Tom Brown's Schooldays* with Swinburne's portrayal of Althaea.

32. *The Collected Letters of D.H. Lawrence*, ed. Harry T. Moore (London: Heinemann, 1962), I, 474.

Mark Spilka

On the Enrichment of
Poor Monkeys by Myth and Dream;
or, How Dickens Rousseauisticized
and Pre-Freudianized
Victorian Views of Childhood

Poor Monkey was the original title of Peter Coveney's book, *The Image of Childhood*, which covers that literary theme from Rousseau to Freud in a manner still unsurpassed. In revising his book for a new edition in 1967 Coveney had chosen his second title for its explanatory value, but his first and more poetic title had been chosen a decade earlier for its happy union of Shakespeare with Henry James.[1] Let me begin my own pondering of the childhood theme with some comments on that extraordinary if obscure conjunction.

"Now God help thee, poor monkey!" says Lady Macduff to her son in *Macbeth* (IV, ii), just before the slaughtering of that innocent and vulnerable family by Macbeth's bloody henchmen. In the prologue to Henry James's novel of 1897, *What Maisie Knew*, a concerned lady similarly responds to Maisie's role as a shuttlecock for divorcing parents: "'Poor little monkey!' she at last exclaimed; and the words were an epitaph for the tomb of Maisie's childhood." Shakespeare's wise and witty child is, of course, literally entombed. After a brief exchange with his mother on his father's apparent desertion of his family, and some apt remarks on the buying and selling of new husbands, he defies his intruding murderers and is quickly slain. But James's ultimately wiser child, waiting as it were in the wings, now moves to the dramatic foreground as the point of view and reflector on her own figurative entombment, which becomes in turn the novel's central agon. Let us take that useful contrast as our paradigm for the enrichment of poor monkeys in the nineteenth century, when childhood first emerged as a major literary theme, thanks largely to the genius, not of Henry James, but of Shakespeare's true Victorian heir, the Inimitable – and therefore highly imitable – Charles Dickens.

I

The innocence and vulnerability of children like Maisie and young Macduff are defining aspects of their role in literature; yet curiously they do not even begin to play that role in any dominant or important way until the late eighteenth and early nineteenth centuries. There are few children, and none of them in leading roles, in the plays of Shakespeare and his contemporaries. There are of course those tragic adolescents, Romeo and Juliet, whom Shakespeare saw as young adults; but even when the adolescent quality of their lovers' world is heightened, as was beautifully the case in the Zeffirelli film of 1968, the point about childhood in that world is that it quickly moves to young adulthood, that the bridge to adulthood is short and swift and may indeed end in early death.

Perhaps the relative brevity of childhood and adolescence is one reason for their delayed entrance as important literary themes. The prolongation of adolescence, the lengthening and complication of the journey into adulthood, are comparatively recent phenomena. If a boy can become a man at thirteen in the old Jewish tradition, if a girl can marry at fourteen in Shakespeare's time, then there is nothing especially problematic about childhood; no great gulf separates children from adults, and the center of life, interest, and significant conflict remains the adult world. Hamlet may question the validity and value of that world and may die in the attempt to cleanse it; but it is an adult world he lives and dies in. So too with Juliet and Romeo; and Lady Macduff's "poor monkey" only heightens the horror of that world with a moment's pathos through his sudden death.

The point in cultural history when childhood and adulthood become separate and opposing worlds is clearly the late eighteenth century, when the industrial revolution begins and the political and social revolutions in France, England, and elsewhere mark the emergence of modern society—an urban, mercantile, and democratic society in which the middle class rises while the upper class falls and the poor shift to the city in great numbers. It is of course the middle class in particular which fosters late marriages; which insists on the extension of educational opportunities for its children; and which keeps them children accordingly for longer periods of time, preparing them—ostensibly—for the increasing complexities of the adult world through a curious and perhaps necessary process of prolonged insulation and isolation from it. On the one hand, then, there is the long, insulated journey toward adulthood, and on the other, increasing complexities and difficulties, confusions and alarums, oppressive levelings and assorted blights, in the adult world itself. The opposition which the French philosopher Rousseau had formulated in theory in the eighteenth century has become more and more a fact of modern society, and has in fact been reformulated in our time by the American maverick Paul Goodman as an opposition which makes for "growing up absurd."[2]

But if the adult world now seems – by all reports – absurd, it had seemed rational enough in the eighteenth century, where all such judgments begin, and its denizens had even been deemed innately benevolent by some observers. The notion of innate benevolence, along with others like it, had been generated by those changing philosophical perspectives on the acquisition of knowledge and identity which Ian Watt discusses in *The Rise of the Novel*.[3] Thus, in that leveling age when kings and bishops toppled off high perches, the already fallen creatures below them were no longer conceived as receivers of given places in a fixed vertical hierarchy, and of given rules for living; they were conceived rather as individual perceivers – born free, equal, and by some lights benevolent   who in learning how to live might shape their own identities and futures in a relatively open and largely horizontal world. The search for new Edens in America and elsewhere, new fortunes in trade, new places in the social sun, and the renewal also in social, economic, political, and religious spheres of the Renaissance emphasis on individualism, contributed to this optimistic view of personal happiness and its rightful pursuit. *Robinson Crusoe* was one eighteenth-century celebration of the individual's athletic capacities for pursuing happiness. *Moll Flanders* and *Pamela*, *Joseph Andrews* and *Tom Jones*, spoke similarly to the resilient powers of thriving individuals. But the notion that such thriving free-born souls were also born benevolent, and thus willing and vigorously able to share their hardwon happiness with less fortunate strivers, was soon questioned.

In *Virtue in Distress* R.F. Brissenden argues that the sentimental eighteenth-century notion of Benevolent Man was quickly undermined by the glaring contradiction of inequities and injustices in a society composed, supposedly, of amiable free-born persons, and that the originally positive meaning of words like "sentimental" was similarly undermined. Worse yet, the sentimental person, the man or woman of feeling or sensibility, was soon recognized as a weak, vulnerable, essentially short-sighted person, rather than a thriving soul, and therefore as fair game for satire or savaging by such as Jane Austen in England and the Marquis de Sade in France.[4] That adverse reaction was, however, almost equally shortlived. As Brissenden fails to note, words like benevolence, sentimentality, and sensibility would regain their positive currency by mid-nineteenth century, particularly in England, where the delayed impact of Rousseau's concept of Original Innocence would be most strongly felt and where the essential features of his outlook would be most thoroughly domesticated.

Rousseau had developed his seminal views in mid-eighteenth century. He believed in the uncorrupted child of Nature, born in a state of innocence and threatened by the corruption of the adult social world. He further associated Nature with innate human qualities like Feeling, Sensibility, and Imagination. Reason had been aligned with such qualities by the original notion of sensibility, but had become divorced from them as the inadequacies of the benevolent view of man became increasingly—indeed, embarrassingly—evident. It was at that point, in what is now more often called an Age of Reason than an Age of Sensibility, that the conflict between sense and sensibility began, and the failure of the age to cure its social ills was attributed by the advocates of sensibility to reason, and by the advocates of reason to sensibility. Our present placard notions of the Romantic opposition to the Age of Reason as the century turned—the opposition, that is, of Nature-Feeling-Innocence-Childhood, on the one hand, to Society-Reason-Corruption-Adulthood, on the other—derive from that conflict, and so obscure Rousseau's actual belief in the rational cultivation of those naturally benevolent aspects of childhood which might eventually offset social ills—a belief so radical, I might add, that it would eventually displace innately Benevolent Man with his much more plausible successor, the Benevolent Child in need of loving nurture, who as Wordsworth early saw, and as Dostoevsky later insisted, was the only possible Father of Benevolent Man.

Consider in this light Rousseau's emphasis on the child as a being important in itself—not a diminutive adult, not a passive creature or a tabula rasa to be shaped wholly by training and experience, as in certain eighteenth-century theories—but a self-active soul endowed with natural tendencies to virtue which needed careful nourishment. Or consider the departure here from still older theories: instead of training a child out of its active ills, its childish or animalistic or innately sinful ways, through reason, the originally benevolent nature of the child was to be more fully developed and drawn out by rational procedures: its natural or spontaneous capacity for feeling, what might be called its *affective* innocence, was to be cultivated, much in the manner of current progressive educational systems. The reversal here of eighteenth-century theories was a reversal also of the severe Christian doctrine of Original Sin, the fallen state of natural vice from which children were to be rescued by rational virtue. Rousseau had replaced this older view, surviving from the Middle Ages, with another Christian doctrine, that of Original Innocence or natural virtue, as evinced in the attitude of Christ himself toward little children. In the nineteenth century, when the Evangelical view of childhood flourished, these doctrines would often exist side by side, in modified forms, as applied to different aspects of sensibility—the sinful passions and the innocent affections. But for the moment the important fact to note is the enormous secular influence of the new doctrine of childhood innocence.

The English Romantic poets, notably Blake, Wordsworth, and Coleridge, transposed this doctrine into poetry quite effectively, and, in the process, gave the childhood theme its first important literary utterance. The appeal of the child in a state of nature to these advocates of feeling, spontaneity, and imagination seems obvious enough. Blake stressed the joys of infancy, expanded them even to the joys of innocent sexuality in later life – an expansion his own culture would reject, but which would be advanced in our time by such neo-Romantics as D.H. Lawrence and Norman O. Brown to a more receptive age. Wordsworth, especially in the Immortality Ode, set a pattern of approach to childhood for future decades in his regret for lost innocence and lost religious vision, in his awareness too of the closing shades of the social prison, and in his adult solace through the "philosophic mind" with its fuller grasp of human sorrow. Coleridge stressed the intuitive, imaginative quality of the child's soul and the need to develop that quality further in adulthood by cultivating the child's capacity for wonder, joy, and spontaneity. Again these placard views are more pliant and complex than I have indicated. The important point is that they flourished among Nature poets, cultivators of solitude and communion with nature and with natural types like peasants and children; and that the Victorian novelists, who are essentially urban, social, or immersed in social and civic conflict, transposed them from that source.

The chief transposition was made by Dickens in novels like *Oliver Twist, Dombey and Son, David Copperfield, Bleak House,* and *Great Expectations* – novels in which the infantile perspective is directly or indirectly employed as the dominant point of view. It was Dickens who made the child the emotional, the *affective* center of fiction and used him or her as his validating touchstone for human worth. It was Dickens too who gave symbolic order to the social disorders of his day, especially in later works where the shades of the social prison, legal maze, or dustheap become controlling metaphors. These two devices of Romantic poetry, the use of the child as affective center and the use of controlling metaphors, were applied by Dickens to urban and industrial culture and its many problems. The full force of his achievement may be seen by comparing his best novels with those of other early Victorians who also record the ravages of industrialism in terms of its toll on childhood. Disraeli, Mrs. Gaskell, and Kingsley, in their social novels, depict hunger, starvation, and death among little children; but none of them is able to convey those afflictions from the child's perspective or to give them focus and concentration through symbolic order; nor are they able to command the emotional and attitudinal range which Dickens brought to his subject. For Dickens was working closer to the emotional heart of the problem – the quality of life, not among the suffering poor, but in the Victorian middle-class home, from which cultural center the nature of Victorian life, its values and aspirations, its tone and direction, were manifestly shaped.

It is from this environment that Dickens' children are usually drawn and then subjected to lower class ordeals, as Dickens himself was in childhood. We must turn to the Victorian home, then, as incidentally Peter Coveney does not, for our most important clues to the nature of the childhood theme and of the several curious splits in sensibility that theme entails.

II

Sociologists speak of the modern home as fragmented, a mere meeting ground and point of departure for its busy inhabitants, a kind of domestic freeway. But in the Victorian age middle-class homes were conceived as proverbial castles, places of refuge and sanctity, bulwarks against an increasingly commercial and urban culture characterized by ruthless economic practices, by the blight of slums and factories where the poor and their children labored for long hours, and by the blight also of prostitution and crime. In Dickens' *Great Expectations* a criminal lawyer's aide named Wemmick wears two faces expressing the split between domestic and urban culture: one face, hard and wooden, with a postal slit for a mouth, he wears in the city; the other face, genial and relaxed, humane and sensitive, he wears in his home, which he literally calls his castle and models along castle lines, with artificial moat and drawbridge and tiny cannons at the entrance. One face is designed to meet the corrupt dehumanizing commercialization of city life; the other the beneficent and genial aspects of domestic life, to which narrow pound the now two-faced Benevolent Man of the eighteenth century has obviously retreated, as indeed he had often retreated in his own time – after long exposure to worldly ills – to more pastoral environs.

As these last thoughts imply, the Victorian home was also conceived as a pastoral retreat. "In the recoil from the City," writes Walter Houghton in *The Victorian Frame of Mind*, "the home was irradiated by the light of a pastoral imagination. It could seem a country of peace and innocence where life was kind and duty natural." "A tent pitch'd in a world not right," said Victorian poet Coventry Patmore; "a bright, serene, restful, joyful nook of heaven in an unheavenly world," said moralist Brockden Brown. Whether urban or suburban, then, the Victorian home continued the pastoral and romantic tradition of the country refuge. But since it was not in fact a country refuge, its pastoral advantages were peculiarly confined and intensified:

> In the home so conceived [writes Houghton], man could recover the humanity he seemed to be losing. Under the intense pressure of competitive life, he felt more and more like a money-making machine, or a cog in the vast mechanism of modern business. . . . But in the home he might escape from this inhuman world. . . . He might feel his heart beating again in the atmosphere of do-

mestic affection and the binding companionship of the family.
. . . Small wonder the Victorian home was sentimentalized [adds
Houghton]. In the reaction from a heartless world the domestic
emotions were released too strongly and indulged too eagerly.
Indeed, it may be only by the unabashed display of feeling that
one can prove unmistakably to all the world, himself included,
that he has a heart.[5]

Thus Houghton explains how and why the eighteenth-century cult of sensibility was domesticated in Victorian times. The result of that process was,
I think, a hothouse atmosphere of intense domestic feeling—an atmosphere,
moreover, in which certain curiously heightened values flourished.

The damaging blows to religion from the advances of science and the
growth of hardheaded materialism had created a moral and religious crisis
in the culture at large. The Evangelical movement as it spread through all
religious sects may be taken as exemplary of the vigorous response to that
dilemma; and yet whatever its enthusiasms, and however commendable its
philanthropic aims, it tended to confuse respectability and diligence with
spiritual grace and so gave sanction to the new commercial ethos. In that
already sacred refuge, the home, moreover, where its chief impact was felt,
it further intensified the hothouse atmosphere by sanctifying domestic roles
and relations. Thus, under the new Evangelical aegis, women took on moral
and religious roles formerly assigned to churchly figures: mother and sisters
were seen as saints and angels, vessels of spiritual perfection, guardians of
religious and moral certitudes which flourished nowhere else. Little children too, under the combined aegis of Rousseau and the evangelists, were
considered pure and untainted, girls more especially than boys since they
seemed daintier and cleaner and had more stake in remaining virginal until
marriage. Even fathers, through their exposure to urban ills, took on religious functions: for when not overindulging their affections they served as
severe disciplinarians of their children and as patriarchal protectors from
encroaching evils. By the end of the century this parental combination of
pious affection and grim correction would seem confusing to many observers, who read its double message in highly critical terms. But in fact new
evils did exist outside Victorian homes, and the Evangelical stress on the
domestic affections, on the one hand, and on strict obedience and harsh
punishment on the other, was designed to meet them. In an age of moral
and religious crisis, affection and correction were, I think, survival strategies, ways of insulating children from a godless heartless world. They were,
moreover, effective strategies, producing a nation which still prizes obedience,
especially in its children (as Margaret Thatcher had occasion recently to remind us), and which in its queues and courtesies and unarmed civic order

is still one of the wonders of the western world. The Victorians managed well, then, in insulating their children from the new commercial ethos — which they also managed to promote. But they were less successful in coping with the chief evil of their day, sexual depravity, which they tended to see as the only evil, or as representative of all others, since it was in fact the last fixed vertical prohibition to survive the fall of kings and bishops in the eighteenth century.

In dealing with Richardson's novels, Ian Watt speaks of that "tremendous narrowing of the ethical scale" in the eighteenth century by which virtue was redefined "in primarily sexual terms," and "chastity, instead of being only one virtue among many, tended to become the supreme one."[6] That narrowing process — the work essentially of the Puritan middle class — would take on the cast of a major fixation in the nineteenth century, and with ample cause. What we now call Victorian prudery was an attitude toward sexuality which developed partly in reaction to aristocratic excesses in the Regency period (1811–1820), but also to the spread of scandalous French novels and the free-love doctrines they promoted, and to the more tangible spread of sexual license and venereal disease. Adultery, seduction, and prostitution were decidedly on the increase. As Walter Houghton notes, some 42,000 illegitimate children were born in one year in England and Wales; 8,000 prostitutes flourished in London alone, 50,000 in England and Scotland, due to starvation wages for women among the urban poor, the maintenance of large armed forces, and the postponement of marriage until young middle-class sons could afford to live like gentlemen.[7] In marriage itself widespread ignorance and lack of birth control devices made sex extremely hazardous in its consequences — large families for men to support, early deaths for women from too much childrearing and childbearing. The prudery was founded then on real fears, on real conditions. But whatever its many justifications, the attitude was there as part of the mixture of feeling in the domestic hothouse. On the one hand, domestic affections were cooked up to a high pitch; on the other, sexual feeling was severely repressed and talk about sex forbidden, the whole matter kept under strict taboo, hidden as it were beneath or behind the voluminous skirts and heavy draperies then in fashion. In the meantime, in the cities, prostitution continued to flourish briskly and openly, and prurient interest in sexuality was evidently widespread, as the lively trade in pornography attests.[8]

These domestic conditions of intensely insulated affection for members of the family, especially those of the opposite sex, and of severe censure for sexual expression of any kind, were just about perfect for producing sexual neurosis in Victorian children. Whether they were diffused or merely diversified by the presence of nannies, cooks, and governesses, numerous siblings and dependents, is hard to determine. It seems evident, however, that whatever normal guilt a child might feel for forbidden feelings, under the Freudian dispensation, would be enormously heightened in such homes, and the chances for later resolution enormously lessened. Married love must have been hell, in any case, in a culture which held that no decent woman should experience sexual feeling, and that a man's sexual responses to his wife were a form of desecration. The frequent appearance of the madonna-prostitute syndrome in nineteenth-century fiction, as in the novels of Thackeray, Dickens, Eliot, and Dostoevsky, or the peculiar love for little girls expressed in the lives and works of Dickens, Eliot, Ruskin, Dowson, Dodgson, Barrie, and James, suggests the depths to which the domestic split between sex and affection had carried. It seems clear that childhood itself had become a problematic and conflictual realm in the nineteenth century; and if writers and readers alike turned to that realm from the commercial harshness and ungodliness of the adult world, and from the unbearably conscious guilts and tensions of marriage, seeking relief in childhood innocence, what they found there—along with the emotional freshness they sought—were childhood versions of the problems from which they fled. In facing and expressing those problems as honestly and effectively as they often did, these writers were mapping out new contours of emotional experience, new aspects of sensibility, new ways also of looking at adult inequities, from which the contemporary world still benefits.

III

Suppose we consider first the most obvious benefit, the precocious childhood view of adult inequities, whether social or domestic. It was Dickens who first identified with the childhood victims of social injustice, and who presented from their point of view, and with the emotional honesty, the innocent directness, the touching vulnerability which can be expressed through that perspective, the absurdities, tyrannies, and obtusenesses of the adult social world. Oliver Twist's workhouse request for more gruel is perhaps the most famous instance: the outrageous request of a sensitive middle-class child that the children of the poor should also be decently fed, a request which still carries its outrageous edge, as our jeopardized school lunch programs today attest. By couching that request in middle-class accents, by placing it on the lips of a genteel orphan boy deprived at birth of his rightful status, Dickens seduced his original class-conscious readers into putting their own children, if not themselves, in Oliver's place—as well they might in an age when social slippage was so common that societies were often formed against it. Consider, among Evangelical societies with railroad titles like "The Ladies Association for the Benefit of Gentlewomen of Good Family, Reduced in Fortune Below the State of Comfort To Which They Have Been Accustomed," and "The Friendly Female Society, for the Relief of Poor, Infirm, Aged Widows, and Single Women, of Good Character, Who Have Seen Better Days," the relevant listing also of "The London Orphan Asylum, for the Reception and Education of Destitute Orphans, Particularly Those Descended from Respectable Parents."[9] In the light of such listings, Arnold Kettle's view that we care in the gruel scene "not because it is Oliver and we are close to Oliver (though that of course enters into it), but because every starved orphan in the world, and indeed everyone who is poor and oppressed and hungry is involved," will not do.[10] Even today it is our middle-class selves, or our middle-class children, as mediated through Oliver, for whom we care first and foremost, as we extend our awakened sympathies to those starved orphans in Dickens' novels, who are not themselves responsible for their dead parents' failure – that is to say, *our* failure – to provide for them whether in worse or better days. Our position, in this respect, is much like that of the Benevolent Man from the eighteenth century, who continues to exist in Dickens' novels, but whose exemplary function – after Pickwick – is to assist, rescue, and above all bear witness to this new center of attention and worth, this new and finer gauge of social gravity, the Benevolent Child.

Oliver's later exposure to London crime, Little Nell's trek through industrial phantasmagorias, Esther Summerson's childhood view of Chancery, that "grown boy" Nicholas Nickleby's view of Dotheboys Hall, suggest further the new way of gauging social conditions. Even with Little Jo, the London sweep with whom Dickens openly asks his more fortunate readers to identify, we interpret the situation of the poor through childlike middle-class eyes. In making us use such eyes, moreover, Dickens exploits our middle-class stake in the domestic affections so as to change our Evangelical, commercial, or utilitarian minds. He uses Rousseau, as it were, as his entering wedge in that assault on our *other* middle-class predilections. Thus Obedience and Forbearance, Diligence and Factuality, are often challenged by his childhood victims of adult inequities. When offered poor nutrition or unrewarding labor or the impoverished abstractions of utilitarian science, these self-active claimants of Rousseauistic rights win our assent by demanding richer fare.

Dickens is often credited with affecting reformist sentiment in his own and future generations through such persuasive fictional assaults. But one historic consequence has gone unremarked. By converting his childhood victims into fledgling rebels, he seems to have set in motion that long historic process whereby a whole generation of self-active children would rebel against our own adult absurdities in the 1960s. Let us call them the Benevolent Generation, in keeping with the Benevolent Man and the Benevolent Child from whence they sprang; but let us add at once that Dickens himself was not quite so Rousseauistic as his rebellious progeny. By mid-career he seems to have discovered that indignant children, however confident of their own innocence and integrity, can behave absurdly too.

Consider in this light his assault on the adult reader's clashing values in *David Copperfield.* With his childish mother and maternal nurse young David enjoys the domestic affections, as that novel opens, which seem proper to his innocent birthright; but when the Evangelical Murdstones control the household, that birthright is usurped and David becomes in their eyes a disobedient criminal to be trained by discipline and punishment out of his innately sinful ways. We rejoice, certainly, when David later escapes these punitive parents and makes his marvellously scary dreamlike way to a more comic domestic sanctuary; but when we learn that he suffers thereafter from an undisciplined heart it may well give us pause. The problem of the undisciplined heart is one that Dickens seems to leave unsolved, unless we grant him the implicit notion that every child has a right to learn about human fallibility from his or her mistakes, and that we as mature and experienced readers may indulge that right, as Dickens himself does so effectively in parts of *Copperfield* and from start to original finish in *Great Expectations.* In doing so, moreover, he credibly expands the infantile perspective, extends it into young adulthood by bringing his childhood victims into situations which not only repeat and amplify their original ordeals, but which now even expose them to their own imperfections.

It is one of the brilliant strokes of *Copperfield* that the harsh stepfather Murdstone is also one of the owners of the wine warehouse at which David later works, and that Murdstone's frightening spinster sister reappears as governess of the girl whom David later wants to marry, the doll-like daughter of another employer like Murdstone, and thus another version of David's unreachable mother. It is one of the nicely educative things about Dickens' novels that parental figures always appear or reappear in positions of social dominance or favor which can then be assessed by domestic tensions and emotions from the childhood period. Thus we twice meet Jaggers and Magwitch as the legal and criminal fathers, respectively, in *Great Expectations;* thus Bounderby, the bully of humility in *Hard Times,* becomes the commercial and marital extension of the utilitarian father Gradgrind; or Krook and the Lord High Chancellor preside as absurdly grotesque fathers over the legal maze in which the orphaned wards mature in *Bleak House.* By keeping alive and sensitive the emotions of maturing middle-class children, as extended to adult inequities of every kind, Dickens domesticates the social scene, retrieves it from dispassionate remoteness, and so develops in us that passionate sense of injustice, and that glimmering or appalling sense of fallibility, we first felt in childhood. He has given social satire a dimension of compassion, pathos, indignation, and indulgent humor which it lacked before he wrote; he has taken it beyond the easy warmth and shrewdness of Fielding, his most obvious eighteenth-century influence, and the intelligent wryness of Swift and other Augustan critics of social follies and personal imperfections.

Let us move on to the advances in psychological fiction, which today seem more spectacular than those in social satire, and which bring us even closer to private imperfections. Though firmly committed to the Romantic cult of childhood innocence, Victorian novelists were too deeply involved with their own childhood experience, and too honest in most of their efforts to evoke it, to rest content with its idyllic aspects. They have given us a number of powerful evocations of the emotional conflicts of childhood, its guilts and fears and psychic damages, for which there is simply no precedent in previous literature. The most important novel in this respect is again *David Copperfield*, where in the first fourteen chapters Dickens moves his hero through a series of surface events which reflect inner problems. An obvious case in point, which I have developed more fully elsewhere,[11] is David's response to the gravestone beneath which his father lies in the churchyard by his childhood home. David feels childish compassion for it "lying out alone there in the dark night" by itself; but when his mother later reads to him in the cold Sunday parlor where his father's funeral was held "how Lazarus was raised up from the dead," David becomes frightened and has to be reassured that the dead are still at rest in their churchyard graves. Still later, when David is a few years older, his mother marries the mysterious Murdstone while David is safely off with his nurse's family in Yarmouth. When he returns home Nurse Peggotty tries to explain what has happened in his absence: "What do you think?" she begins, "You have a Pa!" David's response to this news is astonishingly revealing: "I trembled and turned white. Something—I don't know what or how—connected with the grave in the churchyard, and the raising of the dead, seemed to strike me like an unwholesome wind." Peggotty further explains that it is a *new* father, not the old one risen from the dead; but when David enters the house he finds Murdstone in the Sunday parlor where his father's funeral took place, sitting beside his mother by the fire; and when he later roams outside into the yard he finds that an empty dog-kennel has been filled up "with a great dog—deep-mouthed and black-haired like Him—and he was very angry at the sight of me, and sprang out to get at me."

Let me say again what I have said elsewhere, that this is brilliant psychological fiction. The harsh Evangelist Murdstone has become the risen and revengeful father whom David once viewed with such benevolent compassion. As his name half-consciously attests, he is the murdered man, and thus the vengeful murderer, who comes from beneath the gravestone to punish David and separate him from the loving mother he has so far unquestioningly possessed. His powers—as we learn from earlier scenes—involve those mysteries of sexual attraction which pull the mother out of David's range. In the meantime the boy's hostility and fear suffuse the outward scene. The projective artistry here extends throughout these early chapters, and lends a psychological dimension to David's Evangelical ordeals which makes them unforgettable. Indeed, they constitute a dreamlike sequence of real events which has influenced writers for the last century. Among the many novelists who have followed Dickens' precedent and have given us close accounts of psycho-sexual conflict extending from early childhood into young adulthood, let me mention only George Eliot, Fyodor Dostoevsky, and Henry James in the nineteenth century, and, in our own time, Kafka, Lawrence, Joyce, and Thomas Wolfe. Let me note also that all these probers of the childhood theme proceed on moral and social as well as psychological grounds; all are moved by the desire to find values to mature by in a culture which has lost its hold on moral, social, and religious certainties. As James would argue in "The Art of Fiction" in 1885, and would go on to demonstrate in *What Maisie Knew*, "the development of the moral consciousness of a child" is a psychological "adventure" worthy of adult pursuit.[12] The ground rules for that adventure were set, I think, in *David Copperfield*.

IV

So far I have implied two basic motives for the intense preoccupation with childhood in nineteenth-century fiction. The one which we can honor most today is the desire, just noted, to come to grips with the terms of childhood conflict so as to renew the grounds for value and for selfhood. The other motive, which rests more unthinkingly on the cult of childhood innocence, is nostalgia: the desire to return to a period of conscious innocence, to find relief from adult conflicts by escaping into what seemed, by selective memory, an idyllic realm, and remaining there — preferring it, in fact, to adulthood. There are, I think, a number of valid aspects to such nostalgia, among which is the spirit of pleasurable fun which we associate with childhood and which makes us appreciate the humor of Dickens or Mark Twain or Lewis Carroll. Such pleasure is after all a way of renewing one's sense of well-being and may be another way of affirming selfhood. But there is another aspect of nostalgia which no longer works so well for us, though it led Victorians by the thousands to shed copious tears, and to a second age when the word "sentimental" acquired positive meaning.

In a sense we too experienced a brief revival of sentimentality in the 1960s; but it differed from that of the nineteenth century in its willingness, as the saying then went, to "let it all hang out," in its free and open traffic, for instance, with sexuality and affection, and in its perhaps too easy fusion of those feelings in such popular refrains as "All You Need Is Love" — for as we now know, you also need some way to deal with the repressed hostility behind all that easy love. Victorian sentimentality was by contrast more uniformly repressive in nature, and its expression and reception in the nineteenth century were, I believe, neurotic phenomena. Dickens is again, unhappily, the most influential exemplar. His early novel, *The Old Curiosity Shop*, derives from popular Evangelical tracts on an unlikely subject, the exemplary piety of dying children.[13] It tells the story, accordingly, of the long delicious journey toward death of an incredibly selfless heroine, Little Nell, who is best described as a "domestic saint writ small."[14] The novel itself was one of the most popular fictions of the age, and easily the most influential. To this book we owe George Eliot's Eppie in *Silas Marner*, Dostoevsky's Nellie in *The Insulted and Injured*, Lewis Carroll's Alice, Harriet Beecher Stowe's Little Eva in *Uncle Tom's Cabin*, Johanna Speyri's *Heidi*, Sir James Barrie's Wendy in *Peter Pan*, James's Maisie, and such modern extensions of the type as Shirley Temple in 1930s films like *The Littlest Rebel*, Carson McCullers' Mick Kelly in the 1940s, Salinger's Phoebe and Esme in the 1950s, and, still more recently, Erich Segal's Jennifer Cavilleri, the young woman whose exemplary death in *Love Story* is worked for all its tearful worth. The supposed reversal of the type in Vladimir Nabokov's *Lolita* (1955) and in recent sexually exploitive films like *The Exorcist* must also be mentioned, since my own tale is one of changing tastes and attitudes and reversed taboos which are really forms of cultural continuity.

It should be said at once that most of the above "imitations" are improvements on the original. Eppie is unruly; Nellie is moody and precociously romantic; Alice pouts and gets angry; Shirley sings and dances; Jennifer sasses; Lolita chews bubble-gum. Nell's counterpart in the subplot of *The Old Curiosity Shop*, the Marchioness, a domestic slavey capable of comically muted resentment of her lot, should stand perhaps at the head of this list as an example of what Dickens himself could do when he was not under the compulsion to confer domestic sainthood on children. Indeed, the Marchioness may well have initiated all such saving graces. But from beginning to end Nell herself is characterized by abstract traits – youth, goodness, beauty, long-suffering unselfishness, untiring patience, maternal wisdom, religious serenity – at least some of which no creature her age ever possessed or should possess; and as Aldous Huxley has shown, her death – when we finally get to it – is presented through a threnody of blank-verse rhythms which blot out actuality in idealized praise.[15] Within recent years some of our more resourceful scholars have come to the defense of Dickens' portrait of Nell, but since the turn of the century there has been a general critical consensus that Nell is a sentimental textual blur, and among psychological critics at least, a general attribution of that textual failure to Dickens' personal involvement with Nell's prototype, his wife's young sister Mary Hogarth, who died in his arms after a sudden illness. At this late date in the history of

Dickens criticism I need not rehearse the details of the textual proof of sentimentality, of the biographical proof of its neurotic origins in Dickens' life, or of the modern view of sentimentality—as an effusion of one kind of feeling which inhibits or represses another kind—on which these proofs are based.[16] It seems more important, at this point, to speculate on those cultural attitudes toward the end of childhood innocence which I think we still share with the Victorians, for all our modern reversals, and for which Dickens created the still prevalent mythos.

Victorian preoccupation with the deaths of children was founded, of course, in the very real problem of high mortality rates among them in all classes, but especially among the poor, and with the religious and indeed existential problem of what to make of it. According to one recent theory, what they made of it was a pleasurable social occasion, a radical violation of subjectivity having occurred which dissolved individual limits into funereal communion, or "sacralized intimacy with mankind in general."[17] Thus, thanks to Dickens and the dying Nell, the Victorians in their copious grief enjoyed transcendant communal unity of a kind we no longer share. It troubles me, I must confess, that they enjoyed it through "an erotic movement toward annihilation," the agent of which was a pubescent girl. Why not a grown woman? If the unifying feeling was erotic, as our resourceful theorist argues, surely a sexually mature woman would have provided a greater death-kick, as Richardson's Clarissa did, for instance, for the preceding century, or Segal's Jennifer for our own. The clue to this peculiar reaction lies, I think, in the hothouse nature of the Victorian home, and in the tensions and repressions experienced there, which Dickens shared with and recreated for his readers, and from which he released them through what I would call neurotic rather than erotic violation. How else can we explain such related phenomena as the cult called Love of Little Girls, by which young men at Oxford in the 1880s invited little girls, as opposed to big ones, to their rooms for tea; or the increased popularity of child-prostitutes by that decade, to the point where grown prostitutes began to dress like them to recapture trade;[18] or the odd desire to marry girls of twelve and thirteen exhibited by Victorians like Ruskin and Ernest Dowson or by the hero of Henry James's first novel, *Watch and Ward;* or the even odder desire in Dickens himself to be buried beside his wife's sister, young Mary Hogarth, as if to possess her spiritually in a final post-carnal embrace which would forever preserve their mutual innocence? Indeed, it was that final vicarious possession through death which Dickens gave to thousands of weeping readers as compensation for their own lost childhoods.

However bizarre such innocent necrophilia seems today, the myth that Dickens created for it is still very much with us. In Vladimir Nabokov's *Lolita,* for instance, there is the same regressive flight through the countryside, ending in deathly tribute to childhood innocence, as in *The Old Curiosity Shop;* and behind that flight there is the same old fear of sexual and emotional personhood in adult women, about which our current feminists have much to say. The chief difference between old and new versions of this regressive myth is that Nabokov's narrator denies the little girl's affective innocence, if not his own, until the final pages, and meanwhile ecstatically reveres her precocious sexuality. And even here his sexual apotheosis of her charms, like his ultimate retreat into that modern version of erotic self-annihilation, aesthetic bliss, is merely the obverse—not the opposite—of Dickens' spiritual apotheosis of the dying Nell in blank-verse threnodies. It is, I think, a form of reverse sentimentality, an effusion of one kind of feeling in the narrator so as to deny another in his supposedly tough beloved. Indeed, Lolita's missing affections—or perhaps I should say her short-shrifted affections—are scarcely relevant to his regressive nostalgia, which—like Grandfather Trent's gambling mania in Dickens' novel—needs only the sacred image of the little mother to sanctify the game. As both Dickens and Nabokov seem to have recognized, moreover, it is a deadly and disequal game, and not even the attempt to purge the power lust behind it by killing off those comic scapegoats, Quilp and Quilty, can save its necessary victims.[19]

It takes real as opposed to parodic genius, I would argue, to create a reversible sentimental myth like this one, which has enthralled regressive souls for more than a century, and to go on from there—as Dickens did—to create dreamlike visions of growing up absurd which have enthralled what I am going to call emotionally *progressive* souls over the same two centuries. Are there any connecting links, historically, between these two oddly opposing lines? Certainly *one* link *seems* to have disappeared. The little victim of yesteryear, the little mother whom Dickens more or less invented, is no longer with us in her original saintly form. Along with her older saintly sisters, she was knocked off her pedestal by the feminist movement in the 1890s, by the increased freedom also of sexual expression in serious fiction and—after the first World War—in revolutionary fact, and by the breakup finally of the domestic hothouse itself through these and other social changes. The most paradoxical of these changes, for our purposes, was the increased awareness of the conflictual nature of childhood emotional experience which Dickens initiated in dreamlike form in *David Copperfield.*[20] For as that awareness ran to its modern excesses in recent decades, lo and behold, the little domestic saint returned in modern guise as the little nymphet we now exploit so knowingly in novels, films, and advertisements! It is high time, I hope you will agree, that we get rid of that little incubus—or at least knock her off of her sexual pedestal—by retracing our crazy steps. With Dickens, for instance, it was necessary to work through the regressive myth in order to reach his dreamlike vision of growing up absurd; with us, it seems necessary to reverse the process, to work back through our greater knowledge of sexuality and its unconscious powers to a healthier possession of those tender feelings we now tend to repress, as the Victorians repressed sexuality before us.

To do this we will have to reformulate or perhaps reinvent Sigmund Freud, whose appearance at the end of the last century signalled the return of a doctrine rather like that of Original Sin: the doctrine, that is, of the sexual nature of childhood experience in its unconscious aspects, and of the neurotic nature of family experience in its rivalries and tensions and repressive romances. It was a doctrine with considerable relevance for nineteenth-century culture and the kind of neurotic disturbances it produced, and for those modern cultural analogues like the Jewish home in *The Metamorphosis* and *Portnoy's Complaint* or the Southern home in *The Sound and the Fury* and *Look Homeward, Angel* which preserve hothouse ways. It was a doctrine, moreover, toward which novelists themselves were clearly working even before it was formulated, as Freud himself acknowledged. But having worked with that conscious formulation over the past eighty years, and having suffered from its many excesses in recent decades, it seems necessary now to reexamine the unconscious powers of the repressed affections in our domestic freeways. And for this the achievements of nineteenth-century pioneers like Dickens and Dostoevsky, George Eliot and Henry James, may serve as useful models since they tried, with some success, to preserve the domestic affections while giving us our first honest expressions of early sexual conflict. Indeed, if poor monkeys are a richer fictional breed today, innately loving yet at the same time innately jealous, hostile, vengeful creatures who in learning to cope with their own conflictual natures, along with ours, might well grow up to be something other than regressive or absurd, it is novelists like these—Dickens foremost among them—whom we have to thank for that dreamlike, if not altogether mythical, prospect.

Notes

1. See Peter Coveney, *Poor Monkey: The Child in Literature* (London: Rockliff, 1957); revised and reissued, with an introduction by F.R. Leavis, as *The Image of Childhood: The Individual and Society: a Study of the Theme in English Literature* (Baltimore: Peregrine, 1967).

2. Paul Goodman, *Growing Up Absurd: Problems of Youth in the Organized System* (New York: Random House, 1960).

3. Ian Watt, *The Rise of the Novel: Studies in Defoe, Richardson and Fielding* (Berkeley: Univ. of California Press, 1959). See especially ch. 1, on philosophical realism.

4. R.F. Brissenden, *Virtue in Distress: Studies in the Novel of Sentiment from Rich-*

ardson to Sade (London: Macmillan, 1974). See especially ch. 2, on the definition of "sentimentalism."

5. Walter E. Houghton, *The Victorian Frame of Mind, 1830–1870* (New Haven: Yale Univ. Press, 1957), pp. 344–46.

6. Watt, *Rise of the Novel,* pp. 156–57.

7. Houghton, *Victorian Frame of Mind,* p. 366.

8. See Kellow Chesney, *The Anti-Society: An Account of the Victorian Underworld* (Boston: Gambit, 1970), pp. 16, 307–64; published in Britain as *The Victorian Underworld* by Maurice Temple Smith Ltd. (1972).

9. See Richard D. Altick, *Victorian People and Ideas* (New York: Norton, 1973), pp. 180–81, for these and other Evangelical society titles.

10. Arnold Kettle, *An Introduction to the English Novel* (New York: Harper, 1960), II, 125.

11. See Mark Spilka, *Dickens and Kafka: A Mutual Interpretation* (Bloomington: Indiana Univ. Press, 1963), pp. 177–82.

12. See *Theory of Fiction: Henry James,* ed. James E. Miller, Jr. (Lincoln: Univ. of Nebraska Press, 1972), pp. 41–42. For James's childhood reaction to a reading of the crucial early chapters of *Copperfield* (the "ply then taken was ineffaceable"), see Leon Edel, "The Dickens Imprint," in *Henry James: The Untried Years, 1843– 1870* (New York: Avon, 1978), pp. 98–99.

13. See Samuel Pickering, Jr., *The Moral Tradition in English Fiction: 1785-1850* (Hanover, N.H.: Univ. Press of New England, 1976), pp. 107–22. Pickering focuses here on Legh Richmond's Evangelical tracts, *The Dairyman's Daughter* and *The Young Cottager.*

14. I discuss Nell's domestic saintliness more fully in "Little Nell Revisited," *Papers of the Michigan Academy of Science, Arts, and Letters,* 45 (1960), 427–37; see especially p. 435.

15. Aldous Huxley, *Vulgarity in Literature* (London: Chatto and Windus, 1930), pp. 54–59.

16. See my essay, "Little Nell Revisited," cited in note 14; and see also I.A. Richards' chapter on sentimentality and inhibition in *Practical Criticism: A Study of Literary Judgment* (New York: Harvest, 1929).

17. John Kucich, "Death Worship among the Victorians: *The Old Curiosity Shop,*" *PMLA,* 95 (Jan. 1980), 58–72; my quotations are from pp. 69–70.

18. Chesney, *The Anti-Society,* p. 326.

19. I refer here to the narrator's confession, at the end of the novel, that he has robbed Lolita of her childhood and that she has sobbed nightly after each of their motel couplings. Though he still loves her, even in her bedraggled pregnancy, it is still a deadly and disequal love, as she herself recognizes when she tells him she would sooner go back to his comic double, the honest pervert Quilty, than run off with him again. His vengeful attempt to exorcise the power-lust behind such love by killing Quilty, as Dickens had killed off Nell's nasty sexual pursuer, Quilp, a century before, seems by design a grotesquely comic appeasement of his own guilty conscience; and his subsequent retreat into that modern version of erotic self-annihilation, aesthetic bliss, simply continues that regression in service of the id which has al-

ways characterized his celebration of Lolita's erotic charms. I would argue, then, that Nabokov's sophisticated and parodic art is as nostalgically neurotic here as the Victorian sentimental tradition it ostensibly parodies.

20. By 1848, two years before *Copperfield,* Dostoevsky had arrived at an independent view of infantile sexuality in the unpublished fragment, *Netochka Nezvanova;* but it was not until his return from Siberia, after he had absorbed Dickens' precedent, that he was able to develop his richer view of childhood conflict in novels and tales like *The Insulted and Injured, A Raw Youth,* "A Little Hero," and *The Brothers Karamazov.*

Sara M. Putzell-Korab

Passion between Women in the Victorian Novel

Critical analyses abound on the subject of passion between men and women in Victorian novels. They cover such various loves as Heathcliff and Cathy's grand passion, David Copperfield's misguided attachment to Dora, and Maggie Tulliver's unhappy infatuation with Stephen Guest. Sexual passion between women, on the other hand, has received little scholarly comment. In 1901 the British medical journal *The Lancet* smugly announced, "As yet in this country the novelist . . . has not arrived at the treatment in romance of . . . Sapphism," which it groups with other "diseases . . . found in French novels."[1] Opinion has not altered significantly since then. In 1956 Jeanette Foster remarked that until the end of the nineteenth century the presentation of lesbianism in literature was "nearly an exclusive product of France," while as recently as 1975 Jane Rule's survey of *Lesbian Images* in literature again mentions French fiction but otherwise ignores the nineteenth century.[2] At most, Nina Auerbach's 1978 study, *Communities of Women*, acknowledges lesbianism as "a silent possibility in two or three of the novels."[3] This "silent possibility" deserves further consideration, however, because educated Victorians were aware of it from their reading of French novels, and it is referred to in English literature. Finally, recognizing that the Victorians were aware that women can feel passion for each other may help, as the second half of this essay illustrates, to clarify such ambiguous scenes in Victorian novels as those which occur between Lucy Snowe and other women in Charlotte Brontë's *Villette*.

I

In 1836 *The Quarterly Review* complained of the availability of French novels: "it is notorious that they are advertised in a thousand ways over the

180

whole reading world—when we see them exhibited even in London in the windows of respectable shops—when they are to be had in circulating libraries—when we know, *as we do know*—that they find their way, under the specious title of '*the last new novel*' into the hands of persons wholly or partially ignorant of their real character—nay, into *ladies' book clubs*—we feel that it is our duty to *stigmatize* them."[4] Among the works singled out as liable to "pervert" public as well as private morals is Balzac's *Scènes de la vie parisienne*, which includes the story of "La Fille aux yeux d'or." When the hero and the girl with the golden eyes consummate their passion for each other, he discovers that, although a virgin, she is extraordinarily proficient in the art of love. The solution to this paradox comes when he subsequently finds her lying murdered at his half-sister's feet and realizes that it has been a crime of passion: the two women had been having an affair. Although "La Fille aux yeux d'or" did not appear in English translation until the 1885-93 Boston edition, it was available in a number of French editions. Written as part of *L'Histoire des Treize*, it also served as part of the nucleus of the *Scènes de la vie parisienne* that *The Quarterly Review* maligned. Between 1835 and 1898, "La Fille" appeared in some nine French editions of Balzac's works, including an 1856 Paris edition of the *Scènes* that was reprinted eight times.

Not only Balzac but other major French novelists wrote of sexual passion between women. In Diderot's *La Religieuse* (1796), for example, the Mother Superior of a convent falls in love with and makes sexual advances to a young nun. In addition to seven eighteenth-century editions, including one anonymous English translation (London, 1797), *La Religieuse* went through twenty editions between 1800 and 1870, thus giving credence to Sainte-Beuve's 1844 remark that, although the novel was forbidden reading, everyone knew of her "histoire obscène et douloureuse."[5] Perhaps the most widely known French treatment of a woman's passion for another woman, however, is Gautier's eponymous *Mademoiselle de Maupin* (1835). The novel's bisexual heroine is modeled on Madeleine d'Aubigny who, among other escapades, made love to a young girl, fought duels, and fled from Paris to Brussels in order to escape arrest, only to be expelled from Belgium for what was deemed her scandalous behavior. Although she died in 1707, her story was revived in magazine articles and comedies during the 1830s, as well as in Gautier's novel, which became, according to Enid Starkie, "one of the most famous works of the nineteenth century—certainly one of the most notorious" and "the artistic bible of a whole generation."[6]

Gautier's response to those who feared that works like *Mademoiselle de Maupin* would corrupt young girls points to another source for Victorian awareness that women could desire each other: "Pour leurs filles, si elles ont été en pension, je ne vois pas ce que les livres pourraient leur apprendre."[7]

Girls' schools, like British public schools, thus provided another opportunity for developing passionate attachments to those of one's own sex as well as for observing such attachments. Coquette, the heroine of William Black's *A Daughter of Heth* (1871), brightly explains to her male friend, Whaup,

> Our *pension* was full of mystery and romance . . . because of two German young ladies who were there. They introduced—what shall I call it?—exaltation. Do you know what it is? When one girl makes another *exaltee,* because of her goodness or her beauty, and worships her, and kisses her dress when she passes her, and serves her in all things, yet dare not speak to her? And the girl who is *exaltee*—she must be proud and cold, and show scorn for her attendant—even although she has been her friend. . . . All the *pension* was filled with it—it was a religion, an enthusiasm—and you would see girls crying and kneeling on the floor, to show their love and admiration for their friend.

Whaup cynically observes of this phenomenon "that it was a clever device to let a lot of girls make love to each other, for want of anybody else. It was keeping their hand in, as it were."[8]

Mrs. Craik's more charitable remarks in *A Woman's Thoughts about Women* (1858) indicate that girlhood crushes were hardly confined to the continental pension and were a subject of sufficient English concern to warrant advice about them. Calling such crushes pure but "almost as passionate as first love," Mrs. Craik admonishes, "This girlish friendship, however fleeting in its character, and romantic, even silly, in its manifestations, let us take heed how we make light of it, lest we be mocking at things more sacred than we are aware."[9] If, contrary to Gautier, Mrs. Craik finds the passions of girls innocent of sexuality, she takes a more equivocal view of love between mature women. Again, her advice suggests audience awareness of the possibility of real passion, both platonic and sexual, between women:

> It is the unmarried, the solitary, who are the most prone to that sort of "sentimental" friendship with their own or the opposite sex, which, though often most noble, unselfish, and true, is in some forms ludicrous, in others dangerous. For two women, past earliest girlhood, to be completely absorbed in one another, and make public demonstration of the fact, by caresses or quarrels, is so repugnant to common sense, that where it ceases to be silly it becomes wrong. But to see two women, whom Providence has denied nearer ties, by a wise substitution making the best of fate, loving, sustaining, and comforting one another, with a tenderness often closer than that of sisters, because it has all the novelty of

election which belongs to the conjugal tie itself—this, I say, is an honorable and lovely sight.[10]

Much as she admits the "sustaining" value of love between women, Mrs. Craik seems genuinely concerned about physical expressions of that love, for—in addition to this explicit warning—in her novel *Christian's Mistake* (1865), she holds up to ridicule two older women who behave almost as if they were married to each other. Mrs. Craik's descriptions of such relationships would appear to have come from observation rather than reading, and she includes her audience as observers when she writes in *A Woman's Thoughts* of the "wonderful law of sex—which exists spiritually as well as materially, and often independent of matter altogether; since we see many a man who is much more of a woman, and many a woman who would certainly be the 'better half' of any man who cared for her—this law can rarely be withstood with impunity."[11]

From phrenologists too the Victorians received information and advice on sexual behavior, including that between members of the same sex. *The American Phrenological Journal and Miscellany* advertised a supplement, which I have as yet been unable to locate, on "Amativeness: or Evils and Remedies of Excessive and Perverted Sexuality."[12] Handbooks written for general audiences tend to be discreetly euphemistic when referring to what they label "abuse" and "perversion." One lists as sexual abuses "mis-placed or hopeless love"; another simply says of "perversion," "The abuse and disorderly gratification of this propensity is fraught with innumerable evils, physical, intellectual, and moral."[13] The ultimate discretion is the quiet "etc." that concludes one list of the results of "excess and perversion" of amativeness: "libertinism, sensuality, obscenity, lasciviousness, nymphomania, lust, seduction, prostitution, etc."[14] Writing as a scientist rather than as a popularizer, Franz Joseph Gall, the father of phrenology, is more explicit. The translator of the 1835 American edition from which I have taken the following observation by Gall seems, however, to have considered the passage improper, for he has given it in French. Of homosexuality Gall writes, "J'ai eu occasion d'observer plusieur hommes et plusieurs femmes qui étaient les esclaves de ce gout dépravé. La nuque large et voûtée frappe surtout chez les femmes. Presque toutes les femme livrées a ce penchant ont, en même temps, une constitution robuste et mâle."[15] Like French novels, Gall's observations were accessible to the Victorians: between 1800 and 1853, there were thirteen editions in English of his works or descriptions of his system as well as fourteen French and thirteen German editions.

French novels, schoolgirls' experiences, observation—all are means by which the Victorians learned that women can love women sexually. In addition to these, some important English novels provide sufficient allusions to indicate awareness. In fact, the first English novel, Samuel Richardson's *Pamela* (1740), contains several noteworthy scenes between an aggressively chaste Pamela and an experienced Mrs. Jewkes, set to guard Pamela by her would-be lover, Lord B. The following conversation is representative of the relation between the two women:

> And pray, said [Pamela] . . . how came I to be [Lord B's] property? What right has he in me. . . . Well, well, lambkin, (which the foolish often calls me), if I was in his place, he should not have his property in you long questionable. Why, what would you do, said I, if you were he? – Not stand shill-I -shall-I, as he does; but put you and himself both out of your pain. – Why Jezebel, said I, (I could not help it,) would you ruin me by force? – Upon this she gave me a deadly slap upon my shoulder: Take that, said she; whom do you call Jezebel? [16]

While Mrs. Jewkes' expression of readiness, if she were a man, to take Pamela forcibly may be read as Richardson's method of emphasizing Pamela's peril while limiting the number of scenes between her and Lord B., the similarity between her statement and that of Phoebe to Fanny Hill in John Cleland's *Memoirs of a Woman of Pleasure* (1748–49) suggests that it may also be interpreted as evidence of her own interest in the girl. While awaiting the arrival of her own "*Lord B . . . from Bath,*" Fanny Hill is initiated into the mysteries of sex by an older woman, Phoebe. Fanny's letters recount Phoebe's love-making with physiological precision; her only lament is that Phoebe is not a man. Echoing Mrs. Jewkes, Phoebe herself cries, "Oh! what a charming creature thou are! . . . What a happy man will he be that first makes a woman of you! . . . Oh! that I were a man for your sake!" [17]

That Cleland deliberately parodies and makes explicit what is implicit in Richardson's novel seems clear from his use of "Lord B" as the man for whom Phoebe, like Mrs. Jewkes, is keeping the younger woman. That the potential exists for a sexual relationship between Pamela and another woman is implied not only by this but also by other scenes in the novel. For example, Pamela has already had a close relation with Mrs. Jervis, the housekeeper in her first situation. Afraid of her master's attentions, Pamela asks permission to sleep with Mrs. Jervis, who cries with her over the problem and, according to Pamela, tells her, "I fear more for your prettiness than for anything else; because the best man in the land might love you. . . . She wished it was in her power to live independent; then she would take a little private house, and I should live with her like her daughter." [18] Pamela herself contrasts this non-sexual attachment between Mrs. Jervis and herself with Mrs. Jewkes' overt physical interest in her:

You may see—(Yet, oh! that kills me; for I know not whether *ever* you can see what I now write or no—Else you will see)—what sort of woman that Mrs. Jewkes is, compared to good Mrs. Jervis, by this:—

Every now and then she would be staring in my face, in the chariot, and squeezing my hand and saying, Why, you are very pretty, my silent dear! And once she offered to kiss me. But I said, I don't like this sort of carriage, Mrs. Jewkes; it is not like two persons of one sex.[19]

Pamela's contrasting the two older women in this way clearly indicates her fear that her chastity is endangered by Mrs. Jewkes as well as by Lord B, a presumption underlined by her subsequent refusal to sleep in the same bed with Mrs. Jewkes.

Richardson repeats this situation of a woman's expressing an unwelcome sexual interest to a still virginal heroine in *Sir Charles Grandison* (1753-54), in which "Miss Barnevelt, a lady of masculine features, and whose mind bely'd not those features" addresses herself to Harriet.[20] "Sneeringly spoken of rather as a *young fellow*, than as a woman," Miss Barnevelt expresses contempt for her own sex until she meets Harriet, who reports, "Miss Barnevelt said, she had from the moment I first enter'd beheld me with the eyes of a Lover. And freely taking my hand, squeezed it.—Charming creature! said she, as if addressing a country innocent, and perhaps expecting me to be covered with blushes and confusion."[21] Clearly no innocent, Harriet later imagines Miss Barnevelt writing to "a brother *man*" and describing her as one man would to another: "'Tis the softest, gentlest smiling rogue of a girl—I protest, I could five or six times have kissed her . . . Such a blushing little rogue!—'Tis a dear girl, and I wish'd twenty times as I sat by her, that I had been a man for her sake."[22] Whereas Cleland uses the relation between Phoebe and Fanny to characterize the latter as capable of enjoying another woman yet anticipating further pleasures with a man, Richardson uses the advances of Mrs. Jewkes and Miss Barnevelt to warn his audience that young women have to preserve their virtue against importunate women as well as men.

Comparable scenes can be found in the Victorian novel. In George Meredith's *The Ordeal of Richard Feverel* (1859), for example, Richard's old nurse, Mrs. Berry, expresses her chaste ardor for his young bride as follows:

Berry leaned over her, and eyed her roguishly, saying, "I never see ye like this, but I'm half in love with ye myself, you blushin' beauty! Sweet's your eyes, and your hair do take one so—lyin' back. I'd never forgive my father if he kep' me away from ye four-and-twenty hours just. Husband o' that!" Berry pointed at the young wife's loveliness. "Ye look so ripe with kisses, and there they are a-languishin! . . . You never look so but in your bed, ye beauty! – just as it ought to be." Lucy had to pretend to rise to put out the light before Berry would give up her amourous chaste soliloquy. Then they lay in bed, and Mrs. Berry fondled her, and arranged for their departure tomorrow . . . and hinted at Lucy's delicious shivers when Richard was again in his rightful place, which she, Bessy Berry, now usurped; and all sorts of amorous sweet things enough to make one fancy that adage subverted that stolen fruits are sweetest. . . .[23]

And Berry lies awake after Lucy sleeps, "squeezing the fair sleeper's hand now and then to ease her love as her reflections warmed." Like a schoolgirl's crush, Mrs. Berry's adoration of Lucy leads to thoughts of connubial bliss. Passion between women once again is limited in its physical expression, preparing for and reminding the women of heterosexual passion.

In contrast, Thomas Hardy presents passion between women as an option to be entirely rejected in *Desperate Remedies* (1871). The possessive passion of Miss Aldclyffe for Cytherea is depicted as an obstacle to the latter's happiness. Miss Aldclyffe imagines Cytherea gliding around her body and touching her. Going into Cytherea's room, Miss Aldclyffe embraces her and questions her as to whether any man has ever kissed her. Angered by Cytherea's refusal to answer, Miss Aldclyffe accuses, "'Tis now with you as it is always with girls,' she said, in jealous and gloomy accents. 'You are not, after all, the innocent I took you for. No, no.' She then changed her tone with fitful rapidity. 'Cytherea, try to love me more than you love him – do. I love you more sincerely than any man can. Do, Cythie: don't let any man stand between us. O, I can't bear that!'"[24] Hardy's unsympathetic presentation of Miss Aldclyffe's passion led a *Spectator* reviewer to dismiss her as "a miserable creation – uninteresting, unnatural and nasty."[25] The pejorative "unnatural" indicates that the reviewer at least understood that Miss Aldclyffe's passion for Cytherea is sexual.

When such major novelists as Richardson, Meredith, and Hardy represent women displaying sexual passion for members of their own sex, it is clear that Victorian readers must have been aware of it as a possibility. Whether the useful stage in female sexual development that Mrs. Craik describes or the impediment Hardy suggests, the option seems one of which a significant number of authors and readers would have been conscious.

II

If any Victorian author might have been conscious of passion between women and have accordingly alluded to it in her fiction, it is Charlotte Brontë.

Not only did she live and study at the Pensionnat Heger, a girls' school in Brussels, but she did so at the very time that the story of Madeleine d'Aubigny, Gautier's "Mademoiselle de Maupin," was being revived there. Indeed, Brontë's use in *Villette* (1853) of the name "de Bassompierre," which belongs to a character in Gautier's novel, suggests that she knew the story. Certainly, she had read widely in the kind of French literature that *The Quarterly Review* condemned, for she remarks of one batch of forty French novels that she received, "I have read about half—they are like the rest—clever wicked sophistical and immoral."[26] Finally, she was interested in phrenology, which included the study of such passion, and in 1851 had her own phrenological character taken.[27]

Victorian awareness of sexual passion between women together with the likelihood that Charlotte Brontë would have shared that awareness provides an important context for interpreting the character of Lucy Snowe, heroine of her last novel, *Villette*. Drawn from Brontë's own experience in Brussels and set primarily in a continental pension, the novel chronicles Lucy's progress from frustration and self-repression to a limited fulfillment and acceptance of her lot in life. For a passionate woman such as Lucy, it is a difficult progress. The first man for whom she experiences a strong attraction, Dr. John Graham Bretton, regards her simply as a friend and patient; after a flirtation with Ginevra Fanshawe, Lucy's student and friend, Dr. John marries another of Lucy's few friends, Paulina de Bassompierre. The second and last love of Lucy's life, M. Paul Emanuel, shares her passionate temperament and returns her love, but dies before they can marry. It is thus such a life as Mrs. Craik describes, one in which a woman might well make "the best of fate" by "a wise substitution" of love for another woman. That Lucy appears to reject this option helps to characterize her: while on her own admission both passionate and androgynous, she fears unsanctioned passions and shares the common Victorian belief that true heterosexual love transcends the bounds of mortal existence with a redemptive power.

Lucy's passionate nature is evident from girlhood when young Paulina's emotionally charged reunion with her father affects Lucy so strongly that she wishes the child would "utter some hysterical cry, so that [Lucy] might get relief and be at ease."[28] Later, forced to support herself, Lucy takes a position as a crippled woman's companion and finds her life necessarily confined to two rooms; "almost content," she allows herself to grow "narrowed" to this lot. Once freed, however, by the invalid's death, her spirit shakes "its always-fettered wings half loose" (ch. 6, p. 56). Alone and independent, she gives herself a brief holiday in London before going to Villette, which is modeled on Brussels. There she coincidentally, which is to say providentially, finds employment as a governess then teacher at Madame Beck's "Pensionnat de Demoiselles." Unfortunately, she does not, until M. Paul, find anyone with whom she can share a close emotional relationship. Life thus becomes for her a war in which she must struggle to quell her own longings. She says of herself, "I had feelings. Passive as I lived, little as I spoke, cold as I looked, when I thought of past days I *could* feel. About the present it was better to be stoical; about the future—such a future as mine—to be dead. And in catalepsy and a dead trance I studiously held the quick of my nature." Nevertheless, as she continues to recall, so volatile is her nature that even thunderstorms can arouse a "craving" in her: "At that time, I well remember, whatever could excite—certain accidents of the weather, for instance, were almost dreaded by me, because they woke the being I was always lulling, and stirred up a craving cry I could not satisfy" (ch. 12, p. 114). Into this repressed yet yearning life come not only Dr. John, whose friendly letters inspire in Lucy a brief passionate "idolatry," but also two women, whose behavior would seem to offer Lucy fulfillment through a more assertive, even masculine role—if she so chooses.

Lucy's friendship with Ginevra Fanshaw, a pretty English student and Lucy's only companion at the pension, leads to what Kate Millett has called "one of the most indecorous scenes in the entire Victorian novel."[29] Intellectually an unlikely friend for Lucy, Ginevra is frivolous and ignorant, whereas Lucy is serious and studious. Furthermore, Ginevra is admired by Dr. John, with whom Lucy is initially infatuated. Yet Lucy and Ginevra are quite close. The girl comes to her to show off her clothes and to gossip about her triumphs over men; Lucy readily listens and admires her, even as she criticizes her frivolity. More important, when they are together, Lucy behaves almost like a gentleman towards Ginevra, fetching the younger woman her shawls and supporting her when they walk. Indeed, Ginevra frequently calls Lucy such males names as "Timon" and "Diogenes." Lucy's assumption of this male role culminates in her acting the part of Ginevra's suitor on stage.

Coerced into replacing an absent student in the school play, a farce about a coquette courted by both a fop and a heroic lover, Lucy plays the fop and Ginevra, the coquette. Although Lucy objects strenuously to being in the play and does refuse to act the part in trousers, once on stage she enters even more than is required into the spirit of her part and makes love to Ginevra with an amazing and—for a fop—inappropriate virility. From observing Ginevra's admirer, Dr. John, as he watches the play, Lucy draws out "a history" to inspire herself:

> In the . . . sincere lover, I saw Dr. John. Did I pity him, as erst? No, I hardened my heart, rivalled and out-rivalled him. I knew myself but a fop, but where *he* was outcast *I* could please. Now I know I acted as if wishful and resolute to win and conquer.

> Ginevra seconded me; between us we half changed the nature of
> the role, gilding it from top to toe. . . . I know not what possessed
> me either, but somehow my longing was to eclipse . . . Dr. John.
> Ginevra was tender; how could I be otherwise than chilvalric?
> Retaining the letter, I recklessly altered the spirit of the rôle.
> Without heart, without interest, I could not play it at all. It must
> be played—in went the yearned-for seasoning; thus flavored, I
> played it with relish.   (ch. 14, p. 144)

Encouraged by Ginevra, Lucy thus redirects her passion from a man to a
woman, from Dr. John to the girl, and she does so with enthusiasm, priding
herself that "where he was outcast," she "could please." In the context of
her isolation and of her already rather masculine behavior toward Ginevra,
Lucy's performance seems to indicate that her passionate nature can find
release in relation to either a man or a woman, whichever circumstances
and her own sense of self will allow.

Despite her enjoyment of pleasing Ginevra on stage under the temporary license that the play gives to their flirting with each other, Lucy consciously limits opportunities to express her passionate self. Her intellectual
self is a different matter. Criticized by M. Paul for displaying a masculine
intellect, she says, "Whatever my powers—feminine or the contrary—God
had given them and I felt resolute to be ashamed of no faculty of His be-
stowal" (ch. 30, p. 342). She may not be "ashamed" of her capacity to express passion, but she does consciously regulate the few outlets she is offered for displaying it. Disapproving of "these amateur performances," she
takes "a firm resolution never to be drawn into a similar affair," saying, "A
keen relish for dramatic expression had revealed itself as part of my nature;
to cherish and exercise this new-found faculty might gift me with a world
of delight, but it would not do for a mere looker-on at life" (ch. 14, p. 144).
Her recognition of her enjoyment as a release of her emotional self and her
rejection of it as inappropriate to the life which she elsewhere makes plain
that she believes is divinely ordained for her is comparable to her subsequent rejection of Roman Catholicism and a conventual life. Again, she recognizes in these a means for fulfilling her passionate self, but rejects them
as inappropriate to her life, this time because she is a Protestant who believes
each individual must assume responsibility for her own soul. Commenting
on her liability to accept the temptation to seek solace in the Roman Catholic church, Lucy admits of herself, "Without respecting some sorts of affection, there was hardly any sort having a fibre of root in reality which I could
rely on my force wholly to withstand" (ch. 15, p. 165).

Lucy's determination "to withstand" any deeper relationship with a woman
than her teasing one with Ginevra is indicated not only by her refusal to

perform on stage ever again but also by a scene that she describes immediately prior to her account of the fete at which the play occurs. She begins by explaining that she has chosen "solitude" at the pension even though "each of the teachers in turn made . . . overtures of special intimacy," because the other teachers are either "narrow," "coarse," "egotist[ical]," "corrupt," or "avaric[ious]" (ch. 14, p. 130). Of these teachers, Lucy singles out one, the Parisienne Zélie St. Pierre, for special odium. She mercilessly points out all the Parisienne's faults—her greed, her lack of principles, her laziness, her coldness, her excessive love of pleasure. Her description of the Parisienne's physiognomy implies both coldness in her "well-opened but frozen eye" and excessive sexuality by her "large, prominent chin."[30] Normally tolerant, Lucy gives no other character, not even those who actively oppose her later friendship with M. Paul, the abuse she heaps on the Parisienne. While there are a number of reasons why Lucy might disapprove of this woman, including the Parisienne's unrequited interest in M. Paul, Lucy does not simply disapprove of her as she does Ginevra when the pretty student's interest in Dr. John is temporarily returned. Lucy responds to the Parisienne with what is for her—indeed, for any of Charlotte Brontë's characters—an extraordinary anger coupled with an even more extraordinary curiosity. According to Lucy,

> The Parisienne . . . was prodigal and profligate (in disposition, that is; as to action, I do not know). That latter quality showed its snake-head to me but once, peeping out very cautiously. A curious kind of reptile it seemed judging from the glimpse I got. Its novelty whetted my curiosity. If it would have come out boldly, perhaps I might philosophically have stood my ground, and cooly surveyed the long thing from forked tongue to scaly tail-tip; but it merely rustled in the leaves of a bad novel, and on encountering a hasty and ill-advised demonstration of wrath, recoiled and vanished, hissing. She hated me from that day.
> (ch. 14, p. 130)

Several elements of this indirectly worded passage suggest that Lucy has rejected a sexual advance by the Parisienne. First, she distinguishes the woman's "profligate" disposition from her "prodigal" one. The current meanings of the word "profligate" were wasteful of one's property or sexually licentious. Lucy rules out the former meaning. Furthermore, "profligate" had acquired the connotation of unusual, including homosexual and lesbian, sexual behavior. In condemning French fiction, The Quarterly Review, for example, had made the following distinction in describing almost all of the surveyed novels as making "a lapse of female chastity . . . the main incident":

"there are not ten in which that lapse is not adulterous; in not a few it is accompanied by incest or other *unnatural profligacies.*"[31]

That the Parisienne's profligacy of disposition is sexual is also suggested by Lucy's calling her glimpse of it one at "its snake-head" and describing it as rustling "in the leaves of a bad novel" – "bad" novels being, again, French novels that recounted sexual immorality. Yet Lucy leaves the nature of the Parisienne's immoral disposition vague. Such reticence is inconsistent with any heterosexual immorality, for neither Brontë nor other popular authors of the mid-nineteenth century were that reticent regarding heterosexuality. In *Jane Eyre,* for example, Rochester actually confesses his affair with a French actress to Jane, and Jane thinks more than once about becoming his mistress. Numerous other popular novels, including Dickens' *David Copperfield,* Gaskell's *Mary Barton,* Wood's *East Lynne,* and Reade's *Griffith Gaunt,* depend on clear references to heterosexual affairs.

Finally, that the Parisienne has displayed a "disposition," while not "action," toward a sexual relation with Lucy is indicated by Lucy's reaction. She says she has no knowledge of the Parisienne's action in this regard. She is ignorant of what is being suggested to her and wishes she had taken a cool survey, because, "Its novelty whetted my curiosity." Lucy, the student as well as teacher, has missed an opportunity to observe a phenomenon of which she has been ignorant. She misses it because of her own quick, angry response to the Parisienne – a response that suggests she has felt this demonstration of the "snake-head" to be a direct insult to herself. And her reaction certainly offends the Parisienne, because the woman hates her from that time on.

Coming as it does immediately before Lucy's "tender" scene on-stage with Ginevra, Lucy's encounter with the Parisienne helps to define her relation with Ginevra as chaste as well as to underline her determination to repress her passions until circumstances offer a relationship that she believes not only right, but divinely sanctioned for her.

That relationship develops out of her friendship with the one male professor at the pension, M. Paul Emanuel, whom she comes to regard as her own Emanuel, or savior. When he invites her to share an "intimate and real" friendship in which they will be "kindred in all but blood," Lucy envies "no girl her lover, no bride her bridegroom, no wife her husband" and feels content to give "a sister's pure affection" so long as she can rely on his friendship (ch. 35, pp. 394, 395). Despite others' attempts to block their friendship, M. Paul purchases Lucy her own school and engages himself to marry her once he returns from a necessary voyage. Although a storm at sea destroys M. Paul, it does not destroy the peace he has given her. His promises of love, like his gifts, are to her "a legacy," a "thought for the present" and "a hope for the future," emblematic of the promises of the New Testament; throughout his absence, she is sustained, because "he wrote as he gave and as he loved, in full-handed, full-hearted plenitude," giving with the benevolence of a paternal God "neither a stone, nor an excuse—neither a scorpion, nor a disappointment" (ch. 42, p. 476; cf. Luke 11:9–13). After his death, the days they have spent together sustain her not only as a memory but as a prophetic assurance of the life to come, for, as she says, "Some real lives do—for some certain days of years—actually anticipate the happiness of Heaven; and, I believe, if such perfect happiness is once felt by good people (to the wicked it never comes), its sweet effect is never wholly lost. Whatever trials follow, whatever pains of sickness or shades of death, the glory precedent still shines through" (ch. 37, p. 422). The name of M. Paul's ship, the *Paul et Virginie*, signifies, moreover, that their betrothal, like that of the lovers in Saint-Pierre's novel of that name, is equivalent to the marriage of true lovers, popularly believed to survive death. As a model spinster explains in *Agatha's Husband*, published the same year as *Villette*, if true lovers "never marry, as sometimes happens . . . God will cause them to meet in the next existence. They cannot be parted—they belong to one another."[32]

In living on the memory and assurances of her betrothed, Lucy is a very Victorian heroine. When we take into consideration her passion, her androgyny, and her experiences with Ginevra and the Parisienne, however, we must enlarge our conception of the Victorian heroine from the pure, sexless, repressed figure she has often seemed. Lucy Snowe is fully human. She is furthermore a woman with more than one option for expressing her nature. Her chaste spinsterhood represents not a lack or failure of her nature or even of her circumstances. Her situation is more psychologically, sexually, and spiritually complex than that. Lucy Snowe consciously defines her own sexual identity and does so partly in terms of conventional sanctions but also in terms of what she believes to be right for her.

Even the name of this Victorian heroine suggests the complexity of her nature. Her Christian name might be construed as an allusion to the virginal St. Lucy or Lucia, a representative of that clear vision by which this Lucy controls the other dimension of herself obliquely indicated by her surname. Frequently read as a sign that Lucy has a cold nature that must be taught to feel, the name "Snowe" was, in fact, intended by Brontë to signify that a passionate nature underlies Lucy's cool behavior. To her publisher Brontë wrote, "A *cold* name she must have; partly, perhaps, on the '*lucus a non lucendo*' principle—partly on that of the 'fitness of things,' for she has about her an external coldness."[33] That Lucy displays an "external coldness" implies that within lies no wintry nature, but one of summer heat. Again, the *lucus a non lucendo* principle is that of the absurd etymology by which a thing is named as the opposite of itself, so that for Lucy to be surnamed

"Snowe" signifies an essential fire, such as characterizes Brontë's more famous heroine, Jane Eyre.

Much as the name "Lucy Snowe" subtly signifies a complex psyche in which strong emotional and sexual needs are held in check by a wider Christian vision, so too the scenes with Ginevra and the Parisienne subtly signify what might at first seem an un-Victorian capacity for fulfilling this complex psyche outside a woman's conventional life of marriage and motherhood. Yet even this capacity proves Victorian too once we view Lucy's situation in the multiple context familiar to Brontë's contemporaries for a woman's experiencing passion for her own sex. Lucy's self-controlled capacity for a range and depth of feeling that includes women is presented in the contexts of the pension that nurtured schoolgirl crushes, the spinster's substitution of a female as the object of her affection, the phrenological analyses of passionate and lesbian women, and, of course, those "bad" French novels out of which the Parisienne glides.

If viewing Brontë's portrait of Lucy Snowe in these multiple contexts can enlarge our understanding of the psychological complexity of her nature, then I think we need to consider these contexts as we review the lives of other Victorian heroines and the lives of the actual women who created and responded to them. Surely, if such a major and influential novelist as Charlotte Brontë—not to mention Richardson, Mrs. Craik, Meredith, and Hardy—could allude to passion between women, we may take it to be, however much a "silent possibility," still a significant dimension of female sexuality in the nineteenth century. There has been much discussion of Victorian attitudes toward sexuality and, over the last decade, women's sexuality in particular. To complete our understanding of those attitudes, we need to consider Victorian women, fictional and real, as sexual beings in relation not only to men but also to women.

Notes

1. *The Lancet,* 1 June 1901, quoted in the *Oxford English Dictionary* under "sapphism."

2. Jeanette Foster, *Sex Variant Women in Literature, A Historical and Quantitative Survey* (New York: Vantage Press, 1956), p. 60; Jane Rule, *Lesbian Images* (Garden City, N.Y.: Doubleday, 1975). In *Sexual Heretics, Male Homosexuality in English Literature from 1850–1900* (London: Routledge & Kegan Paul, 1970), Brian Reade remarks similarly that an anthology of lesbian literature would be more difficult to achieve than one of homosexual literature, adding, "So far as England goes in this context, therefore, it is true to say that homosexual literature for all practical purposes is male" (p. 2).

3. Nina Auerbach, *Communities of Women: An Idea in Fiction* (Cambridge, Mass.: Harvard Univ. Press, 1978), p. 7.

4. *The Quarterly Review,* 66 (April 1836), 66.

5. Quoted by Mario Praz in "An English Imitation of Diderot's *La Religieuse* (C.R. Maturin's *Tale of the Spaniard*)," *Review of English Studies,* 6 (1930), p. 429. Praz regards *La Religieuse* as a source for the story of Alonzo in *Melmoth,* vol. 2, ch. 9, citing resemblances between his situation and that of Diderot's young nun. Arthur M. Wilson notes that nineteenth-century anti-clericals, both French and English, welcomed *La Religieuse,* and he gives the number of editions in *Diderot* (New York: Oxford Univ. Press, 1972), pp. 385–87; 782, n. 36.

6. Enid Starkie, *From Gautier to Eliot: The Influence of France on English Litera-ture 1851–1939* (London: Hutchinson, 1960), pp. 27, 29; Starkie adds that Gautier's novel was "considered of topical interest at the time when, according to Houssaye, the relationship between George Sand and the actress Marie Dorval was at the height of its intensity." She cites *Mademoiselle de Maupin,* Balzac's "La Fille aux yeux d'or," and Latouche's *Frigoletta* as sources for Swinburne's *Lesbia Brandon,* which also "deals with sapphic love" (p. 44). René Jasinski recounts the history and notoriety of Madeleine d'Aubigny in *Les Annees Romantiques de Th. Gautier* (Paris: Librairie Vui-bert, 1929), 285–86. D'Aubigny died in 1707, but she was well-remembered a cen-tury later, as indicated by Jasinski's quotation from an 1890 letter: "Au temps de mon enfance on parlait encore de cette virago"; specific revivals that Jasinski mentions are Jules Janin's *Barnave* (1832) and *Memoires* (1836), an 1835 article, an 1839 com-edy, but he notes that there were others (pp. 286–88).

7. Théophile Gautier, *Mademoiselle de Maupin* (Paris: Charpentier, Libraire-Éditeur, 1858), p. 16.

8. William Black, *A Daughter of Heth* (1871; rev. ed. New York: Harper, 1892), pp. 124–25.

9. Mrs. Craik, *A Woman's Thoughts about Women* (London: Hurst & Blackett, 1858), p. 131.

10. Ibid., p. 135.

11. Ibid., p. 138.

12. Vol. 7 (New York, 1845), 408. The supplement was to be "devoted to the evils of sexual excesses in their various forms — matrimonial, promiscuous, and individ-ual" and was to cover "the *whole* ground of this excess, instead of occupying a single field" (p. 409).

13. Mrs. L. Miles, *Phrenology, and the Moral Influence of Phrenology: Arranged for general study, and the purposes of education, from the first published works of Gall and Spurzheim to the Latest Discoveries of the present period* (Philadelphia: Carey, Lea, & Blanchard, 1835), p. 25; and *How to Read Character: A New Illustrated Hand-book of Phrenology and Physiognomy for Students & Examiners; with a Descriptive Chart* (New York: Samuel R. Wells, 1874), p. 39.

14. O.S. Fowler, *Human Science: or, Phrenology* (Philadelphia: National Publish-ing Co., 1873), p. 679.

15. Franz Joseph Gall, *The Influence of the Brain on the Form of the Head,* trans. Winslow Lewis (Boston: Marsh, Capen and Lyon, 1835), III, 169.

16. Samuel Richardson, *Pamela, or Virtue Rewarded.* The Norton Library (New York: Norton, 1958), p. 129.

17. John Cleland, *Memoirs of a Woman of Pleasure* (New York: Putnam's, 1963), p. 15. Compare Book 7 of Sterne's *Tristram Shandy*, which ridicules the affair between an Abbess and a young novice.

18. *Pamela*, p. 19.

19. Ibid., p. 109.

20. Samuel Richardson, *The History of Sir Charles Grandison*, ed. Jocelyn Harris. (1753-54; rpt. London: Oxford Univ. Press, 1972), I, 42.

21. Ibid., I, 43.

22. Ibid., I, 69.

23. George Meredith, *The Ordeal of Richard Feverel*. Signet Classics (New York: New American Library of World Literature, 1961), p. 401.

24. Thomas Hardy, *Desperate Remedies*. Wessex ed. (London: Macmillan, 1912), p. 93.

25. *Spectator* (22 April 1871) in *Thomas Hardy: The Critical Heritage*, ed. R.G. Cox (London: Routledge and Kegan Paul; New York: Barnes and Noble, 1970), p. 5.

26. *The Brontës: Life and Letters*, ed. C.K. Shorter (London: Hodder and Stoughton, 1908), I, 191.

27. See Ian Jack, "Physiognomy, Phrenology and Characterisation in the Novels of Charlotte Brontë," *Brontë Society Transactions*, 15, (1970), 377-91, and Dr. J.P. Browne's "Phrenological Estimate" of Charlotte Brontë (1851) in T.J. Wise and J.A. Symington, *The Brontës: Their Lives, Friendships and Correspondences* (Oxford: Shakespeare Head Press, 1932), III, 256-58.

28. Charlotte Brontë, *Villette* (1853; rpt. London: Collins, 1953), ch. 2, p. 26. All further references are in the text by chapter and page to this edition.

29. Kate Millett, *Sexual Politics* (Garden City, N.Y.: Doubleday, 1970), p. 141.

30. See *How to Read Character* for a typical analysis of the meaning of facial features.

31. Vol. 66 (April 1836), 106.

32. Mrs. Craik, *Agatha's Husband, A Novel* (London: Milner and Co., n.d.), p. 167. Cf. Mrs. Craik's statement in *The Woman's Kingdom, A Love Story* (1869; rpt. London: Hurst and Blackett, n.d.) that for everyone "there is but one true love— leading to the one perfect marriage, or else leading through dark and thorny yet sacred ways to that perpetual virginity of heart and life which is only second to marriage in its holiness and happiness."

33. 11 June 1852, in Wise and Symington.

Wendell Stacy Johnson

Fallen Women, Lost Children: Wilde and the Theatre of the Nineties

"It's not work that any woman would do for pleasure, goodness knows, though to hear the pious people talk you would suppose it was a bed of roses." Shaw's Mrs. Warren is speaking to her daughter Vivie, in the second act of his play about the "fallen woman." Mrs. Warren's profession is prostitution, but by it she has risen in the world, not fallen. So this play represents the inversion of a familiar mid- and late-Victorian theme. A sensual life suggested by the red rose of feminine sexuality which Tennyson finds so fascinating and so terrifying has been reduced to hard work for a hard-pressed woman and no rose garden at all.[1] At the same time that he denies that image, Shaw is playing with and against the stage convention of so much nineteenth-century melodrama, that which has the harlot with a tender heart or at best the erring woman who now seeks redemption.

A standard comment on the late Victorian stage, especially the "problem plays" of Henry Arthur Jones and Arthur Wing Pinero, is George Sampson's: "The only problem for the theatre was that concerning women who had made, or were contemplating, breaches of the Seventh Commandment."[2] And the plays of the 1890s did very often, still, concern women who committed adultery. They were not, ordinarily, working-class prostitutes like the Jenny of Rossetti's poem or the country-lass-gone-wrong of his painting called "Found"; nor middle-class wives such as the one in Augustus Egg's triptych "Past and Present," a strayed woman who is driven from her husband, home, and two (legitimate) daughters; nor again, ordinarily, the artistic or intellectual women who break their marriage vows quite openly like Mary Ann Peacock Meredith and the versions of her in George Meredith's verse and fiction, or who refuse to be legally married like Sue Bridehead in Hardy's *Jude the Obscure*. These figures on the stage, finally, were no latter-day versions of the Browning woman—Pompilia, for example—who is liberated, by an act of romantic daring, from a marriage that enslaves her. They tend, rather, to be seen in relation to Society. That is, not to a whole society but to the socially ascendent classes, where they hold at best ambiguous positions. Disaster, which threatens women who too openly break the sexual code in the Victorian drama, is the disaster of not being received in the best houses. But what they may fear more is that decent society will exclude their children.

The plot structure of social comedy, including melodramatic elements, is inherited by late Victorian playwrights from the earlier stage, Victorian and pre-Victorian. But this particular situation of the woman who has erred becomes in the 1890s, with the impact of Ibsen's realism and increasing skepticism about easy resolutions to the Victorian "woman question," a more than conventional matter. It cannot be resolved as in Browning's dramatic poetry by being placed in the long ago and far away, any more than the problem of what Mill has defined as "the subjection of women" can be resolved by the shifting of tone that Tennyson displays in *The Princess*—moving from sentimentalism to farce to sententious but inconclusive idealizing— and, at a much lower level, Pinero does as late as 1888 in *The Weaker Sex*, diluting the serious matter of women's claims to justice (which the dramatist tentatively acknowledges) with a finally farcical manner.

The English theatre of the 1890s, however, which produced the first stage-worthy plays of literary merit in the century, amounted at its best to more than imitation Ibsen. And its best was not the mature Pinero nor even the early Shaw. Its best was Wilde. Oscar Wilde moves very rapidly in this decade from highly competent comedy-cum-melodrama, witty and well-made in the mode of Scribe—although his wit has been too often taken only as a decoration overlaying the slight and irrelevant plot—to the height of social comedy, *The Importance of Being Earnest. Earnest* is not a freak of genius unrelated to the other plays. In those others, Wilde makes the most of sexual imagery from earlier Victorian poets and sexual conventions from earlier playwrights, distinctly qualifying with his wit both moral associations and moral endings, both aesthetic and social meanings. He introduces paradox to the modern stage, at first, it might seem, with merely perverse playfulness and then at last with critical effect. And it is he who influences, rather than being in any important way influenced by, Pinero and Shaw.[3]

Wilde, before Shaw, turns the cliché of the feminine rose to dramatic and ironic purpose. His once-lily-white and priggish Lady Windermere, after discovering that Mrs. Erlynne "is better than I am," still vaguely longs for the simple Tennysonian contrast between the red rose of earthly experience and the white blossom of lost virginal ignorance (for Tennyson the contrast is not really, at last, so simple) when she speaks of the Garden at Selby as

Augustus Egg, *Past and Present, No. 1*
The Tate Gallery, London

if it were Eden, where "the roses are white and red." Inevitably, by implication, she has come to recognize something of the hybrid in herself. And the irony of that final remark to Mrs. Arbuthnot by the egoist Lord Illingworth in *A Woman of No Importance,* "You gave yourself to me like a flower, to do anything I liked with" — because he did do as he liked — is that the poor rose was taken and sold. Wilde reveals in his way, as Shaw does more bluntly, how vulnerable delicate blossoms all are in an acquisitive society. The erotic use of women suggested by metaphors of roses and involving the reality of beds means nothing like a bed of roses for "fallen" beauties, as not only Mrs. Warren knows.

The plots of *Lady Windermere's Fan* and *A Woman of No Importance* have at their centers these two demi-heroines who have strayed and who have children. Lady Windermere must remain Mrs. Erlynne's unacknowledged daughter, as Gerald is Mrs. Arbuthnot's child but must be Lord Illingworth's unacknowledged son, because both children are illegitimate. A contrast between these women now beyond the social pale (if the truth were known) and the children quite comfortably within it still (so long as the truth is not known) is the basic plot situation for both plays and for at least some dozen other English plays produced between the late 1870s and the second decade of the twentieth century.

II

Three plays of the 1890s provide a specially striking set of parallels: *Lady Windermere's Fan* from 1892, *The Second Mrs. Tanqueray* from 1893, and *Mrs. Warren's Profession* from 1894.[4] There are striking differences, of course, among the three. Wilde's play is essentially a comedy, Pinero's is essentially a melodrama, Shaw's is essentially a problem play that goes beyond Ibsen in its moral and prescriptive attitude toward a social problem: the problem not only of sexual prostitution but more generally of capitalist exploitation. But the comedy has melodramatic and distinctly moral aspects, the melodrama includes some almost Wildean comedy and makes a gesture finally toward confronting its moral problem, while the Shavian indictment is also comic, with its own paradoxical phrases echoing Wilde, and is evidently based upon a familiar melodramatic plot situation.

As for the central characters, the children and the mothers, Lady Windermere is indeed the fallen woman's daughter and Shaw's Vivie the Madam's child, but Ellean is only a stepdaughter to the second Mrs. Tanqueray and she seems almost too legitimate; the maternal figures are strong in their several distinct ways, clever or demanding or crafty. Mrs. Erlynne is consistently sympathetic as well as clever, while Paula Tanqueray is neurotic, often petulant, and Mrs. Warren shrewd and also generous if in her all too commonsensical way still marred by ordinary human greed. Probably most critics today would consider Pinero's the weakest of the plays (Wilde's plot creaks too, but is relieved by the funny and apparently cynical speeches). Yet it is Paula who remains the most interesting of these characters to an actress — an actress who might bring off Ibsen's Hedda or Chekhov's Ranyevska and still find Mrs. Tanqueray a challenge.

The children in each play are nearly too good to be true. Lady Windermere and Ellean can be saved at last, conventionally, from a goodness so simple as to be insufferable; Vivie stays what she has always been, a prig. The shock of learning that her mother is a bawd and her own income derives from the trade in sex is really rather slight, and she is at the end very good, very high-minded. Her views may be admirable in the abstract. Shaw never suggests a sense of the contradiction between those views and her own behavior. Vivie supports herself by doing actuarial work "with an eye on the Stock Exchange," so that hers is in its own way (certainly, for a Socialist) the profession of a bawd and prostitute. In her overriding need for independence which will give economic power, she is unquestionably Mrs. Warren's daughter.

But, finally, the mothers represent in every instance the true focus of the drama. Each of these plays presents a woman who is concerned with gaining or retaining the love of a daughter. Mrs. Erlynne's and Mrs. Warren's daughters are their own, and are illegitimate. Paula Tanqueray has no child of her own, and her stepdaughter is very legitimate. The problem of legitimacy is crucial in each play: what is a legitimate child, what is a legitimate wife, what is legitimate love? Such socially and morally complex questions reverberate here as they do in the poems of Browning and Tennyson, and the novels of Meredith, of Dickens, of Hardy. One thinks of Esther Summerson and Lady Dedlock. One may think as well of the lives and letters of George Eliot, John Stuart Mill, Harriet Taylor.

III

"*Lady Windermere's Fan* has at first sight a definite kinship with *Mrs. Dane's Defence* and *The Second Mrs. Tanqueray*," Allardyce Nicoll comments; but he goes on to distinguish Wilde's comedy from the later plays (Henry Arthur Jones's Mrs. Dane defended herself at the very end of the decade and the century). His assertion that Wilde is wholly uninterested in moral implications, that the quality of his work lies wholly in its witty dialogue, not at all its story, is surely too simple—one cannot abstract what is said entirely from the context, ignoring who says it and in what situation—but Nicoll is certainly right to emphasize the difference.[5]

Wilde's "Play About a Good Woman" is obviously a playing, too, upon the word *good*. What was clear to his audience in 1892 was the hardly new idea that a woman who has erred can yet be generous and so "good," can indeed be morally strengthened through her suffering – and repentence. At the same time, it was and is evident that a sheltered young woman like the Lady Windermere who is first seen "arranging" the roses from Selby "in a blue bowl" can be too neat, too puritanically good to be generously good at all. So much for the obvious. The significant objects in Act I are roses and a fan, the significant speech is Lord Darlington's, not the young puritan's. That lady plays with roses and fans lacking any sense of how fragile flowering nature is; of how fragile, how artificial and deceptive, the social world of fans must prove to be. The "bad" Darlington, she insists, is really "better than most other men" – because she finds him naturally attractive and socially agreeable. Her allowing of "no compromise," her insisting that life is a "sacrament" of love, of sacrifice, is bitterly ironic: she is too shallow to realize that she compromises constantly, accepting Darlington's attentions while denying that she does, or that she will not for a moment consider sacrificing for love a vain conception of herself as saintly, with a heavenly home and perfect husband. Darlington plays with the idea that her being charming makes her puritanical vanity inconsequent; like Wilde himself and like some other great Romantics, he denies the difference between moral and aesthetic. Yet in this play there is a moral meaning determined by manners, by style, just as there is a true story within the predictable plot determined by language, by wit. The "bad" man – and his badness – is the one unresolved ambiguity in the drama, for we are never certain of his attitude toward Windermere's supposed behavior, the young wife's situation, or sexual bondage and freedom, just as he may not be certain or able to distinguish conviction from willful illusion, principle from desire. This "bad" man knows one true thing: that "good" people do "a good deal of harm" both by their Calvinistic dividing of the real world into the altogether bad and the perfectly good and by their making "badness of such extraordinary importance." His genuine wit implies that evil is in everyone and that it is banal. These are altogether serious moral ideas.

The seriousness of these ideas is not lessened by his possibly being in his trivial way quite bad. Nor does the Duchess of Berwick's commonplace observation that men are all bad, followed by the beautifully simple-minded "We're good," respond to anything real. ("Dear Lord Darlington, how thoroughly depraved you are," she exclaims delightedly, as she would to no woman.) She is only accepting that now familiar fictional version of the Fall so that instead of the Fall of Man(kind) it becomes the Fall of Woman: now women are, as in the "madonna-harlot complex," either angelically pure or altogether, but not trivially, depraved. She is happy to observe that the male sex is quite satisfactorily bad "without any exception." Sexually they have the right if not indeed the obligation to be so.

The implication is clear enough, and thus Wilde need not spell it out as

Pinero does, that if "bad" and "good" refer largely to sexual transgressions, then bad men require bad women. Wilde might have had homosexuality in mind as an alternative, and the relevance of these speeches to that subject is apparent (if not so apparent as in *Dorian Gray*), but the subject of course is not touched upon. What his speech on mercenary women, uttered once more by Lord Darlington, implies is also clear enough: Lady Windermere would make an example of Mrs. Erlynne for being mercenary and thus immoral (in blunt words that she cannot use, a prostitute), but she does not reflect on what her rose gardens, her fan, and her title cost, or whether she could have married without there being some such gross considerations.

"A wonderful thing, a fan," she says in Act II, just before Mrs. Erlynne drops hers. The final business of the fan, that artificial turning point of the play, is just as stagey as the earlier scene where the wife finds and overreacts to her husband's other bank book, with its record of payments to the other woman. But the fan, as Wilde's title indicates, carries more meaning.

Fans, prettily arranged like flowers, are still works of artifice, not natural, and they define this social world of good and bad: they are usefully useless, they hide and hint, they are maneuvered to forbid or flirt, and they become in this play the decorative masks that sum up both manners and morals. A fan may serve good manners that amount to bad morals, egoism, and self-serving tricks. A fan may also mask for better purposes, just as a lie like Mrs. Erlynne's about the fan is a self-sacrificing sign of love.

At the end of Act II Lady Windermere is persuaded that her husband has "broken the bond of marriage" and decides that she will "break its bondage." She is very different from the Browning heroine who breaks that bondage and from the Meredith heroine who refuses it, because her response is based on a momentary misunderstanding and not an actual experience of tyranny or gross injustice. (But then Othello acts on no more evidence, for the handkerchief is as flimsy as the bank book and, later, the fan.) Her motive seems to be as much hurt pride as moral indignation. Whether her lover believes the gossip or not, he still believes her perfectly "good"; his attraction to the young woman appears to outweigh Darlington's intermittent wit. In Act III that is evident. He "moralizes," as Cecil Graham complains, about his good Lady Windermere. And in that act the contrast between wit and plot does seem a strain as the skeptical and supposedly frivolous commentator becomes all at once conventional. The basic and not altogether admirable motivations come to contradict the brittle intelligence of the speeches. It now can be seen that this plot is a cliché the paradoxical and comic comments mock; yet the speaker is no single voice—there can be no consistently antimoralizing moralist without his standing outside the drama, outside the world he lives in—but a pervasive sensibility which speaks in several voices, often the voices of those who speak more wisely than they know.

In the action of the fourth and final act, mockery takes over again, and it is the clever lie of Mrs. Erlynne that saves a situation from both disaster and cliché, from a moral and aesthetic shambles. The apparently good woman is humbled, but the supposedly bad one does not drift away in a golden glow of motherly martyrdom. Mrs. Erlynne has to carry it off. At the end she wins Lord Augustus and worldly status, not only to save a comedy but also to display a truth. And what is the truth that the ignorant daughter, who is in a way like the mother's younger impetuous self, is not finally mature enough to understand? It is simply that virginal flowers and delicate fans cannot outlast either natural generosity (the unsentimental essence of a mother's love) or good sense, which is learned—is artificial, even, a matter of wit in the two and ultimately identical senses of wisdom and style. Mother knows best.

IV

All of this artful complication means that Wilde has made of the fallen woman and her child not something trivial, not a ridiculous vehicle for irresponsible paradox, any more than he has used the subject to exploit sensational and pathetic possibilities, as Pinero does, or to state a case, as Shaw. He is recording an actual world, a strictly limited society, with its falsehoods and pretenses and, in spite of everything, its comic possibilities: the possibility, above all, of shaping life as a true comedy with a successful ending through honest vision as well as sensible deception.

There is little of the comic in *Mrs. Tanqueray,* and it does not allow for a happy ending. Yet in that play Pinero is conscious of Wilde—it was written while Wilde's piece enjoyed considerable success in the theatre—and even tries to use some Wildean dialogue. In the first act of Pinero's melodrama Cayley Drummle has a little of a Darlington's or Illingworth's accent when he comments on the dubious Miss Hervey, now Lady Orreyd—

> who would have been, perhaps has been, described in the reports
> of the Police or the Divorce Court as an actress. Had she
> belonged to a lower stratum of our advanced civilization she
> would, in the event of judicial inquiry, have defined her calling
> with equal justification as that of a dressmaker—

and on the loss of social standing suffered by a man who marries such a woman:

> You may dive into many waters, but there is *one* social Dead Sea—!
> JAYNE. Perhaps you're right.
> DRUMMLE. Right! Good God! I wish you could prove me otherwise!
> Why, for years I've been sitting, and watching and waiting.

MISQUITH. You're in form tonight, Cayley. May we ask where you've been in the habit of squandering your useful leisure?

DRUMMLE. Where? On the shore of that same sea.

But this is all much coarser than anything in Wilde, and not surprisingly the would-be wit Drummle becomes in the succeeding three acts a conventional and a naive sentimentalist.

In those acts Aubrey Tanqueray is revealed as himself a sentimentalist and a remarkably confused one; his daughter Ellean as the predicted cold young woman—her confusion, when she settles tentatively with a distracted father she has never known and a neurotic stepmother who hungrily demands her filial love but whom she never can know, is at least understandable; and Paula Tanqueray as a person equally victimized and maddening. Paula's resentment of Mrs. Cortelyou for her apparent snub, given vent in Act II, is intensified when that old friend of her husband and the first Mrs. Tanqueray takes Ellean abroad; and Act III brings matters to a climax with the appearance of Hugh Ardale.

Hugh is in effect a plot device. His presence shows how fragile the present Mrs. Tanqueray's reputation is, for he is her former lover. It also reinforces the tension between Paula and Ellean with a curious version of the love triangle, in which illicit love cancels out innocent love which conflicts with maternal love which is frustrated by the memory of the illicit past. All of this plot conflict is arbitrary and conventional. Neither Paula nor Hugh—nor, for that matter, Tanqueray—will shatter Ellean's innocence, which is really simple ignorance and just as false as Lady Windermere's smug "goodness"; it is already clear that under these circumstances Act II must end badly for everyone.

It does. The woman who has been wronged (and Tanqueray believes that Paula's touches of the coarse derive from that experience) must be marked and so further wronged. She can, specifically, claim no legitimate child. In some degree this familiar plot of the theatre is so because it is a plot, so to speak, of the society; it may sound like theatrical bathos, but for all the self-dramatizing tone there is still something in Paula's remark, "I believe the future is only the past again, entered through another gate."

And Paula Tanqueray is not at the end wholly unrelated to Hedda Gabler. She is, however, very much a lesser relation, and this is distinctly a lesser play. Its weakness is heard in the last speeches of Aubrey and Ellean, which try to answer a problem but can only seem feeble. Aubrey rails against the abuse of vulnerable women by amoral men, but without the point and quite explicit social purpose of a Shaw. He simply blames all upon the casual womanizer, indicting Ardale.

Curse him! Yes, I do curse him—him and his class! Perhaps I curse myself, too, in doing it. He has only led "a man's life"—just as I, how many of us, have done! The misery he has brought on me and mine it's likely enough we, in our time, have helped to bring on others by this leading "a man's life!"

The outburst is not merely witless moralizing, and it disposes of the really rather witless "wit" of Drummle upon actresses and dressmakers; still, the ambiguity of "his class" remains tantalizing, for this is neither an insight into guile nor an all out attack on social and economic wrongs. And when Ellean, chastened, cries, "I helped to kill her. If I'd only been merciful!" she has only a rather vague sense of mercy, not much wisdom or understanding that she can refer to.

These reactions are odd, half-ironic comments on the suffering and suicide of Paula Tanqueray. The play could, and can, come to life if the actress playing Paula can communicate enough inner complexity—that of the wronged, self-indulgent, intensely maternal and frustrated, intensely neurotic woman—to overcome the all too clearly "worked up" plot with its too simply theatrical tricks.

V

The trick of *Mrs. Warren's Profession* is theatricality partly inverted. But only partly so. Here again the daughter may appear to be of sterner moral stuff than the older woman who now longs to be maternal, but this is again in part because her existence in society has been secure. Here the daughter figure is taken by Shaw the moralist to be really the good, at least the better, person, for she is uncorrupted. Her mother's corruption by being a prostitute she can accept as a necessary evil; she cannot accept the acquiescence in the way of this world, in fact the greedy ambition, that has made her mother a bawd as well, a capitalist living off the prostitution of others. So where Wilde makes an illegitimate daughter see something of the hard facts of life and accept not the moral purism but the moral good sense of comedy, and where Pinero makes the legitimate child and stepdaughter see those facts with a pathetic hope that mercy may help (as her father curses male egoism but offers no solution in wit or policy for it), Shaw essentially returns to a true "Victorian" moral stance. His Vivie will not, seeing such social facts, accommodate herself in any way to them, at least not in her rhetoric; neither will she simply lament them. She is more willful than witty, more stern than merciful to her own household. *Mrs. Warren's Profession* is one of the "Plays for Puritans" in a somewhat different sense, perhaps, than Shaw intended. He and Vivie *are* sexual and social puritans—as much as, say, Karl Marx was, and in principle no doubt admirably so. Shaw's moral conviction is firm, even if his sense of life's complications, its paradoxical admixture of harsh and cold with cosmic possibilities, is never subtle.

It is Shaw, not Wilde, for whom comic paradoxes are beside the point, amounting to a kind of decoration or relief. (He even fails to make much of the plot's comic potential, of the perhaps incestuous attraction between Frank and Vivie—are they brother and sister?—in the way a Fielding, for example, does.) His play is as contrived as either Wilde's or Pinero's, as quintessentially Victorian in theme, and much more High Victorian in its message, which is neither sophisticated nor diluted.

The plot generally follows the well-made plan of those others. In Acts I and II a mature woman and her daughter have just met, the daughter is admired by a young man who woos her, and the young woman learns of her mother's dark past—as Lady Windermere and Ellean learn such truths, although very gradually and not fully. The daughter recognizes the shallowness and the crudeness of her mother's old companions. She can at best be only tentatively reconciled to the "poor old mother" who is partly that and partly still a lively, sexual, and yet a socially and personally frustrated woman.

Act III, with the slightly comic but much more pathetic clergymen, Frank's father, the ineffectual Praed, and the brutal bully Crofts all gathered, shows the daughter Vivie in contrast with them and their world of greed, hypocrisy, and—with the baby-talking lover—sentimentalism. For her this is all quite intolerable. It seems inevitable that Vivie will remove herself and be alone in Act IV.

In that last act she counters Frank's feeble attempts at wit in the bad imitation of Wilde—"I'm not a fool in the ordinary sense: only in the Scriptural sense of doing all the things the wise men declared to be folly, after trying them himself on the most extensive scale"—and Mrs. Warren's maternal appeals, so reminiscent of Mrs. Erlynne's but more yet of Paula Tanqueray's. Vivie chooses still to be alone. She chooses in effect to be an orphan. Where Windermere's wife was ignorant of her true mother, and Ellean transformed hers into a saint in heaven, unable to accept the evidently less than saint-like surrogate on earth, this young woman who refuses to be involved with the fallen and truly culpable must simply and clearheadedly deny her own role as a daughter. Her judgment may be sound, but her manner suggests that she can stand outside class, a family, outside not only Society of the narrow fashionable sort but outside all society as it now is.

Incidentally, Vivie rejects Praed's "Gospel of Art," a thin parody of Wilde and Pater, as well as Croft's "Gospel of Getting On" that Matthew Arnold scorned. Praed's dithyrambic is wholly beside the point:

I feel bound to tell you, speaking as an artist, and believing that the most intimate human relationships are far beyond and above the scope of the law, that though I know your mother is an unmarried woman, I do not respect her the less on that account. I respect her more.

(Failing to understand the real nature of Mrs. Warren's life and livelihood, he *does* take the metaphor of the passionate roses seriously still.) And Crofts has stupidly tried to corrupt Vivie in a way she can easily resist, with his own "philosophy of life," his reminding her of the Crofts Scholarship endowed by profits from sweatshops, his pointing out that "no man can offer you a safer position." But in their hopelessly muddled or crudely selfish ways, these men are talking about people. Vivie is as fastidiously unaffected by human obligations in the specific sort as any aesthete in a garret, as much devoted to getting on in her own profession as any crude entrepreneur. She is unsparing of mother and lover: "Now once for all, mother, you want a daughter and Frank wants a wife. I dont want a mother; and I dont want a husband. I have spared neither Frank nor myself in sending him about his business. Do you think I will spare you?" She is cold. She is moral. She is earnest.

And finally, although the comparison seems almost inevitable with those other plays about mother- and daughter-figures, the seemingly fallen woman and the supposedly pure, *Mrs. Warren's Profession* presents in its earnestness an even more interesting, an even more telling, contrast with Wilde's one great play. Vivie acts the orphan; Jack Worthing is one.

VI

One of the curiosities in the criticism, or more properly, non-criticism, of Wilde's plays is the assertion, often merely the assumption, that *The Importance of Being Earnest* is a brilliant trick of "insolent" paradox — far removed except in being insolent or mannered from his lesser work but sharing what one egregious commentator calls the "fundamental insincerity" of it all.[6] There is really a progression from the earnest Lady Windermere to the not so earnest Ernest.

That thematic progression can be charted by reference to the characters and plots of each play. The clever Mrs. Erlynne protects her illegitimate daughter from disgrace and from too much knowledge, manipulating events so that the playacting and the play can conclude with comedy triumphant. It is comedy still based in part on ignorance. The conscientious Mrs. Arbuthnot protects her illegitimate son from the degrading honors offered by his own father and is obliged to let him know the truth, in a play full of moral and specifically biblical language. It is also a play with, now, more psychological range: Mrs. Arbuthnot has been transformed from being rather like Hester Prynne to being almost like Portnoy's mother; Gerald's beloved Hester herself becomes a virtual Ruth to Mrs. Arbuthnot's Naomi, transformed as the other daughter-figures are from being a prig who is outraged by the sins of the mothers into being one able to say, "God's law is only Love," and she says so with the full knowledge that Lady Windermere lacks. The play ends as a modified and somber comedy—if comedy at all—about parents and children: "Children begin by loving their parents. After a time they judge them. Rarely if ever do they forgive them."

The next play is also about falling, loving, judging, and forgiving. But it develops into something different. *An Ideal Husband* has no relationship of mother and child. It has no fallen woman who is basically good—the fallen Mrs. Cheveley is genuinely bad—and it is darker and more complicated in plot, more problematic as a play. It is more contrived, even, than the earlier ones; its moments of cynicism are more serious, its explicit morality is more forced. It is yet fuller, too, of verbal paradoxes because far from being a distraction quite irrelevant to plot, these passages underline the intensely and unresolvedly paradoxical nature of the whole.

In fact, *An Ideal Husband* has such earnest moralizing—by that means precisely it risks being called a profoundly immoral play—that it seems less like *Earnest* than the earlier plays do. But it is a necessary part of the movement toward that climax. It puts aside Wilde's recurrent theatrical subject of legitimacy and inheritance in order for him to come back to that theme with fuller control over its anxiety-producing ambiguity. Puzzling and, for all its bons mots, remarkably confused in tone as to parody and preaching— in dramatic plausibility it is easily the least successful of Wilde's plays, as if the thickness of the plot might distract from the murkiness of the moral— it nevertheless clears the air. It does so, that is, for Wilde; its own gaseous mixture of platitude with playfulness, facts about power and greed with ideals about good conventional behavior, remains thick and murky on the stage. Here, for the first time, what was only tentatively earnest and even by implication moralistic in the plots is flatly so, and the audience hardly knows whether to wince or laugh. Is this parody indeed, or a perverse sermon? Wilde reverses the idea of pure women made impure, with always flawed men wanting them to be like virginal roses, and makes it the idea of ideal men shown to be really corrupt, with naïve women urging *them* to be the saints. He does so only to come back at last to just the same cliché but with a savage conclusion: men love and need power, as Sir Robert Chiltern does, and at best are compromised by that need; all this being so, their lives are more valuable than women's—for power is everything—and so poor, pure women who have only love, not "intellect," must sacrifice themselves for these strong, power-greedy men. This is the ultimate cynicism couched in terms both sexual and social. For better or worse, sheer potency and not maternal love, not sexual love, certainly not love of truth, must conquer all. We may nod or shudder, but the point is clear. Mabel Chiltern's rejecting the "ideal husband" (that her brother certainly is not), means only that she can love just a real, fallible person; yet that is not the same as Gertrude Chiltern's accepting a power broker who may one day be Prime Minister.

All the unlikely turns of plot—the old letter Mrs. Cheveley wants to use against Sir Robert, the brooch as bracelet that betrays her thievery because of loyal if at last conventional Lord Goring, the foolish intercepted note written by Gertrude, this battery of claptrap—lead to the wry and twisted fact. The fact is that a happy marriage within this society is defined as a marriage of male power and female complacence. The Chiltern family has no children.

In *Earnest,* there is a child without parents. Wilde's first two English plays are about parents and children, *An Ideal Husband* about couples without children—while the mother-daughter relationship, the illegitimacy and even incest, the lust for power variously touched upon in these comic melodramas finds a dark expression in Wilde's *Salome*—and the one wholly successful play is about children without having any seriously realized marriage of the sexes yet. The promise of marriages all round at the end is the funniest of burlesques on the conventions imposed by comedy, although the promise *is* what motivates all.

Still, there is one thematic complex that appears in all the plays. They resemble one another when they seem not to. *An Ideal Husband,* for instance, is filled with references to the filial relationship which its plot virtually ignores: in all the serious talk about the corrupting force of the modern, of "this century," both Mabel and of all people Mrs. Chevely have some things to say about the drawbacks and advantages of kinship and especially about parents and children: "Fathers have so much to learn from their sons nowadays," says Mrs. Chevely in an affected version of just what other characters and plays have straightforwardly said. And *Earnest* would pose for Victorian audiences at once the question of the foundling, his legitimacy, his parentage.

Wilde's theme of legitimate family relationships, of love in kinship but also the need for links of definition—for both fallen woman and a lost child like Jack Worthing—is summed up in both its seriousness and its silliness (when wrongly and too earnestly regarded) by his funniest and finest play. The perfect comic comment on the more vulnerable aspects of *Lady Windermere's Fan* and *A Woman of No Importance*—and, to anticipate, *Mrs. Warren's Profession*—with their misunderstandings, pathos, and righteous posing, is a scene in Act III when Jack speaks to the Miss Prism who, improbably, abandoned him in error at Victoria Station.

JACK (*in a pathetic voice*). Miss Prism, more is restored to you than this handbag. I was the baby you placed in it.

MISS PRISM (*amazed*). You?

JACK (*embracing her*). Yes . . . mother!

MISS PRISM (*recoiling in indignant astonishment*). Mr. Worthing! I am unmarried!

JACK. Unmarried! I do not deny that is a serious blow. But after all, who has a right to cast a stone against one who has suffered? Cannot repentance wipe out an act of folly? Why should there be one law for men and another for women? Mother, I forgive you. (*Tries to embrace her again.*)

Here, then, is the perfectly ironic version of the old familiar theme, the fallen woman and lost child. The situation can be so comic because it is based on a mistake: as Miss Prism objects, "There is some error." In this play about illusions and absurdities — where, even so, deluding fans and delicate flowers are replaced by food, by the nourishment promised or given with cucumber sandwiches, bread or cake, and muffins, which suggest the ordinary needs of real life — the ordinary assumptions and sad probabilities are denied. In reality, most Victorian foundlings are impoverished bastards, just as most lovers lack those titles or names their loved ones want and most lies do not accidentally prove to be true. The comedy that relies on outrageously improbable happy solutions, such as the *deus ex machina* (the gipsy who knows the truth, the traveling peddler with his tale of Joseph Andrews' parentage) or poor fuddled Miss Prism, ironically confirms life's grim realities by saying, "never mind, but pretend otherwise."

It says that if not only sexuality but all of life is not a bed of roses, if the relation of erring parent and lost child may be that of alien as much as kin, if one's daily bread is sometimes sour dough rather than cake or muffins, that may not be the most important thing. Newly christened Ernest is delighted by his name but is in earnest only about being just himself, one who can still, at the end, *play* wittily on words. Lady Bracknell suspects him still of triviality; so have most of Wilde's earnest reviewers and critics.

Beds of roses, fallen women, and fortunate foundlings belong in sentimentalists' plays and books. This play is no lurid melodrama, but it is a play with recurrent references to the lurid novel which trades in sexual sensation. Love, even a rather childish doting love, is Cecily's redemption from indulging in such fantasies of dark sensation and sin. Manners more than the book of Army Lists prove Uncle Jack's legitimacy.

Notes

1. The sexual flower imagery in Tennyson, which E.D.H. Johnson comments upon in his often-cited note—in *PMLA*, 64 (1949), 1222–27—is dealt with at greater length in my *Sex and Marriage in Victorian Poetry* (Ithaca: Cornell Univ. Press, 1975), pp. 110–84.

This essay on Wilde and late Victorian theater is one result of work made possible by a generous grant from the University of California, in the Wilde collection of the William Andrews Clark Memorial Library at UCLA.

2. *The Concise Cambridge History of English Literature* (Cambridge: Cambridge Univ. Press, 1941), p. 758.

3. Samuel C. Chew's assertion that Wilde, "always the opportunist," copied Ibsen by way of Pinero, is unsupported; it betrays Chew's all but irrational bias against Wilde. See *A Literary History of England*, the work of Malone, Baugh, Brooke, Sherburn, and Chew (New York: Prentice-Hall, 1948), p. 1481.

4. *Mrs. Warren* was of course long banned from public performance in England and was first seen by a general audience in 1905, in New Haven, Conn.

5. See vol. 5, on the period 1850–1900, in Allardyce Nicoll's *History of English Drama* (Cambridge: Cambridge Univ. Press, 1946), especially pp. 190–91.

6. Chew, *Literary History*, p. 1480; Chew's part of the *Literary History* includes Wilde only in brief and only under the heading "Aestheticism and Decadence," devoting just one sentence to *The Importance of Being Earnest*—this in a work that gives two pages to the plays of Jones and Pinero (and not one word to Wilde under its heading of Drama)! With rare exceptions the critical treatment of Wilde as dramatist has been silly, subsumed under biography of a kind more often journalistic than informative, or hostile. The recent exceptions are some thoughtful essays by Richard Ellmann, Epifanio San Juan's *The Art of Oscar Wilde* (Princeton: Princeton Univ. Press, 1967), which includes illuminating and intelligent accounts of all the works, and Christopher S. Nassar's study *Into the Demon Universe* (New Haven: Yale Univ. Press, 1974), which can sometimes be tendentious in its dealings with individual plays—he makes *Salome* a touchstone in his emphasis upon the negatively Romantic, or demonic, force in Wilde—but is consistently fascinating.

It may well be that the serious critical consideration of this one major Victorian dramatist (as well as the great wit of the age) is now in its beginnings.

Thomas F. Boyle

"Morbid Depression Alternating With Excitement": Sex In Victorian Newspapers

For much of this century the epithet "Victorian" has been synonymous with, as Walter Phillips put it in 1918, "an almost incredible smugness and prudery."[1] In recent years, however—most dramatically since the publication in 1966 of Steven Marcus' landmark study of nineteenth-century sexuality, *The Other Victorians,* and with the steady flow of previously suppressed pornographic works which have been released in the past two decades under liberalized laws of censorship—this one-dimensional image has begun to fade. Indeed, nowadays, "Victorian" seems to have taken on, to the purveyors of the mass-media at any rate, lasciviously sinister overtones, conjuring up images of whore-infested gin mills, upper-class sodomites and flagellants, and spectral sexual psychopaths. However accurate this revisionary scenario may be, the belief endures that Victorian sexuality remained hidden, or at least suppressed, from the general population. Even Marcus states, of "the secret life of sexuality," that "although it is true that the Victorians could not help but know of this, almost no one was reporting on it; the social history of their own experiences was not part of the Victorians' official consciousness of themselves or their own society."[2]

In this context, the experience of opening the files of the newspapers which graced the breakfast and tea tables of respectable (and other) Victorians leaves the modern reader perplexed and fascinated: the police reports of mid-nineteenth-century newspapers consistently offer graphically detailed accounts of the sexual misbehavior of all classes of the citizens of the "Age of Improvement." Some of the more sensational weeklies are devoted to little else. And having access (as I do through the generosity of Gordon N. Ray) to a nine-million-word collection of clippings of *only* police and trial accounts (kept between 1839 and 1862 by a Scots gentleman named Bell Macdonald who subscribed to papers from all over the British Isles)[3] is to confront, besides violent crime, a compendium of vice including seduction, rape, adultery, transvestitism, illegal abortion, prostitution, bigamy, sadism, and indecent exposure.

Beyond its obvious interest as entertainment or as a curiosity, this archive offers significant rewards to the serious scholar. There are of course, at first glance, certain problems implicit in working with such material. It may appear irresponsible, for example, to attempt to characterize a twenty-three-year period, even in the most qualified way, on the basis of journalistic accounts that were often as not aimed at the baser elements in the populace, which are certainly factually unreliable in part, and which appear in the context of an amateurish editorial project of dubious consistency — one full of gaps (particularly in regard to source information) and of apparently unmanageable proportions. While this is a reasonable objection, it is in fact strikingly manifest after turning only a few pages that these clippings do provide meaningful insights into unresolved historical and cultural issues. And nowhere is this more apparent than in the reports on sexuality.

In the first place, as I have implied, the very existence of such newspaper accounts provides a historical footnote which is not only at odds with the received view of the period, but also rearranges the emphasis of more enlightened recent studies. Moreover, the presence of these accounts leads one to investigate the few available pieces of external evidence on the subject and, in doing so, to discover that Macdonald was collecting and clipping his newspapers during the formative years of modern journalism. Technological innovations such as the telegraph and railway came into their own in the 1840s and changed forever the nature of the reporter's profession. Legal changes in the 1850s — such as the demise of the Stamp Duty and the breakdown of the expensive distinction between "news" and "opinion" papers — had a like effect on editorial and marketing practices. The debacle of the Crimean War in 1854 became symbolic of a rising iconoclasm and general discontent with establishment policies among the newly prosperous and literate middle class, and this of course was enhanced by the telegraphed reports from the Crimea of the Special Correspondent of the *Times*. In any case, the reader of Macdonald's clippings is provided with a first-hand view of the growth of the newspaper industry in Britain from a situation in which papers were generally expensive, short on print, full of dated news, and given to supporting the strictures of established beliefs, to one in which papers were cheap, the news was "hot," and editors were increasingly willing to take positions subversive to conventional wisdom and practice, especially in light of the public awareness of low doings in all places — high and low — which the papers provided.

What has this to do with sex? The sexual beliefs — or fantasies — of official Victorian orthodoxy were central to the preservation of the stability of social institutions, of dogma in science and religion, of the positions of the intellectual commissars on the monthly reviews; and the mere presence of *vertabim* testimony from rape or bigamy or adultery cases tended to undermine this stability. Indeed the papers, to a degree commensurate with their growth (and the increasing amount of sexually oriented newsprint Macdonald managed to clip), went far beyond this, particularly after 1854, and their anti-establishment editorializing underlined not only the conflict between the "official" and "real" accounts of Victorian sexual tastes, but also suggested, implicitly and explicitly, that new radical visions – of the sensual and psychological natures of man, of the social structure of England, and of the metaphysical makeup of the universe – might be in order. Indeed, it is not stretching the point to propose that these "low" and "sensational" newspapers played a profound role of cross-fertilization with such contemporary works of genius as *Origin of Species* and Dickens' last works. At the very least, they penetrated more effectively than we have heretofore realized the Victorian façade of the domestic ideal and set some prominent equilibriums spinning. As one editorialist had it in 1859, in the pages of the daily papers the

> most marvellous and melodramatic events are mingled with the occurrences of everyday existence, and each law or police reporter is an Asmodeus who flies over the housetops with hundreds of Don Cleophases under his wing and unroofs all London, for the curious public to contemplate next morning at breakfast time . . . [what is] enacted at every hour of the day and night in London, to the amazement of a community who discover that they have lived so long in indifference or in ignorance of the wonders taking place around them, and to the triumphant confirmation of the aphorism that truth is strange and stranger than fiction.[4]

II

Inevitably, some of what we find in these columns we already know, or have suspected. Mayhew's prostitutes, grifters, and eccentrics are ever-present. The abysmal living conditions in the slums provide a distressing complement to the stories of child-beating and starvation. The cruel oppressiveness of institutional life – from the hospital to the workhouse to the ragged school, from the courtroom to the prison or asylum, the sort of material which informs government Blue Books and the protest novels of Mrs. Gaskell or Charles Reade (not to mention Dickens) – is re-enacted daily in newsprint. What strikes the reader first, however, is what is *not* expected: the steady parade of prosperous and reputable yet lascivious Victorians through these courts, and the even-handed, worldly ways in which they are handled by judges and reporters alike. One of the more amusing, though not untypical, cases of the period illustrates this nicely, as well as providing some insights into the role played by the history of Divorce Law in Victorian sexuality and into public attitudes to such matters. In the courtroom report, an upholsterer named Lyle brought suit in August 1857 against his business partner, a Mr. Herbert, who had been boarding in his house, for Criminal Conversation. A suit for "Crim. Con.," as adultery was popularly known, was an action brought by a plaintiff to recover damages from a defendant for having "seduced and debauched" his wife. Lyle, having become suspicious of his wife, had hired an unemployed cabinetmaker, one William Taylor, to observe her conduct with Mr. Herbert. Taylor and Lyle rented a room in the next house which happened to be adjacent to Mrs. Lyle's bedroom. Taylor, according to his own testimony,

> then bored a hole in the party wall, but this was of no use, and he fixed up an apparatus with an index attached to it that would indicate when any person got into the defendant's bed. He could tell by this apparatus whether one, two, three, or four persons got into the bed. (*A laugh.*) He called the apparatus an indicator. (*Laughter.*) On the night of the 18th of June he was watching with his ear to the hole, and the indicator acted. (*A laugh.*) The lever fell according to the weight. (*Laughter.*) It first informed him that one person got into bed, and then that a second person had done so. (*Renewed laughter.*) He immediately proceeded to the roof, and entered by the trap-door, took the servant by the hand, opened the door of the defendant's bedroom, tore down the curtains, and turned the bull's-eye (a policeman's lantern) upon them. (*A roar of laughter.*) Mr. Herbert and Mrs. Lyle were in bed together. Mr. Lyle was at this time making the best of his way to the place. . . .

Under cross-examination, Taylor acknowledges that he and the wounded husband had been blithely drinking gin-and-water while waiting for the device — which the judge, in his summing up, was to refer to as a "crimconometer" — to act; and that after the offending adulterers had been discovered,

> he and the plaintiff and several others went to a public-house and had some drink. . . . Believed that after the discovery was made, they had a glass of brandy-and-water all round. (*A laugh.*) After this, they all went back to the house. There was gin and water on the table. He stole a bottle of gin from Mr. Herbert's bedroom at the time of discovery. (*A roar of laughter.*) It was Mr. Lyle's gin, and he had his authority for taking it. They had pickled salmon,

A MERRY TALE FROM CROYDON.

One of the strangest trials for adultery ever recorded took place on Tuesday at the Croydon Assizes. The plaintiff was a young man, a Mr. Lyle, who carries on business as an upholsterer in Charlotte-street, Fitzroy-square, London; and the defendant is a Mr. Herbert, a gentleman of Croydon, rising fifty. The latter had gone into partnership with the former, and at length, under pretence of seeing more closely to the business, obtained a bedroom at Mr. Lyle's, and settled in town. The real object of this seems to have been the seduction of Mrs. Lyle. On the 27th of May, while his wife was at Birmingham, a telegraphic message came to the warehouse of Mr. Lyle, to the following effect:—"E. D. Herbert, Esq. Private—important—immediate. Meet me at the Euston-station by the 1·45 train. I could not come any sooner.—M. A. POWELL." The signature to this message was in the name of the sister of Mrs. Lyle; but it appears to have been sent by the plaintiff's wife. She arrived in London by the train referred to, but did not make her appearance at her husband's house until the following day, and the assumption was that she and Mr. Herbert had passed a guilty night together. Mr. Lyle, with the assistance of his servants and some of his friends, then watched his wife; and the proceedings they took, as related by the witnesses, caused frequent roars of laughter among the auditors. One of the watchers, named William Taylor, said:—"He remembered Mr. Lyle making some communications to him upon the subject of the conduct of his wife on the morning of her departure for Birmingham. Witness had previously mentioned something to him upon the same subject, and arrangements were made to detect the parties. A room was first taken in Cumberland-street, at the back of Charlotte-street, but this was not found to answer, and another was afterwards taken next door by witness. He then bored a hole in the party wall, but this was of no use, and he fixed up an apparatus with an index attached to it that would indicate when any person got into the defendant's bed. He could tell by this apparatus whether one, two, three, or four persons got into bed. (A laugh.) He called the apparatus an indicator. (Laughter.) On the night of the 18th June he was watching with his ear to the hole, and the indicator acted. (A laugh.) The lever fell according to the weight. (Laughter.) It first informed him that one person got into bed, and then that a second person had done so. (Renewed laughter.) He immediately proceeded to the roof, and entered by the trap door, took the servant by the hand, opened the door of the defendant's bedroom, tore down the curtains, and turned the bull's-eye (a policeman's lantern) upon them. (A roar of laughter.) Mr. Herbert and Mrs. Lyle were in bed together. Mr. Lyle was at this time making the best of his way to the place, and Mrs. Lyle rushed upstairs to her own room. On the following day, witness saw Mr. Herbert in the plaintiff's house, and he said he was prepared to pay for his guilt, and it was a pity that there was such a fuss made about it." Cross-examined: "The 'indicator' was an invention of his own. He had not taken out a patent for it. (Laughter.) Since this discovery, he had been living with Mr. Lyle. Mr. Lyle was watching the 'indicator' while he (witness) was looking through the hole. (Roars of laughter.) An hour and a half elapsed before the instrument began to act, and during that time they drank some gin and water. He suggested that the parties should have every facility afforded them in order that he might detect them. Would swear that he did not sit upon the tiles dressed in woman's clothes in order to watch Mrs. Lyle and the defendant. He made a rough model of the 'indicator,' but he was not aware whether it was in court or not. After the affair had been discovered, he and the plaintiff and several others went to a public-house and had some drink, but he did not see Mr. Lyle smoke a cigar. Did not know whether he smoked a cigar or not. Believed that after the discovery was made, they had a glass of brandy-and-water all round. (A laugh.) After this, they all went back to the house. There was gin and water on the table. He stole a bottle of gin from Mr. Herbert's bedroom at the time of the discovery. (A roar of laughter.) It was Mr. Lyle's gin, and he had his authority for taking it. They had pickled salmon, gin, and tea, but he could not say whether the meal was supper or breakfast, but it was more like breakfast than supper, because it was in the middle of the night. By witness's advice, Mr. Her-gin, and tea, but he could not say whether the meal was supper or breakfast, but it was more like breakfast than supper, because it was in the middle of the night. By witness's advice, Mr. Herbert was allowed to remain in the house all day after the transaction, and he took his boots away in order that he might not leave. (*A laugh.*)

The case is, on one level, pure bedroom farce, and the audience treats it as such. The judge himself, while struggling to maintain decorum, is visibly amused. Nor is he blinded by any prudish moral outrage. With tongue-in-cheek he finds for the plaintiff, the cuckolded Mr. Lyle, and then awards him damages of one farthing, "the lowest coin in the realm." The newspaper sardonically headlines the piece "A Merry Tale from Croydon."[5] Certainly the very existence of such an account (printed, the piece avers, throughout Britain) suggests a decidedly un-Victorian spirit abroad.

More important, the newspaper calls the attention of its readers to just this point, noting that "a day rarely passes without the unfolding of some curious tale of crime and horror, or of debauchery and dissipation" in the court reports, and that such cases transmit a sobering message:

> The grotesque character of the details drew inextinguishable laughter from counsel, jury, and gallery auditors; but, as we have often before had occasion to remark, it is useless to blind our eyes to these disease spots in our system. The case presents a strange aspect of our boasted conjugal life—of that domestic bliss which is vindicated by actions for damages, and watched over by "crim-conometers."[6]

It also becomes clear that the writer is not addressing only a sexual issue, but the cash interest which informed it and which had doubly polluted Victorian England's "boasted conjugal life." By probing further in *Lyle* v. *Herbert,* we realize that the one-farthing damages represent not only a judge's down-to-earth sense of humour, but also a recognition that the Criminal Conversation statute had been debased into a confidence game in which a needy or greedy husband might throw his attractive young wife into the path of an older, richer man and thereby make a profit out of his own cuckoldry. In many such cases, money in pocket, the offended husband and violated wife might live happily, and prosperously, ever after. This is an obvious reading of Lyle's convivial mood on the discovery of his wife's infidelity.

In fact the Divorce Act which went into effect 1 January 1858 was passed largely in response to these abuses. In a speech in 1857 in favor of liberalized divorce legislation, the Marquess of Landsdowne lamented "the monstrous assumption that the loss of affections of a wife is to be treated as a loss of

ordinary chattel, and is to be compensated in pounds, shillings, and pence."
The continuing publication of these cases, he went on, was "that great stigma
upon the legislation, the manners, habits, and customs of this country,"
which "is represented in all other countries of the world as an indication
of, I will not say degraded, but of the loose, sordid, and selfish principles
which prevail in this country."[7]

Nor were all of the Crim. Con. cases so merry as the tale from Croydon.
Indeed many were so lewd and presented such a Swiftian vision of the brutish-
ness of humankind that today's most sensational tabloids would be more
likely to bowdlerize them than did the Victorian press. In one such example, a soldier named Ling brought suit against an older fellow officer named Croker. Ling had been stationed in India when his wife took up with
Croker back in England. Letters written by each of the men to Mrs. Ling
are produced in the trial. The prosecution uses Croker's to portray him—
with his own words—as the heavy-breathing lecher. In one *billet-doux,* after
offering his paramour a detailed home remedy for an upper respiratory infection, he warms to the task:

> Mind and obey this positive order; it will do you all the good in
> the world, and before long cover your dear little bones with good
> hard flesh; you will be yourself again; and when we meet, the
> more ready and willing to do "is moffie." (A phrase in Hindo-
> stanee) How I long for the time that will find your sweet little
> self cuddled up in my monster arms, lip to lip; and slowly emerg-
> ing from a scene of exquisite delight! What think you about all
> this; and have you consented to the wish expressed in my last? I
> am sure you have, dearest. You would not disappoint in even the
> most disagreeable act, if you hoped that by it I should be for a
> moment gratified. This is the only thing left to comply with;
> when I tell you it will be a great satisfaction I am sure you will
> surrender unconditionally; and on my part, and on the instant, I
> promise you the most perfect bliss and unconditional indulgence
> in any way you please, even to a greater extent than that compris-
> ed in your last act. Do you recollect it? And how delighted you
> were at the perceptible result. Next time you shall dispose of it as
> you fancy; as a further inducment, I will tell you one or two
> things you are ignorant of.[8]

The wounded husband's missives are in part expurgated, but his coarsely
venal scheming is as manifest as Croker's lust. He writes from his tent in
India before his estrangement from Mrs. Ling: "There is a Mrs. C— out
in these parts—the only petticoat almost that I have seen since I left home.
She is a —— pretty woman. You may remember her husband in India. She

lives with any one I believe. Last evening I had her to dinner but found to my disgust that the —— blackguard Smith (his servant) had taken ***."

After his return to England, and about to pursue his claim as the wounded husband, his particular charm has not diminished:

> You see what a —— of a scrape you have got me into with that —— mother of yours. I shall take Mrs. C's advice and burke the whole matter —— providing you agree to certain conditions, the only ones upon which I will allow that cursed scoundrel C. to escape. Between you, I care not how, I require that the 250 £. which you have spent be immediately placed to my account at Cox's. Powell's receipt for which must be sent me, and that in two months from this time you place at my disposal the further sum of 300 £. available should I desire it. Solely and entirely upon these terms alone, do I consent to squash the damnatory evidence of your guilt.[9]

In this trial, it is proved that Mrs. Ling had in fact moved in with Croker. As a consequence of such condemnatory evidence Croker is ordered to pay Ling 1,000 pounds for having alienated his wife's affection. Ling subsequently was to bring his suit to the still very expensive and generally inaccessible divorce court. Mrs. Ling defended herself—one wonders why by this time— by countering that her husband had had an affair aboard ship from India to Europe while she was confined with their youngest child, and *before* she had taken up with Croker. She was not able, however, to produce concrete proof of her charges, and Ling was granted his divorce one day after Mr. Lyle of Croydon received a farthing for having contributed the crimconometer to Victorian Progress.

Contrary to the Marquess of Lansdowne's expectations, the coming of the Divorce Law a few months after these trials did nothing to bring to the newspapers a renewed respect for Britain's pretense to total respectability. Many more Victorians than had been anticipated rushed to Sir Cresswell's divorce court, and the details were published as enthusiastically as had those in the Crim. Con. proceedings. In 1861, after only three years under the new law, one newspaper editor was able to comment:

> It is impossible to look back upon the history of our divorce and matrimonial causes without a sensation of shame and humiliation. Never before in the national annals was there such a catalogue of evil passions and revolting vices—such chronicle of petty meanness, of crawling lies and subterfuges, of wretched spite, of scandalous collusion, of base and villainous motives. This narrow tribunal of Westminster Hall is the dissecting room of English

morality. There the skin is stripped off; there the muscles are laid bare; there the sharp knife severs and keen probe penetrates; there when the ghastly labor is over, we come to the grinning skull and fleshless bones.[10]

And it was not only the petitioners in the divorce and criminal courts who filled the newspaper columns and suggested to the public and literary establishment the basic instability of the official version of English society. Upper class *demimondaines* might be shrugged off as unfortunate but inevitable leftovers from Regency amorality. Less easily dismissable were events like the public meeting called—and reported widely in the papers—to discuss the "Confessional in Belgravia." At St. James Hall in 1858, before a large all-male crowd, including at least fifty peers, two hundred members of Parliament, and innumerable clergymen, an Anglican curate was charged in absentia with luring women—particularly attractive young widows—into a darkened drawing room outfitted with candles and a make-shift altar, donning a surplice and sash and bidding the women kneel before him and confess the most intimate details of their sexual lives and fantasies, asking "questions . . . so grossly indecent as to be unfit for publication [which] created a great sensation in the meeting." The self-appointed prosecutor justifies bringing the case to a public hall because it is necessary that the "bishops of our Church should see the danger of allowing these clergy once to overstep those bounds which separate . . . the Reformed Protestant Church from the Church of Rome. (*Loud cheers*) It is like a man who begins dram drinking. He goes on step-by-step and at last ends in *delerium tremens*. These 'holy fathers' have long been in a happy *delerium;* and I think when this case becomes known the *tremens* will begin."[11]

And so the clippings go on, for 1500 pages. A farmer is sued, a few miles from Thomas Hardy's birthplace, for breach of promise by a destitute laborer's daughter who had borne him a child; he had accomplished the seduction in question by constantly and ostentatiously driving his herd of bullock and sheep past her front porch.[12] A young merchant rents rooms in Camden Town, dons lady's drawers, a white crinoline petticoat, a lady's dress, and spends his evenings standing near the window with a wreath of roses around his head, exhibiting himself in a manner that his landlady finds "too disgusting and offensive to particularly describe."[13] Hugh Rowley, son of Lord Longford, "a black sheep of the aristocracy" and devotee of "peg top trousers and Inverness wrappers," sits smugly mute in divorce court as his wife provides shocking details of his "cruelty, adultery, and desertion." Then, the divorce having been granted, Rowley sues his now ex-wife for perjury in another court, a charge for which, if convicted, she will go to jail. Had he challenged the truth of her allegations in the divorce proceedings, he would have not been free of an undesirable mate, nor could he have wreaked such a punitive revenge.[14]

So the pietistic self-representations of the Victorian establishment were daily and voluminously negated. There appeared to many to be no question that, as in James Hannay's 1856 remarks on William Palmer (the respectable surgeon who also happened to be a mass-murderer, adulterer, and sire of countless bastards), "the devil is still extant, will travel by rail as readily as by old coach, and hides his hoofs, jauntily, in patent leather."[15]

III

The devil, in these particular incarnations, is clearly a lively fellow. The documentation of his — or her — exploits in the newspapers, however, strikes more and more of a somber note as one reads on. The dominant mood of the Victorian world of illicit sexuality, it becomes clear, was often one of insistent and unmistakable pathos. Sex is ultimately neither titillating nor sensationally shocking; it is, rather, a kind of dismal swamp, honeycombed with quicksand and teeming with predators. An 1853 case headlined "The Outrage at the War Office,"[16] for example, tells not of a military scandal, as we might expect from the headline, but of the critical wounding of a four-year-old girl, stabbed in the "private parts" as she squatted to urinate over a grating at one of the war office buildings. The housekeeper is charged with inflicting the injury from her quarters below stairs. Acts combining brutality and sex — like this one — from which one can easily infer a variety of symbolic patterns, are, sadly, not exceptional in Bell Macdonald's clippings. They take place, after all, in a world which, beneath the pretense of sanitized respectability, is randomly violent and suffers from inadequate or nonexistent hygienic conditions in which public relief of bladder and bowels is commonplace. The ultimate sense conveyed here is not "outrage," but doleful resignation. How many other ground floor and below-stairs habitations were treated as sewers? How many other such defensive-aggressive transactions were taking place — understandably — minute by minute?

Another case, pithily titled "Ignorance and Depravity," illuminates this mood further. I quote it in full:

> Isaac Rushford, aged forty-two, was indicted at York for feloniously administering a quantity of seeds of paradise to Kitty Littlewood, with intent to procure abortion, at East Ardsley on the 2nd of February last. The prisoner lived in Dewsbury Road, Leeds, and had got a reputation as a wizard. The prosecutrix having been unwell for some time, and the doctors she employed doing her no good, acting on the advice of a neighbor she went with her father to Leeds to consult the prisoner. The prisoner, as

the prosecutrix described it, "ruled her planet and gave her some pills." Not improving under his treatment, she sent for him to Sheffield, and the prisoner told her she would never prosper until she went to live at West Ardsley—a place near Leeds and easily accessible. She and her father accordingly went to live at West Ardsley and there the prisoner frequently saw her. At first he gave her some medicine, which he said was for palpitation of the heart. He then told her she would never be well unless she suffered him to have connection with her. This she refused several times. She afterwards re-moved to East Ardsley, and the prisoner continued to attend her, and at length she permitted him to have an improper intercourse with her, on his representation that she never would get well unless she did. On one occasion he gave her something which stupefied her, and it was on that occasion that the intercourse commenced, and it was afterwards continued for some time. At length she became in the family way and the prisoner then brought her a quantity of the seeds of paradise, and told her to make a tea of it and drink it. She did so, and had a miscarriage on the 26th of March. On another occasion after that the prisoner brought her a bullock's heart and some shoemaker's awls. He burnt the heart, and said the awls were to keep her enemies off. She was to place them under her pillow and wear them in her pocket. He also sent her two pieces of parchment as charms, and said one would get her a young man, and the other was to prevent her being bewitched. She gave him 5 pounds for these. The learned counsel objected that there was no proof of the administering of the drug by the prisoner. His lordship overruled this objection, and the jury found the prisoner guilty. His lordship said it was quite lamentable to think that such an amount of ignorance should prevail. Such practices must be severely punished. The sentence of the court was that he be imprisoned eighteen calendar months, with hard labor.[17]

No one will deny that Kitty Littlewood and Isaac Rushford, at least as they are presented here, can be characterized as "ignorant" or "depraved." Yet something is missing. There is another level of meaning, to these terms, in this setting, which insinuates itself more deeply into the consciousness. The judge's pronouncements, after all, do seem a bit disingenuous in the context of the Victorian courtroom as we have come to know it from these newspapers—a compound, indeed, of hypocrisy and self-delusion. The clichés of the headlines seem consistently misdirected, the product of a society vigorously self-conscious but not at all self-aware. As the outrage at the war office might more appropriately be aimed at sanitary conditions and practices, so the judge in this case might better lament the apparent failure of *both* the educational and legal systems to cope with social realities, including the terrible poverty which is so often apparent. The judge's platitudes seem an attempt to distance himself from the real question: what has this depressing saga of mean Midlands lodgings and seeds of paradise, of sun-signs and shoemaker's awls, of pills and bullock's hearts, to do with fornication? And what in turn has fornication to do with eighteen months at hard labor? And what has any of this to do with Victorian progress?

One thinks here of *The Other Victorians* and the way in which these news clippings further illuminate the significance and pervasiveness of the "displacement and denial"[18] which Professor Marcus finds at the heart of both official and illicit Victorian sexual writing. His analysis of a passage describing the Cremorne "pleasure" gardens in Chelsea (a notorious haunt of prostitutes and swells) in William Acton's 1858 treatise on prostitution might well apply to many of these court reports:

> [There is] a peculiar confusion; one is never quite certain of the source or location of its intense and frozen sadness. The depression is there in the scene itself, but it is also present in Acton, and not merely as a response to what he is observing but as something he has brought to this event and projects onto it. This inability to separate out satisfactorily what one must call the subjective and objective components of an experience indicates, I think, a dimmed consciousness, and, further, a disinclination to examine the contents or meaning of one's responses.[19]

In Marcus' psychoanalytical reading, the sort of behavior which we might be inclined to deplore as hypocrisy is largely unconscious, a question of an inability to deal with sexuality rather than of deviousness. Certainly we must agree with Marcus that the result of these attempts to "master the subject"—as did Henry Spencer Ashbee in his "massive" and "obsessional" bibliography of pornography, or as in the case of that paradigm of apparent philistine hypocrisy, Dickens' Podsnap—is "to reproduce on another level and in a symbolic way the original chaos and disorder they were intended to bring under command."[20]

J.H. Plumb, having read Marcus and *My Secret Life*, sees these matters in plainer terms. What *My Secret Life* makes manifest (as, perhaps more intensely, do the newspapers) is that one can only understand the deep-seated and evangelical nature of the Victorian ideology of respectability if one understands the gross reality which it set itself in opposition to. Indeed one can see the "official consciousness" in this light as a justifiable act of defensive self-preservation (in some ways parallel to the violent aggression of the housekeeper at the war office). Plumb, noting that "poverty and destitution were always so close to Victorian men and women that they easily became the victims of those members of the propertied class who wished to debauch them,"[21] writes that, in part as a result of this unpleasant social reality, "the Victorian youth was presented with endless opportunity for sexual indulgences"[22] and that the newly prosperous middle classes were desperately afraid of sliding back into the slough where sensuality and slavery were often synonymous.

These points are nowhere better illustrated than in these newspaper police reports, one of the saddest (strikingly so, especially since the superficial details of the case are so sexually titillating) examples of which is an 1855 case from Kingston. A fifteen-year-old "young gentleman" named Elton was accused of "feloniously assaulting" Mary Elizabeth Crawley, seventeen, a servant at the rectory home of his clergyman uncle, with the assistance of two other servants, Elphick the groom, and Miss Fenn, the cook. The content of Crawley's testimony, at first glance, bears close resemblance to contemporary pornography, from *My Secret Life* to *The Pearl*:

> While witness and Fenn were undressing, Elton came in and passed to his own room, and witness locked her door. She and Fenn then went to bed and directly afterwards Elphick came into the room, and unlocked Elton's door, and said to him, "George, you come in and lie on Fenn's side." Witness said that if they did so, she would tell Mr. Sugden [her master, husband of Elton's sister], and Elphick replied, "Oh no, you won't." Elton then came to her bedside. He was undressed and he got into bed. Witness screamed as loud as she could, and the prisoner Fenn put her hand over her mouth, and Elphick held her while Elton committed the assault with which he was charged. . . . Fenn [then] told her it was no use complaining, it was done now, and could not be undone. Elphick then told her that unless she consented to similar treatment a second time she would be sure to be in the family way and Fenn confirmed what he said; [and then] Elphick assaulted her in the same manner Elton had done. This all took place without her consent. . . ."[33]

In spite of the bawdy promise of the piece, in the end—once again—we are left with a distinctly sour aftertaste. Crawley's predicament is a tragic indictment of the social context in which she appears to be trapped. It is soon clear that she has been at least the victim of religious bigotry—she is a Catholic—if not sexual ill-usage. She has had no privacy; her biological ignorance is pathetically exploitable. The prosecutor seems more concerned in his histrionic way with the likelihood of such indignities taking place in the house of a clergyman on a Sunday than with the emotional or physical welfare of the girl whose interests he is supposed to represent.

Crawley is then subjected to a severe cross-examination by the defense, "the greater portion" of which, the reporter notes, is "not of a character fit for publication." The defense hammers at the point that Crawley, as well as Elphick and Fenn, had been for some time sexually experienced, and that Elton's poor uncle "merely appeared to have the misfortune to be troubled with a parcel of immoral and debauched servants."

The judge's summing up to the jury dwells on two points: first, that "in all such cases a most essential ingredient for the consideration of the jury was the conduct of the woman who complained about the outrage both before and after it occurred"; second, he takes pains to assure the public that the arrangement of the bedrooms in the Reverend Sugden's house had in no way contributed to the incidents that had taken place within. The jury, after "a short deliberation," finds the young gentleman not guilty.

Whether Crawley's story is true is not the point here. Rather it is how decidedly unappetizing the story becomes. The girl's position, appearance, and story cry out for sympathy; yet we find no evidence that these are given serious consideration. We are implicitly asked by the recounting of details to *care* about *all* of these children and instead we see the inexorable closing of ranks against the religious and economic outcast without reference to her human condition.

These accounts, then, whether of sadism, exploitation, or debauchery, provide an extensive, frequently insightful, documentation of the sad confusion which so often characterized the Victorian transition into the modern world. And precisely because they do focus on such sensitive issues as sex and violence, the clippings most dramatically define the daily conflict between the humanitarian impulse and the repressive rigidity of officialdom against a background of intolerable social reality. Indeed, presented in an accessible and comprehensive format, an archive such as Macdonald's clippings can stand beside such eminent achievements as Dickens' protest novels or Matthew Arnold's social criticism—neither of which, being part of the established order itself, had the freedom to deal explicitly with sexual matters—not only as indictments of the Victorian official consciousness but as the basis for a serious attempt to understand its contradictory nature.

IV

Just as the significance of newspaper journalism has been generally minimized as a source for scholars,[24] so has it been overlooked that the *issue* of the accuracy and value of news reporting, especially in terms of the relationship between sex and violence and the official culture, was much on the minds of the mid-Victorian reading public. For example, in 1862 the

MARLBOROUGH STREET.

ALLEGED INDECENT EXPOSURE.—On Monday, *Annie
Mercom*, one of the numerous foreign prostitutes who frequent Regent-street, was charged with indecent exposure.
Police-constable Tarrant, A 299, said: About five o'clock
en Saturday, while on duty in Regent-street, he saw the
prisoner walking along the street with her clothes raised
in such a manner as to expose the leg above the knee. He
distinctly saw the defendant's flesh, and he noticed that
every now and then she twitched her clothes higher. He
then took her into custody. The defendant, through Mr.
Albert, the interpreter, denied the charge. She might
have lifted her dress to avoid the dirt, but she made no
intentional exposure; indeed, that was impossible, as she
wore drawers. Mr. Bingham asked the constable if he
was quite certain he saw the defendant's flesh? The constable said he was positive he saw the flesh, and that the
clothes were lifted to attract the attention of gentlemen to
her legs. Mr. Bingham said the conduct of foreign prostitutes in Regent-street and the Haymarket had become so
shameless and notorious that he was determined to deal
with cases like the present, when fully established, with due
severity. He should therefore commit the defendant to
hard labour for seven days. Mr. Lewis, of Great Marl-
borough-street, shortly afterwards made an appeal to the
magistrate to induce him to commute the imprisonment
into a fine. Mr. Bingham replied that Mr. Lewis might
inflict pain on his feelings, but he would not induce him to
alter his decision. Mr. Lewis then gave notice of appeal.
The drawers, which the defendant still wore, which were
short and loose, were impounded by order of the magistrate, to be produced in case the appeal was prosecuted.

More Zeal than Discretion.

At Marlborough Police Court, a few days ago, Edwin
Hawkes, a young man described as an artist, living at
Paddington, was charged before Mr. Broughton, under
the following circumstances:—It appeared that the prisoner, who had been walking behind two females,
deliberately placed his hand upon their legs beneath
their clothes, this was in Charles street, Westbourne
terrace. The girls, who were frightened, ran away, but
the prisoner was taken into custody by Doble, 174 D,
who witnessed what had taken place. The affair
occurred in the afternoon between two and three o'clock.
It was stated to the magistrate that the prisoner had
already suffered three months for a like offence. The
prisoner, on being asked what he had to say, made this
curious and perfectly original defence:—"A year or two
ago he saw in the street a lady's bootlace unfastened; he
politely made known to her the fact, and offered to do it
for her. She consented, and while he was lacing the
boot carefully examined the contour of her leg and ankle.
The swell of the calf and the graceful delicacy of the
ankle made, alas! too deep an impression upon his mind,
for he must confess that whenever he had since had "a
chance of a leg," he could not refrain from pursuing his
professional studies in spite of his remembrance of his
former punishment, "My conscience," said he, "is
perfectly clear. I have done no harm, nothing approaching to an indelicate thought ever entered my mind. My
strong passion is, as an artist, to draw ladies' legs."
Mr. Broughton, who expressed himself most strongly
with regard to the conduct of the prisoner in the pursuit
of his artistic studies, remanded him for further inquiry
for a week with liberty to give bail for his reappearance.
Being unable to procure sureties, the amorous and
enthusiastic artist was committed.

French critic E.M. Forgues published a review of British fiction which pointed out the resemblance between the more sensational contemporary English novels and the newspaper reports from Sir Cresswell's divorce court. Perhaps, Forgues suggested, the British should moderate their arrogant moral complacency a bit since much of the world now saw them as "the angels of adultery."[25] The *National Review* sprang to the defense of British culture, asserting that Trollope's novels were truly representative of both literature *and* life in England, being "concentred upon well-to-do, decorous, and deservedly prosperous people, who solve, with a good deal of contentment and self-satisfaction, the difficult problems of making the most of both this world and the next. . . ."[26]

A couple of years later *The Christian Remembrancer*, explicitly addressing sensation novels (denounced as "newspaper novels"[27] by the Dean of St. Paul's) written by women such as Miss Braddon and Mrs. Henry Wood, lamented:

> In one and all there is appeal to the imagination, through the active agency of the nerves, excited by the unnatural or supernatural. But the abnormal quality need not outrage physical laws, exceptional outrages of morality and custom may startle much in the same way. Bigamy, or the suspicion of bigamy, is sensational as fully, though in a lower field, as are ghosts, and portents; it disturbs in the same way the reader's sense of the stability of things, and opens a new, untried vista of what may be.[28]

In 1855 Mrs. Oliphant, reviewing *Psychological Inquiries* by Benjamin Brodie (Surgeon to the Queen; President of the Royal Society) in *Blackwood's*, used the opportunity to attempt to define—admiringly—received opinion on the human psyche according to Brodie. The human consciousness is separated into the Brain, "seat" of "sensations," the "organ of our instincts and appetites," a manifestation of our lower nature; and the Mind, full of "thoughts" which have "their seat only in the spiritual essence." These products of the Mind link us with God and the afterlife, separating humankind from animals. Oliphant, at this point, puts her finger on the obvious question and asks rhetorically, through Brodie, what of "the instincts and appetites which we possess in common with other animals? Have we no cerebral organ for *amativeness, alimentiveness, combativeness, destructiveness,* and the like?" The answer is that this sort of instinct "is a stumbling block that must be removed from our path. It lies there, a mysterious something between sensation and thought."[29]

I have cited these instances—literary, religious, and scientific—to demonstrate in relevant specific fields some attributes of the "official consciousness." In the case of the response to Forgues, we see a remarkable ability to mount an inflexible, unrealistic defensive position in the face of mere common sense. We also see in the reference to the "afterlife" the extraordinary degree of overlap which existed between literature and religion. In *The Christian Remembrancer* and *Blackwood's* pieces we see the same interaction between science and religion. If a novel about bigamy, by its effect on the "nerves," disturbs the "reader's sense of stability of things, and opens a new, untried vista of what may be," what was unsettled by such newspaper accounts as we have seen? The point here is, in Mrs. Oliphant's terms, that there is no "special place" for sexuality in the universe as conceived by Victorian orthodoxy. Admitting carnal desire as normal human behavior would suggest, in this system, that the privilege of afterlife, of Godliness, is not necessarily reserved for prosperous Christian humanity. In this sense the Victorian world as we encounter it is a "world without psychology," to use Marcus' terms, a world of "organs and physiology in which everything is convertible into matter."[30] Sexuality must be either denied or reduced to some quantifiable malfunction of the human organism.

V

What is perhaps the most curious case to emerge from the early years of the divorce court also raises the most challenging questions about the ultimate nature of these sexual-spiritual conflicts. In *Robinson* v. *Robinson and Lane* (1858), Mr. Robinson accused his wife of committing adultery. He named as co-respondent the family hydrotherapist, a Dr. Lane, who had a fashionable practice at Moor Park, Surrey (the house in which Jonathan Swift had been employed by Sir William Temple), and who numbered among a prosperous clientele one Charles Darwin.[31] The Robinsons had married — she a wealthy widow — in 1844 and had moved about in respectable circles at a series of residences in Blackheath, Edinburgh, Boulogne, and Reading. They had met Lane in 1850 and had renewed their acquaintance in 1854, at which point Mrs. Robinson, at least fifty and not always in good health, became a regular client at the thirty-one-year-old Lane's establishment. In 1857 Mr. Robinson "made a discovery which opened his eyes. He discovered a diary written by his wife containing an extraordinary narrative of her impure conduct."

It is this diary which constitutes most of the evidence at the divorce trial of 1858, an Ecclesiastical divorce already having been obtained through presentation of the same material. The most significant passages for the prosecution concern a visit to Moor Park in October 1854. They testify to what Mrs. Robinson, a disciple of phrenology as well as hydrotherapy, had in an earlier entry described as the "preponderance of amativeness in her character."

Oct. 7, Sunday—Fine sunny warm genial day. . . . Dr. Lane asked
me to walk with him. . . . I still lingered, but at last joined him,
and he led me away and alone to our private haunt, taking a
wider range, and a more secluded path. At last I asked to rest,
and we sat on a plaid; and read Atheneums, chatting meanwhile.
There was something unusual in his manner, something softer
than usual in his tone and eye. . . . The sun shone warmly down
on us; the fern, yellow and brown, was stretched away beneath us;
fine old trees in groups adorned the near ground, and far away
gleamed the blue hills. I gave myself up to enjoyment. I leaned
back against some firm, dry heather bushes, and laughed and
remarked as I rarely did in that presence. All at once, just as I
was joking my companion on his want of memory, he leaned over
me and exclaimed, "If you say that again, I will kiss you." You
may believe I made no opposition, for had I not dreamed of him
and of this full many a time before? What followed I hardly
remember—passionate kisses, whispered words, confessions of the
past. Oh God, I never hoped to see this hour, or to have any part
of my love returned. Yet so it was. He was nervous, and
confused, and eager as myself. At last we raised ourselves and
walked on happy, fearful, almost silent. We sauntered, not
heeding where, to a grove of pines, and there looked over another
view beautiful as that on this side, but wilder.

A week later, after a series of daily assignations, in the woods, the library,
and the back of a horse-and-buggy:

The Doctor, after talking some little while appeared to return to
his former kind feelings for me, caressed me, and tempted me,
and finally, after some delay, we adjourned to the next room and
spent a quarter of an hour in blissful exictement. I became nearly
helpless with the effects of his presence, could hardly let him
depart, wept when he made me try to obviate consequences, and
finally bade him a passionate farewell. I was alone. Passion-wasted
and sorrowful, sleep was far from me; that night I tossed, and
dreamed, and burned till morning, too weary and weak to rise."[32]

The defense lawyers assert that the diary is a "mere hallucination," and
present a series of witnesses to prove it. Certainly, if one reads Mrs. Robinson's ecstasies closely, they are suspiciously evocative of the set nature pieces
and Keatsian excesses of the late eighteenth and early nineteenth centuries.
That the woman's record of iniquity might represent a wishful fantasy rather

than a morbid or diseased reality presented perhaps greater problems for the official view of such things, since it suggested a more threateningly willful and conscious act – something, indeed, which could not easily be explained away in materialistic terms. In any case, it presented even thornier problems for the judge.

In the first place, the Law of Evidence prevented Dr. Lane from testifying (presumably because he would be asked to testify against himself). Next, as Mrs. Robinson's lawyer pointed out, "the case against Dr. Lane rested on nothing but Mrs. Robinson's diary which [also] could not be admitted against him; and it might, therefore, happen that Dr. Lane would be dismissed on the ground that no adultery was proved against him, and Mrs. Robinson would be divorced on the ground that her adultery with Dr. Lane had been proved. He need hardly say what a state of jurisprudence such a state of things would represent." Finally, a series of medical witnesses appeared to testify that a woman of Mrs. Robinson's years, with her history of ovarian problems, might very well suffer from a "malady" (Dr. Ralph Colp, a Darwin scholar, notes that this kind of "insanity" was then called "erotic monomania") which caused her mind to be "in a state of morbid depression alternating with excitement."[33]

This latter phrase – at once diagnostical and ideological – is particularly appropriate for an overview of Victorian sexuality. As we have seen, the antics of a licentious populace were denied or repressed so vigorously that even conventional conjugal sex became a source of chaos and fear.[34] The coexistence of excitement and the bourgeois drive to repress it resulted in a confused morbidity which drove all who came within its influence into chaotic retreat. The spectacle of Mrs. Robinson, whose sexuality is so real and, at the same time, unreal, was positively indigestible. This was not merely a metaphorical reality. Since the legal system could not "take her in," as it were, Mrs. Robinson paradoxically "won" her days in court because a divorce could be granted only with concrete proof of adultery. The establishment was hoist with its own materialistic petard. The judge noted sadly at the conclusion of the trial that Mr. Robinson "remained burdened with a wife who had placed on record the confession of her misconduct or, at all events, even taking the most favorable view, of unfaithful thoughts and unchaste desires."[35]

There is no record – that I know of – of what happened to the Robinsons after the trial. But by the 1860s, it is now clear, awareness of the retreat from orthodoxy had become general, spurred by sexually related developments. Darwin's work was upsetting Mind-Brain theorists and their relegation of "instinct" to the lower orders. Pornography, while burgeoning, was deteriorating into a materialistic abstraction. Even Freud, who forty years later was to establish the importance of instinct, devised his theories of infantile sexuality (we are now told by J.M. Masson, who has studied his previously suppressed letters) in an effort to shift "the emphasis from a real world of sadness, misery, and cruelty, to an internal stage on which actors performed invented dramas for an invisible audience of their own creation."[36] And Dickens, in the words of J. Hillis Miller, concluded his career attempting to come to terms with an England "being slowly destroyed because it cannot find strength to rid itself of the tangible, material presence of the dead forms of the past,"[37] and, as a consequence, in his last completed work, *Our Mutual Friend* (1864–65), presents a world of "verbalized consciousness"[38] which is "altogether fictive,"[39] in which the characters "transform their real situations into fictive situations which free them from the steady pressure of reality."[40] Certainly one must agree with Miller that these qualities place Dickens "on the threshold of the twentieth century."[41] In a like sense, the wide publication of Mrs. Robinson's graphically reconstructed Romanticism is a comparable phenomenon. No less so is the mid-Victorian journalists' insistence that reports of crime in popular newspapers had blurred the line between fact and fiction. These indeed must be seen as contributing one of the fundamental steps from the hierarchical universe of Victorian orthodoxy to what we now call Modernism.

Notes

1. Walter Phillips, *Dickens, Reade and Collins: Sensation Novelists* (New York: Columbia Univ. Press, 1919), p. 93.

2. Steven Marcus, *The Other Victorians* (New York: Bantam 1967), p. 102.

3. "Various Trials Cut From Newspapers," 5 vols. clippings collected by W. Bell Macdonald. Lockerbie, Dumfrieshire, Scotland, 1839–62. These volumes are hereafter referred to as "Trials."

Macdonald (1807–1862) was laird of Rammerscales, a great country house which still stands in the south of Scotland. He earned a B.A. from Glasgow University, then studied medicine and served as a surgeon in the Royal Navy before he succeeded to Rammerscales on the death of a maternal uncle in 1837. A dedicated linguist and classical scholar, he devoted the rest of his life to his translations and his book collection. By the time of his death, he had amassed more than 6500 volumes in his library. The eclectic nature of his pursuits is evident in these clippings, which include journals representing most conceivable geographical and cultural interests in Great Britain.

In 1920, 1500 volumes from the library, including these five, were sold at auction. The five are now in the collection of Professor Ray. Some 5000 volumes remain in the old library according to the current Macdonald of Rammerscales. They include a number of other collections of newspaper clippings on a variety of subjects.

4. "Trials," V, 33. Asmodeus and Don Cleophases appear in Le Sage's *The Devil with Two Sticks.*

5. "Trials," IV, 61–62; 64–65.

6. Ibid., IV, 64.

7. Ibid., IV, 65.

8. Ibid., IV, 11.

9. Ibid., IV, 11.

10. Ibid., V, 349.

11. Ibid., IV, 139–40.

12. Ibid., III, 27.

13. Ibid., IV, 150.

14. Ibid., V, 20–21; 58–68.

15. "Great Britain," *New York Daily Tribune*, 8 July 1856, p. 3.

16. "Trials," III, 2.

17. Ibid., IV, 66.

18. Marcus, *The Other Victorians*, throughout.

19. Ibid., p. 11.

20. Ibid., p. 55.

21. "The Victorians Unbuttoned," in *In The Light of History* (Boston: Houghton Mifflin, 1973), p. 244.

22. Ibid., p. 246.

23. "Trials," III, 223.

24. Even Richard Altick, who makes such wonderful use of the resources of popular culture, notes in *Victorian Studies in Scarlet*, that he has chosen in his research not to take "laborious recourse to the files of contemporary newspapers and hastily compiled books, where the risk of unreliability is higher anyway."

25. "Degenerescence du roman," *Revue des Deux Mondes*, 40 (August 1862), 692.

26. "Orley Farm," *National Review*, 16 (January 1863), 27–40. Reprinted as "Trollope as the Voice of the English Middle Class," *Anthony Trollope: The Critical Heritage*, ed. Donald Smalley (London: Routledge and Kegan Paul, 1969), p. 168.

27. H.L. Mansel; "Sensation Novels," *Quarterly Review*, 114 (April 1863), 261.

28. "Our Female Sensation Novelists," *The Christian Remembrancer*, 46 (July 1863), 211.

29. "Psychological Inquiries," *Blackwood's Edinburgh Magazine*, April 1855, pp. 411–12.

30. Marcus, *The Other Victorians*, pp. 32–33.

31. See Ralph Colp, Jr., "Charles Darwin, Dr. Edward Lane and the 'Singular Trial' of Robinson v. Robinson and Lane," *Journal of the History of Medicine and the Allied Sciences*, 36 (April 1981), 205–13.

32. "Trials," IV, 137.

33. Ibid., IV, 138.

34. In Acton, according to Marcus, sex "is thought of as a universal and virtually uncurable scourge," *The Other Victorians*, p. 28.

35. "Trials," IV, 251.

36. J.M. Masson, in a speech to a meeting of the Western New England Psychoanalytical Society, June 1981. Quoted by Ralph Blumenthal, "Did Freud's Isolation,

Peer Rejection Prompt Key Theory Reversal?" *New York Times*, 25 August 1981, pp. C1, 2.

37. J. Hillis Miller, *The Dickens World* (Bloomington and London: Indiana University Press, 1973), p. 169.

38. Ibid., p. 304.

39. Ibid., p. 306.

40. Ibid., p. 308.

41. Ibid., p. 293.

Howard W. Fulweiler

"Here a Captive Heart Busted": From Victorian Sentimentality To Modern Sexuality

D'ailleurs elle devenait bien sentimentale. Il avait fallu échanger des miniatures, on s'était coupé des poignées de cheveux, et elle demandait à present une bague, un véritable anneau de mariage en signe d'alliance éternelle. Souvent, elle lui parlait des cloches du soir ou *des voix de la nature;* puis elle l'entretenait de sa mère, à elle, et de sa mère, à lui. Rodolphe l'avait perdue depuis vingt ans. Emma, néanmois, l'en consolait avec des mièvreries de langage, comme on eût fait à un marmot abandonné.

—Gustave Flaubert, *Madame Bovary*

It is now apparent that imaginative literature has been on a peculiar kind of journey for some two hundred and fifty years—a sentimental journey. Extensive research is not required to discover the presence of sentimentality everywhere in the literature of the last two centuries. For instance, the greatest French novel of the nineteenth century, *Madame Bovary*, is about a woman who travels the sentimental road, while its author is deeply concerned with sentimentality as a modern problem. Emma Rouault, a shallow young farmer's daughter, marries Charles Bovary, a dull middle-class doctor. Feeling herself to be separated from a sense of belonging and meaning in her life, she attempts foolishly to find fulfillment in a sentimental obsession with "Romance," a pursuit represented in the novel as artificial and empty. Emma's increasingly desperate pursuit of her lovers—the inexperienced student Léon, and the worldly, self-centered Rodolphe—and her growing isolation from her husband and child bring her anxiety to levels of unbearable intensity. Emma's downfall, however, comes about, ironically, not in climactic scenes of passion with her lovers or husband, but as a result of her inept attempts at financial manipulation as she attempts to gratify her craving for frivolous material possessions, clothes and jewels. Grand passion is portrayed not only as illusory in itself, but as the natural companion of a trivial middle-class hankering for feminine finery. Emma commits suicide by eating arsenic stolen from M. Homais, the local apothecary and next-door neighbor. Her death is not a glorious *liebestod* but a painful process of physical degradation punctuated by vomiting.

Flaubert created in this novel a haunting nineteenth-century emblem of the human heart gone astray. Emma's anxious search for genuine feeling in her sterile bourgeois surroundings suggests failure in the relationships

234

which have traditionally provided meaning and emotional satisfaction: religion, friendship, family, and especially marriage, which in some way includes and represents the others. The power of the novel grows out of the bleak isolation of all the characters—not only Emma Bovary, but her husband and her two lovers.

Flaubert of course described the plight of Emma in all its spirit-numbing detail with no trace of sentimentality in his own narration. Sentimentality is not Flaubert's style, but his target. It is Emma's sentimentality, her inauthentic but pathetically intense appetite for emotional gratification which brings about her destruction. "The reasons of the heart," to borrow Pascal's pre-Enlightenment and pre-Romantic phrase, have gone awry. Anxious overemphasis on romantic love has ended in disaster.

A parallel with more universal consequences may be found on the other side of the Atlantic. If Emma Bovary's sentimental fixation on romantic love brings about domestic disaster, it was, we remember, Mark Twain's opinion that a Southern fixation on the sentimentality of Sir Walter Scott helped to bring on the catastrophe of the Civil War. In the case of Twain, one might see a continuing attack on sentimentality as the informing structure of the author's work as a whole. Twain's *Huckleberry Finn*, perhaps the best-known American novel of the nineteenth century, levels a massive attack on the sentimentality of its age. Although the anti-Romantic burlesque—"Here a captive heart busted"—of the concluding chapters of *Huckleberry Finn* is sometimes described as an aberration, the sentimental pictures and poetry left to posterity by Miss Emmeline Grangerford, a dead fifteen-year-old who "kind of pined away," are central to the novel. There was a crayon drawing, Huck tells us, "where a young lady was at a window looking up at the moon, and tears running down her cheeks; and she had an open letter in one hand with black sealing-wax showing on one edge of it, and she was mashing a locket with a chain to it against her mouth, and underneath the picture it said 'And Art Thou Gone Yes Thou Art Gone Alas.'" It will be remembered that this artist was also the author of "Ode to Stephen Dowling Bots, Dec'd," a poem dedicated, as Huck says, to a boy "that fell down a well and was drownded."

> They got him out and emptied him;
>   Alas it was too late;
> His spirit was gone for to sport aloft
>   In the realms of the good and great.

Huck comments that "if Emmeline Grangerford could make poetry like that before she was fourteen, there ain't no telling what she could a done by-and-by. Buck said she could rattle off poetry like nothing. She didn't ever have to stop to think."[1] The reader of *Huckleberry Finn* is made to realize, of course, that the sinister underside of this false sentiment is not only the brutal injustice of a society based on slavery, but the homicidal mania of the Grangerfords and the Shepherdsons in their fixation on family honor.

As we have seen, Flaubert in *Madame Bovary* focuses on sentimentality as the topic of his book, as the tragic flaw of his heroine. Similarly, sentimentality is the object of Twain's satire in *Huckleberry Finn*, as it is in so much of his work, both early and late. But what must interest both the historian and the critic far more than Flaubert's pitiless anatomy of sentimentality and Twain's laughter at it is the nearly universal appearance of sentimentality *not* as an object of attack, but as perhaps the most characteristic aspect of nineteenth-century art and nineteenth-century artists. I do not refer only to easy targets, such as Bloodgood Haviland Cutter, Twain's "Poet Lariat" of *Innocents Abroad*, or Julia A. Moore, "The Sweet Singer of Michigan," but to literary giants of enduring value—Wordsworth, Thackeray, Whitman, Tennyson, Dickens, even Twain himself on occasion. One remembers the possibly apocryphal remark attributed to Flaubert: "*Madame Bovary c'est moi!*"

The fact is that sentimentality is not simply a critical term; it is also historical. Sentimentality in literature can hardly be said to exist before the latter part of the seventeenth century; it becomes common in the second half of the eighteenth century. As everyone knows, Victorian literature represents the triumph of literary sentimentality, which then begins—or so we are sometimes told—a sharp decline in the twentieth century. Although this latter generalization may need further investigation, there is no doubt that it is a widely accepted truism. No one accuses Chaucer of sentimentality—or Shakespeare or Donne. The love story of Aeneas and Dido is passionate but not sentimental. Dante's intellectual intensity is matched by powerful sentiment but not sentimentality. Medieval romances are about love, but they are not sentimental.

What is sentimentality? Sentimentality in literature is not simply an excess of emotion or feeling. Instead it consists in focusing upon individual emotions or fresh experiences and transforming them into more generalized notions or "ideas." For example, the fresh experience of alienation, disorientation, and homelessness suffered by many in the eighteenth and nineteenth centuries is transformed into a general idea, frequently imaged in imaginative literature in the vicissitudes of friendless orphans or persons abandoned by their families to a cruel world. Two representative characters come at once to mind: Clarissa Harlowe and Oliver Twist. *Oliver Twist* and *Clarissa* are still recognized as great novels because their title characters continue to convey fresh experience with emotional depth and intellectual intensity. On the other hand, all readers recognize sentimentality in them as well: occasional flatness, even triteness, the tear jerker as calculated mechanism. In terms of literary history Richardson is not only recognized by many as the father of the English novel, but also as the father of sentimentality. If Richardson is its father, Dickens is certainly its greatest and most popular exponent.

To take a different example, one might consider a well-known character from ancient literature. Mary Magdalene, for instance, appears in the New Testament as a fresh insight, a new possibility for experience—a prostitute who is capable of loyalty and spiritual vision. By the end of the nineteenth century, her literary descendants have degenerated to a sentimental category: the whore with a heart of gold, now a code rather than a character. It is apparent, of course, that sentimentality always involves a kind of reduction, a movement toward the trite. It offers not an excess of emotional experience, but the reduction of the experience to something like a slogan.

It is crucial to remember that sentimentality is not merely an aberration of less gifted writers. It is a commonplace in the work of the greatest artists of the eighteenth and nineteenth centuries. I believe it is the chief characteristic of twentieth-century literature as well, although it takes a new and perhaps more virulent form, as I shall try to explain in due course. In any case, all must agree on the central importance of sentimentality in an eighteenth-century giant like Samuel Richardson or in nineteenth-century writers like Dickens and Tennyson, possibly the most widely read of serious artists in modern times. The latter two are imaginative writers of power, depth, and intellectual substance, who seem to suffer in twentieth-century eyes from a similar aesthetic schizophrenia. Dickens' *Bleak House* is disfigured by the mawkish sentimentality of Esther Summerson. Tennyson's career as a whole is seriously flawed by his domestic idyls. This circumstance in the case of the two most representative Victorian writers is more than a chance coincidence of parallel private neurosis. It is not explained by simple reference to "Victorian sentimentality," although that term is worth our closest attention.

If the eighteenth and nineteenth centuries ushered in the age of sentimentality in literature, creating a gulf between the sensibility of Richardson, Tennyson, or Dickens and that of Shakespeare, Chaucer, and Milton, western consciousness has evolved even further in the twentieth century. Striking the proper balance between intellect and emotion has seemed so difficult a problem for serious writers in our own time that they have commonly given up the attempt. A curious bifurcation divides the contemporary literary landscape: there does in fact remain an outright sentimentality of the Victorian type; it is separated from what is called "serious literature," which affects a manner self-consciously cerebral. Erich Segal's *Love Story* squares off against Pynchon's *Gravity's Rainbow;* Harlequin romances contrast with *New Yorker* fiction. Poetry readers must cultivate a taste for the Spartan but *au courant* fare of the little magazines or slop up the treacle of

Rod McKuen. There is an interesting connected phenomenon to which I shall return: the more consciously cerebral literature of serious contemporary artists often associates itself—surprisingly—not only with the head but also with the genital area as well, avoiding the heart only in ritualized purification from possible taint of Victorian sentimentality.

Literary sentimentality points toward a large problem for modern consciousness, a pervasive difficulty in harmonizing what George Eliot's Adam Bede called "notions and feelings." The difficulty often turns into anxiety and sometimes panic that one may not be able to feel anything at all. Hence Emma Bovary's frenetic obsession with foolish love affairs. By means of a messy suicide she can be certain as she vomits away her life that at least her feelings are authentic. Similarly the emptiness of rural southern life in nineteenth-century America invites first the apparently innocent, though false, sentiment of Emmeline Grangerford, then the less innocent and more spurious values of her murderous family, and finally calls forth the grandiose and apocalyptic heroics of the Civil War. Abraham Lincoln was not engaged in idle small talk when he greeted Harriet Beecher Stowe as the little lady who started this great big war.

It is worth our while here to remind ourselves of what sentimentality is about. We have seen what it is. Does it have a characteristic subject matter? Yes indeed. Although sentimentality in the eighteenth and nineteenth centuries is sometimes directed toward animals, toward nature and the natural man, toward religion, or toward the memory of a supposed happy and organic society of the past, these are not its chief topics. The most important subjects, and those I wish to address, are the same in not only the eighteenth and nineteenth centuries, but the twentieth century as well. They are the status of women, romantic love, marriage, and the family. In the nineteenth century we find an apotheosis of the domestic values: an ecstatic deification of women, marriage, and family. Interestingly, the importance of these values is commonly indicated only in their absence or distortion. Ann Douglas, in her wonderfully suggestive study, *The Feminization of American Culture*, says that sentimentalism "asserts that the values a society's activity denies are precisely the ones it cherishes."[2] One might add that the values a society most loudly proclaims are those it fears it has lost. A common theme for Dickens and Tennyson, for instance, is a lonely search for the domestic values mentioned above by fictional characters who have been disinherited.

Tennyson's most popular poem is a case in point. *Enoch Arden* is the story of a poor orphan boy who grows up to marry his childhood sweetheart, Annie, to the unspoken sadness of Philip Ray, another playmate who also loves her. Enoch is shipwrecked on a voyage to earn money for his poor family. Philip helps Annie and her children in Enoch's absence, and at last after eleven and a half years he marries her. Enoch is finally rescued and returns, an alien to his family, whose happiness he can only observe from a wall behind Philip's house. Enoch ekes out a lonely existence so as not to disturb Philip and Annie, revealing his identity only in death. Although this soap opera displays Tennysonian genius, it is the epitome of Tennysonian and Victorian sentimentality. It is also a parable of Victorian alienation with its bleak vision of the accelerating breakdown of the family and the older organic society. In Dickens' work Oliver Twist, David Copperfield, and Pip, taking their solitary journeys through hosts of surrogate parents in search of a family paradise, are analogous parables. Josiah Bounderby's rejection of his mother in *Hard Times* is another emblem of a widely shared anxiety about the collapse of the family in the face of the Industrial Revolution. Richardson's *Clarissa*, the massive foundation of modern fiction, fits this dominant sentimental pattern. Its thousand-plus pages all deal with the difficulties of a young woman who has been separated both spiritually and physically from her family.

Now before forging ahead with our story we must go backward for a moment. The sentimental journey which has been undertaken by modern literature since the early eighteenth century and which is still continuing in the twentieth has a historical background which must be considered if we are to understand the recent past and the present. C.S. Lewis wrote wisely in his seminal study of medieval consciousness, *The Allegory of Love*, that "Humanity does not pass through phases as a train passes through stations: being alive, it has the privilege of always moving yet never leaving anything behind. Whatever we have been, in some sort we are still."[3] In that faith in the organic unity of human consciousness, as well as its development in history, let us—I hope not too superficially—consider for a moment what many believe to be one of the truly important transformations in the history of human consciousness and its perception of the relation of the sexes. Although there is considerable controversy as to exactly *what* happened and the degree to which it happened, there seems little reason to doubt that something very important began to take place in the eleventh century in the western psyche's perception of women and what we now call romantic love. "French poets. . . ," Lewis wrote, "discovered or invented, or were the first to express, that romantic species of passion which English poets were still writing about in the nineteenth. They effected a change which has left no corner of our ethics, our imagination, or our daily life untouched, and they erected impassible barriers between us and the classical past or the oriental present. Compared with this revolution the Renaissance is a mere ripple on the surface of literature."[4]

The new kind of "courtly love" discovered by the medieval poets is certainly the foundation of what we now call "romantic love" but, in its emphasis on an extramarital setting, quite different from the ordinary middle-class tradition of the nineteenth and twentieth centuries: "Boy meets girl; they fall in love; difficulties arise; difficulties are overcome; plot resolved by marriage." In the Middle Ages, the "same woman who was the lady and 'the dearest dread' of her vassals was often little better than a piece of property to her husband. So far from being a natural channel for the new kind of love, marriage was rather the drab background against which that love stood out in all the contrast of its new tenderness and delicacy."[5]

This curious circumstance leads us to another well-known interpretation of the discovery of romantic love in the Middle Ages, that by the French scholar, Denis de Rougemont, who felt that the development of the tradition led to the "inescapable conflict in the West between passion and marriage" and to the dangerous and destructive worship of passion itself, so prominent in western literature since the inauguration of romantic love in the Middle Ages.[6]

Thus Lewis finds the medieval discovery and celebration of the Lady and romantic love a revolutionary step in the expansion of human possibilities and a crucial deepening of human consciousness while de Rougemont regards these phenomena, in their association with passion and their neurotic tendency toward histrionic suffering, nothing short of a calamity for the western psyche. Both writers agree, however, that something momentous happened. The ancient world offers no example of a love affair like that of Tristan and Iseult. Ovid's *Art of Love* is nothing like the courtly love tradition; to the modern mind it appears to have little to do with love at all. Cynical and satirical, its chief topic is sexual attraction—from a male point of view. There are no "Ladies," or even women that one might marry or cherish—only "girls" to be won over. Love in Ovid is seen as sexual love to be pursued, but also as a foolishness, a madness, or a sickness. Ovid also wrote a book called "The Remedies for Love." Like the courtly love of the Middle Ages, it has nothing to do with marriage, but unlike the Middle Ages, it points to no theophany as does Dante's love for Beatrice. Neither does it present an opportunity for responsibility or charity, such as that taken by Chaucer's lovers in "The Franklin's Tale."

Chaucer's "Franklin's Tale," incidentally, with its revolutionary application of the new tenderness and sensitivity of courtly love to love in marriage, anticipates another stage in the evolution of human consciousness. The rise of the middle class and the coming of the Protestant Reformation, to name two causes out of many possible, began to turn the energies released by the discovery of romantic love towards marriage and the family. Strict medieval ideals of chastity on the one hand, paradoxically accompanied by adultery and the worship of women on the other, came to be replaced by the ideal of conjugal affection.

It is sometimes said that the heroic and chivalric interests of earlier western literature came to be domesticated in the late seventeenth and eighteenth
century. This is undoubtedly true, but even more interesting is the fact that
the tradition of romantic love also became domesticated in a new ideal of
love in marriage, typified in Milton, but spreading throughout European
culture in the eighteenth century.[7] The enormous popularity of Richardson reflects the change, even as *Pamela* and *Clarissa* helped to bring it about.
We must make no mistakes here. Contrary to the strongly held opinions of
the "moral majority," the modern nuclear family is not really the ancient
basis of our society, which has been recently shaken by liberal modernism.
It is an institution which has evolved to primary importance only in the
eighteenth and nineteenth centuries. In the last few years two works of historical sociology have made this fact quite plain. I refer to *Centuries of Childhood: A Social History of Family Life* by Philippe Ariès, and Lawrence Stone's
magisterial *The Family, Sex and Marriage in England 1500–1800*.[8] The thesis of Ariès' book is that despite the fact that the nuclear family in the nineteenth and twentieth century is popularly supposed to be in decline, the
"study of modern demographic phenomena" has led to "a completely contrary conclusion" (p. 10). Ariès' argument, based on medieval and later art,
demographics, and contemporaneous personal accounts, is that it was not
until the thirteenth century that childhood began to be discovered as a separate category of life. An analysis of medieval and renaissance art led Ariès
to the further conclusion that the modern concept of the family "was unknown in the Middle Ages, that it originated in the fifteenth and sixteenth
centuries, and that it reached its full expression in the seventeenth century"
(p. 353). Both Ariès and Stone agree that the larger concept of the kin-
oriented, extended family, with its emotional and spiritual emphasis on the
blood line, was probably the only concept of a family character much considered in the Middle Ages. Stone's detailed study is focused on the change
from this more open "lineage family" to the rise of what he calls "affective
individualism" and the "companionate marriage," which in turn brought
about the closed "nuclear family," the norm for the last two centuries (pp.
4–8, 325–405). The shift from the older kin-oriented extended family to the
modern nuclear family follows that new stress on love in marriage that occurred in imaginative literature.

And what has all this to do with sentimentality? These are some of the
outer circumstances which surround its growth. They are related to other
external circumstances and causes, economic, political, religious, and psychological, which it would take many essays like this one to be able to consider. Some of these circumstances would have to do with actual historical
events and tangible material forces; some would have to do with the history
of ideas, as in some of the religious and literary influences already cited.

It is my aim here to outline what I consider to be the inner circumstances and causes of the developments we have been discussing, the psychic transformations within or behind the sentimental journey of modern literature. I am concerned with the evolution of consciousness rather than the history or ideas or the temporal procession of events. What follows is indebted to the thought of Owen Barfield, who, along with some other twentieth-century thinkers such as R.G. Collingwood, Julian Jaynes, Thomas Kuhn, Erich Auerbach, Claude Levi-Strauss, and Erich Neumann—to name only a few—has concerned himself with this subject.[9]

What is meant by the term, "evolution of consciousness"? The foundation of Barfield's account of human consciousness lies in something quite simple: he takes seriously and follows out the logical consequences of a nearly universally acknowledged axiom of modern epistemology. The axiom is usually recognized as self-evident as soon as it is stated: What we see, or feel, or touch, or hear in the world around us cannot be identical with what is actually there. There must necessarily be a difference between appearance and reality. The physical sciences, for instance, stress the difference between the *actual* structure of the universe and the *appearances* which are presented by that structure to ordinary human consciousness. Similarly, a good deal of philosophy, certainly since Kant, and a good deal of literary criticism since Coleridge have emphasized the participation of the human mind in the creation, or evocation of these phenomena. Since the discovery of quantum mechanics, twentieth-century physics has emphasized the same thing. To put it another way, our perception is not only a passive thing which is done *to* us by our senses, but it is also an active thing which we do in part by thinking. In the graphic arts the French Impressionists actually attempted to put on canvas the creative function of the mind in seeing.

The things we perceive, then, are the outcome of 1) whatever is *actually* there; 2) our sense-perceptions; and 3) the selecting, ordering function of our minds; they are in fact "representations." We distinguish between real things and hallucinations when others perceive the same representations. The truth is that the familiar world which we see and know around us— trees, rainbows, blue sky, animals, and people—is a system of collective representations.

Collective representations do not exist separately from the individuals who make up a particular social group. Their existence, however, does not depend on any particular individual. In this way collective representations are like language. Like the words of a language, they are shared by members of a particular social group and are passed on from one generation to another, evolving only gradually during the centuries, but thereby resulting in what I have called the evolution of consciousness, as opposed to the mere history of ideas. It must in fact follow that the familiar world experienced by one culture will be somewhat different from that experienced by another.[10]

Although there are many possible applications of this account of consciousness and its historical development, one drawn from anthropology, but with philosophical and psychological aspects, is especially significant in the present context. Noting the common anthropological observation that primitive people seem not to perceive in the same way that we do, Barfield suggests that "in the act of perception, they are not detached, as we are, from the representations. For us the only connection *of which we are conscious* is the external one through the senses. Not so for them."[11]

And this brings us to a key term in Barfield's vocabulary and in that of some of his anthropological tutors: *participation.* Participation may be defined here as the "extra-sensory relation between man and the phenomena," the non-material connection between human beings and what is ordinarily called familiar nature. It is a commonplace in anthropology to recognize that primitives participate in their environments in a way quite different from modern man. We are reminded, however, that modern man also of necessity must "participate" in his environment, since it is composed of collective representations. Yet there is an important difference. What is most characteristic of phenomena in the twentieth century and what especially distinguishes them from those of the past is that our participation in them, and thus their representational nature, is excluded from our immediate awareness.[12]

The evolution of consciousness of western man, then, may be understood in the light of his gradual development away from "original participation," the immediately experienced sense of belonging observed in primitive people. In arriving at logical thought patterns and the more efficient modes of manipulation upon which civilization is based, modern man has suppressed his awareness of the representational reality of the universe. As an increasingly convenient fiction he has come to regard his phenomena as facts, totally independent of his own consciousness. Participation, which is admitted on all sides as a logical necessity, has simply been elbowed out of modern consciousness, much in the same way that Freud held that certain sexual materials are pushed out of our conscious minds into the unconscious.

As may have been anticipated, the burden of the remainder of this essay will be to show how the loss of participation in modern times is the cause of modern loneliness and existential *angst* on the one hand and the triumph of literary sentimentality on the other. As the last vestiges of original participation ebbed away, sensitive thinkers and artists began more and more desperately to try to recover what traces of it they could. Some of these attempts involve the enormous imaginative and intellectual efforts of the Romantic Movement, some the less authentic products of sentimentality, and some the confusion of the two.

For various reasons the nineteenth century seems to have registered the high point of the distress. In England the first half of the century witnessed devastating external changes which increased the impact of inner ones. The formal collapse of the older, participative and organic system of Christendom occurred as a result of such events as the Catholic Emancipation Act, the repeal of the Test and Corporation Acts, and the great Reform Bill of 1832, all outward manifestations of a decay that had been increasing steadily for three centuries. The losses could be sensed in areas both more personal and more universal than those suggested by formal changes in the legal constitution. As mentioned earlier, the extended, kin-oriented family of village or feudal manor began to shrink to something quite different. Among the upper classes, great county families unified by the participating sense of "blood" began to feel their coherence and vitality draining away. One thinks of the unmarried brother and sister, Mr. and Miss Thorne, in Trollope's *Barchester Towers,* pathetically clinging to the value of blood and family, as the Thornes of Ullathorne die out in their generation. "Blood," in its older, comprehensive sense, leads us to a renewed understanding of what "loss of participation" means. It means losing the perception of an extrasensory link to Nature itself. Thomas Aquinas assumed not only that Nature was God's creation, but that the Natural Law which bound men and animals together was a divine law, partaking of eternal mind as well as of matter. "Blood" for the author of the Doctrine of Transubstantiation was a sacramental sign of man's extrasensory relation to both God and Nature. Mr. and Miss Thorne's sentimental and eccentric obsession with blood is a pallid remnant of the earlier universal assumption.

Victorians who were sensitive to the subtle shifts in basic consciousness around them felt themselves increasingly cut off, increasingly bereft of the sense of belonging – not just belonging to a church or to an organic state, but to Nature as well. This growing change in perception of the world engendered a search for the remnants of belonging, for the links that might still connect human beings to Nature and to the past, in which an organic relationship to Nature was felt to have been unbroken. The more sensitive the seeker, the more frantic the search or, paradoxically, the more strident the searcher's insistence that nothing had changed after all – that God, man, and Nature still maintained the same old relationship. A conscious intellectual insistence on this relationship – which had once been an immediate experience – as a notion or idea is the characteristic source of Victorian sentimentality and of literary sentimentality as a whole. It is prominent in the sentimentality of certain aspects of Protestant fundamentalism; it is prominent in the Tractarian effort to revive a medieval Catholic Church to which

Victorian Englishmen belonged after all. It exists to a certain degree in Tennyson's or Ruskin's Toryism. It exists in anxious Victorian anti-vivisectionism on the one hand, and in Sir Edwin Landseer's animal portraits on the other. It exists in the busted captive hearts Mark Twain laughed at; it helps to form the vision of a natural paradise on the river to which Huck and Jim flee in their escape from nineteenth-century civilization. It is the driving force behind Emma Bovary's pathetic quest for romantic love.

The search for participating links and the corresponding insistence that the links still held firm grew most intense (and thus sentimental) in the area of women, romantic love, and the family. Most of what is now regarded as sentimentality in Dickens and Tennyson is centered around these subjects—one thinks of Rose Maylie, Little Nell, the Queen of the May, Dora. The enormous genre of the seduction novel in all of its manifestations is a related phenomenon. Conversely, one thinks of the remarkable avoidance of women and romantic love in the work of the classic nineteenth-century American novelists, as described by Leslie Fiedler and by Ann Douglas.[13] It is my view that as human beings began unconsciously to experience successive losses of participation in Nature, in the Church, and, by the eighteenth and nineteenth centuries, in the extended family, there came to be only one place left for it: the nuclear family. The special emphasis on the nuclear family, with its all-powerful father, its compliantly sweet mother and obedient children, isolated from the organic connections that united the older extended family, is a Victorian creation, an example of the intellectualized insistence on participation that is at the root of sentimentality. It is this emphasis which began to insist, formally and consciously, on specialized roles for family members. Children's literature and newly devised pursuits suitable for females are peculiarly Victorian. All of this may be seen as an effort, a desperate effort, to define the nuclear family as a defense against final isolation and alienation in a mechanized world.

In any case I would like to insist on two points. First, the loss of a sense of participation in western consciousness is a genuinely important event with far-reaching consequences, a kind of catastrophe of modern times, despite its association with rational thought and the development of civilization. Human consciousness seems to have traded a kind of servitude, through a servitude at home in its world, for a new freedom, but a freedom characterized by a disconnected homelessness and anomie. This loss is related not only to the sentimental journey we have been discussing but also to the emotionally and intellectually disorienting solipsism of the modern world. The second point I would like to make is that the consciousness of the Victorians was different from our own. It is not simply that they had different beliefs about the world, though of course they often did; it is that they saw a slightly different world. Although twentieth-century readers may find parts of Dickens or Tennyson sentimental, most Victorians did not. It is worth remembering that George Eliot wept upon reading Tennyson's "Guinevere." Thomas Henry Huxley, John Tyndall, and John Stuart Mill, hardly sentimentalists, were all ardent admirers of Tennyson. Sensitive Victorians were drawn to admire works which sometimes seem sentimental to the twentieth century for the same reasons Victorian authors were moved to write them.

But one may reasonably object that the same general lack of a sense of participation still exists in the twentieth century. *Why,* then, do modern readers see some nineteenth-century works as sentimental, while intelligent Victorians did not? The answer to this question has two parts. The first part is suggested by a commonplace of literary history. Dickens and Tennyson, to continue with two representative Victorian examples, were perhaps the last authors of major stature who attempted to be not only "serious" artists, but popular ones. By a curious irony of fate they were nearly the first who had the opportunity to write for a mass reading public, but were among the last consciously to attempt to do so. It is a fact of literary history that literature in the twentieth century split into two streams, as observed earlier: the serious and the popular. In the popular stream sentimentality of the Victorian sort is not dead at all, but still finds an enormous audience, as is evidenced in books like Segal's *Love Story* or in the nearly universal response to the television series of a few years ago, *Roots,* which dramatized those powerful issues of women, family, and connection to Nature much as the better Victorians did, with depth, intelligence, and considerable sentimentality. The title *Roots* itself suggests the unconscious yearning for that sense of participation we have been discussing. These examples, nonetheless, are one half of a divided stream. The other half is the cerebral "serious" literature mentioned earlier. It is not so surprising that twentieth-century critics, accustomed as they are to reading only one half of the divided stream—the serious half—should either discreetly ignore the other half which they find still imbedded in the admittedly "serious" Victorian artists, or should search for a posthumous psychoanalysis to explain a divided Tennyson, a divided Dickens, or a schizophrenic Mark Twain.

The second half of the answer is more speculative than the first and involves an enlargement of the conventional understanding of sentimentality. Although this part of the answer is speculative, it seems inevitable if we accept the notion of an evolution of consciousness which has increasingly repressed the older sense of participation. The Victorians were obsessed—to the point of sentimentality—with women and family because women, with their biological links to Nature, have been viewed traditionally as the guardians of the inchoate processes of the earth. They have been the traditional preservers of the status quo, the maintainers of the identity of the family, both extended and nuclear, as well as the source of evolutionary change in the future. The sometimes sentimental attribution of superior moral powers to women, the representatives of Nature, may be seen as an attempt to re-establish the older notion of the comprehensive, participative Natural Law assumed by St. Thomas Aquinas, and assumed in a somewhat different form by Aristotle in his *De Anima*. Marriage, as is well known, has been a common symbol for the integration of human values with the natural order from the Old Testament to the Romantic poets. As the general sense of participation became more and more obscured in modern times, the Victorians became fixated on its remnants—especially in the nuclear family, in which a person could still have a sense of belonging, an extrasensory relation with his surroundings.

Unfortunately, however, as the sense of participation had earlier faded along with the diminished importance of the Church, the feudal system, and the extended, kin-oriented family, so in the nineteenth century it began to weaken further in the perceived weakening of the nuclear family. It was nearly impossible for any but the most influential to obtain a divorce in the first half of the nineteenth century. A hundred years later divorce was commonplace. The shrillness of the Victorian defense of the family suggested the defenders' anxieties. As an assumed sense of participation in the nuclear family became less universal in the twentieth century, its assertion in literature appeared more and more sentimental to twentieth-century readers. Does this fact signal an end to sentimentality in serious twentieth-century literature? Have we come at last to the end of the sentimental journey of modern literature? Not quite.

The interesting thing about sentimentality as it appears in artists like Dickens or Tennyson—I exclude poor writers or intentionally manipulative ones—is that they themselves are quite unaware of it. They do not set out consciously to write sentimentally. Is it possible, therefore, that twentieth-century writers, even serious writers, engage in a kind of sentimentality of which they are unaware, just as their predecessors were? I believe this to be the case. As the universal perception of being a part of Nature in an extrasensory as well as a sensory way began to collapse in modern times, it took refuge in smaller and smaller areas. If Christendom collapsed, there was always the extended family. If the extended family broke down in the Industrial Revolution, the nuclear family with its participative relation between man, woman, and child, could still be relied on, even refurbished and enhanced. But what if the nuclear family itself should collapse, as it has shown signs of doing in the twentieth century? What if it, too, is only a sociological accident? As the divorce rates skyrocket and traditional sex roles become confused or reversed people worry that not only romantic love but love itself may be only an illusion, masking sordid physiological necessities. Is there any part of the older relationship in which a now desperately cornered human being, lost in a mechanical world, can find that participative link to Nature and to his fellow human beings which justifies and gives meaning to his mechanical sensory link to it? Yes, of course there is: sexuality itself. The intense and increasingly shrill emphasis on sexuality is the twentieth-century development of Victorian sentimentality. Contemporary fears of loss or inadequacy are apparent in every Sunday Supplement discussion of middle-class sexual activity. Sexual sentimentality will surely be seen also as a keynote of twentieth-century imaginative literature. Now, of course, it is rarely recognized as sentimental at all. Good twentieth-century writers share the unconsciousness of good Victorian writers that parts of their work are sentimental. In fact they think an increased emphasis on sexuality just the opposite of sentimentality, in much the same way that Tennyson regarded his domestic idyls as a realistic antidote to the high-flown "sensibility" of his eighteenth-century predecessors. Poor writers manipulate sexual sentimentality in the twentieth century as their grandfathers manipulated domestic sentimentality in the nineteenth.

It is not surprising, therefore, that the great spiritual physician of the twentieth century should come forward to explain civilization's discontents through the bizarre theory of an incongruous but destructive family romance leading to social anarchy. Lacking the historical perspective to see beyond the middle-class Victorian nuclear family, Dr. Freud developed his theory that the family's power, its mystery, as well as its tendency to sickness, was grounded in a single reality repressed from ordinary awareness—its sexuality. Moreover, Freudian theory connected this physiological explanation of the universal modern malaise—in a brilliant paradox—to the spiritual, nonsensory side of man, an hypothesized "unconscious," which links us all to a common nature, an unfallen Garden of Eden, to which all belong and in which nothing is forbidden. In an age in which participation is repressed, both doctors and writers tend to suppose that any deep relationship *must* be sexual in nature, even though unrecognized as such. All of this is a clear parallel to the evolution of consciousness as reflected in literature from the mid-nineteenth century to the mid-twentieth.

Sexual sentimentality takes two opposite courses, which have a polar relationship. Baudelaire, the French contemporary of Tennyson and Dickens, demonstrated a version of Victorian anxiety by simply reversing the sentimental themes of the latter to excite a similarly sentimental sense of shock at the loss of traditional relationships. W.H. Auden wrote more profoundly than he knew in comparing the two poets. "The aspects of Tennyson that are now so distasteful to us, the 'schoolmistress Alfred' of *The Miller's Daughter* and *Guinevere,* the schoolboy Froggie-hater of *Riflemen Form,* are the counterpart of the 'shocking' Baudelaire to whom the sole pleasure in love was the knowledge of doing evil and who hoped to conquer solitude by inspiring universal horror and disgust."[14]

D.H. Lawrence is, sentimentally, the natural successor to Dickens and Tennyson. A serious writer, he focused on the issue of failing participation just as surely and genuinely as they did. For him, the now thoroughly mechanical, rationalized—yet fragmented—world contained only sexuality as a link to nature, a link important not just because of its sensual aspects but because of its paradoxical spiritual principle of integration of the human personality. As in the case of so many divided Victorian artists, there are also two Lawrences. There is the more fully controlled artist of, say, *Women in Love,* and then there is the more strident, more schematic, more sentimental Lawrence of *Lady Chatterly's Lover,* who reduces fresh experiences to "ideas," and who frantically attempts to recover man's roots in the past and his link to Nature through the worship of copulation, conducted by a liturgy of four-letter words of Anglo-Saxon origin.

Sexual sentimentality may be discerned in a spectrum running from *Playboy* and the solemn "how to" manuals (which replace Victorian domestic handbooks), through the obligatory bedroom scenes in Book-of-the-Month selections, to the more self-conscious sexual sermonizing of writers like Henry Miller. It appears everywhere to some degree in serious twentieth-century literature: Joyce, Hemingway, Faulkner, Updike. The pattern has been recently repeated in the changing subject matter offered on television soap operas.

A pathetic emblem of the effects of sexual sentimentality is the "American girl" of the 1980s—still as unsatisfied as Emma Bovary was, but no longer able to believe in romantic love—protesting her computerized environment by uttering stridently those once-secret and sacred four-letter reminders of our ancient connection to Adam and Eve in the Garden of Eden.

And where do we go from here? How much longer will the sentimental journey last before the western psyche can adjust its sad disarray of mind and heart? I hope our deliverance will be soon, but I fear that Huckleberry Finn may have outgrown Miss Emmeline Grangerford in the nineteenth century only to turn in our own time to sporting with Miss Brooke Shields in the Blue Lagoon. And like poor Jim at the end of Mark Twain's masterpiece, an entire culture is still chained up in a flimsy slave cabin constructed of false sentiment—"a captive heart busted."

Notes

1. *Adventures of Huckleberry Finn,* ed. Sculley Bradley, Richmond Croom Beatty, E. Hudson Long (New York: Norton, 1961, 1962), pp. 83–85.

2. Ann Douglas, *The Feminization of American Culture* (New York: Knopf, 1977), p. 12.

3. C.S. Lewis, *The Allegory of Love: A Study in Medieval Tradition* (London: Oxford Univ. Press, 1936; rpt. New York, 1976), p. 1.

4. Ibid., p. 4.

5. Ibid., p. 13.

6. Denis de Rougemont, *Love in the Western World*, trans. Montgomery Belgion (New York: Pantheon, 1956), p. 8.

7. See Jean H. Hagstrum, *Sex and Sensibility: Ideal and Erotic Love from Milton to Mozart* (Chicago: Univ. of Chicago Press, 1980), especially pp. 14, 15, 47, 67.

8. Philippe Ariès, *Centuries of Childhood: A Social History of Family Life*, trans. Robert Baldick (New York: Knopf, 1962); Lawrence Stone, *The Family, Sex and Marriage In England 1500–1800* (New York: Harper & Row, 1977).

9. Erich Auerbach, *Mimesis: The Representation of Reality in Western Literature*, trans. Willard R. Trask (Princeton: Princeton Univ. Press, 1953); Owen Barfield, *Saving the Appearances: A Study in Idolatry* (New York: Harcourt, Brace, 1957); R.G. Collingwood, *The Idea of History* (Oxford: Clarendon Press, 1946); Julian Jaynes, *The Origin of Consciousness in the Breakdown of the Bicameral Mind* (Boston: Houghton Mifflin, 1976); Thomas Kuhn, *The Structure of Scientific Revolutions* (Chicago: Univ. of Chicago Press, 1962); Claude Levi-Strauss, *The Savage Mind* (Chicago: Univ. of Chicago Press, 1966); Erich Neumann, *The Origins and History of Consciousness*, trans. R.F.C. Hull (New York: Pantheon, 1954).

10. Barfield, *Saving the Appearances*, pp. 17–20, 33.

11. Ibid., p. 11.

12. Ibid., p. 40.

13. Douglas, *Feminization of American Culture*, pp. 5 and passim; Leslie Fiedler, *Love and Death in the American Novel* (New York: Criterion, 1960), pp. xix–xx, 35–36, 215–16, and passim.

14. *A Selection from the Poems of Alfred, Lord Tennyson*, ed. W.H. Auden (Garden City, N.Y.: Doubleday, 1944), p. xx.

John Maynard

The Worlds of Victorian Sexuality:
Work in Progress

Sexuality in Victorian Society

Since at least the publication of Strachey's *Eminent Victorians* there has been
no lack of recognition that Victorian society, more than others, is to be characterized by a peculiar attitude toward sexuality. Strachey's case studies of
respectable Victorians slyly suggested that Victorian society generally pushed
normal sexual urges underground and reaped, in return, a harvest of com
pulsive or even mad behavior dominated by hidden instinctual needs. Few
observers of the Victorian scene after Strachey have failed to point out the
unusual degree of sexual restraint imposed upon social life and published
literature alike. Biographers in Strachey's tradition have carried the pursuit
of repressed sexuality, hypocritical idealism, and psychological distortion
from the eminent to the great Victorians – sometimes unwisely, but who can
deny, for instance, a broad connection between Ruskin's obsessive youthful
idealism and his extreme sexual innocence? Who can doubt, to take another
example from the many that offer, that Elizabeth Barrett's lingering disease
in her father's house at Wimpole Street was as much the result of an arti-
ficially prolonged sexual childhood as of physical ailment? Meanwhile, the
idea of Victorianism as the antithesis of modern sexual attitudes has been
entrenched in the popular conception and common language. In common
usage Victorian means sexually ignorant or repressive. The Victorian woman,
that rather multiplex and complicated phenomenon, has become stereotyped
into the mere model of all that the modern woman is not, or at least wishes
not to be. Such are the views, scholarly and popular, of Victorian sexuality,
one would almost wonder how the human race survived the period.

Its physical survival can perhaps be attributed to the heroic efforts of all those matrons who lay still and tried to think of England. Psychological survival, in our century's predominant view of the Victorians, is said to have demanded more: going underground, into the social underworld of Victorian deviance and prostitution or the literary underworld of erotic fantasy and commercial pornography. Certainly there was a large other world of Victorian sexual life whose complexities have only recently begun to be explored by serious historical researchers. Few studies of the Victorian underworld have been free from the sensationalism of the subject. Histories of sexuality tend, almost by the nature of the subject, to fall somewhere between storehouses of odd facts and gilt-edged pornography. Most fail to observe the close relations between overworld repression and underworld release. Gordon Rattray Taylor, *The Angel-Makers: A Study of the Psychological Origins of Historical Change 1750–1850* (London: Heinemann, 1958), avoids many of these faults but insists on his interesting but somewhat shaky superstructure of psychohistory with its periods of patrist and matrist psychological types—more broadly elaborated in his *Sex in History* (1954; rpt. New York: Vanguard, 1970). Ronald Pearsall, *The Worm in the Bud: The World of Victorian Sexuality* (Toronto: Macmillan, 1969), is the fullest compendium of fact and anecdote regarding sexual issues in the Victorian period. Pearsall's interesting gleanings from primary sources are not always adequately evaluated and presented in a coherent argument. (Pearsall's *Public Purity, Private Shame: Victorian Sexual Hypocrisy Exposed* [London: Weidenfeld and Nicholson, 1976] is essentially a popular survey.) Eric Trudgill, *Madonnas and Magdalens: The Origins and Development of Victorian Sexual Attitudes* (New York: Holmes & Meier, 1976), looks especially at ideas of woman in the Victorian period, but also surveys Victorian theories of sex, the changing balance of prudishness and adventuresomeness in public attitudes toward sex, as well as literary issues.

The most useful general introduction to historical issues concerning sexuality in the nineteenth century is Jeffrey Weeks' deceptively brief chapters on the nineteenth century in *Sex, Politics and Society: The Regulation of Sexuality Since 1800* (London: Longman, 1981). This is less an attempt at a full history than it is a comprehensive survey of the still very sparse sources in social history; it is also a cogent rethinking of the historical issues by the light of Foucault's ideas of the construction of discourses on sexuality in historical periods, and the tendency to increasing societal promotion and regulation of sexuality in modern times. Weeks plots the development of a respectable, middle-class family sexual system that attempted to channel and regulate sexuality, first at home, and then, later in the century, in society at large. Yet he rightly sees this middle-class family system as in itself diverse and in competition with other sexual systems—that of other classes, or of a deviant group such as homosexuals, or more generally, of the sexual radicals who challenged it—which to some extent it helped to create. Peter Gay's forthcoming full length study of sexuality in Victorian England, America, and the Continent should likewise help bring a more comprehensive and more critical historical perspective to bear on the subject. Keith Thomas, "The Double Standard," *Journal of the History of Ideas,* 20 (1959), 195–216, provides clear analysis of one idea and a good deal of historical material. Sex in Scotland in the nineteenth century is surveyed interestingly by J.C. Smout, "Aspects of Sexual Behaviour in Nineteenth-Century Scotland," in A. Allan MacLaren, ed., *Social Class in Scotland: Past and Present* (Edinburgh: John Donald, 1976), 55–85.

Of broader studies, Denis de Rougemont's equally classic works, *Love in the Western World,* trans. Montgomery Belgion, rev. ed. (1956; rpt. New York: Harper and Row, 1974) and *Love Declared: Essays on the Myths of Love,* trans. Richard Howard (Boston: Beacon, 1964), still present an important and challenging thesis of the origin of romantic and adulterous love in the traditions of courtly love. Wayland Young, *Eros Denied: Sex in Western Society* (New York: Grove Press, 1964), is an unsystematic history, mostly a history of ideas, that argues for sexual freedom. Vern L. Bullough, *Sexual Variance in Society and History* (New York: John Wiley, 1976), is more systematic and historical but relatively breezy. Like Taylor and Young, he argues that Western society has been, on the whole, unusually restrictive. Michel Foucault's more recent, *The History of Sexuality. Volume I: An Introduction,* trans. Robert Hurley (New York: Pantheon Books, 1978), is a prolegomenon to a full historical study in progress that has already borne fruit in Weeks' work, and generally offers a better model in its conception of competing discourses creating sexuality in an age than do the simplistic ideas of repression/revolution or of psychohistorical periods offered by other historical thinkers. As a theoretical statement it is weakened by its disregard for the scientific discourse on sexuality provided by modern psychology since Freud, by historical and cross-cultural approaches to different societies' forms for sexuality offered by anthropology—e.g., the classic Clellan S. Ford and Frank A. Beach, *Patterns of Sexual Behavior* (New York: Harper, 1952), or Donald Symons, *The Evolution of Human Sexuality* (New York: Oxford Univ. Press, 1979)—by the physiological studies of Masters and Johnson or of John Money on gender differences and the endocrinology of sex, or even by the philosophical discussion of sexuality begun by Sartre and Thomas Nagel (see Alan Soble, ed., *The Philosophy of Sex: Contemporary Readings* [Totowa, N.J.: Rowman and Littlefield, 1980]). And there are, of course, sociological studies such as Kinsey's or the plethora of serious or popular surveys since, especially the more theoretical work of Gagnon and Simon. Foucault might rightly observe that most of these are essentially culture-bound to the state of sexuality of our time; yet observations such as Kinsey's on class differences in sex or on the range of preference from homosexual to heterosexual do suggest some broader visions of that elusive thing, human sexual nature, which is probably not, in matters of sexuality, the infinitely moldable set of body parts enjoying themselves that Foucault's theory suggests. On the whole, Lawrence Stone's full historical study of the period preceding the nineteenth century, *The Family, Sex and Marriage in England 1500–1800* (New York: Harper and Row, 1977), comes closest to being an adequate history of sexuality. The most detailed history to date, it is focused on social facts rather than on ideological positions or study of miscellaneous works of erotica. Stone traces broad swings between what he calls patriarchal repression and affective individualism, with the nineteteenth century generally in the former phase. His generalizations sometimes threaten to obscure the fineness of his perception of the historical complexity of a period, especially in his observations forward to the nineteenth century. His study is complemented by Jean-Louis Flandrin's work on family and sexuality in France, *Families in Former Times: Kinship, Household and Sexuality,* trans. Richard Southern (Cambridge: Cambridge Univ. Press, 1979), especially in his contrasts between Catholic sexual morality and the more liberal English Puritan position that rather early authorized a union of marriage with love and sexual pleasure.

On specific subjects, the large and complex issue of nineteenth-century prostitution is ably surveyed by E.M. Sigsworth and T.J. Wyke, "A Study of Victorian Prostitution and Venereal Disease," in *Suffer and Be Still: Women in the Victorian Age,* ed. Martha Vicinus (Bloomington; Indiana Univ. Press, 1973), pp. 77–99. Three recent studies—Judith R. Walkowitz, *Prostitution and Victorian Society: Women, Class and the State* (New York: Cambridge Univ. Press, 1980), Frances Finnegan, *Poverty and Prostitution: A Study of Victorian Prostitutes in York* (Cambridge: Cambridge Univ. Press, 1979), and the briefer study by Arthur J. Engel, "Immoral Intentions: The University of Oxford and the Problem of Prostitution, 1827–1916," *Victorian Studies,* 23 (1979), 79–107, which looks at the special and interesting case of town-gown prostitution—provide the first substantial evidence on prostitution from studies in local history. Brief anecdotal surveys may be found in Vern L. Bullough, *The History of Prostitution* (New Hyde Park: Universe Books, 1964) and Kellow Chesney, *The Victorian Underworld* (London: Temple, Smith, 1970), pp. 307–64. Cyril Pearl, *The Girl with the Swansdown Seat* (New York: Bobbs-Merrill, 1955), an early popular study of the Victorian underworld, discusses the courtesan world of London. Fraser Harrison, *The Dark Angel: Aspects of Victorian Sexuality* (New York: Universe Books, 1977), is broadly suggestive about the impact of the Victorian sexual underworld on different classes. Trudgill looks at the changing societal and literary image of the prostitute. Full studies of two highly publicized campaigns on prostitution, Josephine Butler's crusade for repeal of the Contagious Diseases Act and William Stead's journalistic war against child prostitution, are provided by Paul McHugh, *Prostitution and Victorian Social Reform* (New York: St. Martin's, 1980), and Michael Pearson, *The Age of Consent: Victorian Prostitution and its Enemies* (Newton Abbot: David and Charles, 1972), as well as by Walkowitz, who looks at the repeal crusade in two specific cities. Deborah Gorham, "The Maiden Tribute of Modern Babylon Re-examined: Child Prostitution and the Idea of Childhood in Late-Victorian England," *Victorian Studies*, 21 (1978), 353–79, takes a penetrating look at child prostitution as a crux in changing Victorian attitudes toward the age of sexual awakening and as a way of distinguishing between working class and middle class sexuality.

Constance Rover, *Love, Morals and the Feminists* (London: Routledge & Kegan Paul, 1970), explores ninetenth-century feminists' avoidance of sexual issues, whether birth control, marital reform, or personal sexual liberation, and she looks at contributions in these areas by women not associated with organized feminist groups.

On Victorian homosexuality there are studies by H. Montgomery Hyde, *The Love that Dared Not Speak its Name: A Candid History of Homosexuality in Britain* (Boston: Little, Brown, 1970), and Jeffrey Weeks, *Coming Out: Homosexual Politics in Britain from the Nineteenth Century to the Present* (London: Quartet Books, 1977); also the Introduction to the anthology by Brian Reade, *Sexual Heretics: Male Homosexuality in English Literature from 1850 to 1900* (London: Routledge & Kegan Paul, 1970), pp. 1–56. A broad survey is offered by A.L. Rowse, *Homosexuals in History: A Study of Ambivalence in Society, Literature and the Arts* (New York: Macmillan, 1977). Colin Simpson, Lewis Chester, and David Leitch, *The Cleveland Street Affair* (Boston: Little, Brown, 1976) offer a detective story approach to a full study of the most sensational homosexual case before Wilde; see also H. Montgomery Hyde, *The Cleveland Street Affair* (New York: Coward, McCann and Geoghegan, 1976). David Hilliard, "UnEnglish and Unmanly: Anglo-Catholicism and Homosexuality," *Victorian Studies*, 25 (1982), 181–210, looks in detail at the controversial issue of homosexuality in one area of Victorian religion. Lesbianism in the nineteenth century is briefly and somewhat inadequately discussed in Lillian Faderman, *Surpassing the Love of Man: Romantic Friendship and Love Between Women from the Renaissance to the Present* (New York: Morrow, 1981). (Works on homosexual writers are presented under "Sexual Discussion in Victorian Literature," below.)

That other ancient subject, incest, is briefly considered in Anthony S. Wohl, "Sex and the Single Room: Incest Among the Victorian Working Classes," in Anthony S. Wohl, ed., *The Victorian Family: Structure and Stresses* (New York: St. Martin's, 1978), pp. 197–216. See also Bryan Strong, "Towards a History of the Experiential Family," *Journal of Marriage and the Family* (1973), pp. 457–66. On the perversions, there is a full study of flagellomania that justifies its notoriety as a Victorian and English preoccupation: Ian Gibson, *The English Vice: Beating, Sex and Shame in Victorian England and After* (London: Duckworth, 1978). John R. Gillis, "Servants, Sexual Relations, and the Risks of Illegitimacy in London, 1801–1900," *Feminist Studies*, 5 (1979), 142–73, gives an interesting and detailed account of sexual mores among domestic servants, a record quite different from stereotypes of seduction and betrayal of downstairs females by upstairs males. Broader surveys of the perplexing issue of rising illegitimacy rates in the earlier nineteenth century are made by Peter Laslett in *The World We Have Lost* (London: Methuen, 1971) and *Family Life in Earlier Generations: Essays in Historical Sociology* (Cambridge: Cambridge Univ. Press, 1977) and in the fine summary account by Weeks, *Sex, Politics and Society*, pp. 59–67, whose ch. 4 provides generally the best account of sexuality and the working class.

The Underworld of Victorian Literature

Mario Praz's *The Romantic Agony*, first published back in 1933, trans. Angus Davidson, 2nd ed. (London: Oxford Univ. Press, 1951), and Steven Marcus's well-known *The Other Victorians: A Study of Sexuality and Pornography in Mid-Nineteenth-Century England* (New York: Basic Books, 1966), a work that indulges our normal tastes for both pornography and moralizing against pornography, have interestingly illuminated some parts of the Victorian literary underworld. Marcus's explorations of both *My Secret Life* and the nineteenth-century physician-sexologist William Acton follow Young's earlier work. Pearsall (*The Worm in the Bud*) also analyzes a variety of kinds of Victorian pornography. David Loth's *The Erotic in Literature* (London: Secker and Warburg, 1962) is a competent general history of pornography. His conclusion, that increased repression and censorship stimulated an increased outlet in pornography, seems generally sound. H. Montgomery Hyde, *A History of Pornography* (New York: Farrar, Straus and Giroux, 1964) is an equally well-written brief survey. See also Michael Perkins, *The Secret Record: Modern Erotic Literature* (New York: Morrow, 1976), who argues that pornography is a repressed and debased form of a more constant erotic literature. Reade includes some examples of homosexual writings that represent, or approach, a special class of pornography. The fullest lists of nineteenth-century works of pornography were compiled by "Pisanus Fraxi" (Henry Spencer Ashbee) in privately printed bibliographies of the nineteenth century: *Index Librorum Prohibitorum* . . . (1877); *Centuria Librorum Absconditorum* . . . (1879); *Catena Librorum Tacendorum* . . . (1885). A greatly abridged edition of all three with an interesting account of Ashbee was issued as *Forbidden Books of the Victorians*, ed. Peter Fryer (London: Odyssey, 1970).

My Secret Life, which was almost certainly not written by Ashbee, was privately printed in eleven volumes ca. 1888-1894. The full text was published by Grove Press in 1965. E. and P. Kronhausen, *Walter: The English Casanova* (London: Polybooks, 1967) is a selection and commentary. Jerome Meckier, "Never in Lapland: A Clue to the Nature of *My Secret Life,*" *English Language Notes,* 16 (1978), 166–77, argues for its novelistic, artistic qualities.

Victorian Censorship

Against the Strachcyan picture of the Victorian driven by unfilled sexual urges into depression or compulsive behavior, we can set our friend Walter of that eroto-epic of the Victorian man of pleasure, *My Secret Life,* a figure of huge sexual actualization but driven underground and in his own way as compulsive as the fervidly repressed Victorian. Between these pendant extremes, apollonian and dionysian with a vengeance, what we do not yet see very well is how the Victorian who did learn to live with his or her sexual needs within the complicated divisions of the society experienced maturation and the sexual life. If most Victorians were neither Florence Nightingales on the one hand nor Walters on the other, what more representative forms of coming of age under Queen Victoria can we describe? Or, to put this in terms of Victorian literature, what visions of sexual experience do we find in the nonpornographic, serious writing of the day?

The answers to these questions may seem obviously to lie on the other side of a well-known barrier: the Victorians' reverence for, or prostration before, the ideal of reticence. Many writers have explored the large world of Victorian censorship and prudishness, though none has given an entirely balanced picture of the conflict between restraint and expression that really marks the age. The spirit has too often been polemical—another kick at the dead horse of Victorian prudery—rather than properly historical. Most, however, do see the origins of prudishness and censorship before the Victorian period. See "The Pattern of Literary Prudery" in Trudgill, pp. 204–47; Peter Fryer, *Mrs. Grundy: Studies in English Prudery* (London: Dennis Dobson, 1963), especially on linguistic prudishness; and Loth (*The Erotic in Literature*). Lionel Stevenson, "Prude's Progress," *Virginia Quarterly Review,* 13 (1937), 257–70, though only a brief study, is still the closest thing to a balanced, historical assessment of the specific forces at war over censorship. Maurice J. Quinlan, "Reformers," in his *Victorian Prelude: A History of English Manners: 1700–1830* (New York: Columbia Univ. Press, 1941), ch. 9, outlines the pre-Victorian period. Richard Stang, "The Cheek of the Young Person," in his *The Theory of the Novel in England 1850–1870* (New York: Columbia Univ. Press, 1959), ch. 5, sketches attitudes towad censorship in Victorian novelists and critics; see also Mario Praz, *The Hero in Eclipse in Victorian Fiction,* trans. Angus Davidson (London: Oxford Univ. Press, 1956), a more controversial statement of the impact of prudish forces on Victorian fiction. Noel Perrin's fine study of what was called castrating literary classics before that word itself was castrated from nineteenth-century usage, *Dr. Bowdler's Legacy: A History of Expurgated Books in England and America* (New York: Atheneum, 1969), provides a very readable history not only of Harriet and Thomas Bowdler's erasures but of the rise and fall of the entire nineteenth-century expurgating industry; his justifiable dislike for their sins of omission does not blind him to the sinners' motivations for their labors of editorial love.

Varieties of Victorian Sexual Lives and Ideologies

Only the rare, almost unique, voice of a Walter takes us into anything like the realities of Victorian sexual life. We have no Victorian Masters and Johnson, no Kinsey; in literature we have no *Sons and Lovers*, not even a *Peyton Place*, certainly no Anaïs Nin or Henry Miller. Yet there are scraps and pieces being gathered here and there about the Victorians' well-hidden private lives and private participations, and these seem generally to indicate that the rigid division between a majority of prudes and a minority of deviants is more modernist myth than reality. One illuminating peep we can take into the sex lives of ordinary Victorians, a survey of sexual attitudes and experiences of Victorian American woman conducted by a female doctor Clelia Mosher who did have some of Kinsey's instincts (though not the courage to publish her results), indicates that there may have been a large world between repressive overculture and deviant sexual underworld: Jane MaHood and Kristine Wenburg, eds., *The Mosher Survey: Sexual Histories of 45 Victorian Women* (New York: Arno Press, 1980). Mosher's information suggests that the Victorian angel in the house was not so much less sensible about sex than the Victorian woman in the street as has been supposed. The women she questioned spoke quite directly about the reality of a female sexual response and the majority affirmed the pleasure of sex, especially with increasing experience.

Our growing knowledge of special aspects of Victorian life seems likewise to be blurring the rigid dichotomy between overworld and underworld that our century had seemed to see. For instance, detailed study of prostitution suggests that working-class young women often went in and out of street-walking as a stage in their lives perhaps closer to adolescent sexual exploration than to career prostitution.[1] Until late in the century, when prostitution began to be the very distinct and separate profession that it is in our century, there was in fact not the rigid sense of an uncrossable barrier between the fallen woman and her respectable sister that we think of as especially Victorian—at least not among the majority working class. More generally, we are perhaps coming slowly to realize that in this issue as in all others there was no single Victorian type; rather, there was a great range of class, regional, family, or personal varieties of sexual experiences.

By the same token, it seems clear that it is not true, as we earlier thought, that there was a single, unchallenged prudish position among Victorians who claimed to offer expert knowledge on sexual matters. Familiar "Victorian" ideas, such as the notion that women were either angels or fallen creatures, that women are passive in sex, that birth control is unnatural and immoral, that masturbation is unhealthy and dangerous, may have been the most prominent or even majority opinions. But such issues raised strong discussion, debate, or protest, and it was the protesters or their successors who eventually began to carry the day at the end of the period. Peter Gay, "Victorian Sexuality: Old Texts and New Insights," *The American Scholar*, 49 (1980), 372–77, in a review of the Arno Press reprint series on sex, marriage, and society, has recently reminded us that "expert" Victorian opinions on sex hardly represent a monolithic ideology. In this respect, as Gay rightly observes, Marcus's extensive presentation of the opinions of one expert, Dr. William Acton, has had the effect of seeming to simplify a complicated age. A similar criticism was made by Brian Harrison in "Underneath the Victorians," *Victorian Studies*, 10 (1967), 239–62, and more recently by Weeks in *Sex, Politics and Society*, pp. 40–41. Marcus's stress on Acton followed that of Peter T. Cominos, "Late-Victorian Sexual Respectability and the Social System," *International Review of Social History*, 8 (1963), 18–48, 216–50; however, Cominos sees a more complicated competition of various sexual positions in the Victorian period, with a system of respectability tending to make headway among middle classes against the earlier double standard. See also his less important "Innocent Femina Sensualis in Unconscious Conflict," in Vicinus, ed., *Suffer and Be Still*, pp. 155–72. Morse Peckham, "Victorian Counterculture," *Victorian Studies*, 18 (1975), 257–76, follows Cominos in seeing a competition of new respectability with older forms of hypocritical constraint or license. He comes close to Foucault and Weeks' insight in seeing that all positions represent an unusual emphasis on sexuality itself. Carl N. Degler, "What Ought to Be and What Was: Women's Sexuality in the Nineteenth Century," *American Historical Review*, 79 (1974), working mostly in an American context, gives a fuller view of the dissenting opinions, in favor of sex and asserting women's sexual pleasure, that challenged Acton's position; he also cites the then unpublished Mosher report. F. Barry Smith, "Sexuality in Britain, 1800–1900: Some Suggested Revisions," in Vicinus, ed., *A Widening Sphere*, pp. 182–98, discusses English opponents to Acton's position and suggests areas of future research. R.S. Neale, *Class and Ideology in the Nineteenth Century* (London: Routledge & Kegan Paul, 1972), pp. 121–42, also challenges the idea of a monolithic middle class and middle-class opinion. The tentative conclusions of Degler, Smith, and Neale would seem to be that Acton's position was a prominent new conservative one but that it was never an orthodoxy and was continually challenged by other doctors and experts as well as by the common sense and common practices of Victorian lovers, married and unmarried. Of the popular general histories of Victorian sexuality most accept too readily the idea of one respectable orthodoxy. Trudgill often seems drawn between taking Acton as an orthodox voice of his society and accepting his own insights into the pluralism of the attitudes he reports. Harrison offers occasional information on various Victorian rebels, though he also relies excessively on Acton. Among relevant broad histories of sexuality, Milton Rugoff, *Prudery and Passion* (New York: Putnam's, 1971), specifically on America, gives a good sense of the variety of competing sexual attitudes and practitioners in the Victorian period in both America and England. Rugoff's general metaphor for sexuality in history, the conflict of repression and passion, fits centrally the Victorian age.

Further information on advocates of liberal attitudes toward sex can be found in accounts of the controversy over contraception. See Norman E. Himes, *Medical History of Contraception* (1936; rpt. New York: Schocken Books, 1971); Peter Fryer, *The Birth Controllers* (New York: Stein and Day, 1966); Angus McLaren, *Birth Control in Nineteenth-Century England* (London: Croom Helm, 1978). Fryer provides more information on theories of controllers and their opponents; Himes is more technical; McLaren provides a fuller social context. J.A. Banks, *Prosperity and Parenthood: A Study of Family Planning Among the Victorian Middle Classes* (London: Routledge & Kegan Paul, 1954), like his later work on *Feminism and Family Planning in Victorian England* (New York: Schocken, 1964), co-authored with Olive Banks, is a technical sociological study of factors leading to population limitation. See also Banks' *Victorian Values: Secularism and the Size of Families* (London: Routledge and Kegan Paul, 1981), that maintains the position that feminism did not affect the growth of family planning. On the relations between feminism and birth control there is also Rover's study (*Love, Morals and the Feminists*).

General studies of Victorian medical authorities on sex have been made by Alex Comfort, *The Anxiety Makers: Some Curious Preoccupations of the Medical Profession* (Camden, N.J.: Thomas Nelson, 1967), and by the more comprehensive work of John S. Haller, Jr., and Robin M. Haller, *The Physician and Sexuality in Victorian America* (1974; rpt. New York: Norton, 1977), actually dealing with both English and American doctors.

The Hallers also give an authoritative account of Victorian medical wars on masturbation and nocturnal emission, author issue on which there was not one but a variety of Victorian positions. See also Ben Barker-Benfield, "The Spermatic Economy: A Nineteenth-Century View of Sexuality," in

Michael Gordon, ed., *The American Family in Social-Historical Perspective* (New York: St. Martin's, 1973), pp. 336–72 (in the American context, with information on clitoridectomy and female castration); R.H. Macdonald, "The Frightful Consequences of Onanism: Notes on the History of a Delusion," *Journal of the History of Ideas*, 28 (1967), 423–31; E.H. Hare, "Masturbatory Insanity: The History of an Idea," *Journal of Mental Science*, 108 (1962), 2–25. Bibliographies of Victorian commentary and advice on sex, marriage, gynecology, bodily and moral purity, and sexual psychology are provided by Gay (the Arno Press reprints) and, more comprehensively, by Barbara Kanner, "The Women of England in a Century of Social Change, 1815–1914: A Select Bibliography, Part II," in Vicinus, ed., *A Widening Sphere*, pp. 222–23, 225–26, 246–49, 261–63, 267–68. (An earlier bibliography by Kanner in Vicinus, ed., *Suffer and Be Still*, compiles Victorian works on prostitution, pp. 189–90.)

Sexual Discussion in Victorian Literature

If it is not true that there was one common Victorian sexual lifestyle or one sexual ideology, it is also not true, to turn again from the age to its creative artists, that serious Victorian writers did not attempt, within the constraining ideas of literary decorum of the time (or against the restraints on publication), to pose and discuss the problems of sexual experience as they found them. Wendell Stacy Johnson has recently surveyed the considerable body of Victorian literature that discusses directly or worries over issues of sexuality and called attention to the sexual complications that troubled and excited Victorian writers' lives as much as they have those of writers of our century. See his *Sex and Marriage in Victorian Poetry* (Ithaca: Cornell Univ. Press, 1975), and his more popular *Living in Sin: The Victorian Sexual Revolution* (Chicago: Nelson Hall, 1979). Johnson's general studies of sexuality and Victorian literature should open the way to others, such as those in the present volume, that look in detail at the sexual lives of major Victorian writers and at the complex ways in which they develop the artistic means to discuss sexual issues within the constraints of Victorian censorship. Except for Walter Houghton's brief survey in *The Victorian Frame of Mind* (New Haven: Yale Univ. Press, 1957), pp. 353–72, the only other general discussion of sex in Victorian literature is Russell M. Goldfarb, *Sexual Repression and Victorian Literature* (Lewisbury: Bucknell Univ. Press, 1970). It is weakened by his relentless quest for hidden or unconscious meanings. Harrison offers a number of readings of Victorian literary works as well as observations of paintings. Sally Mitchell, *The Fallen Angel: Chastity, Class and Women's Reading, 1835–1880* (Bowling Green: Bowling Green Univ. Popular Press, 1981), takes as her subject the representation of unchaste women in Victorian fiction. Her broad analysis of both middle class and more popular (penny weekly) reading of works by known and little known writers demonstrates the restraints that forced respectable writers formally to condemn or punish all but marital sex; it also provides very broad evidence of the preoccupation with sexual subjects, moral and immoral – often quite explicitly stated – in respectable reading and some sense of the varying content of the fiction in relation to different class audiences and to changing views of women and emerging feminist concerns. Richard D. McGhee, *Marriage, Duty & Desire in Victorian Poetry and Drama* (Lawrence: Regents Press of Kansas, 1980), an essay on Victorian poets' use of the theme of marriage as a locus for the reconciliation of duty and desire, offers valuable insights into the nature and quality of desire in different writers. McGhee's work may be profitably read with Tony Tanner's exciting exploration of the unbinding by desire of the contract world of marriage in his *Adultery and the Novel* (Baltimore: Johns Hopkins Univ. Press, 1979), a book that focuses on adultery in Rousseau, Goethe, and Flaubert, yet offers a conceptual framework for issues of sexuality in the nineteenth-century novel generally. More wide-ranging but less satisfactory is Judith Armstrong, *The Novel of Adultery* (New York: Barnes and Noble, 1976), also more concerned with continental than English works.

A.O.J. Cockshut, *Man and Woman: A Study of Love and the Novel, 1740–1940* (New York: Oxford Univ. Press, 1978), broadly surveys sexual issues in the novel, evidently not an entirely congenial task. Patricia Ball's *The Heart's Events: The Victorian Poetry of Relationships* (London: Athlone Press, 1976) offers sensitive readings of Victorian poetry focusing on ego relations in love and somewhat understating writers' appreciation of the strength of sexual forces.

Reade's anthology (*Sexual Heretics*) gives selections of literature on homosexuality. On the general emergence of a homosexual literature at the end of the century, see Rupert Croft-Cooke, *Feasting with Panthers: A New Consideration of Some Late Victorian Writers* (London: W.H. Allen, 1967). Timothy d'Arch Smith, *Love in Earnest: Some Notes on the Lives and Writings of English "Uranian" Poets from 1889 to 1930* (London: Routledge & Kegan Paul, 1970), moves from William Johnson Cory, Symonds, and Carpenter to little-known pederastic (and by and large pedestrian) poets of the early twentieth century. Jeffrey Meyers, *Homosexuality and Literature 1890–1930* (Montreal: McGill-Queens Univ. Press, 1977), looks at the subject of homosexuality in major writers, both homosexual and heterosexual. See also individual biographies of Carpenter, Symonds, and Wilde. Ian Young, *The Male Homosexual in Literature* (1975) is a bibliography. The literature of lesbianism has been competently catalogued by Jeanette Foster, *Sex Variant Women in Literature* (1956; rpt. Baltimore: Diana Press, 1975) and by Gene

Damon, Jan Watson, and Robin Jordan, *The Lesbian in Literature*, 2nd ed. (Reno: The Ladder, 1975); see also the relevant sections of Faderman.

Bigamy, an issue of far more interest to the Victorians than to the twentieth century, has been competently studied in the context of the novel of the 1860s by Jeanne Fahnestock, "Bigamy: The Rise and Fall of a Convention," *Nineteenth Century Fiction*, 36 (1981), 47–71.

The subject of the prostitute in literature is considered by Trudgill in a broad survey of novels, by Mitchell, and by Martin Seymour-Smith, *Fallen Women: A Sceptical Enquiry into the Treatment of Prostitutes, their Clients and their Pimps in Literature* (London: Thomas Nelson, 1969), a rather breezy, uncritical work. Praz, *The Romantic Agony*, looks at a few serious English writers who chose sado-masochistic themes, especially Swinburne.

Nothing on the nineteenth century approaches the insightfulness of Jean H. Hagstrum's *Sex and Sensibility: Ideal and Erotic Love from Milton to Mozart* (Chicago: Univ. of Chicago Press, 1980). The Romantic period has been looked at broadly by Gerald Enscoe, *Eros and the Romantics: Sexual Love as a Theme in Coleridge, Shelley and Keats* (The Hague: Mouton, 1967), who argues that the Romantics anticipate a modern positive vision of sexuality. Nathaniel Brown, *Sexuality and Feminism in Shelley* (Cambridge: Harvard Univ. Press, 1979), turns a commentary on Shelley's *A Discourse of the Manners of the Antient Greeks* into a model exploration of sexual issues, unusually in touch with twentieth-century studies of sexuality. On the transition to modernism see Charles I. Glicksberg, *The Sexual Revolution in Modern English Literature* (The Hague: Martinus Mijhoff, 1973), a study limited by its simplistic conceptual model of repression-revolution. Lloyd Fernando, *New Women in the Late Victorian Novel* (University Park: Pennsylvania State Univ. Press, 1977), provides interesting relations between late Victorian literature and sexual libertarian ideas such as those of Karl Pearson. Gail Cunningham, *The New Woman and the Victorian Novel* (New York: Barnes and Noble, 1978), follows Rover's (*Love, Morals and the Feminists*) useful distinctions between nineteenth-century feminism in economic and political areas and personal, sexual liberation to define what is new in the sexual and psychological novel of the New Woman; the connections she makes to major figures such as Hardy, Gissing, and Meredith are especially interesting. Samuel Hynes, *The Edwardian Turn of Mind* (Princeton: Princeton Univ. Press, 1968), pp. 149–208, provides a useful survey of the literature of sexual liberation at the beginning of the twentieth century.[2]

Relevant broader studies of erotic literature are John Atkins, *Sex in Literature: The Erotic Impulse in Literature* (New York: Grove Press, 1970) and *Sex in Literature: Volume 2: The Classical Experience of the Sexual Impulse* (London: Calder & Boyars, 1973), an unsystematic but bright and lively survey of themes in erotic literature and of the erotic literature of Greece and Rome. Laurence Lerner, *Love and Marriage: Literature and Its Social Context* (New York: St. Martin's, 1979), explores Denis de Rougemont's (*Love in the Western World*) conception of the opposition between passion and the social form of marriage by a wide-ranging, lively discussion of English literature with many examples from Victorian works. His treatment of English attempts to join love, sex, and marriage (to "marry Iseult") – which follows Flandrin's sociological observations on the difference between English and Continental, Puritan and Catholic, sexual ideologies – is especially interesting. Leo Bersani's *A Future for Astyanax: Character and Desire in Literature* (Boston: Little, Brown, 1976), not unlike Norman O. Brown though in a different and very contemporary critical mode, makes a case for the liberation of desires from social or personal rigidities and eloquently plots the emergence of a deconstructed character open to varied desires in nineteenth- and twentieth-century French and English literature. On more explicitly pornographic literature there are also the works by Loth (*The Erotic in Literature*) and Perkins (*The Secret Record*) mentioned above. Finally, Maurice Charney, *Sexual Fiction* (New York: Methuen, 1981), like Perkins, argues for serious literary study of a genre or subgenre of fiction focused on sex. Studying representative fictions about sexual actions from *Fanny Hill* to *My Secret Life* to *Lolita,* he resists Marcus's sense that works classed as pornography by their appearance in restrictive societies are necessarily subliterary. Charney argues that literature on sex may be more or less explicit about sexual acts, but the critic's business, as with any kind of literature, is with defining and exploring its quality, not with arbitrary classifications that place one kind of sexual work within, and another without, the pale of literature.

What we have been finding out about sexuality in Victorian society and literature is generally commensurate with Michel Foucault's observations that western culture had been deeply affected by, or afflicted with, an extensive social and political discourse centered on the idea of sexuality long before the sexual revolution of the age of Havelock Ellis, Freud, and D.H. Lawrence. We need not go as far as Foucault in viewing sexuality as a creation of western culture to acknowledge that he is essentially correct in seeing in the entire Victorian world, from overworld of prudes to the underworld of libertines, a profound preoccupation of the age (as of our age) with sexual subjects.

With our broadening view of the importance of sexual issues in the Victorian age and our simultaneous sense of the complexity and variety of Victorian sexual attitudes and practices, we may very well be at a particularly creative moment in the study of Victorian sexuality. While historians follow up on the pioneering work of the past twenty years in carefully documented, precisely defined studies of various individual aspects of Victorian sexual life, literary historians and critics may be able to look at the place of sexuality in Victorian literature free from the old stereotypes of opposing prudery and lechery. Victorian people and Victorian writers were not mainly like Thackeray's famous mermaids in *Vanity Fair*, all angel above water, "proper agreeable, and decorous" and all monster's hideous tail below, "writhing and twirling, diabolically hideous and slimy." They wanted to define some appropriate place for sexual experience in their lives; in their serious literature they often attempted to explore and define the nature of the sexual life. Beneath the quieting restraints on explicit public writing about sex they expressed various viewpoints and argued their differing positions just as writers have in our century. Our challenge is to look now, without polemics and presuppositions about what Victorian sexuality was but with live critical intelligence, at the variety of sexual issues and visions of sexual experience presented in Victorian literature. Above all, we now need more careful studies of individual authors and works to see what they said about sexual issues and how they said it. With the clarity provided by such studies, we may eventually be able to make out a more satisfactory, far less simplified picture than we have had so far of the complexity of the Victorians' sexual experience and their writing about that experience.

Notes

1. Walkowitz, ch. 10 (also pub. in Martha Vicinus, ed., *A Widening Sphere: Changing Roles of Victorian Women* [Bloomington: Indiana Univ. Press, 1980], pp. 72–93). Finnegan's studies of prostitutes in York paint a grimmer picture of the difficulty prostitutes faced in finding alternate livings in another city. Both note that the ordinary prostitute served men of her own class more than Walter's; their studies look at the class-bound ordinary prostitute catering to army or navy rather than the upwardly mobile London horsebreaker.

2. I have chosen not to extend this list by citing works on individual authors, such as Gerhard Joseph's excellent *Tennysonian Love: The Strange Diagonal*, Samuel Southwell's more controversial *Quest for Eros: Browning and "Fifine,"* or recent biographical studies of lesser figures, such as Havelock Ellis or J.A. Symonds, whose lives and works are obviously of central importance to sexual issues. Such studies, unlike these general materials, are easily discoverable in standard bibliographical sources for the individual writers.

Contributors

SUSAN BEEGEL, Adjunct Professor of American Civilization at the University of Massachusetts at Boston, has published journal articles on Victorian poets and American novelists, as well as on composition pedagogy.

THOMAS F. BOYLE, Associate Professor of English at Brooklyn College, City University of New York, regularly presents papers and publishes articles on sensationalism in Victorian fiction and journalism. He has co-edited a text anthology, *The Urban Adventurers*; his first novel, *The Cold Stove League,* was published in 1983.

JENNI CALDER, of Scotland, is the author of the biography *Robert Louis Stevenson: A Life Study.* Her many books include *There Must Be a Lone Ranger: The American West in Myth and Reality; Stevenson and Victorian England; Robert Louis Stevenson: A Critical Celebration;* and *Women and Marriage in Victorian Fiction.*

GEOFFREY CARTER, Assistant Professor of English, The George Washington University, teaches Victorian literature. His current research interests include Freudian and Marxian perspectives on literature and theories of narrative with respect to Carlyle's *French Revolution.*

ELLEN MILLER CASEY is Professor of English at the University of Scranton in Pennsylvania. She has published articles on Braddon's *Not Wisely But Too Well* and on Dickens as editor of *All the Year Round.* She is currently working on British fiction of the 1880s as reflected in reviews of the period.

266

MORTON COHEN, Professor Emeritus of the City University of New York, edited *The Letters of Lewis Carroll* and has written extensively on Lewis Carroll's work. He is presently writing a biography of Carroll.

HOWARD FULWEILER is Professor of English at the University of Missouri at Columbia. Besides numerous articles on Victorian literature he is the author of "The Oxford Movement" in *Victorian Prose: A Guide to Research*; and *Letters from the Darkling Plain: Language and the Ground of Knowledge in the Poetry of Arnold and Hopkins*.

ALAN P. JOHNSON, Associate Professor of English at Arizona State University, has published essays on various Victorian writers in journals such as *Victorian Poetry* and *Dickens Studies*, and has been associated with *English Literature in Transition: 1880–1920*, serving as associate editor from 1976 to 1982.

WENDELL STACY JOHNSON, Professor of English at Hunter College, has published extensively on nineteenth-century literature. His books include *The Voices of Matthew Arnold*; *Gerard Manley Hopkins: The Poet as Victorian*; *Living in Sin: The Victorian Sexual Revolution*; and *Sex and Marriage in Victorian Poetry*.

RICHARD McGHEE, Professor of English at Kansas State University, is the author of *Marriage, Duty and Desire in Victorian Poetry and Drama* as well as numerous articles on Victorian poetry.

LORALEE MACPIKE is Associate Dean of Graduate Studies and Associate Professor of English at California State College, San Bernardino. She is the author of *Dostoevsky's Dickens*, a frequent book review for *West Coast Review of Books*, and is completing a book-length study of childbirth as a metaphor in the nineteenth-century novel.

JOHN MAYNARD, Chairman of the Department of English at New York University, is the author of *Browning's Youth* and various articles and reviews on Browning and on nineteenth-century literature. He has been working on a study of sexual discussion in major Victorian literature. His book on Charlotte Brontë and sexuality will soon be published by Cambridge University Press.

SARA PUTZELL-KORAB, Associate Professor of English at Georgia Institute of Technology, is the author of *The Evolving Consciousness: An Hegelian Reading of the Novels of George Eliot* and co-editor of *The Crisis in the Humanities: Interdisciplinary Responses*. She is currently exploring fictional and scientific sources for Eliot's later novels.

MICHAEL SLATER is a Senior Lecturer at Birkbeck College, University of London. Formerly the editor of *The Dickensian,* he is presently the Chairman of the Trustees of the Dickens House Museum. Besides editions of *Nicholas Nickleby* and Dickens' Christmas books, his publications include the *Dickens 1970 Centenary Essays*; *Dickens on America and the Americans*; and *Dickens and Women.*

MARK SPILKA is Professor of English Literature at Brown University. His many publications include *The Love Ethic of D.H. Lawrence*; *Dickens and Kafka: A Mutual Interpretation*; *Towards a Poetic of Fiction*; and *Virginia Woolf's Quarrel with Grieving.*